THE SPANISH CIVIL WAR, THE SOVIET UNION,
AND COMMUNISM

STANLEY G. PAYNE

The Spanish Civil War, the Soviet Union, and Communism

YALE UNIVERSITY PRESS   NEW HAVEN & LONDON

Published with assistance from the Louis Stern Memorial Fund.

Designed by Rebecca Gibb. Set in Scala by Duke & Company. Printed in the United States of America by R. R. Donnelley & Sons.

Library of Congress Cataloging-in-Publication Data
Payne, Stanley G.
The Spanish Civil War, the Soviet Union, and communism / Stanley G. Payne.
p. cm.
Includes bibliographical references and index.
ISBN 0-300-10068-X (hardcover : alk. paper)
1. Communism—Spain. 2. Communism—Soviet Union. 3. Communist International—History. 4. Soviet Union—Relations—Spain. 5. Spain—Relations—Soviet Union. 6. Spain—History—1868–1931. 7. Spain—History—Republic, 1931–1939. 8. Spain—History—Civil War, 1936–1939. I. Title.
HX343.P39 2004
946.081'3'0947—dc22
2003018761

A catalogue record for this book is available from the British Library.

The paper in this book meets the guidelines for permanence and durability of the Committee on Production Guidelines for Book Longevity of the Council on Library Resources.

10 9 8 7 6 5 4 3 2 1

To the memory of Burnett Bolloten (1909–1987)

Contents

Preface

The policy and intervention of the Soviet Union have long remained among the least explored and most controversial aspects of the Spanish Civil War. Seizure of most of the German documents in 1945, together with the general accessibility of the Italian state data, provided opportunities years ago to resolve the major problems associated with the German and Italian intervention. In the Soviet case, access to copious documentation in the Comintern and military archives was restricted to favored Soviet scholars, and only very limited material drawn from them appeared in Russian-language publications on the Spanish conflict. A new opportunity was created by the collapse of the Soviet Union, which, at least for a number of years, greatly broadened access to most, though not all, Soviet archives.

The availability of previously inaccessible documents has made possible several important new publications. The first was *Queridos camaradas* (1999), the excellent study of Comintern policy in Spain by Antonio Elorza and Marta Bizcarrondo, which resolved a number of problems for the first time. This work was followed by a key collection of Soviet documents, *Spain Betrayed* (2001), prepared by Ronald Radosh, Mary Habeck, and Grigory Sevostianov, which illuminates both political and military affairs. Other works have appeared in several languages.

This book is the first broadly synthetic account of Soviet policy and its relation to the revolutionary process in Spain during the 1930s. By combining new Soviet data with Spanish and other sources, it broadens the perspective on that conflict.

I gratefully acknowledge the pioneering work of the scholars who have ventured into the field before me, notably my former doctoral student Daniel L. Kowalsky, whose excellent account of the relations between the Soviet Union and the Spanish Republic during the Civil War I hope will soon be published. Their research has helped to make this book possible. The manuscript has been read and criticized by Juan Linz and Michael Seidman, and has profited considerably from their advice. Barbara Salazar edited the manuscript with altogether unusual care and skill.

I dedicate the book to the memory of my cherished friend and colleague Burnett Bolloten, an altogether extraordinary man who devoted much of his life to collecting and studying data on the Spanish conflict. His work remains indispensable to its understanding.

Abbreviations

ANV	Acción Nacionalista Vasca (Basque Nationalist Action)
AO	Alianza Obrera (Worker Alliance)
BOC	Bloc Obrer i Camperol; Bloque Obrero y Campesino (Worker-Peasant Bloc)
BPA	Bloque Popular Antifascista (People's Antifascist Bloc)
CADCI	Centre Autonomista de Dependents de Comerç i Industria (Autonomist Center of Commercial and Industrial Employees)
CEDA	Confederación Española de Derechas Autónomas (Spanish Confederation of Autonomous Right Parties)
CGT	Confédération Générale du Travail (General Confederation of Labor)
CGTU	Confederación General del Trabajo Unitario (General Confederation of United Labor)
CNT	Confederación Nacional de Trabajo (National Confederation of Labor)
CPA	Concentración Popular Antifascista (People's Antifascist Association)
CPSU	Communist Party of the Soviet Union
CSR	Comités Sindicalistas Revolucionarios (Revolutionary Syndicalist Committees)

DGS	Dirección General de Seguridad (General Security Administration)
ECCI	Executive Committee of the Communist International
ECPP	Estat Catalá–Partit Popolari (Catalan National People's Party)
FAI	Federación Anarquista de Iberia
FCC-B	Federación Comunista Catalano-Balear (Catalan-Balearic Communist Federation)
FCI	Federación Comunista Ibérica (Iberian Communist Federation)
FET de las JONS	Falange Española Tradicionalista y de las Juntas de Ofensiva Nacional-Sindicalista (Traditionalist Spanish Phalanx and of the Leagues of National-Syndicalist Offensive)
FJS	Federación de Juventud Socialista (Federation of Young Socialists)
FNTT	Federación Nacional de Trabajadores de Tierra (National Federation of Farmworkers)
FNUT	Federación Nacional de Uniones de Trabajadores (National Federation of Workers' Unions)
FOUS	Federación Obrera de Unidad Sindical (Worker Federation of Syndical Unity)
FSL	Federación Sindicalista Libertaria (Libertarian Syndicalist Federation)
FUA	Frente Unico Antifascista (Sole Antifascist Front)
GABOC	Grupo de Acción del BOC (Action Group of the Worker-Peasant Bloc)
GEPCI	Gremios y Entidades de Pequeños Comerciantes e Industriales (Guilds and Small Business and Industrial Entities)
GPU	Gosudarstvennoi Politicheskii Upravlennie (State Political Directorate; Soviet secret police, predecessor of NKVD)
GRU	Glavnoye Razvedovatelnoye Upravlenie (Main Intelligence Administration; Soviet military intelligence)
ICE	Izquierda Comunista de España (Communist Left of Spain)

ICL	International Communist League
IRA	Instituto de Reforma Agraria (Institute of Agrarian Reform)
JCE	Juventud Comunista de España (Communist Youth of Spain)
JCI	Juventud Comunista Ibérica (Iberian Communist Youth)
JIR	Juventudes de Izquierda Republicana (Republican Left Youth)
JONS	Juntas de Ofensiva Nacional-Sindicalista (Leagues of National-Syndicalist Offensive)
JSU	Juventud Socialista Unificada (United Socialist Youth)
KGB	Komitet Gosudarstvennoi Bezopasnosti (Committee of State Security; Soviet secret police, successor to NKVD)
KPD	Kommunistische Partei Deutschlands (Communist Party of Germany)
MAOC	Milicias Antifascistas Obreras y Campesinas (Worker-Peasant Antifascist Militias)
NEP	New Economic Policy
NIC	Non-Intervention Committee
NKVD	Narodnyi Komissariat Vnutrennikh Del (People's Commissariat of Internal Affairs; Soviet secret police)
OCE	Oposición Comunista de España (Communist Opposition of Spain)
PCC	Partit Comunista de Catalunya (Communist Party of Catalonia)
PCE	Partido Comunista de España (Communist Party of Spain)
PCF	Parti Communiste de France (Communist Party of France)
PCOE	Partido Comunista Obrero de España (Communist Worker Party of Spain)
PNV	Partido Nacionalista Vasco (Basque Nationalist Party)
POUM	Partido Obrero de Unificación Marxista (Worker Party of Marxist Unification)
PSOE	Partido Socialista Obrero Español (Spanish Socialist Worker Party)

PSUC	Partit Socialist Unificat de Catalunya (United Socialist Party of Catalonia)
PSUE	Partido Socialista Unificado de España (United Socialist Party of Spain)
RILU	Red International of Labor Unions (Profintern)
SB-L	Sección Bolchevique-Leninista (Bolshevik-Lenin Section)
SIM	Servicio de Inteligencia Militar (Military Intelligence Service)
SPD	Sozialdemokratische Partei Deutschlands (Social Democratic Party of Germany)
UGSOC	Unió General de Sindicats Obrers de Catalunya (General Union of Worker Syndicates of Catalonia)
UGT	Unión General de Trabajadores (General Union of Workers)
UMRA	Unión Militar Republicana Antifascista (Republican Antifascist Military Union)
UPA	Unió Provincial Agraria (Provincial Agrarian Union)
USC	Unió Socialista de Catalunya (Socialist Union of Catalonia)

THE SPANISH CIVIL WAR, THE SOVIET UNION,
AND COMMUNISM

Soviet Policy and the Comintern in the Early Years

1917–1925

THE SOVIET REGIME was consolidated by revolutionary civil war and theoretically devoted to the expansion of the revolutionary process throughout the
world. Lenin postulated that by 1917 the entire world had been brought into
the capitalist sphere, and thus a great deal of it held or would soon hold the
potential for socialist revolution, inaugurating what Arno Mayer has called the
era of "international civil war."[1] Consolidation of the Communist regime in
Russia and the founding of the Communist International, accompanied by
revolutionary agitation and outbreaks in other countries, provoked grave concern abroad, a preoccupation that strongly influenced European politics throughout the interwar period and during much of the rest of the twentieth century.

Yet revolution was much more easily proclaimed than carried out, and as
early as 1920 Lenin called for "peaceful coexistence" in Soviet foreign relations.
While some analysts would later claim that peaceful coexistence was merely
standard terminology for what anticommunists would later call "cold war," as
early as the 1920s it was being alleged that the Soviet government had lost or
was losing the goal of world revolution as a dominant priority and was more
and more concerned with internal development and security. Whenever this
idea was advanced in the West, however, another initiative to extend Soviet political or territorial influence or to advance the revolutionary process would follow in a few months or years.

The peculiar Soviet combination of Russian messianism and imperialism
with the expansionist revolutionary ideology of Marxism-Leninism produced

a policy that the Russian scholars Vladislav Zubok and Constantine Pleshakov have called the "revolutionary-imperial paradigm," the guiding orientation of Soviet policy for seven decades, from 1917 until after 1985.[2] Such a basic orientation did not, however, result in constant Soviet promotion of civil war abroad or direct military conflict. Peaceful coexistence rather meant a split-level policy of normal peaceful diplomatic and economic relations on the one hand and indirect efforts to infiltrate, subvert, and foment revolutionary activity on the other.

During the first two decades of the Soviet Union, Soviet policy abroad may be divided into four periods. The first, consisting of the initial revolutionary struggle at home and abroad from 1917 to 1923, was followed by a period that more fully introduced the split-level policy of peaceful coexistence accompanied by somewhat diminished Comintern revolutionary activity. The "Third Period," announced in 1928, introduced no change in regular diplomacy but increased the emphasis on Comintern revolutionary activity. After this strategy proved disastrous for Communist interests, a fourth phase in 1935 sought antifascist diplomatic and military alliances abroad for collective security, flanked by a new Comintern policy seeking "popular fronts" with other worker parties and bourgeois democrats to complement Soviet diplomacy and to advance Communist politics. The collective security/popular front phase then came to a crashing end in August 1939 with the signing of the Nazi-Soviet Pact, which put an end to antifascism until the disaster of the Nazi invasion of the Soviet Union, the conditions for which Stalin's diplomacy had so blindly created.[3]

The Soviet regime initially strove to consolidate itself amid conditions of mounting civil war in 1918 while it was a quasi-ally of imperial Germany. Though the West viewed Germany as the leading reactionary power in Europe, German nationalists had often conceived of their program as a revolutionary force, bringing a new culture, a new moral order, and a new international framework to the world. German policy during World War I consistently aimed to subvert existing imperial structures and their allies through subversive and revolutionary designs. The Germans attempted to undermine the British and tsarist empires by encouraging the Muslims to revolt in the eastern Middle East, Central Asia, and British India, in military alliance with Turkey.[4] They tried to incite revolutionary Mexico against the United States so as to tie down the Americans in the western hemisphere. They made a modest attempt to disrupt social and economic relations in the Entente's largest neutral trading partner, Spain, by inciting deadly violence in Barcelona's labor relations. The only measure that yielded success was their guarantee of free transit to Lenin and provision of financial support for his subversion of the Russian Empire. Leaders of imperial Germany were not blind to the Bolsheviks' ultimate ambitions, and at one point in 1918 General Ludendorff, who dominated much of Germany's policy, even suggested sending minor German forces to finish them off. They could have done so rather easily, but the Kaiser and other German leaders opposed the idea.

German aid, primarily financial, provided important assistance to the Bolsheviks. The subsequent peace with Germany had to be purchased by massive territorial and economic concessions, and by mid-1918 Lenin was even looking for German military assistance in prosecuting the Russian civil war. As Lenin had hoped, the German triumph in the east lasted less than a year, though the collapse of imperial Germany was brought about by the triumph not of proletarian revolutionaries but of the Western capitalist powers. For the next twenty years, Communist and fascist revolutionaries would, each in their own way, work to reverse this outcome.

The final phase of World War I, followed by extreme disorder in Central and Eastern Europe, opened new opportunities for revolution. The creation of the Red Army early in 1918 was followed some months later by a Soviet announcement that "our Red Army must become the nucleus of a World Proletarian Army." On October 3, 1918, Lenin dispatched a letter to the Central Committee of the Communist Party calling for "an army of three million" to spearhead an "international workers' revolution." He would in fact soon need an army of more than three million simply to win the Russian civil war, and after the Allied victory in the west he quickly responded by offering new economic and territorial concessions to guarantee peace with the Allies and terminate their support of White counterrevolutionaries.[5]

By the winter of 1919, however, revolution seemed to be on the march once more. Lenin told the Eighth Party Congress in March 1919 that the Soviet Republic was "living not merely in a state, but in a system of hostile states," so that it was "inconceivable that the Soviet Republic should continue to exist for a long period side by side with imperialist states. Ultimately one or the other must conquer." When in the following month a *Räterepublik* or soviet republic was temporarily declared in Munich, he was euphoric, declaring that "our victory on an international scale is now completely secure," even though the revolution had not yet triumphed militarily in much of Russia. By July he even announced that the period of trial was nearly over, for "next July we shall greet the victory of an international Soviet republic."[6]

The Soviet leadership did not assume, contrary to some of their more naive pronouncements, that a worker army could simply vanquish the capitalist-imperialist world in a war of conquest. The overthrow of capitalism would require the initiative of revolutionary workers in almost every country, and to that end delegates of the new Bolshevik-style communist parties convened in Moscow on March 4, 1919, for their first meeting as the Communist International, or Comintern. All but nine of the fifty-one delegates were already living in Russia.[7]

As Aleksandr Vatlin has observed, "The concept of the Third International was fundamentally different from those of its two predecessors: it pushed to the forefront a subjective factor and the use of a lever of social transformations. . . . The emphasis was shifted from the thesis of revolution as a midwife of history to the thesis of the party as a midwife of revolution. It was . . . a transfer of Russian ideological extremism originating from the 'Narodnaia Volia,'" or "People's Will," the founding Russian revolutionary movement of the 1870s.[8]

Abroad a revolution triumphed only momentarily in Budapest, but in 1920 the defeat of a Polish attempt to seize much of Ukraine opened the way for a Red Army offensive into the heart of the new Polish republic. Unlike some of the more euphoric Soviet leaders, however, Lenin realized the risk involved in this venture. Success would depend not merely on military victory but on a rebellion by Polish workers.[9] By July Lenin nonetheless thought things were moving along magnificently. He told Stalin that "the situation in Comintern is splendid . . . [and] it is time to encourage revolution in Italy. . . . For this to happen, Hungary must be sovietized, and maybe also the Czech lands and Romania." Communization of Poland could carry over to Lithuania and Germany. True, the new revolutionary thrust might run out of momentum, but even if it failed for the moment, it would "teach us about offensive war. . . . We will help Hungary, Italy and at each step we will remember where to stop."[10]

Within this perspective the Second Congress of the Comintern convened in Petrograd and Moscow from July 19 to August 7, 1920, and this was the occasion on which the Soviet leadership forced member parties to approve the famous "Twenty-one Conditions" of Communist orthodoxy. The member parties were required to remove systematically from membership any reformists and centrists; to pledge to combine legal and illegal activities; to establish cells in trade unions; to adopt the Bolshevik principle of "democratic centralism" with iron discipline and conduct periodic purges of "petit bourgeois" elements; to support unconditionally every Soviet republic; to change their official party names to Communist; and to recognize that "all decisions by congresses of the Communist International as well as by its Executive Committee are binding on all parties."[11] The Comintern was governed by a Presidium, an Executive Committee (ECCI), and a Political Secretariat, and by the following year had set up its own trade union confederation, the Red International of Labor Unions (RILU), or Profintern.

Collapse of the offensive into Poland altered the stance of the Soviet government, if not of the Comintern, and in November 1920 the term "peaceful coexistence" was introduced. The equivalent setbacks for the Comintern were first the rapid collapse of the Bela Kun Communist-Socialist dictatorship in Hungary in the summer of 1919, followed by failure of the revolutionary "March Action" in 1921 in Germany, home of the largest Western European Communist party (Kommunistische Partei Deutschlands, or KPD), which had announced its participation in "the most vast civil war in world history."[12] In 1921 Lenin introduced the New Economic Policy (NEP) for the Soviet economy, a new Anglo-Soviet trade agreement marked the first accord with a major capitalist country, and regular diplomacy moved to the fore.

Despite these setbacks, the Comintern did not retreat in its policy. By December 1921 it had adopted the revolutionary strategy of the "united front from below," pursuing the goal of forming Communist "united fronts" directly with workers who might belong to other trade unions or parties, bypassing noncommunist organizational structures altogether. This strategy provoked splits in trade union movements all over Europe, drew criticism from foreign Communist leaders, and in the long run achieved little. Though revolutionary actions would also be attempted in Estonia and Bulgaria, the last significant opportunity for the Comintern in postwar Europe came amid the turmoil of the French invasion and hyperinflation in Germany during 1923, when the KPD even engaged in limited cooperation with Hitler's National Socialist Party. Though Comintern leaders had been the first to grasp the full potential for political stigmatization of the new terms "fascism" and "fascist" arising from Mussolini's government in Italy, they also recognized certain key similarities between such a movement and Communist parties.[13] The final KPD revolt proved abortive, and would be the last insurrectionary gesture in Germany.

After the failures of the first five years, the Fifth Comintern Congress insisted on full "Bolshevization" of member parties, requiring strict centralization and control from Moscow. Member parties were not required to reproduce every feature of Sovietism in total detail, but they did have to adopt the basic features, with other measures depending on circumstances. Its most central component was the absolute orthodoxy and unswerving loyalty of foreign party leaders. From the Kremlin's point of view, successful Bolshevization was probably not fully completed until the following decade.

The death of Lenin brought no lessening of revolutionary orthodoxy. The manifesto of the Second Comintern Congress had declared that "the international proletariat will not sheathe its sword until Soviet Russia is incorporated as a link in the World Federation of Soviet Republics." The new constitution of the USSR in 1924 declared the Soviet government to be the nucleus of a world state. The *Small Soviet Encyclopedia* of 1930 explained that the world proletariat was international and tied to the USSR. "That is why every country in which a socialist revolution was concluded will enter the USSR," though this feature was later dropped from the Stalinist constitution of 1936.[14]

The only effective military action to set up a satellite state beyond the Soviet frontier had been the invasion of Outer Mongolia in 1921 by a mixed force of the Red Army and a new Soviet-organized Mongolian army, but Outer Mongolia was not added to the USSR. Instead, it became a "people's republic," a new formula for the first full stage of new satellite regimes in lands not deemed propitious for the direct establishment of Soviet-style socialism. The new Mongolian government organization had initially been formed in the Soviet Union in March 1921. After successful military occupation of Outer Mongolia a few months later, it took control, transforming itself into what was called a "people's revolutionary government." This was not a formally socialist government but was defined as representative of an advanced form of the "democratic revolution" that preceded socialism. It remained in theory a quasi-theocratic monarchy under a figurehead Mongolian chief of state. The standard designation for the puppet state of Outer Mongolia was "a bourgeois democratic republic of a new type,"[15] terminology that was to emerge again in Spain during 1936–37. By 1924 the Outer Mongolian regime had become officially a people's republic firmly under Communist control after a series of purges that eliminated a good many of the original Mongolian Communist leaders. Military and security forces were fully under Soviet control and key institutions were dominated by Soviet advisers. After 1945 the designation would be changed to "people's democracy," in line with the nomenclature of the new Eastern European states.[16]

Soviet policy abroad became less activist during 1924, the year in which Stalin introduced the doctrine of "Socialism in one country." The Soviet Union would concentrate increasingly on internal development, though Stalin also emphasized that for the "complete victory of socialism . . . the united efforts of the proletarians of several countries are necessary."[17] The first task of Communists abroad, however, was now to defend the Soviet Union; promoting foreign revolution, while still a goal, was secondary. In relations with other worker parties, the Comintern introduced in 1924 the tactic of "united front from above," opening the way to negotiated fusions rather than subversive Communist takeovers from below.

Despite the fact that in the same year Fascist Italy became the first significant power to recognize the Soviet Union officially, "fascism" in general was a major foe and, despite the temporary dallying with the Nazis (who had been defined more blandly as "ultranationalists"), antifascism became a major feature of Comintern propaganda. Fascism was often painted with an undiscriminating brush, so that almost everyone but Communists became some sort of hyphenated fascist, most notoriously social democrats. Such Communist pejoratives had a long history, going back to Lenin's invention of such terms as "social patriotism" and "social chauvinism" to describe the policies of defensist Russian Social Democrats during World War I. As early as November 1922, a few weeks after Mussolini's march on Rome, *Izvestia* used the term "social fascist" to characterize the Italian Socialist Party. Early in 1924 Grigory Zinoviev, secretary of the Comintern, began to adopt the term, and it was soon repeated by Stalin, who defined social democrats as "objectively the moderate wing of fascism," "not antipodes but twins."[18] Such invective was scarcely designed to facilitate the united front from above.

"In 1925 the emerging Bukharin-Stalin duumvirate detected a 'temporary' and 'relative stabilization of capitalism' in Western Europe and North America," based on new technology and economic growth. This perception made peaceful coexistence even more appropriate, at least for the time being. The Fifth Plenum of the ECCI in March–April 1925 "tacitly recognized . . . a transitional stage between revolutions," with no imminent opportunities for the moment.[19]

War remained nonetheless inevitable, and, with the "temporary stabilization" of capitalism, the doctrine of a future "second imperialist war" began to take form. Capitalist imperialism allegedly inevitably produced war. Its first great struggle had been World War I, but another would have to follow—one of only two key prognostications that Marxism-Leninism ever got right. In 1925 Stalin declared that in the next great conflict between capitalist powers the Soviet Union would eventually participate, "but we should be the last to do so. And we should come out in order to throw the decisive weight in the scales, the weight that should tip the scales."[20] Such a war would soon be termed the next "icebreaker" of world revolution, as indeed it would prove to be, and Stalin would eventually seek to maneuver Soviet policy toward participation in it along the lines that he first outlined in 1925.

CHAPTER TWO

Communism and Revolution in Spain

1917–1931

AT THE TIME the Comintern was organized, Spain was not particularly high on its agenda, but Comintern agents were sent to Madrid at the close of 1919 to take the lead in setting up a Communist party of Spain one month later, earlier than Communist parties were organized in many other countries. In Spain the Comintern faced an unusual combination of circumstances, in which four factors may be identified as the most salient: Culturally, Spain was part of Western Europe, but of its most underdeveloped part. Economically, it was part of a largely agrarian and backward Southern Europe, a very large and somewhat artificial category that extended from Portugal across to the Balkans and also had certain features in common with Eastern Europe. Politically, Spain had one of the longest "modern" political histories in the world, liberal constitutional and parliamentary government having been introduced as early as 1812, though this history had been one of frustration and sometimes of failure, liberalism having broken down altogether with the imposition of the dictatorship of Miguel Primo de Rivera in 1923. Finally, socialist ideas and trade union activity also had an extensive history in Spain, dating from the 1830s and 1840s, but here the failure was even more acute. Socialism was weak, and the main trade union and revolutionary force was anarchosyndicalism.

Marxism had a lengthy history in Spain, but with little to show for it. The Partido Socialista Obrero Español (Spanish Socialist Worker Party, or PSOE) had been formed in 1879, and the small Unión General de Trabajadores (General Union of Workers, or UGT) of skilled workers was set up nine years later. The

PSOE leadership had initially been close to the Guesdist Marxist current in France, and the party was a founding member of the Marxist social democratic Second International in 1889. In many ways it was a typical party of the Second International, Marxist and revolutionary in theory, pragmatic and relatively social democratic in practice. Spain long lacked a significant industrial working class, and the PSOE, like most Second International parties, showed little interest in or aptitude for organizing farmworkers. It did not manage to place its leader, Pablo Iglesias, in parliament until 1910, and even then only through electoral alliance with the Republicans. The UGT had difficulty organizing as many as 100,000 workers. During World War I the Spanish party paralleled the pro-Entente, defensist position of its French counterpart, becoming strongly interventionist, linking the future possibilities of socialism in Spain to victory by the Western democracies. In Spain's own turbulent 1917—marked by military dissidence, political protest, and severe labor unrest—the Socialists attempted to lead a general strike but were unable to do so effectively.[1]

The key difference in Spanish labor was that the majority sector was anarchosyndicalist. Though revolutionary anarchism had enjoyed a certain vogue in several countries during the late nineteenth century, it was Spain that emerged as the chief center, followed by Italy and later to some extent by Russia and Poland. The notionally oxymoronic phenomenon of "organized anarchism" developed in Spain in several forms, ranging from vegetarian discussion societies to small conspiratorial cliques of bomb throwers and terrorists to a much more broadly structured worker organization of anarchosyndicalism; that is, the combination of anarchist political ideas with syndicalist worker organization. The latter tendency emerged in Spain as early as the 1870s, though it did not develop into a mass movement until 1917–18. The first groups of the 1870s and 1880s were suppressed by the Spanish state, and in following years anarchist terrorism became focused on Barcelona.[2]

The Confederación General del Trabajo (National Confederation of Labor, or CNT), organized in 1911, was eventually dominated by anarchosyndicalism as it grew into the first mass worker movement in Spain, temporarily enrolling possibly as many as 700,000 members after the industrial expansion of World War I. During its first decade the CNT was an unstable amalgam of anarchosyndicalists, Marxist-influenced revolutionary syndicalists, a certain number of "pure" anarchists (though these people also formed separate groups), and a considerable number of pragmatic syndicalists, with revolutionaries coming increasingly to the fore after 1917. Spain had also been one of the targets of German revolutionary strategy during World War I, and money from German agents may have been instrumental in sparking the first killing of a Barcelona industrialist by anarchosyndicalist *pistoleros* (gunmen) in 1917. For the next six years Barcelona was the site of violent class struggle between CNT pistoleros, assassins hired by the industrialists, and activists of the Carlist/Catholic Sindicatos Libres (Free Syndicates). There were massive strikes and nearly three hundred political killings during these *años del pistolerismo* (gunmen years), social tension and violence playing a role in provoking Primo de Rivera's *pronunciamiento* in 1923.[3]

The strongest response to the Bolshevik coup d'état in Russia in November 1917 came at first from the "pure" anarchists and anarchosyndicalists, who initially confused the strange-sounding Bolsheviks with Russian anarchists and assumed they were destroying the Russian state. Spanish Socialists, like social democrats generally, were more restrained, still focused primarily on the military victory of the Entente. Their interest in Russia increased immediately after the Allied victory in November 1918, and in the following months worker groups held a series of pro-Bolshevik meetings in quite a large number of Spanish cities.[4]

These meetings coincided with the greatest strike wave in Spanish history to that point, as social conflict in the largest centers was accompanied by widespread agrarian disturbances in the south. Those disturbances began in 1918, were resumed the next summer, and continued at a lower level into 1920. The striking farmworkers rioted, burned barns, and destroyed other property, but they committed little violence against persons, as anarchosyndicalist activists did in the cities. Farmworkers sometimes declared themselves to have been inspired by "Russia"—however vaguely—and there was little doubt that a sort of myth of the Russian revolution had entered Spain, as elsewhere. Some farmworkers and smallholder activists apparently thought that the Bolshevik principle meant primarily land to the peasants, though some small collectivist entities were briefly established before the disorders were finally put down by military forces over the three years 1918–20. This period became known hyperbolically as the *trienio bolchevique* (Bolshevik triennium) in the southern Spanish countryside, though it was not truly Bolshevik and did not amount to a full triennium, lasting at most from the spring of 1918 to the spring of 1920.[5]

Moderates and conservatives became increasingly alarmed. The Republican Marcelino Domingo called Spain "the Russia of the West," and an American correspondent reported that "present-day Spain has much in common with pre-revolutionary Russia." José Ortega y Gasset would later write that elites were as weak in Spain as in Russia (an erroneous analysis) and that Russia and Spain represented "the two *pueblo* [common people] races of Europe."[6] These distortions indicate the ease with which even a truly great intellectual could be confused by these developments, and in fact a series of books and pamphlets invoked the supposed similarities between Russia and Spain.

The Bolsheviks made their first appeal to the Spanish left in January 1919, two months before the Comintern was founded. They addressed themselves not to the anarchosyndicalists but to "the left elements in the Spanish Socialist Party."[7] In fact the great bulk of the Spanish Socialists followed what is usually termed the "revolutionary reformism" of Pablo Iglesias, which had for some years maintained an electoral alliance with middle-class liberal Republicans, though without losing sight of the eventual goal of socialism. An extensive debate on the course to follow concerning the Comintern took place within the Socialist Party during the summer of 1919. A compromise was finally hammered out by the time the party congress met in December, according to which the PSOE would remain within the Second International but would work to bring the two internationals together. The strongest support for Bolshevism was among the young, and a few days later the Fifth Congress of the Federation of Young Socialists (Federación de Juventud Socialista, or FJS) voted unconditional adherence to the Comintern (which would not adopt the Twenty-one Conditions until the following year), deepening the dilemma for the party.

At its national congress in December 1919, the CNT, eager to join an organization as revolutionary as the Comintern, nevertheless reaffirmed its own non-Marxist identity as "a firm defender of the principles sustained by Bakunin" and made its final decision dependent on the Comintern's holding a genuinely representative international congress.[8]

The Bolshevik leaders were completely ignorant of Spanish conditions and at that point were fixated on extending the revolution to Germany, and thence to other parts of Western and Central Europe. The Party leaders in Moscow hoped that the Spanish party congresses might prove to be harbingers of revolution, but a few months later they concluded that the divisions within the Spanish working-class movement limited it at the present time to achieving no more than a "Spanish revolution of 1905"; that is, in Marxist-Leninist parlance, a "bourgeois democratic revolution."

At the same time, Spain was too large and potentially too important to ignore. Thus the first Comintern agent, the subsequently well-known Mikhail Borodin (pseudonym of Mikhail Gruzenberg), arrived in Madrid before the end of 1919, accompanied by an assistant introduced as Jesús Ramírez (pseudonym of the American socialist Charles Phillips, who had learned Spanish in

Mexico).[9] The first postwar congress of the Second International had been postponed until July 1920, and in the meantime both the Comintern and some of the radical pro-Bolshevik Young Socialists were eager to take action. With the Comintern's encouragement, by the end of February 1920 the national committee of the FJS, dominated by leaders in Madrid, decided to convert the entire Federation of Young Socialists into an official Partido Comunista de España (Communist Party of Spain, or PCE), and did so on April 15. Most Young Socialists in other parts of the country balked at this unrepresentative action, however, so that no more than about a thousand of the more than five thousand members of the FJS actually joined the nascent PCE. The initial PCE was fairly typical of the small ultraleft groups that formed the first foreign Communist parties, but in Moscow Lenin realized that their extremism might be counterproductive. To have any chance at power, a fledgling Communist party would have to aim at forming a coalition government with the broader left (as in Hungary in 1919) and then try to dominate it. Thus in April Lenin issued his oft-cited pamphlet *"Left-Wing" Communism: An Infantile Disorder,* condemning revolutionary extremism.[10]

The PSOE, which had grown in the past year from 16,000 to 53,000 members, was the main hope of the Comintern, and at the 1920 congress the party passed a resolution to join the Third International, while stipulating it would retain full autonomy and continue to work to bring the two internationals together. The UGT rejected the new policy in August 1920 and called for a special congress of unification with the CNT. Nonetheless, by the summer of 1920 three Spanish delegations had been dispatched to Moscow, representing the PSOE, the CNT, and the nascent PCE. In general, only the PCE's delegates were favorably impressed, and by the following year both the PSOE and CNT had decisively rejected the Twenty-one Conditions, spurning any association with the Comintern.[11]

A small number of pro-Communist members rejected the Socialists' decision. Regarding the PCE not illogically as a handful of political militants who lacked any real association with workers, they persuaded a few UGT members to join them in a separate Partido Comunista Obrero de España (Communist Worker Party of Spain, or PCOE). When a unity effort failed, both groups sent delegations to Moscow, but after a new Comintern agent had managed to reunite them, in January 1922 a tiny radical sector split off from the original PCE under the extremist intellectual Juan Andrade to form a separate Grupo Comunista Español. The top Comintern official in Western Europe, Jules Humbert Droz, was then dispatched to Madrid in May. He managed to reunite the

Communists, and would remain the chief supervisor of the Spanish party for nine years, until the coming of the Republic. Fragmentation would nonetheless remain a problem.

All the while the CNT was carrying on the principal revolutionary activity in the country. Despite its final rejection of the Comintern, it harbored a small but dynamic current of "Communist syndicalists," led by Andreu Nin and Joaquín Maurín. Nin was a young journalist who, amid the turmoil that attended the violence in Barcelona, temporarily became general secretary of the CNT and briefly one of its most influential leaders.[12]

The other leader of the Communist syndicalists became the most original figure in the history of Spanish revolutionary Marxism. Born of an Aragonese father and a Catalan mother in northeastern Aragon in 1896, Maurín at first trained for the priesthood and then taught school very briefly. Tall, eloquent, idealistic, and with a commanding physical presence, he stood out as a natural leader. One of his chief biographers has judged that "his errors, his indecision, his contradictions sometimes led him to adopt confused positions, but he always maintained the orientation and level of analysis that made him one of the rare examples of an original analyst" of Spanish Marxism.[13]

Maurín became a Leninist partly through his reading of Georges Sorel, who helped convince him of the need for revolutionary dictatorship and violence. He early adopted the position, however, that the vehicle of revolution in Spain must be a reconverted anarchosyndicalism, its syndicates playing the role of soviets, which otherwise could not be constituted in Spain. Like his slightly older colleague Nin, Maurín soon turned to revolutionary journalism, first in Lérida, where he directed the weekly *Lucha social*, which cited Sorel more frequently than Marx, and where he gained a small but radical and devoted following despite his youth, and later in Barcelona. He soon found himself the chief leader of the Catalan section of the CNT, and at a secret national plenum of the CNT in Lérida in April 1921, it was decided by a vote of 10 to 7 to send a second delegation to Moscow, this time to attend the first congress of the Profintern (the Comintern's trade union organization), which would meet in July. At this conclave the Spanish delegation, led by Nin and Maurín, found itself the second largest group after the Soviets themselves, and played a not inconsiderable role. Though they sought to maintain the CNT's independence, Nin and Maurín were dazzled by the spectacle of revolutionary Russia, its iron dictatorship and organized legions of workers and soldiers. The rampant human misery that had so appalled Angel Pestaña, the earlier CNT delegate to the Comintern, they chose to ignore, apparently accepting it as the temporarily necessary condition of a true workers' revolution. Their CNT colleagues in Barcelona were less impressed, however, and reacted very negatively to the Profintern resolution declaring "organic solidarity" with the Comintern.

After Nin was temporarily arrested in Germany on the return trip, Maurín succeeded him at the age of twenty-five as general secretary of the CNT; he in turn was arrested by Spanish police in February 1922. Maurín's version of the future Spanish revolution, which he set forth in the pamphlet *El sindicalismo a la luz de la revolución rusa* (Syndicalism in the light of the Russian revolution), was published three months later. It contended that a workers' revolution must rely on the syndicates, but only as the main instruments of a more centralized political struggle. Central state power, which Maurín tended to refer to as "the organization," could then become federalized in accord with anarchosyndicalist principles. This approach seemed to represent an effort to combine Marx with Bakunin. It emphasized the Bolsheviks' reliance on professional revolutionaries but was careful to avoid the word "party" (anathema to anarchosyndicalists), while insisting that syndicalist morality must be based on the concept of collective violence. According to Maurín, "the class struggle means the systematization of the doctrine of collective violence." He was certain that the new order would soon be installed in Europe by mass revolutionary violence, declaring in *Lucha social* on April 29, 1922, that "Russia, within a few years—if the proletarians of Europe have not already learned how to destroy their own states— will issue forth from its frontiers, its youth filled with energy and singing, and will carry out the great liberating revolution, the war that will put an end to all wars and all injustice."[14]

CNT leaders officially rejected this approach, together with any association with the Profintern, at a national congress in June 1922, and before the end of the year Maurín had struck out on his own, helping to organize a small group of fractions of CNT syndicates willing to join the Profintern. He also remained in close contact with Nin, who served as Spanish representative on the Comintern's ECCI from 1922 to 1925, temporarily substituted as first secretary of the Profintern, and was beginning to play a role in the PCE as well. Maurín's new group became the nucleus of an entity that styled itself Comités Sindicalistas Revolucionarios (Revolutionary Syndicalist Committees, or CSR) and started a new weekly, *La Batalla,* in December 1922. The CSR also included a few schismatics from the PCE and had nuclei in Lérida, Valencia, Asturias, Vizcaya, and Burgos. They had been inspired by the initiative of Pierre Monatte in forming a CSR group within the French Confédération Générale du Travail (General Confederation of Labor, or CGT) and enjoyed some degree of Soviet financing, like the regular PCE. The Comintern did not officially endorse the CSR but had earlier espoused the tactic of creating Communist fractions within other syndical groups. Maurín declined to become an official member of the CSR, however, in order to preserve his potential relationship with the CNT.[15]

Meanwhile the left wing of the reunited PCE was becoming more dominant and was strongly oriented toward violence, particularly in Bilbao, one of its two strongholds. The bodyguard of Oscar Pérez Solís, leader of this tendency, was even responsible for shooting and killing a Socialist worker at the Sixteenth Congress of the UGT in November. That same month the Fourth Congress of the Comintern officially endorsed the tactic of the "united front from below," introduced a year earlier, which required Communist parties to attempt to fuse with members of other worker groups whom they could steer toward creation of revolutionary worker governments. In Spain the goal was a United Front with members of the UGT and CNT. The PCE leadership, however, opposed collaboration with social democrats, at least until imposition of the Comintern line, so that, as Gerald Meaker observes, "the Spanish Party had by now acquired a minor notoriety among the Bolshevik leaders for its dissensions and leftist tendencies."[16] Thus at the Fourth Congress, the PCE, with 5,000 members, was given only three votes, while the British party, with approximately the same membership, enjoyed seven. Conversely, the united front was not extended to the final elections of the Spanish parliamentary monarchy in April 1923. Maurín and a few others recommended an electoral alliance with middle-class Republicans, though such an alliance was categorically prohibited by Comintern tactics, and the result was complete isolation of the PCE. After another round of violence in Bilbao, however, unity was restored between the main sector of the PCE and the ultraleft of Pérez Solís. In Bilbao, as elsewhere, the PCE was weak in real workers but included a disproportionate number of very young militants. In Bilbao they were formed into action groups that by 1923 were primarily responsible for making that city the leader in Spain in political violence per capita, and second only to Barcelona in the absolute number of incidents. A disproportionate amount of this violence was directed against Socialist leaders and workers who opposed the Communists. A general strike attempted on August 23 brought massive repression, ending with a shoot-out at the barricaded party headquarters in which some twenty Communists were killed or injured and another seventy arrested. In the final phase of the parliamentary system the PCE, like the much larger CNT, had exhausted itself with sterile extremism.

The advent of the dictatorship rendered all political parties impotent, but none was dissolved. The PCE's weekly, *La Antorcha*, continued to be published until 1927, though the CNT's *Solidaridad obrera* was closed by the authorities in May 1924. Maurín maintained a certain degree of collaboration with the CNT, and by 1923 was already viewed with enmity and jealousy by PCE hierarchs, who considered him too independent. In a pamphlet published in Paris in 1924, *L'anarcho-syndicalisme en Espagne,* he offered the standard Marxist interpretation of anarchism, holding that it represented a backward culture of idealism supported by immigrant workers from the underdeveloped south. These people were in need of acculturation and modernization, and particularly of instruction in the materialist culture of Marxism. Though Maurín as usual strongly supported effective revolutionary violence, as in the Soviet Union, he condemned anarchist violence as irrational and self-destructive, observing of the repression in Barcelona that "these monstrous crimes of capitalism were no more than a reaction to the anarchists' tactics of terror; the latter, by their incomprehension of class struggle, by their group actions, had been the principal cause of the great tragedy."

Maurín anticipated a much more extensive debate between Marxists and anarchists in several issues of the Barcelona journal *L'Opinió* in 1928, the most extensive discussion of the origins of Spanish anarchism and of its relative success to that point.[17] This discussion deserved to be placed in a broader context. Catalan anarchism had been initiated not by illiterate immigrants from the south but by semi-educated Catalan workers and by a sector of the intelligentsia. In Spain the weakness of the modern state and its lack of penetration made it all the easier for anarchists to conceive of the state as a null or negative factor, easily dispensed with, a source neither of progress nor even of decisive power. Moreover, Spanish society had a long tradition of localism and particularism, pactist and confederal on the national level and often enjoying de facto self-governance on the local level. Anarchosyndicalism therefore developed roots both in the backward agrarian south and in modernizing, industrializing Catalonia. In each case the process was probably encouraged by the broader social and cultural context. From the mid–nineteenth century the lower middle classes and urban workers in parts of Andalusia had sometimes been strongly attracted to a radical republicanism that was highly individualistic, egalitarian, and anticlerical, serving to create an environment more propitious for a libertarian movement among the lower classes. Moreover, Andalusian anarchism did not appeal merely to the most immiserated but also to a somewhat broader cross section of society, while early twentieth-century Catalonia was rife with individualism and with political particularism on the bourgeois level, a situation perhaps not totally unassociated with the growing libertarianism of workers.

In Spain the anarchosyndicalists' success was partly predicated on the Socialists' failure. The UGT had originally been centered in Barcelona, but the
Madrid leadership of the movement found Catalonia uncongenial and eventually
withdrew the organization to the Spanish capital. Early Spanish socialism was
narrow, rigid, and unimaginative. Its partisans quarreled with trade union
moderates in Catalonia as well as with incendiary anarchists, and long failed
to develop a strategy to reach the largest and poorest proletariat, located not in
the cities but in the southern latifundist countryside. While the UGT held to
the restrictive craft union principle, the CNT in 1919 adopted the *sindicato
único* (industrial unionism), maximizing its mobilizational potential.[18]

Finally, the anarchosyndicalists of the CNT were more successful in developing a revolutionary syndicalism simply because they were more radical and
more violent, even sometimes visiting their violence on workers who refused
to join their ranks. Anarchosyndicalist violence and revolutionism became
self-perpetuating, generating a self-radicalization of industrial relations that
frequently forced the issue and provoked a polarization of worker attitudes
and actions that could never have assumed the same form through peaceful
trade union means, such as those normally practiced by the Socialists. Anarchosyndicalists thus demonstrated a capacity for revolutionary self-generation that
the more moderate and disciplined Marxists simply did not possess. Though
organization and unity were always problems for anarchosyndicalists, the very
looseness of their structure allowed them to survive repression and later recon-
stitute themselves relatively quickly. Nor were they as "unmodern" or "anti-
modern" as Marxists claimed, for their industrial syndicates placed about as
much emphasis on modern technology as did the Socialists.

Maurín represented the CSR at the Third Congress of the Profintern,
where he agreed with one of the Soviet leaders that Spanish anarchism constituted "a support for fascism." The Profintern defined a new policy of the "united
trade union front," stipulating that Communist syndicates should strive to
merge with other labor groups. Meanwhile, the Comintern simultaneously
convened its Fifth Congress in Moscow. Maurín enjoyed good relations with
the Comintern leaders, who considered him definitely a Communist, even if
he was not a PCE member, and protected him from rivals in the Spanish party.
Though the CSR were supposed to merge with the Communist syndicates,
an exception seems to have been made in Maurín's case and his tiny group
continued to exist separately until 1926, at least on paper. Maurín was quite
optimistic about the new syndicalist strategy, but the four CSR workers who
accompanied him to Moscow refused to put on the same blinders when they

looked at the new Soviet society. All were repelled, and on their return a schism developed in the CSR, now weaker than ever.

By October 1924 Maurín had worked out a deal whereby the remaining cells of the CSR in Catalonia, with about one hundred members, would be permitted to join the PCE as a discrete Federación Comunista Catalano-Balear (Catalan-Balearic Communist Federation, or FCC-B). On this basis he attended a national plenum of party leaders the following month in Madrid, where Oscar Pérez Solís and other Bilbao representatives joined him in denouncing the passivity into which the party had fallen under the Primo de Rivera dictatorship. This stance echoed the line of the recent Fifth Congress, which had emphasized the need to complete the Bolshevization of Communist parties, while denouncing social democrats as the "left wing of fascism." Under this pressure the entire central committee resigned in December 1924, to be replaced by a new central commission, with Maurín and other representatives of the FCC-B momentarily dominant; Andreu Nin of the Profintern closely cooperated with them. For the first and only time, Communist leadership briefly passed to Barcelona, but, as in 1922, Maurín was arrested almost as soon as he became a national leader. Detained in January 1925, he spent nearly three years in jail, and leadership passed to José Bullejos of the Vizcayan section, who would be general secretary for nearly eight years.[19]

It was in this time of the PCE's passivity and weakness that the leaders of Estat Catalá, the most radical sector of Catalan nationalism, turned to Moscow. Francesc Macià had organized Estat Catalá as a separatist movement that sought to combine ultranationalism with a populist opening to the left.[20] He and Jaume Carner met with Nikolai Bukharin, secretary of the Comintern, during October–November 1925. They agreed on a common program of action against the Spanish government and, according to Carner, the Comintern chiefs "pledged to support economically all the expense of organization, preparation and propaganda for the revolution in Catalonia and in all Spain."[21] Leaders of the Comintern, Estat Català, and the PCE signed a six-page revolutionary pact on November 15, with Nin providing one of the two signatures for the PCE. The agreement stipulated that the signatories would set up a revolutionary committee and publish a manifesto calling for abolition of both the dictatorship and the monarchy, creation of a *república federativa popular*, recognition of the right to independence of Catalonia and the Basque Country, abandonment of the Moroccan protectorate, complete freedom of association, expropriation of the great latifundia in order to give land to peasants, and the creation of workers' councils in industry. The central committee for the revolution was to be composed of representatives of Estat Català, the radical Basque nationalist youth organization Aberri, the PCE, the CNT, and the Juventud Comunista de España (Communist Youth of Spain, or JCE), and it would in turn develop a Revolutionary Military Committee, with a six-point plan for insurrection in Madrid. This pact was then formally ratified by the Comintern leadership on November 25, though they warned that extensive preliminary agitation must be carried out. When the Catalan representatives returned to Spain, however, the plan began to unravel. Leaders of the CNT and of Aberri were reluctant to join forces with Communists, and the Moscow directors continued to emphasize delay until the plan became a dead letter.[22]

In 1926 the Comintern set up a special "Latin Section" (Romansky Lendersekretariat in the Russo-German argot used by the ECCI) for southwestern Europe. By 1932 continental European countries were organized in six regional groups, the head of the Latin Section being the Bulgarian Stoian Minev, whose most common pseudonym was Stepanov. He would later play an important role in Spain during the Civil War. In earlier years, the Comintern chieftains had had high hopes for communism in Italy, but the rise of fascism soon killed them, while France remained completely stable, its Communist party steadily losing support. Thus Spain rose slightly in the comparative interest of the Comintern, though heretofore it had invested scant resources there, and the party had been fractious, divided, and sometimes self-destructively ultraleft.[23]

Clandestinity under the dictatorship did not encourage unity. By 1925 the PCE leadership in Madrid was divided into three factions, while a new group of dissidents in Paris constituted themselves as the Grupo Comunista Español. As secretary general, Bullejos did, however, manage to achieve greater unity in Madrid, and then sought to gain control of the FCC-B in Barcelona. That proved more difficult, and the Madrid leaders began a campaign against the incarcerated Maurín, whom they resented: they charged him with lacking adequate understanding of Marxism-Leninism and being too sympathetic to Trotsky. Maurín had met Trotsky on his first trip to Moscow in 1921, had clearly been impressed by him, and visited him on each succeeding trip. Trotsky, for his part, while falling into disgrace in Moscow, was especially interested in Spain, which he viewed as the crucial revolutionary stepping-stone to Latin America. Moreover, Maurín was closely associated with the Russo-French leader Boris Souvarine (who had just been expelled from the French Communist Party) and would soon be engaged to Souvarine's sister, while also maintaining contacts with leaders of the French CSR, who had also adopted a dissident position. The loyalty purge conducted by Bullejos weakened the PCE further, and in 1927, just after Trotsky was expelled from the Communist Party of the Soviet Union (CPSU), the leaders of the PCE's executive commission committed the gaffe of asking the Comintern to add Nin to its membership, apparently not grasping how closely he was identified with Trotsky.

Maurín was released from prison in October 1927 and soon moved to Paris, where he married Jeanne Lifshitz, Souvarine's sister. By March 1928 the PCE leaders' campaign against him reached full throttle; he was accused of "schismatic activity," "relations with the police," and "leaving Spain without authorization from the central committee of the PCE."[24] Maurín then went to Moscow to plead his case. The Comintern's control commission gave him a clean bill of health and told the Spanish leaders it was not "admissible" to treat a comrade in that way. The Comintern leaders were apparently more concerned than those of the PCE to establish a worker base in Catalonia. Maurín remained in Paris as a correspondent of *Izvestia* and director of the new Comintern publishing house, Ediciones Europa-América, started at the beginning of 1929.

After Bullejos was arrested in 1928, the Comintern temporarily replaced him with the ultraorthodox Gabriel León Trilla, whose authoritarian manner touched off new dissidence. In Barcelona schismatics formed a separate Partit Comunista de Catalunya (Communist Party of Catalonia, or PCC). When the PCE's Third Congress met in Paris in August 1929 and embraced the standard Comintern goal of establishing a "democratic dictatorship of workers and peasants," Maurín objected that after the fall of the dictatorship in Spain the goal should be a "federal democratic republic," since the votes of the progressive petite bourgeoisie would be indispensable. The congress flatly rejected that idea and refused even to recognize Maurín, objecting that he lived in Paris and was a member only of the French Communist Party. Nonetheless, when a special party leadership conference met in March of the following year during the post–Primo de Rivera interregnum, it proposed a broader and more moderate interim program, calling for a political amnesty, legalization of the party, a free press, the right to assembly and to strike, and civil rights for women and soldiers; the Comintern immediately slapped it down. Dmitry Manuilsky, on behalf of the ECCI, admonished that "in Spain you have an excellent proletariat, such as perhaps we lacked in Russia," but that the PCE itself amounted to no more than "a few little groups, but not a communist party. That is the tragedy."[25]

Under the limited freedom of 1930, the FCC-B resumed regular activity and Maurín petitioned that his membership in the party be recognized, but the PCE leadership refused unless he publicly confessed numerous errors. Instead Maurín and the FCC-B called for a special "workers' republic" that would establish an alliance to complete the bourgeois democratic revolution and prepare for the socialist revolution—a proposal in fact slightly to the left of the eventual popular front tactic adopted by the Comintern itself in 1935. But in 1930 it constituted a "rightist deviation," as did the call for internal democratization of the PCE. Maurín finally broke with the party in a letter of July 5, though at the same time he informed leaders in Moscow that he was "at the entire disposition of the Communist International."[26] In Barcelona about 95 percent of the FCC-B membership remained with Maurín; no more than 5 percent left to form the new Catalan section of the PCE. As before, the ECCI was not eager to lose the only noteworthy Communist nucleus in Catalonia. After Maurín rejected the PCE's charge of Trotskyism, the Comintern sought to resolve the dispute, eventually inviting Maurín to Moscow to settle the problem, but he refused. Maurín also rejected the new PCE tactic of creating a Comité de Reconstrucción de la CNT, saying it was absurd to think that any significant part of the CNT could simply be reconstituted under PCE control; and with the coming of the Republic in 1931 he again called for completion of the bourgeois democratic revolution rather than immediate imposition of the Comintern's socialist revolution line. The ECCI finally expelled him on July 3, 1931, not for Trotskyism (as the PCE leaders would have preferred) but for following what was termed "a liberal Menshevik line."[27] By that time the FCC-B and the schismatic PCC had come together to form a new independent Communist party in Catalonia, the Bloc Obrer i Camperol (Worker-Peasant Bloc, or BOC).

CHAPTER THREE

Communism and the Second Republic

1931–1934

AFTER THE NEP stabilization period of the early and middle 1920s, the Soviet Union began to undergo its second major phase of radicalization as Stalin consolidated his personal power and undertook major new socialist initiatives, beginning with the collectivization of agriculture in 1928. Creating a sense of domestic and international crisis was fundamental to the new radicalization. Events of the preceding year had stimulated such an atmosphere, for in 1927 the Chinese Communists suffered catastrophe when their erstwhile Nationalist allies turned on them and drove them underground, while the Soviet government artificially contrived a war scare with Britain. By 1929 Stalin declared that the Soviet Union must develop a world-class military establishment as soon as possible to avoid being, as he put it, "crushed."

Stalinization affected the Comintern as well. As early as the Seventh Plenum of the ECCI in November–December 1926, it had been announced that the world revolution was bound to proceed through three phases: the initial revolutionary upheavals (roughly 1917–21), the current temporary stabilization, and an inevitable new crisis of capitalist contradictions, which would shift the workers of the world to the revolutionary left. The Sixth Congress in 1928 made this interpretation official policy, announcing that a new "Third Period" had opened: a new crisis of capitalism was at hand to make the world situation "objectively revolutionary."[1]

The Comintern program of 1928 stated that the path to world revolution would develop through four distinct categories of societies: (1) "highly developed or advanced capitalist societies"; (2) societies of medium capitalist development; (3) "dependent, colonial, or semi-colonial societies"; and (4) "very backward, primitive societies." The definitions were vague, but countries such as Germany, France, Britain, and the United States clearly belonged to the first class, so they would be able to proceed rapidly to the "proletarian-socialist" revolution. The third category included countries with little or inadequate industry, with "feudal-monarchical relations" or the "Asiatic mode of production" in both economy and government, and under imperialist economic domination. In this category there could at first be only peasant revolutions against feudalism and "pre-capitalism," together with national independence movements. These movements would eventually "grow over" into socialist revolution, but only after several stages of growth and development that lay in the future. Countries in the fourth category were largely African and for the time being lay outside the pale of revolutionary activity.[2]

The greatest confusion or uncertainty lay in the discussion of the second category of countries, which included such lands as Japan, Spain, Poland, Hungary, and the Balkan states. The tendency in Comintern analysis was more generally to divide countries into two major divisions of capitalist and colonial countries, with the category 2 countries of medium development constituting a secondary category of the capitalist world, "to be discussed only in so far as they showed variations from the characteristics of the advanced capitalist countries." In the lands of medium capitalist development "semi-feudal agriculture" was combined with a certain level of industrialization, resulting in "uncompleted bourgeois-democratic revolutions."[3]

Generally speaking, the Comintern defined two paths to revolution: one was the direct Communist-led socialist revolution; the other and perhaps more common one was the Communist-led bourgeois-democratic revolution, which would rapidly "grow over" into the socialist revolution. Generally speaking, the first route was supposed to be feasible only in the most advanced countries. Heretofore there had been a Communist-led "bourgeois-democratic revolution" (strictly according to Marxist-Leninist definitions) only in Outer Mongolia, which had been at best a category 3 country (if that), and hence not very applicable to the optimistic new revolutionary schema. Consequently the "new type of democratic republic" or "people's republic," Mongolian style, was scarcely even mentioned, though it would regain centrality seven years later, when the socialist-revolution strategy of the 1928 program was replaced by the new Popular Front tactic in 1935.

At the 1928 congress the emphasis lay on the new opportunities for socialist revolution, and consequently delegates from Poland and Bulgaria (where Communist terrorists had tried to blow up the entire Bulgarian government three years earlier) protested that their countries—whatever the level of economic development—had already achieved most of the preconditions for a socialist revolution. The Comintern held that in both types of revolution the Communist Party must bring the majority (sometimes called the "decisive strata") of the proletariat under its own influence. In a concession, the leadership granted that the Bulgarian party had done so at least in part, and the final program of the Sixth Congress concluded that "in *some* of these countries [in the second category] there is possible a process of a more or less swift growing together of the bourgeois-democratic revolution into the socialist revolution," with particular reference to Poland and Bulgaria.[4]

For certain countries in the second category, the final program specified the possibility of "types of proletarian revolution, but with a greater number of tasks of a bourgeois-democratic character." As far as Japan and Spain were concerned, the best that could be foreseen was that a future bourgeois-democratic revolution might soon "grow over" into a socialist revolution. A Spanish delegate at a subsequent plenum of the ECCI declared that the bourgeois democratic revolution in Spain remained incomplete in three key respects: persistence of large landholdings, the unresolved problem of national minorities, and a blocked political system of "feudal monarchy."[5]

The Comintern also stressed the role of allies in the revolutionary process, and the potential allies that received the most attention were the peasantry and national minorities. Peasant revolts were seen as generally playing "a very great—and sometimes decisive—role," a role, in fact, that was considered a major difference between first- and second-category capitalist countries. Next in importance were national minorities; Communist parties were instructed "to come out unequivocally on the side of full national independence for the minorities," as Lenin had done in 1917. The third general sector of allies lay in the urban petite bourgeoisie, though relations with this sector involved so much complication and contradiction that the concept of alliance with it was left largely undeveloped.

The 1928 theses involved the usual Communist carrot-and-stick approach, emphasizing the importance of peace proposals and disarmament. It was frankly stated, however, that this approach was not intended to disarm the proletariat, for generalized civil war in capitalist countries was inevitable. Disarmament proposals served two functions, one being to expose the true policy of the capitalist powers, and the other in certain circumstances to provide a brief breathing space for the Soviet Union. The official history of the Soviet party defined as just wars those for social revolution and national liberation. In a subsequent published letter to Gorky of January 17, 1930, Stalin wrote: "We are *for* a liberating, anti-imperialist, revolutionary war despite the fact that such a war, as is known, not only is not free from 'the horrors of bloodshed' but abounds in them."[6]

The primary emphasis in the 1928 program was on the growth of conflict, especially within capitalist societies. Comintern spokesmen referred to the growth of "state capitalism" and of "fascization" and "radicalization." "Fascization" was defined as the "terrorist dictatorship of big capital," as "direct dictatorship, ideologically masked by an 'all-national idea.'" Fascization employed social demagogy and might even appear to be temporarily anticapitalist but was above all counterrevolutionary. "The chief task of fascism is the destruction of the revolutionary vanguard, i.e., the Communist strata of the proletariat and their cadres." This effort would only produce rapid radicalization, as the Third Period intensified contradictions within capitalism, sharpened the class struggle, and led inevitably to imperialist war.[7]

With the launching of the official anti-Bukharinite campaign in 1929, Stalin identified himself fully with the strategy of the Third Period. That strategy brought renewed emphasis on the "united front from below," an about-face from the "united front from above," which had been the Party's policy since 1924. That policy had permitted common action with other worker groups, while the united front from below recognized unity only with the ordinary members of other movements, who were to be incorporated directly into Communist groups, bypassing their own organizations. This strategy was accompanied by renewed emphasis on identifying social democracy as "social fascism." The Soviet foreign minister, Georgy Chicherin, grasped the artificiality and destructiveness of that idea, and apparently wrote in protest to Stalin in June 1929, but the concept of social fascism was officially endorsed at the Tenth Plenum of the ECCI the following month.[8]

The Third Period was accompanied by a more aggressive military strategy. The main action occurred in northern Manchuria, where the Chinese government began to seize control of the Soviet-owned Chinese Eastern Railway. A Red Army corps of approximately 100,000 troops was formed on the Manchurian border and moved across in a series of actions between August and October 1929, routing the much more poorly prepared Chinese. The resultant Soviet dominance over northern Manchuria became the catalyst for the Japanese invasion of Manchuria two years later, ostensibly to remove the Soviet menace.[9] Japan's response would become so overwhelming that a few years later Stalin pulled back, withdrawing from Manchuria altogether. The complete failure of Soviet policy in northern Manchuria would run parallel to the total political frustration of the Comintern during the Third Period.

The other armed Soviet action was an abortive incursion into Afghanistan in May 1929. Some 800 Red Army troops disguised as Afghans crossed the border nominally to restore a claimant to the Afghan throne, but the would-be king soon abandoned the enterprise. While otherwise friendly countries such as Iran and Turkey manifested alarm, the operation was quickly aborted.

The key country in Europe remained Germany, where the number one enemy was the German Social Democratic Party (Sozialdemokratische Partei Deutschlands, or SPD), which collaborated fully with democratic parliamentarianism, was the chief mainstay of the German Republic, and strongly supported a foreign policy oriented toward other Western democracies. For its assault on the Republic the KPD had meanwhile developed its own fascist-style political militia, the Rote Frontkämpferbund (Red League of Front Fighters), known as "storm troopers of the proletariat," whose highly militarized uniforms went fascist shirt movements one better and helped to qualify the KPD as the foremost movement of social fascism. By 1927 it had developed the clenched-fist "red front" salute and had become increasingly aggressive at a time when Hitler's National Socialist movement was growing only very slowly.[10] After the Socialist police chief of Berlin banned mass outdoor political rallies, a KPD riot produced a major street battle in the German capital on May Day 1929, leaving some thirty dead. The KPD's Twelfth Congress, in June 1929, declared categorically that "Social Democracy is preparing . . . the establishment of the fascist dictatorship."[11]

Meanwhile official Soviet and Comintern policy professed only peaceful intentions. "On no occasion did the Comintern state or suggest that the USSR should undertake an offensive revolutionary war," nor did it maintain that war between capitalist countries should be encouraged merely to foment revolution. The 1928 program denounced as "senseless calumnies" the notion that Communists were seeking to spark a war among capitalists to encourage revolution, though at the end of the following decade Soviet policy would seek to do exactly that.[12] The accelerated militarization that accompanied the First Five-Year Plan also played a role, the Comintern painting a picture of an increasingly powerful Soviet Union whose might compelled respect by capitalist powers.[13] The Soviet government sought a series of nonaggression pacts with other European countries that would guarantee it time to develop its own resources—a situation that the Comintern claimed would inevitably benefit the world revolution. During 1931–32 the Soviet leaders signed nonaggression pacts with Finland, Lithuania, Latvia, Estonia, France, and Poland.[14]

At the beginning of the new decade, the main threat of instability came on the Soviet Union's Asian frontier. During 1929–30, while the Soviets were adventuring in Afghanistan and northern Manchuria, the Muslim rebels that their opponents called *basmachi* (bandits) renewed their activity in parts of Soviet Central Asia and the Caucasus. The main threat in Central Asia had been put down by 1931 and the Soviets signed a nonaggression pact with Afghanistan, but guerrilla bands appeared again in the Caucasus in 1932. In this situation the Soviets responded to Japan's aggression in Manchuria in 1931 with appeasement. Stalin ceased sending arms to China and offered Japan a nonaggression pact. After a very hostile response by the United States to Japan's takeover of Manchuria, the Soviets hoped for a conflict between Japan and the United States, which would relieve any pressure on the Soviet eastern frontier.

For the Comintern, the most active Asian front was French Indochina, where the Indochinese Communist Party had been reunited in 1929. The Comintern was heavily involved in several mutinies and revolts there in 1930, with inevitable harm to relations with France. As Jonathan Haslam has written, "Two irreconcilable objectives—peaceful coexistence and class warfare—were being pursued by different arms of the same authority."[15]

No such problem existed vis-à-vis China, where the Chinese Communists were engaged in full-scale revolutionary civil war, which led to temporary establishment of a Chinese Soviet Republic in 1931 (even though this initiative made nonsense of the four categories of the Comintern's 1928 program). The Soviets could provide little assistance, however, and in the next few years the Chinese Communists grew steadily weaker. One new opportunity did arise for the Soviets in the far western fringe of China, a militarily more accessible area, in December 1933. Some 2,000 Red Army troops, partly dressed as civilians, intervened in Sinkiang to restore a Chinese warlord who had been deposed by native Muslim forces. Soviet "advisers" remained there (in conditions somewhat similar to those of Spain three years later) and exercised considerable influence until they were finally ordered out in 1942.[16]

Ironically, during this period the Soviet Union's best relations with any of the larger powers were perhaps with Fascist Italy, which was eager to collaborate with it against French influence. The Soviet government had been actively pursuing an international disarmament policy, and Italy was the only power strongly to back Soviet inclusion in any potential international program.

For the Comintern the chief battleground remained Germany, where the KPD took an intransigent revolutionary position. Onset of the Great Depression and the severe crisis that developed in Germany were deemed objective proof of the accuracy of the Comintern's analysis and of that country's revolutionary possibilities. Even the rapid rise of Nazism was accepted as only weakening the bourgeois system further. An editorial in *Pravda* on September 16, 1930, declared that though the National Socialists represented "the bourgeoisie," they "had successfully used 'anticapitalist slogans'" and were winning over voters, "especially the young." Hence they should be seen as "fighters for the social liberation of the masses, for the overthrow of the Versailles Treaty and the Young Plan yoke," both of which were also being combated by Communist policy.[17] The rise of National Socialism was seen as positive because it weakened French influence and the possibility of any future Franco-German rapprochement. Even if it constituted fascism, it merely represented the last gasp of the bourgeoisie and need not be feared, since its appearance represented the prelude to an inevitable Communist victory. Thus Communists and Nazis would sometimes make common cause against the Social Democrats and the democratic republic, and the policy of "united front from below" may even have had the effect of permitting rank-and-file Nazis and Communists occasionally to work more easily together. Similarly, the Soviet government was opposed to any Western effort to improve Germany's finances, because, as Karl Radek said in *Izvestia* on July 10, 1931, anything that reduced conflict among the Western powers was bad for the Soviet Union.[18]

With each passing month, nonetheless, the latent conflict between Communists and Nazis moved to the fore, and ultimately most of the street violence that occurred in Germany during the Depression crisis consisted of battles between the two, frequently lethal.[19] These conflicts in no way prevented the KPD from supporting the Nazi demand for a plebiscite to oust the Socialists from control of the Prussian government. A plebiscite was finally held in August 1931 but was won by the Socialists. The fact that the Rote Frontkämpferbund was the principal foe of the Nazis in the accelerated street fighting in Germany had the nominal effect of vindicating Communist "antifascism," all the while that the Comintern insisted that the main enemy and hence the principal "fascists" continued to be the Socialists. Indeed, street conflict with the Nazis had to be toned down to some extent by 1932 simply because the Nazis were becoming so numerous. In Moscow the Eleventh Plenum of the ECCI in March–April 1932 reaffirmed that the highest level of struggle against fascism was the fight against the "cretinism" of parliamentary democracy. After two and a half years of crisis in Germany the Soviet leaders concluded that things were going well: the Republic and democracy were clearly weaker, the KPD vote had increased to nearly 18 percent, and by November 1932 the Nazi vote had begun to decline.[20]

Spain had long held a lower priority for the Comintern, and even the collapse of the Primo de Rivera regime and the opening of an uncertain new constituent period in Spanish government did not immediately change that. The exiled Trotsky, who had visited Spain in 1916 and long sustained an interest in its revolutionary possibilities, was more perceptive. "As usual," he observed, "the leaders of the Comintern started out by overlooking Spanish events. Manuilsky . . . only recently declared that the Spanish events do not deserve attention. There you are! In 1928 these people declared France to be on the eve of revolution. After having long accompanied funerals with wedding music, they could not but greet a wedding with a funeral march. . . . When it appeared, nevertheless, that the events in Spain, not foreseen in the calendar of the 'third period,' continued to develop, the leaders of the Comintern were simply silent." Then the Comintern's Manuilsky did a "180-degree turn," announcing in *Pravda* on December 17, 1930, that the government of Dámaso Berenguer, briefly prime minister of Spain, was a "fascist regime." Trotsky correctly pointed out that it was simply a right-wing military government of the old style, adding, "Once there is a ready epithet, why bother to think?" The Comintern then began to practice the self-deception that "the Spanish proletariat" was adopting the Communist program, and that the formation of "peasant soviets" was now at hand.[21]

The Tenth Plenum of the ECCI coincided with the downfall of the monarchy and the inauguration of the Second Republic, bringing formal recognition by the Comintern that Spain was now one of five European countries (the others were Germany, Poland, Hungary, and Bulgaria) in which revolution was actively on the march. Spain suddenly leap-frogged Japan on the Comintern list, though later that year the central committee of the Japanese Communist Party declared that Japan was also now ready for socialist revolution. The Japanese government, however, was truculently refusing to sign a nonaggression pact with the Soviet Union, and the Comintern would therefore not permit any new revolutionary offensive in Japan. Thus in March 1932 its West European bureau announced that the Japanese party was mistaken. Japan, it said, combined both feudalism and capitalism with a powerful, relatively independent monarchy that supported both feudal landlords and the capitalist bourgeoisie, but was not subservient to either. The bourgeois-democratic revolution had not yet arrived fully in Japan, so it was clearly not prepared for proletarian revolution.[22]

Regarding Spain, the Comintern held to its analysis of 1928, according to which the country still had to complete the bourgeois-democratic revolution, but now it added that capitalism and existing institutions had been so weakened that Spain was poised to pass rapidly from the bourgeois-democratic revolution to the proletarian-socialist revolution. Therefore the Spanish Communist Party must do nothing to defend the new bourgeois pseudodemocratic capitalist republic or to ally with the Spanish Socialists, whose collaboration with the new regime revealed a degree of "social fascism" equivalent to that of the German Social Democrats. Instead it must engage in all-out revolutionary agitation among workers and peasants to prepare as soon as possible for a "Soviet Spain."[23]

An extensive literature by travelers to the Soviet Union already existed in Spain, as in other European countries, and the coming of the new republic—which enormously heightened expectations of change in many sectors of the population—coincided with a new explosion of Marxist literature. The Comintern greatly increased its propaganda activities; Maurín's Ediciones Europa-América was moved from Paris to Barcelona, and numerous new editions of Marxist works were issued, even by a noncommunist publisher such as Editorial Cénit. Soviet cultural diffusion increased considerably, together with Soviet broadcasts in Spain, and new front organizations proliferated.[24] Chief among them was the Asociación de Amigos de la URSS, set up in April 1933, whose members included various Spanish cultural luminaries and Socialist leaders such as Luis Jiménez de Asúa and Juan Negrín. Within three months it gained a membership of 7,000 and continued to grow.[25] This expansion naturally heightened alarm among conservatives over the growth of the Communist menace.

Comintern advisers were nonetheless fit to be tied over the situation of the PCE itself, which seemed incapable of significant new initiatives. A variety of tactics were devised to try to jump-start the party, but nothing seemed to work. The basic Comintern strategy called on the Spanish party to copy the Soviet experience as closely as possible, forming a network of soviets to create a kind of USSR of Iberia, with nominally autonomous republics for Castile, Portugal, Catalonia, the Basque Country, and several other regions as well. The idea was to transcend the democratic republic rapidly by championing a "democratic worker-peasant dictatorship" that would overcome what Comintern advisers saw as the "feudal and Asiatic residues" in Spain.[26] Thus several violent

May Day demonstrations took place in 1931, most notably in Seville (one of the few cities where the PCE had any strength at all), where the army was called out and a number of people were killed.

The PCE leaders were summoned to Moscow that month and interrogated about Spanish conditions, concerning which the Comintern officials revealed gross ignorance. Bullejos was bewildered when Manuilsky asked if feudal overlords still required Spanish peasants to do forced labor, and was admonished by the Comintern hierarchy that "there is more feudalism in Spain than you think."[27] On May 19 Manuilsky presented the Spanish leaders with a lengthy report demanding that the screws be tightened in the party organization. It denounced the leaders for failure to act like true Bolsheviks and introduce a slogan demanding the forming of soviets. They talked back to Comintern officials when they did not even understand their own country: Bullejos had insisted to Manuilsky (quite accurately) that there were no direct residues of feudalism in Spain, thus revealing that they hid the truth from themselves. Manuilsky decreed that Spain still suffered from aspects of overt feudalism: personal servitude, forced labor, internal tariffs, and "religious orders as in the Middle Ages" were some of the principal figments of his imagination. He announced that Spain under the Republic really resembled the Russia of Nicholas I (an extraordinary idea even for a Comintern official, Nicholas's Russia having been a total autocracy that had ended in 1855). A land as backward as Spain still had to pass through the bourgeois-democratic revolution, but as rapidly as possible; the Republic itself was unable to complete the Marxist-Leninist version of the bourgeois-democratic revolution, having inaugurated only a bourgeois counterrevolution. The task of the PCE was to move Spain rapidly forward, extending the bourgeois-democratic revolution—however deformed —into the "dictatorship of the workers and peasants." It must make clear to Spaniards that the constituent assembly about to be democratically elected merely represented the disguise of the monarchist counterrevolution. It must build a network of revolutionary committees and a worker revolutionary guard so as to create a Soviet Spain resembling the Russia of 1917 as soon as possible.

All efforts to follow this injunction over the summer failed, so the leaders were summoned back to Moscow in October. Manuilsky informed them in an essay that "the Spanish revolution has great international importance. It threatens French imperialism, which is fixed between the revolutionary movements in Spain and Germany. On the other side of the Channel is found the revolutionary movement being unleashed in England. The fate of the Spanish revolution is therefore closely tied to the problems of the entire international revolutionary movement." Bullejos tried futilely to convince the Comintern leaders that Spain was dominated not by feudalism but by a bourgeoisie that was carrying out a bourgeois counterrevolution rather than a monarchist one. This explanation merely led Manuilsky to reminisce grimly that the first Spanish "Communists" to come to Moscow in 1920 had been anarchists. As it was, he said, the present inept leadership of the PCE was the chief "obstacle to the Bolshevization of the party."[28]

What infuriated the Comintern leaders was that the only real revolutionary outburst in Spain during the Republic's first year was the failed insurrection of January 1932 by the Iberian Anarchist Federation in alliance with the National Confederation of Workers (FAI-CNT), the PCE having proved impotent. To Moscow, the FAI-CNT initiative demonstrated that Spain had a "revolutionary proletariat," or at least a potentially revolutionary proletariat, but that the PCE was not an effective Bolshevik party.[29] The Comintern bosses believed that this situation had enough potential to merit closer supervision. The Italo-Argentine Vittorio Codovilla, a native speaker of Spanish, who would be known to the PCE as Medina, was made adviser to the leadership in Madrid, while the able Hungarian Comintern operative Erno Gero (known in Spain as Comrade Pedro) was sent to Barcelona to try to expand the almost nonexistent Communist presence in the largest center of radical worker activity. When the Fourth Congress of the PCE convened in Seville on March 17, 1932, Bullejos, still apparently bewildered by some Comintern directives, was reconfirmed for lack of an alternative, but several new figures were brought into the party's politburo. The most important was José Díaz, a former CNT official in Seville, who since his entry into the party five years earlier had demonstrated unswerving loyalty. The paper that Codovilla prepared for the congress explained that the Republic was being supported on the right by the monarchists and on the left by the "social fascists" of the PSOE, that the present administration of Manuel Azaña was a mere "government of transition to the open dictatorship of the haute bourgeoisie," which would soon become a "clear-cut fascist dictatorship." In order to defeat the counterrevolution—that is, Republican democracy—they must create revolutionary committees throughout the country, organize shock brigades to send out among peasants, and use both initiatives to set up soviets all over Spain, just as though the civically, economically, and culturally more advanced Spain of 1932 were only the backward Russia of 1917.[30]

When a feeble military revolt was attempted against the Republican government in August 1932, Bullejos and the PCE leadership stumbled badly once more, in the opinion of the Comintern. They attempted to rally support for the Republic in danger, launching the slogans—the PCE at this point could do little more than launch slogans—"Defense of the Republic" and "Revolutionary defense of the Republic." Codovilla insisted it should be "Long live the soviets," but to Bullejos and some of the other party leaders that seemed absurd; they could not imagine how the possible overthrow of the Republic could be in the party's interest. After being denounced by Codovilla as a counterrevolutionary, the hapless Bullejos had to resign, as did two other top leaders. At a meeting on August 19 the politburo once more declared total loyalty to the Comintern, but also decided by a vote of 7 to 2 that the former leaders should not be characterized as counterrevolutionaries, a move that further infuriated Codovilla. Together with several other figures, the three were then recalled to Moscow. While they were absent Codovilla arranged a new meeting of the politburo on September 27, which by this time had been properly coached to return a total denunciation. The Comintern authorities then officially expelled the old leaders from the party at the end of October.[31]

The autumn of 1932 became the time of the *gran viraje*, or big shift, in PCE leadership, as new figures of greater subservience but also of equal or greater energy were elevated to the top levels. José Díaz, who earlier had helped to bring a part of the Seville CNT into the party, was promoted from head of the organization in Andalusia to secretary general, a position he would hold throughout the following dramatic decade.[32] The young Bilbao firebrand Jesús Hernández, one of the first Spanish graduates of the Lenin School in Moscow, was given command of the party's Agitprop Department, while Vicente Uribe was made editor of the party newspaper, *Mundo obrero*. The first significant woman leader in the party, Dolores Ibárruri, the separated wife of a Socialist miner in the Basque Country, was made head of the women's secretariat and the only female member of the politburo. Years earlier, she had published her first article on the worker movement at Easter and so adopted the nom de plume Pasionaria. She would be widely known by that name as she eventually became the dominant figure in Spanish communism and the most important woman in twentieth-century Spain.[33] The prime qualifications for these appointments were unconditional subservience to the Comintern and a high level of zeal in executing Comintern policies. The new leadership would abundantly manifest these qualities over the next seven years. It was this new leadership that would merit this judgment of Antonio Elorza and Marta Bizcarrondo: "One can no longer truthfully speak of the history of the Communist Party of Spain, but of the history of the Spanish section of the Communist International."[34]

A seven-member secretariat of top party administrators would now meet weekly with other high officeholders; a secretariat for illegal activities was established to advance a plan to create new "national" Communist parties in Catalonia and the Basque Country. The basic goal would remain the establishment of a worker-peasant government in Spain as soon as possible, based on a nominal congress of soviets. The initial program of the revolutionary regime would be not to institute full socialism but to confiscate large landholdings, nationalize large industry and banking and transportation, and dissolve all religious orders.[35]

Manuilsky is said to have earlier declared to Spanish students in the Lenin School in Moscow: "You are a state in which there are numerous nations. You have the Basques, the Gascons [sic], you have Andalusia and Morocco." In order to infiltrate all the nationalist and regionalist movements, the Communists promised full self-determination to all potential separatist areas. The new Partit Comunista de Catalunya was organized in 1933, and at its first congress a year later claimed to have 800 members. Similarly, a Comintern decree of July 27, 1933, instructed that a PC-Euzkadi was to be set up, though "clearly understood on the same basis as the Partit Comunista de Catalunya for its integration into the Communist Party of Spain." The Basque party might be used as a small revolutionary wedge against France, with the goal of including the three Basque departments in southwestern France in a new revolutionary "Union of Basque-Navarrese Socialist Republics." Thus the Basque-Navarrese Federation of the PCE was transformed into the PC de Euzkadi during the course of 1934, though its Basque secretary general, Juan Astigarrabía, would later complain that he enjoyed no independence whatsoever.[36]

Throughout 1932–33 the standard Third Period policies remained in force. The perception of the Soviet leadership was that the Depression was continuing to worsen, hastening the "general crisis" of capitalism, though it might also hasten war. Social democracy as "social fascism" remained the number one enemy, though this grotesque policy generated more than a little discontent among some ordinary Communists. In Germany, for example, lower-level activists on several occasions tried to form "Antifa" or antifascist action agreements with local Social Democrats, but always without official KPD support. In Bohemia, Czech Communist unions won a major strike through alliance with Social Democrat leaders, though this united front from above contradicted Comintern policy. More typical of that policy was the KPD's collaboration with the Nazis in the big Berlin transport workers' strike of November 1932.[37] During the early 1930s it was the exiled Trotsky who insisted that "real fascism," meaning the Nazis, was becoming the main danger, but such a concept remained heretical.

Thus in Spain the main enemy was still the PSOE, the social fascist party par excellence. The new tactic of the PCE at the start of 1933 was to try to form direct workplace committees in factories and shops (Comités de Fábrica y de Campesinos), bypassing the syndicates in order to develop the nuclei of future soviets. The triumph of Hitler at the close of January had no effect on the Comintern, which ruled as late as December 1933, at its thirteenth plenum, that there had never been any viable choice between bourgeois democracy and fascism in Germany, since the two were interchangeable.

The Hitler triumph nonetheless had more than a little psychological effect on ordinary Communists in a number of countries, and the ECCI did momentarily relax its strictures against the united front from above in March 1933. When the Madrid section of the PSOE held a meeting on March 15 to try to unify the efforts of the left against fascism in Spain, Communists were allowed to attend and momentarily proposed the formation of joint "Comités y Milicias Antifascistas." On the following day, the PCE's central committee published an open letter in *Mundo obrero* on the need for a general worker united front against the danger of fascism in Spain, the idea now being a united front from above in which the PCE would play the leading role. On March 19 the party held a meeting in the Frontón Central to launch its Frente Unico Antifascista (Sole Antifascist Front, or FUA), but the Socialists had no interest in joining a front dominated by Communists. The Comintern leadership was soon dissatisfied with the results of such ploys in various countries, and canceled the tactic by May.[38] In Spain, however, the FUA, once launched, was allowed to continue, though it was composed exclusively of the PCE, the Juventudes Comunistas (Young Communists), the Communist Comité de Unidad Sindical, and the Liga Atea (Atheist League), a Communist front modeled on the League of the Militant Godless in the Soviet Union (and hence originally called in 1932 La Liga de Los Sin Dios). It managed to rope in a few notable noncommunist intellectuals, nonetheless, and theoretically it was the FUA that initiated formation of the Milicias Antifascistas Obreras y Campesinas (Worker-Peasant Antifascist Militias, or MAOC), the new Communist militia organization, on an extremely modest basis.[39]

Thus by the spring of 1933 "fascism" had become more prominent in PCE discourse than ever, but substantive confusion abounded. Who was a real fascist? Were there in fact any real fascists? The Socialists were still often called social fascists, while the democratic Republic was itself labeled fascist or "fascistoid." The liberal democrats of Alejandro Lerroux's Radical Party were "integral fascists." Conversely, the FAI-CNT repaid Communists in their own coin, employing the same sort of conflation. For *Solidaridad obrera*, the main CNT mouthpiece, both "reaction" and Stalinist communism were "fascist," as at various times were the moderate left ("Republican fascists") and the Socialists ("social fascists"). By 1933 almost everyone in Republican Spain was calling his opponents fascists, though the only genuinely fascist movement, the Juntas de Ofensiva Nacional-Sindicalista (Leagues of National-Syndicalist Offensive, or JONS), was very much smaller than the PCE.

During 1933 the PCE absorbed two small revolutionary parties, the Izquierda Revolucionaria y Antiimperialista (Revolutionary and Anti-imperialist Left) of the Peruvian journalist César Falcón, which had scarcely a thousand members, and the Partido Social Revolucionario of José Antonio Balbontín and Ramón Lamoneda, which may have had 3,000 members. The PCE claimed to have increased its membership from 11,756 in March 1932 to 19,489 a year later, but much of this increase was doubtless fictitious. Though the party did pick up a fair number of new members, many did not remain very long, and recruitment was often stronger in poor agrarian provinces than in urban centers. By the middle of 1933 the party had fewer than 2,000 members in Madrid, though more than twice that number had passed through the membership lists in the capital during the past two years. Of 1,500 new members in Granada province, scarcely as many as 500 remained in the party.[40] Records indicated that the party's trade union affiliate, the Confederación General del Trabajo Unitario (Unitary General Confederation of Labor, or CGTU), had 36,935 members by the end of 1932.[41]

Mid-1933 was a time of rapid change in Spanish politics as the governing left Republican–Socialist coalition began to weaken and the overt radicalization of part of the socialist movement began. On July 28, 1933, the Spanish administration and the Soviet government exchanged formal notes of de jure recognition, but regular diplomatic relations and an exchange of ambassadors had still not been completed when Azaña fell two months later, and these initiatives were frozen by the administrations that followed. Diplomatic relations with the USSR would not be fully established until after the Civil War began.

The second Republican elections of November 1933 were a disaster for the left; only the PSOE maintained a significant parliamentary representation. The Republican electoral law strongly favored coalitions, but the left was fragmented. The PCE remained isolated, thanks to the policy of the Comintern, which controlled the party's electoral campaign. The PSOE, as usual, was denounced as counterrevolutionary social fascism, and Francisco Largo Caballero, the former labor minister who was now moving to a revolutionary position, was scorned as the author of "fascist laws" and "the chief hangman of the Spanish revolution." Thus the party failed to elect a single candidate, though in the second round of balloting the PSOE and PCE overcame their mutual antipathy to form a Frente Unico Antifascista in Málaga, making possible the election of a Communist physician, Dr. Cayetano Bolívar, who became the first PCE parliamentary deputy. Altogether Communist candidates drew nearly 200,000 votes, centered especially in Madrid, Vizcaya, Andalusia (Córdoba, Málaga, and Seville), and Toledo.[42]

For the Comintern, the prospect was growing steadily more somber. Not only was the Hitler dictatorship consolidating itself—contrary to all Soviet predictions—but the capitalist economies had begun to improve slightly. Manuilsky admitted to the Seventeenth Congress of the CPSU that "the lowest point of the economic crisis" had passed by the end of 1932.[43]

The Comintern was out of ideas, so the basic line continued. Several of the new Spanish leaders were invited to the Thirteenth Plenum of the ECCI in Moscow at the end of 1933. Hernández, the youngest but the best trained and possibly the brightest, made the principal Spanish presentation, but the greatest attention was drawn by Ibárruri. On her first visit to Moscow she delivered an impassioned address in Spanish; though the ECCI members scarcely understood a word, they were impressed by her style and intensity. Several of them raised the question whether the party line in Spain was too extreme, and even Ibárruri, though never given to question Moscow's directives, drew attention to the PCE's total isolation. The decision of the ECCI nonetheless remained rigid. Stepanov, head of the Latin Section, repeated the standard line—whether directed toward the CNT or the PSOE—that "in Spain it is the anarchosyndicalists above all who are active in the fascist movement."[44] The new recruit Balbontín left the PCE in March 1934 over this kind of tactic, insisting that it must learn to ally with other worker parties, and even with middle-class left Republicans. More and more ordinary Communists in Spain, France, and elsewhere were beginning to raise the same question.

CHAPTER FOUR

From Revolutionary Insurrection to Popular Front

1934–1936

THE ATTEMPT to develop an independent, more original and imaginative Marxism-Leninism adapted to Spanish circumstances was carried on by Joaquín Maurín and the Bloque Obrero y Campesino (Worker-Peasant Bloc, or BOC), formed in Barcelona in March 1931. The name of the new group stemmed from the original Comintern ploy of 1923 to form a Groupe Ouvrier et Paysan (Worker and Peasant Group) as an electoral front for the French Communist Party. The BOC set itself the goal of forming "a Great Worker-Peasant Party," with the political nucleus formed by the independent Catalan Communist FCC-B, while the BOC—as in the earlier Comintern strategy—was to form a broader mass organization. Maurín and his colleagues argued that this was the most useful strategy, since direct Bolshevization on the basis of the party alone had failed in both France and Spain.

The FCC-B had conceived of itself as a classic Leninist party, though largely independent of the Comintern and totally divorced from it by 1930, organized by cells and practicing "democratic centralism," which in its case seemed to reflect a degree of intraparty democracy lacking in orthodox Comintern-affiliated parties. Members of district *(comarca)* and provincial groups could be elected directly by members, and the secretary general was directly chosen by a party congress.

Maurín explained his analysis of the situation most clearly in *La revolución española,* which appeared at the close of 1931. He judged the basis of the bourgeois-democratic revolution to be weak in Spain. Since the bourgeoisie itself

was feeble and the working class divided, the current Comintern policy of proceeding directly to the "democratic dictatorship of the proletariat and the peasantry," collapsing the bourgeois-democratic revolution as directly as possible
into the socialist revolution, made no sense. On that basis, the bourgeois-
democratic revolution would simply collapse at the hands of the counterrevolution (as it finally did in 1939). Given such weakness, the bourgeois-democratic
revolution could be completed only by the "armed working class," which must
seek unity to assist this process, not by direct collaboration with the bourgeoisie
on bourgeois terms but by pressing this process forward to its highest and
strongest stage. This would require breaking the power of the church and the
army, distributing all land to the peasants, and providing self-determination
(at least in theory) to the national minorities. In the process the Spanish working
class was to form "revolutionary worker-peasant juntas" that would begin to play
the role of soviets, but the principle of the democratic revolution must initially
be respected, since in 1931 most Spanish workers, after the experience of the
Primo de Rivera dictatorship, insisted on political democracy. By "political democracy" Maurín did not mean individualist liberal democracy, for safeguarding
and completing the bourgeois-democratic revolution was a matter not merely
of freedom or constitutional guarantees, but of breaking the power of conservative interests and creating a society that would be oriented toward the working
class, together with the petite bourgeoisie and the national minorities; only
then could Spain begin to proceed toward the socialist revolution. Since the
FCC-B/BOC basically rejected liberal democracy, this analysis seemed like the
merest splitting of hairs to the non-Marxist outsider, but to the BOC revolutionaries it called for a fundamentally different approach to working-class politics.

The basic FCC-B/BOC program therefore set forth such revolutionary
goals as giving all land to those who worked it, recognizing self-determination
for national minorities, arming a worker militia, controlling industrial production
by the syndicates, and nationalizing banking, mines, and transport. This program was to be carried out in conjunction with the consolidation of the bourgeois-democratic revolution; and only after that revolution had been completed
would it be possible to talk of establishing a worker-peasant republic, which
could move on to the socialist revolution.[1]

The BOC drew fewer than 20,000 votes in the elections of 1931—only a
fraction of the PCE's—but a month later was demanding "all power to the
worker organizations." It judged the functioning of liberal democracy very
harshly, declaring by August that repression was worse under the Republic
than under Primo de Rivera. It agreed with the Comintern that social democrats

were the worst enemies of the workers, and continued to place great hope in the CNT, which it publicly urged to take power through juntas or workers' councils that could play the role of soviets.

After the small dissident Agrupación Política Madrileña, which had split from the PCE in 1930, collapsed at the beginning of 1932 and most of its members rejoined the main party, the only remaining dissident Leninist sector was the tiny Spanish group affiliated with the former Soviet left opposition, which had constituted itself as the Oposición Comunista de España (OCE) in Belgium in 1930. Its strongest personality, Andreu Nin, did not, however, agree with fractionalist tactics and sought a major organized alternative, basically in line with Trotskyist policies. He asked to join the FCC-B but was rejected as excessively sectarian, too narrowly tied to Trotskyism. Trotsky's own idea at this point was that the OCE should work to take over the PCE. He judged Maurín to be "a comical personage with provincial reflexes, corrupt doctrines and primitive slogans."[2] The FCC-B, conversely, respected Trotsky himself, even as it judged Trotskyist guidelines to be narrow and mistaken. The OCE then transformed itself into the Izquierda Comunista de España (Communist Left of Spain, or ICE) in March 1932 as a formally Trotskyist party, still claiming to be a dissident fraction of the PCE (though not affiliated with the Comintern) while simultaneously the only real alternative to it.[3]

By the beginning of 1932 the BOC claimed to have 6,000 members but probably enjoyed no more than half as many. With its tiny supporting sectors in Madrid, Asturias, and Valencia, it organized a so-called Federación Comunista Ibérica (FCI) for the entire peninsula in April 1932, and at the same time merged the cell structure of the FCC-B with the BOC, the two being known henceforth exclusively as the BOC. Though its spokesmen occasionally applied the Soviet term "social fascists" to the Spanish Socialists, Maurín was careful never to do so himself, and in June 1932 the BOC paper *La Batalla* for the first time denounced this Soviet practice. As the Nazi tide rose in Germany, it also denounced the suicidal Comintern-dictated policy of the KPD, identifying it with the policies of bureaucratization and mass repression in the USSR, while the ECCI in turn issued a secret but lengthy denunciation of "renegade communism," its catchall term for Maurín, the BOC, and the tiny Trotskyist group of Andreu Nin.[4] The BOC claimed to espouse a sort of pure "Leninist" revolutionary position, declaring that Trotskyism was scarcely any better than Stalinist Sovietism, for it too supported "mechanico-centralist methods."[5]

One of the BOC's main goals, like that of the PCE, was to destroy "Spanish imperialism" by freeing all regions of the peninsula from the oppression of the imperial Spanish state formed in the early modern period. It called for an "Iberian Union of Socialist Republics," a free union of the socialist republics of Castile, Catalonia, Andalusia, the Basque Country, Portugal, Gibraltar, Aragon, the Balearic islands, Murcia, and Valencia. Far from being merely fragmenting or balkanizing, this plan was declared simply to be the Leninist model of the great Russian revolution (again differing little from the Comintern formulation). By 1933, however, the BOC leadership began to take a more moderate line, supporting separate states only for the "historic nationalities," mainly the Catalans and Basques. This plan in turn became a major bone of contention with the FAI-CNT, whose most radical elements promised armed insurrection against any attempt to sever Catalonia from Spain. The BOC was hostile to radical left Catalanism as inherently bourgeois, but Catalan was the language of most BOC members, though Maurín rarely wrote in it or spoke it in public. The BOC then denounced the autonomous Catalan government inaugurated in 1932 as treasonous and lacking sufficient autonomy, and insisted that it should have its own army. In October 1932 an erstwhile "revolutionary" sector of Estat Català split off to form EC-Partit Popolari (ECPP), declaring that it stood for a completely autonomous worker-peasant government in Catalonia and sympathized with the Comintern, but this move merely increased fragmentation. In Catalan regional elections in November the BOC drew only 20,000 votes; the Esquerra (Left Catalan) coalition amassed ten times as many.[6]

The BOC liked to see itself as the political organization of revolutionary workers in Catalonia and the CNT as the economic organization, but the Oposición Sindical Revolucionaria it had set up within the CNT in 1931 enjoyed scant success. Maurín's analysis of anarchosyndicalism remained simplistically Marxist, as he continued to term it a product merely of "agrarian, precapitalist" society. Nin occasionally did better, relating it to Catalan "economic individualism." At the beginning of the Republic the BOC had tentatively supported the FAI, the elite organization of anarchist activists, but soon denounced its revolutionary adventurism. Faístas in turn sometimes assaulted BOC meetings and there were frequent altercations, but by mid-1933 inept revolutionary extremism had caused the FAI to lose over half its members nationally and proportionately even more in Catalonia. The BOC's own efforts to develop a syndical arm at first enjoyed little success; its only achievement was in Lérida province, where its Unió Provincial Agraria (UPA), mainly of farm renters and sharecroppers, had about a thousand members. Decline of the CNT finally gave the BOC the chance to convene its own Congreso Regional de Sindicatos in October 1933, where it claimed to represent no fewer than 30,000 workers.[7]

The BOC's alliance policy called for a revolutionary worker *frente único* from above, rejecting the Comintern policy of union from the base as a futile attempt at Communist domination, which would be destructive in any case. As the Hitler regime consolidated itself in Germany during 1933, the BOC insisted that the Comintern's policy was based on fantasy, whereas Spain had a brighter future. In Spain the workers had not been defeated, the petite bourgeoisie had not rejected democracy as in Germany, and there was no fascist party of any consequence. The new Catholic Confederación Española de Derechas Autónomas (CEDA; Spanish Confederation of Autonomous Right Parties), though growing rapidly, was clerical and conservative, so that the reaction in Spain retained a rightist rather than a fascist character.[8]

This was a fundamentally sound analysis, but the first fascist scare in Spain developed in Madrid, first with the slow growth of the tiny JONS organization and then with the attempted publication of a weekly called *El Fascio*, prompting the first major concern about fascism among Socialists and formation of the isolated Communist Frente Unico Antifascista (FUA). At that time the BOC decided to organize an Alianza Obrera contra el Fascismo (Worker Alliance against Fascism) in Barcelona, made up of three small entities: the BOC, the even smaller (approximately thousand-member) Unió Socialista de Catalunya (USC), consisting mainly of white-collar employees, and a very small dissident syndicalist group.

This initial Alianza Obrera was minuscule and at first inconsequential, but it was the first genuine alliance of revolutionary worker groups, however limited. For the general elections of November 1933 the BOC formed an alliance with the Catalan sector of the PSOE, but its candidates drew only 24,000 votes —scarcely any more than earlier. Victory by the right cast a pall over the entire left, where disunity had been fatal. The BOC therefore immediately preached the need to form a broad worker front. On December 9 in Barcelona it took the initiative in forming a new and more extensive Alianza Obrera, composed of the BOC, the Catalan sector of the PSOE, the Catalan UGT, the USC, the Sindicatos de Oposición *(treintistas)*, the Federación Sindicalista Libertaria (FSL) (the latter two formerly of the CNT), the ICE, and the Unió de Rabassaires of Catalan vineyard sharecroppers. Its announced goal was to defeat fascism and advance the socialist revolution, and it expanded to Valencia in February 1934.

The Alianza Obrera's first major action was a general strike "against fascism" in Catalonia in March 1934. The action affected forty cities—enough to draw notice. But the Unió de Rabassaires withdrew, saying that the action was too drastic, while the treintistas declared that they would never again support such a tactic; in the future they would join only a general strike aimed directly at revolution.[9]

Though this was the first true revolutionary coalition, the main new factor within the Spanish left in 1934 was the radicalization of the Socialist Party. With the coming of the Republic in 1931, the PSOE had collaborated with the government, taking a position that put them to the right even of the French Socialists at that time and brought them close to the German or Scandinavian Social Democrats. Even those parties had not yet worked out all the de facto contradictions between their reformist policies and their theoretical Marxism, and the PSOE lagged even further behind in that regard. Always an orthodox Second International Marxist party, before 1931 it had never gone beyond electoral alliances with bourgeois republicans. There had been some division within the party when it decided to remain in the governing coalition in mid-1931 and no absolutely clear doctrinal position had been adopted. The general thinking was that the Republic would naturally lead to socialism, so that the bourgeois-democratic revolution could rather peacefully grow over into the socialist revolution. On July 1, 1931, *El Socialista* had reiterated that "above all else we are Marxists," the noted party intellectual Luis Araquistain had declared that the party would eventually move to the dictatorship of the proletariat "when appropriate," and the new Socialist deputy Juan Negrín had declared that the party could achieve "a dictatorship under democratic forms and appearances," yet in practice nearly all the activities of the PSOE had been similar to those of the Northern European Social Democrats.[10]

At the PSOE's Thirteenth Congress in 1932 the problem of reform within a parliamentary government had been extensively debated; there was talk of moving "rapidly to its termination," and of the need for Socialists to march directly toward "the full conquest of power," but representatives of only sixteen of the fifty-one districts of the party voted at that time to leave the government.[11] During 1933, however, both economic and social conditions deteriorated and the parties in power suffered considerable attrition. By March 1934 the UGT, which at one time numbered nearly a million members and had been favored by the Republic's new reformist legislation, had dwindled to only 397,000 dues payers, though its overall following remained a good deal greater than that.

Socialist activity under the Republic had by no means been altogether free of violence, particularly during the electoral campaign of 1931, but party leaders first seriously debated a revolutionary course at the Young Socialist Summer School at Torrelodones (Madrid) in 1933. The philosophy professor Julián Besteiro, veteran leader of both the party and the UGT, a moderate considered to be one of the party's few experts in theoretical Marxism, remained loyal to the classic Second International position. Besteiro opposed continuation in government but declared that a violent revolutionary policy would be an even greater aberration, a "collective madness"; an attempt to impose the dictatorship of the proletariat would prove a "vain childish illusion." He pointed to all the failures of revolutionary maximalism outside Russia and implored, "Is there no way to escape this dictatorial madness that is invading the world?"[12] But the veteran UGT leader and Republican minister of labor Francisco Largo Caballero declared that the recent policy had been a mistake and that the party must return to revolutionary Marxism, and even the more moderate party centrist Indalecio Prieto declared categorically that Socialist collaboration in any kind of bourgeois republican government "has definitively ended."[13] Nonetheless, there was no great pressure to abandon the existing government until it collapsed soon afterward. The growing restlessness found in Spanish society during the Republic cannot be fully understood without reference to the demographic changes taking place. Like the Weimar Republic during its later years, Spain at that time was experiencing the effects of the largest generation of young adults in its history, the consequence, in Spain as in Germany, of the relatively high birth rate of the early twentieth century combined with improved living conditions and reduced emigration. Whereas Spain's workforce incorporated 252,000 young adults in the five years from 1921 to 1926, the figure a decade later was 530,000, more than twice as many.[14] This unprecedentedly large contingent of young people grew increasingly restive, and would form the lance point of radicalization on both left and right.

The mood of the electoral campaign of 1933 differed considerably from the one two years earlier. Some Socialists talked of revolution; spokesmen of the extreme right made authoritarian threats against parliamentary government, and they were joined by José María Gil Robles, leader of the Catholic CEDA. The campaign was also marked by much more violence than that of 1931, and the Socialists were its main practitioners. Largo declared at one point that "we are in a full-scale civil war," and all those killed were rightists, with the exception of one Communist killed by a Socialist when he made the mistake of shouting criticism in a Socialist meeting. From November 1933, even the moderate left began to act to thwart constitutional government in Spain, beginning with the effort of the left Republicans and Socialists to obtain cancellation of the election results as soon as it became clear that they had lost. Electoral defeat strongly reinforced the radicalizing current within the PSOE.

Some historians have argued that the most decisive single development in the history of the Republic before the Civil War was this shift in Socialist policy during 1933–34, though there is no agreement concerning the causes of the change. Some ascribe it primarily to the new danger from the right, while others point to the influence of events in Central Europe after Hitler consolidated his regime and a rightist dictatorship was established in Austria, marking the defeat of what had been the two strongest Socialist parties in continental Europe. The deepening of the Depression in 1932–33 is sometimes also cited. Still others point to the beginning of the Socialists' radicalization in the summer of 1933, a phenomenon not specifically related to the chronology either of foreign affairs or of domestic electoral losses, but apparently stemming from the political weakening of their coalition with the left Republicans, the increasing frustration met by Republican reform initiatives, and the loss or threatened loss of governmental power. Ever since 1932 some leaders had been emphasizing that the PSOE was not just a reformist party, while the argument of "tailism"—that the leaders were pushed along by the increasing radicalization of the base—is not fully convincing. The leadership increasingly talked of change in policy from the summer of 1933, yet when the time came, they would have no difficulty in ignoring radical demands from the Federación Nacional de Trabajadores de Tierra (FNTT), the farmworkers' union, by far the largest national Socialist syndicate. There is no doubt that frustration with the outcome of Republican reform was a serious factor. The new labor laws had greatly benefited organized labor, but the deepening of the Depression—though not so severe in Spain's urban economy—reduced possibilities sharply, and during 1933 landowners took the offensive in the countryside.

Santos Juliá has written:

> It may be useful to remember in this context that the first statements by Socialist leaders about the need to take over all power or to win it by any means necessary—which naturally did not exclude the use of violence—had nothing to do with this presumed fear of the threat of fascism. Socialists began to elaborate the discourse of winning power as soon as they were excluded from the government, when it seemed that it would be the Radical Party that would take over the presidency. At that time no one identified the Radicals with fascism. . . . It was enough that the Socialists felt excluded from the responsibility of governing for them to announce their new intentions: such a change, though only beginning, is incomprehensible unless one keeps in mind the fact that they all

considered the Republic their own creature, which they had a right
—above and beyond any elections or popular vote—to govern.[15]

Thus by the end of 1933 a growing sector of the Socialists had begun for
the first time to embrace what they would call "Bolshevization." In a widely
distributed speech of December 31 Largo Caballero declared that "the difference
between [the Communists] and us is no more than words."[16] Even though the
Socialists had had nothing to do with the last of the three anarchist revolutionary
mini-insurrections that month, some Socialists had begun to talk of doing the
same thing. The left Republican leader Manuel Azaña noted in his diary on
January 2 that such talk was absurd, since the Socialists were simply not numerous or strong enough to take over Spain, but the next day El Socialista thundered:
"Harmony? No! Class war! Hatred of the criminal bourgeoisie to the death!"
Luis Araquistain, the leading intellectual among the Socialist revolutionaries,
founded a new journal, Leviatán, in May to provide theoretical justification for
the new line. Its first issue stressed that violence was indispensable.

Julián Besteiro and some of the veteran leaders of the UGT still opposed
radicalization. Besteiro understood that the rapidly developing Spanish society
had entered a kind of danger zone between mere underdevelopment and the
mature conditions for peaceful social democracy. In a major address the previous
summer he had said that Spanish workers still reflected much of the destructive
reaction characteristic of the earlier stages of industrialization, even though
the Spanish economy had reached a level of development that would not permit
it to be readily "won" directly by a single revolutionary class. Spain in 1934 was
hardly Russia in 1917. Besteiro warned correctly that conditions in Spain were
more similar to those of Italy in 1920, when the occupation of factories by Socialist trade unionists had served merely to provoke a triumphant fascist reaction.

On January 13 the Socialist executive commission approved a new ten-
point revolutionary program, which called for

1. Nationalization of the land
2. Major priority for irrigation projects
3. Radical reform of education
4. Dissolution of all religious orders, with seizure of their property
5. Dissolution of the army, to be replaced by a democratic militia
6. Dissolution of the Civil Guard
7. Reform of the bureaucracy and a purge of anti-Republicans
8. Improvement of the condition of workers but no nationalization of
   industry at this time

9. Tax reform, with the introduction of an inheritance tax
10. All these changes, to be initiated by decree, to be ratified by a new
    democratically elected legislature

Before the end of the month, the revolutionary *caballeristas* took over the UGT, ousting Besteiro and his moderate allies, and on February 3 a revolutionary committee was formed under Largo Caballero.[17] News from abroad only made them more determined: on February 6 twenty demonstrators died in a Paris riot unleashed by the radical right, which ended with Senegalese troops patrolling the French capital, and later that month an insurrection by Socialists against the new authoritarian regime in Austria was completely crushed.

The Revolutionary Committee declared that its insurrection must have "all the characteristics of a civil war," its success depending on "the scope that is achieved and the violence with which it is carried out."[18] Madrid was organized by neighborhoods, with key points targeted and lists of people to be arrested drawn up. The committee planned to use thousands of militia in Madrid, with the complicity of some Assault Guards and Civil Guards, some of the insurrectionists to wear Civil Guard uniforms. The committee made use of a handbook earlier prepared by Marshal Mikhail Tukhachevsky and other Red Army officers, which had been published in Spanish in 1932 as *La insurrección armada*, under the pseudonym A. Neuberg, as part of Third Period policy.[19] The Socialist Youth (FJS), which held three of the ten seats on the committee, was to play a leading role in what would prove to be the best-armed insurrection to take place anywhere in interwar Europe. The FJS was to organize much of the Socialist militia, and its leaders were more directly influenced by readings on the Bolshevik Revolution and were more deeply attracted to the Communist Party than any other part of the movement.[20]

One genuine revolutionary worker alliance already existed: the Alianza Obrera (Worker Alliance), set up in December by Maurín and his associates in Barcelona and later extended to Valencia. Maurín met with Largo Caballero and other Socialist leaders in Madrid in January, and Largo Caballero returned the visit in Barcelona the following month. A fundamental divergence nonetheless existed: Maurín intended the Alianza Obrera to become the vehicle of a large new revolutionary Marxist-Leninist force of a new type; Largo and the Socialist leaders conceived it simply as an umbrella organization for an insurrection in which the dominant role would be played by the Socialist Party.

The CNT, as usual, refused to join any revolutionary action not aimed directly at achieving the anarchist goal of libertarian communism. The only exception came in Asturias, where severe depression in the mining industry and other problems had helped produce the highest rate of strikes in the country. There Socialist and anarchist syndicates had collaborated in the general strike of 1917 and participated in a number of joint actions under the Republic. Thus on March 31 the Asturian sections of the CNT and UGT signed an unusual alliance that created a joint provincial front called the Alianza Revolucionaria for revolutionary action to install "a regime of economic, political and social equality founded on federalist socialist principles," a unique attempt to synthesize the revolutionary aspirations of Marxist socialism and anarchosyndicalism.[21]

On May 5 *El Socialista* announced formation of the Alianza Obrera (AO) in Madrid for "the struggle against fascism in all its forms and the preparation of the working-class movement for the establishment of a federal socialist republic." This national organization united the Socialists with the forces of the original Alianza Obrera in Barcelona and Valencia, repeating its formula under which each member organization was free to carry on its own activity and propaganda independently, but with a general committee in each region for mutual coordination, the regional committees ultimately to choose an AO national committee. Because the CNT abstained everywhere save in Asturias, however, elsewhere the AO consisted largely of the Socialists and a few very small allies, mainly in Catalonia.

The middle-class left Republicans were also moving left. In February the Partido de Acción Popular, the Partido Radical Socialista Independiente, and most of the Partido Republicano Gallego joined to form Izquierda Republicana (Republican Left). Azaña's inaugural speech of February 11 called for greater state regulation of credit and finance, control of certain industries by state agencies or even possible nationalization, expansion of public works, broader agrarian reform but with clearer exemptions for small and medium owners, and creation of a national state economic council. Azaña still called himself "bourgeois," but his party had become social democratic. At the end of June the new Juventudes de Izquierda Republicana (JIR; Republican Left Youth) held their first congress, defining their group as "leftists, democrats, and parliamentarians, in that order," and declaring that leftist goals took precedence over parliamentary democracy, if necessary.[22] Meanwhile the democratic center in Spain was fragmenting further, as the left Radical Diego Martínez Barrio formed his own Partido Radical Demócrata (soon to become Unión Republicana) and the eminent jurist Felipe Sánchez Román organized a small new Partido Nacional Republicano, more moderate than either of the two preceding parties.

During the first months of 1934 the main Socialist violence was directed against the small new fascist movement, Falange Española, which had been formed the preceding October. At least nine Falangists were killed, mostly by Socialists, between November 1933 and June 1934, when the Falangists carried out the first retaliation killing. Yet despite the fact that the Socialists engaged in increasing violence and were preparing for a major revolutionary insurrection, it was the Falangist center in Madrid that the police raided on July 10; they arrested sixty-seven Falangists.[23]

By mid-1934 the Socialists' most frequent justification for violent action was the supposed danger of fascism. Such discourse was very recent, for the sage of the party, Julián Besteiro (like Maurín earlier), denied that there was any serious danger of fascism in Spain. In June 1933 Largo Caballero had told the International Labor Organization that "in Spain, fortunately, there is no danger of fascism," pointing out the absence of any significant demobilized army, of any great masses of urban unemployed, of strong nationalism, of militarist programs, or of potential leaders.[24] As recently as April 1934 Araquistain himself made the same points in an article in the prestigious U.S. journal *Foreign Affairs.*

Though the fascist menace was frequently invoked, AO leaders made it clear that the main motivation was simply socialist revolution. Segundo Serrano Poncela of the FJS wrote in *El Socialista* on June 29 that the AOs

> have no abstract or partial objectives. They will not be used to achieve worker political victories within bourgeois democracy. They are rather the insurrectional preparation for the winning of power. The AOs are an instrument of insurrection and an organism of power. Along with the radical differences between them and the Russian soviets, one may nonetheless find a similar spinal column. The Communists always insist on the organization of soviets to prepare the insurrectional conquest and subsequent support of worker power. Above all else, this is what the Alliances seek.

The difference between Russia in 1917 and Spain in 1934, he declared, was that Russia lacked a substantial number of well-organized proletarian groups, so that it was forced to create new organs such as the soviets. In Spain the well-organized Socialists and their allies were already prepared for such a role.

Conversely, G. Munis (Manuel Fernández Grandizo), possibly the number two theorist of the Trotskyist ICE, after Nin, soon published a pamphlet, *¿Qué son las Alianzas Obreras?* which criticized the Socialist thesis as too "optimistic" in maintaining that "the ascendant process of the revolution is following its course." Munis stressed that the forces of the right were much stronger in present-day Spain than they had been in Russia in 1917. He urged the AOs to work to create full unity among all the worker groups and build a unified paramilitary force, but not to launch a general insurrection. A much wiser course, said Munis, would be to work for the dissolution of parliament and new general elections to weaken the right, which might make it possible to extend leftist power first through political means.

The Communist Struggle to Break Out of Isolation

The Spanish Communists remained almost as isolated as ever. Through the first half of 1934 the Comintern consistently followed its Third Period strategy, and thus the PCE continued with its revolutionary demands, constant encouragement of strikes, and efforts to set up new "factory and peasant committees" as the forerunners of soviets. Tactics continued to emphasize the united front from below. The panoply of front organizations remained active, as well as the very small Frente Unico Antifascista, their only mini-alliance. The PCE had apparently been the first leftist organization to begin to form an armed revolutionary militia, the Milicias Antifascistas Obreras y Campesinas (MAOC; Antifascist Worker and Peasant Militias), initiated on a very modest basis in 1933. On May 16, 1934, the MAOC called for the organization of a unified worker antifascist militia, but since the PCE refused to join the AOs, the Communists could be accused of showing interest only in "partial" and "not seriously revolutionary" activities. That was the burden of an announcement by the executive committee of the Young Socialists, who were otherwise well disposed toward them. Rhetorically the tables had been turned on Spanish Communists, some of whom were becoming increasingly disturbed by the situation. The PCE leadership continued to denounce what it called the inauthentic "leftization" (izquierdización) of the Socialists, who might now be draining away militant workers from the Communists. Through July and into August they loyally followed the Moscow line of denouncing their rivals as "social fascists."[25]

The Comintern line was first altered in France, where the growing strength of the radical right and the Paris riot of February 6 had stimulated interest in genuine unity of action against fascism among Socialists and Communists alike. French Socialists had never moved quite so far in the direction of reformism as had their Spanish counterparts during 1932–33. As early as 1925 the French leader Léon Blum had defined his theory of the "exercise of power," which rejected participation in a government not led by Socialists but was willing to accept leadership of a coalition including nonsocialists. The first such democratic Socialist-led coalition would respect the law and not try to end capitalism but concentrate on major legislative initiatives to aid workers. The French party had strong pacifist tendencies, despite its support of the government during World War I, and its leaders were strongly anti-Soviet; Blum and others were convinced that the Soviet regime would even promote major war to advance its interests. Nonetheless, both Socialist and Communist leaders increasingly believed that the two parties should work together against fascism and the radical right in France. The French leaders were now the most influential national sector in the Comintern, whose own directors were beginning to reveal some doubts about the exclusivist Third Period policy. Thus the French Communist leaders were permitted to negotiate their first agreement with the Socialists at the end of June, which finally led to a formal unity pact against fascism on July 27. It should be pointed out, however, that some of the top French Socialist leaders remained quite wary of their Communist counterparts. Paul Faure, general secretary of the Socialist Party from 1920 to 1940, detested Communists, whom he considered barbaric, un-French, and "agents of Moscow." Moreover, he informed the press on November 13, in France "the fascist peril is perhaps not so real. . . . Fascism in France is in retreat." He was of course fully correct.[26]

At this point the Latin Section in the Comintern began to become excited about the possibilities opening up in Spain, where the situation was potentially moving much farther to the left than in France. One source of encouragement was the recent success in penetrating the left-liberal intelligentsia, among whom a variety of front organizations were operating. Communist publication had achieved a significant volume, and the party had in its ranks one of Spain's leading young poets, Rafael Alberti, and enjoyed the sympathy of other leading figures. Even more important was the militancy of the Socialists and other worker organizations. The Comintern informed the PCE leaders on July 2 that the radicalization of Spanish affairs now provided an opportunity for the PCE to achieve hegemony on the left. Though the AOs did not constitute a valid strategy, the numerous pro-Communist sectors among the Socialists might be used to persuade the PSOE to adopt the Communists' program, and if it did, the PCE might then enter the AOs as part of its own revolutionary strategy.[27]

On July 12 the PCE leaders proposed to Spanish Socialists an agreement similar to that of their French counterparts, but rejected membership in the AOs, insisting that the Socialists should join a separate alliance with the Communists. When this overture was rejected, the Spanish Communists repeated their proposal once more—their sixth appeal of the year to the Socialists. The

AOs were strongly denounced as the very opposite of a united front from the base, though in both of their July appeals the Communists publicly called the Socialists "comrades" for the first time.[28]

The PCE leaders showed increasing interest in a change in tactics, and Díaz led a new delegation to Moscow. They arrived on July 31 and remained in the Soviet capital for twelve days. The Soviet chieftains fretted and fussed but could not bring themselves to accept a basic tactical change, apparently receiving not the slightest encouragement from Stalin. The PCE had little new to say publicly during August, but ceased to attack the AOs directly and made few public references to "social fascism." On August 29 the funeral of a central committeeman who had been killed by Falangists then became the first major public occasion of fraternization between Communists and Socialists. Some days later they held their first joint rally to protest a new decree by the Ministry of the Interior banning participation of minors in political groups.

The Comintern finally decreed a change in tactics in mid-September, and on the 15th the PCE announced in Madrid that it was entering the Alianza Obrera. The Comintern's complete message, which arrived the following day, did attach some strings. It insisted that the AO should be called "Worker-Peasant Alliance," must adopt every point in the PCE program, and should employ the slogan "All power to the Alliance." The PCE was not to renounce the goal of forming soviets as soon as possible, but should participate in any local AO or resulting AO government that accepted its program. These points arrived too late, for type was already set for *Mundo obrero,* which carried the PCE's full announcement early on the 17th. This announcement did urge the formation of soviets, of factory and peasant committees, and of a worker-peasant government. Nonetheless, as Antonio Elorza and Marta Bizcarrondo have pointed out, joining the radically revolutionary AOs did not involve any drastic change in Communist tactics, but simply joined together a new united front from above with standard revolutionary goals. The PCE made much the same argument: the revolutionary movement of the AOs would lead directly to the formation of soviets. This announcement was accompanied by a large joint meeting of Socialist and Communist Youth in Madrid's Metropolitano stadium on the 16th to lay the groundwork for a united revolutionary militia.[29]

The Socialists were themselves not so unified as they claimed. When the FNTT, their farmworkers' syndicate, had attempted a general strike early in June, other Socialists had not supported it, and after a week the strike collapsed. Seven thousand strikers were arrested. Most were soon released, but the failure of the strike left the Socialist forces gravely weakened in southern Spain.[30]

The Revolutionary Insurrection of October 1934

The signal for the insurrection was the announcement on October 4 of a new coalition government that would include three Catholic rightists, totally unacceptable to all the left. The rebellion that followed enjoyed the direct support of the Catalan government as well as the indirect support of the left Republicans, foreshadowing the Popular Front. In Madrid leaders of the left Republican parties dispatched almost identical notes to the president announcing that they were "breaking off all relations with the existing institutions" of the Republic. Azaña had moved to Barcelona, which he calculated enjoyed the greatest security for the left.

The Alianza Obrera came out in revolt the night of October 4 but its efforts were poorly coordinated, despite much planning and more than a little collecting of arms. The program of the insurrection was never announced, and in fact was not published until January 1936. In part it counted on the standard *pronunciamiento* tactic to either neutralize or gain the support of part of the army and police, but such support failed to materialize. There was no remote comparison between the Russian army of 1917—gigantic but demoralized by three years of defeat, millions of casualties, and bad leadership—and the modest but relatively coherent Spanish army of 1934, well rested, not yet profoundly divided, and with its morale still high. Nor did the populace generally respond. Spanish society was suffering from the Depression, but less than some other countries, and was not undergoing severe crisis, other than political divisiveness. By comparison with Russia in 1917, Spain was a semiprosperous Western capitalist country in which most of the population still supported legal institutions and social order.

The general strike in Madrid was at first reasonably effective, but most of the workers and their leaders stayed home. There was a plan to seize key points, and the Young Socialists had supposedly organized as many as 20,000 militia members, but they were irregularly armed. Attempts to seize centers of power immediately broke down into no more than irregular skirmishing, and the arrests of a list of key people were never carried out. All military barracks remained loyal to the government and no arms were distributed to workers. A few barricades were put up in worker neighborhoods and Young Socialists carried on sniping for some forty-eight hours, but revolutionary masses in the streets were not to be found.

In Barcelona the Alianza Obrera found an ally in the Catalan government. Resuming the insurrectionary planning that had dominated left Catalanism before 1931, it had made plans of its own for revolt on behalf of total autonomy within a federal Spain.[31] The BOC had made only very limited progress in its paramilitary activities, which it had begun in 1931. In 1933 direct-action squads called GABOCs (Grupos de Acción del BOC) had been formed, some members of which were armed with pistols. There had been many minor actions and skirmishes, and BOC leaders talked of "antifascist militias" and "future revolutionary battalions," but the reality was very modest. Maurín did not initially approve of the plan for insurrection, saying as recently as September 30 that any attempt to seize power immediately would be "criminal," but the BOC agreed to participate at the last moment. At ten o'clock on the night of October 4 Maurín announced at the Socialist Party headquarters: "Either fascism or the social revolution!"[32] Yet the Catalan government had failed to develop effective paramilitary forces, and in Barcelona the revolt was quickly suppressed by a resolute military commander. In other parts of Catalonia the BOC was a little more effective, initiating general strikes and even a few local government takeovers, but in the other areas the revolt was also rapidly suppressed, leaving altogether some thirty dead.[33]

Largo Caballero's revolutionary committee had named revolutionary commissions for all provincial capitals, but most cities remained quiet, while Socialists in the southern countryside were exhausted from their recent failed strike. In Aragon some anarchist groups did engage in outbursts, and in a general strike from October 6 to 9, anarchosyndicalists briefly declared libertarian communism in a few small towns in Zaragoza. Altogether, there was bloodshed in twenty provinces. Aside from Asturias, the most serious revolts occurred in the two industrialized Basque provinces of Vizcaya and Guipuzcoa, and in Palencia and León. In Guipuzcoa Socialists temporarily took control of the towns of Mondragón and Eibar and declared the revolution. Miners held part of Palencia province and León for several days. More minor revolts took place in Córdoba, Huelva, Albacete, Santander, Cádiz, and Murcia and in three other provinces.[34]

The great drama of the 1934 insurrection occurred in Asturias, where a united Worker Alliance, strongly supported by the CNT, set up the first effective revolutionary commune in Western Europe since 1871. In the mining districts 70 percent of the workers were unionized, had suffered depressed conditions, and had proportionately led all Spain in strike activity under the Republic.[35] The mining areas were quickly seized and more than 20,000 worker militiamen mobilized. Though many at first lacked weapons, they successively gained more arms from each police post overrun, eventually acquiring the Trubia artillery works and twenty-nine cannon. On October 6 they moved into Oviedo, the provincial capital, a city of 80,000 garrisoned by 900 troops and 300 policemen. The local military and police commanders, somewhat weak and divided, undertook a system of passive defense organized around nine strong points. Most of Oviedo, including the center, was occupied by 8,000 militiamen. In the "liberated area" they officially declared the proletarian revolution, abolished regular money, and instituted a revolutionary terror that took approximately forty lives, mostly of clergy. As the struggle continued, portions of the city were blasted apart by shelling, bombing, and dynamite. Though lack of coordination deprived the revolutionaries of support from UGT contingents in nearby León and Palencia, the government was not able to respond until a small relief column began to move south from coastal Gijón on October 11, supported by two squadrons of the Spanish air force and also apparently by the first military use of the helicopter. The city was reoccupied by October 13.

The revolutionaries' regional committee decided to abandon Oviedo that day, but the Communists protested, blaming the other forces for "desertion," until they finally had to admit that there was no alternative. On the following day, October 12, the Communists and a group of Young Socialists then improvised a second regional committee in the nearby town of Sama to stop the retreat. Some militiamen who had abandoned their positions were arrested, then allowed to go back to the fight. The Asturian Communists belatedly tried to form a disciplined new "red army," and even began to talk of Soviet intervention, but their effort soon became hopeless.[36] The sharpest fighting took place between the 14th and 17th as army troops began to seize control of the district that dominated access to the mining basin to the southeast of Oviedo. Finally a new committee was organized to negotiate surrender on the 18th. The army and Civil Guard then made a thorough sweep of the mining region, arresting thousands.

The best estimates indicate approximately 1,200 fatalities for the revolutionaries, 1,100 of them in Asturias. Deaths among the army and police totaled approximately 450, primarily in the same region. The revolutionaries carried out at least 40 murders in Asturias, where at least as many revolutionaries died in summary executions. A total of 107 persons were killed in Catalonia (of whom 78 died in Barcelona), approximately 80 in Vizcaya and Guipuzcoa, 34 in Madrid, 15 in Santander, 10 in León, 7 each in Albacete and Zaragoza, and very small numbers elsewhere. In all Spain at least 15,000 arrests were made—a figure doubled by leftist propagandists, who included 15,000 common criminals under normal detention among the revolutionary detainees. The government announced recovery of 90,000 rifles, 30,000 pistols, and 41 cannon, as well as a number of automatic weapons. About 15 million pesetas was stolen from banks, of which only about a third was ever recovered; the revolutionaries smuggled several million out of the country and destroyed considerable property. In Asturias hundreds of prisoners were subjected to beatings and in some instances torture; several were beaten or tortured to death. Some sniping at troops and police continued for days and not all arms were ever recovered; petty guerrilla actions continued in Asturias into 1935.[37]

Numerous members of the armed forces were also arrested, beginning with six senior commanders of the army and Civil Guard garrisons in Asturias, all of whom were sentenced to prison. In addition, one junior officer and one soldier received long sentences for having joined the revolutionaries. Eleven more junior personnel were also punished, two for having joined the revolutionaries. Leftist sympathies were distinctly more widespread among naval personnel, seventy-two of whom were arrested and prosecuted. Conversely, the only military personnel directly punished for excesses in the repression were four Moroccan *regulares*, summarily executed by their commander.

The Aftermath of the Revolt

The revolution had been a major disaster for the left. Thousands of its people had been arrested and many killed, its leaders had fled or been arrested, and many (though not all) local Socialist Party and UGT headquarters had closed. For the time being, the left was eliminated as a political force. The enterprise had had two justifications, one being the need for revolution, the second the need to strike against the sinister "fascistic" intentions of the CEDA. If those intentions were as strong as the left insisted, the CEDA would now have an easier opportunity than ever. The revolt not merely eliminated the left momentarily but weakened the center as well, leaving the initiative in the hands of the right.

The CEDA, unlike the worker left, was legalistic in its tactics. As Spain's leading fascist intellectual wrote later in 1935, much of the Spanish right "appeared to be fascist, but, in many cases, was essentially antifascist" because of its aversion to violence, while a large part of the Spanish left "appeared to be antifascist, but was, in many of its characteristics and objectives, essentially fascist" because of its inclination to use violence and its rejection of legality.[38]

Historians have almost universally condemned the revolutionary insurrection, and so did the more moderate Socialist leaders afterward.[39] The party leaders, however, had agreed before the revolt that in the event of failure, they would disclaim all responsibility and insist that it had been a spontaneous action of the people.[40] Consequently, the only leader who publicly accepted responsibility for his deeds was the Catalan president, Lluis Companys.

Foreign Hispanists such as Gerald Brenan and Gabriel Jackson have called the insurrection the first round of the civil war of 1936.[41] The primary reason that the attempt to impose a new revolutionary hegemony failed was that it lacked popular support. In 1934 there was no "natural climate" of civil war in Spain. Serious political division does not necessarily imply civil war. The climate for insurrection developed between 1934 and 1936. Through 1934 the Republic's basic problem was how to achieve democracy, whereas after that time it became how to avoid civil war.

From October 1934 until the next elections, in February 1936, Spain was filled with lurid atrocity stories and apocalyptic propaganda by both left and right. The right emphasized the violence of the revolutionaries and their murder of priests and other civilians, while the left stressed brutal behavior by the troops in the mining district, summary executions, alleged military atrocities against miners' families, and continued harsh mistreatment of some of the prisoners.[42] Many of the charges by both sides were valid, but there were frequent exaggerations as well, particularly among the leftist publicists, who seem never to have reflected on the extensive freedom they enjoyed to carry on their propaganda. The insurrection captured the imagination of part of the European left and was widely publicized abroad; Albert Camus penned a drama titled *Révolte dans les Asturies*. The Comintern underwrote a good deal of this propaganda, and while Socialist leaders denied involvement to avoid prosecution, Communist spokesmen stepped forward to claim the leading role of their coreligionists.

Though the initial repression in Asturias was as brutal as the insurrection had been, government power all the while remained in the hands of a centrist liberal democrat president and a centrist liberal democrat prime minister. In Barcelona the rebellion had been crushed not by a reactionary authoritarian but by the local commander, General Domingo Batet, a Catalan and a liberal. Though the failure of the insurrection left the CEDA with greater influence than before, it was unable to use that influence on behalf of a systematically harsh repression.

In fact, a good case can be made for the proposition that the repression, though initially harsh in the mining basin, was generally too mild and ineffective. The center-right administrations that governed Spain from October 1934 to December 1935 followed a rightist and counterreformist socioeconomic policy and kept thousands of prisoners in jail, but made little effort to suppress the revolutionary organizations that had carried out the insurrection. Consequently the revolutionaries were soon back in business in full force. The Republic's repression in 1934–35 was in fact unprecedentedly mild in modern Western European history—the mildest of any liberal or semiliberal state challenged by major violent revolutionary subversion in nineteenth- or twentieth-century Europe. In 1871 the Paris Commune had been drowned in an enormous sea of blood, much of it from thousands of persons arbitrarily executed. The tsarist repression of the Russian revolution and the mass terrorist outburst of 1905–7 was proportionately more moderate than that in France but was nonetheless severe, involving some three thousand executions. The Feikorps and other elements that repressed the German revolutionary disorders of 1919–20 acted with greater severity than did the Spanish Republic, as also did tiny democratic Estonia, which carried out numerous executions after the attempted Communist takeover of December 1924. The response to Socialist maximalism and Communist revolution in Italy and Hungary was the immediate surge of authoritarian forces, which created new regimes that perpetuated repression. In Spain the Republic maintained relatively uninterrupted constitutional government, the right largely continued to obey the constitution, support for fascism was minimal and did not increase, the repression was soon attenuated, civil liberties were soon restored, and the defeated forces were then given the opportunity to regain power through fair electoral means. The leaders of the Radical Party refused to let the right push them into a harsher repression, while the president of the Republic intervened directly to ensure a more benign policy. As in the case of Germany in 1932–33, a more genuine repression might have been the only way to save the Republic, for once the left returned to power, constitutional order and legality began to disappear. Thus the failure to punish the revolutionaries was of no permanent benefit to liberal democracy in Spain and may have hastened its destruction. Atrocious as was the repression of the Paris Communards in 1871, for example, it may have assisted the early stabilization of the middle-class French Third Republic during the 1870s and 1880s.

The case of Finland provides an interesting comparison. Finland underwent a brief but vicious revolutionary/counterrevolutionary civil war in 1918, replete with atrocities. The victorious rightists at first instituted a vigorous repression that took a deadly toll. The number of leftists who died was proportionately even greater than the number slain by Franco's Nationalists during the Spanish Civil War. The Finnish right, however, was essentially liberal and parliamentary, a product of the civilized nineteenth century rather than of the extremist twentieth century. The elements most responsible for the bloodshed, the Communists, were outlawed but a democratic parliamentary system was then instituted. The Socialists, under new social democratic leadership that eliminated Bolshevik residues, then emerged in the elections of 1920 as the largest single party in Finland, becoming a mainstay of Finnish democracy and helping to lead the subsequent struggle to maintain Finnish independence against the Soviet Union.

The differences between the Finnish and Spanish cases are instructive. The Finnish repression was much more severe than the repression of 1934, and at first even more repressive than Franco's repression of 1936, but it was more precisely targeted and soon came to an end. Finland's hard-core violent revolutionaries, the Communists, were permanently disenfranchised. In Spain most revolutionaries, including all the revolutionary organizations, were given full freedom during the course of 1935. In Finland the bulk of the worker left responded coherently and responsibly, reconstituting itself as a fully social democratic movement. In Spain the worker left defiantly maintained its revolutionary posture, using the elections of 1936 as a means to expedite extraconstitutional measures. In Finland it became possible within two years to institute a functional liberal democracy that embraced the full national political spectrum. Such a development was simply impossible in Spain; there the right was more extreme than in Finland, while the left continued to invoke violent revolution.

Failure of the Center-Right Government in 1934–35
Though the center-right coalition government of 1934–35 soon moderated repression, it was nonetheless a political failure that fell between two stools. It failed to repress its enemies effectively, yet it also failed to follow the ultimate logic of its own moderation; it did little to conciliate the left and encourage it to join any new constitutional consensus. This contradiction was due to the basic differences between center and right. While the center might otherwise have tried to conciliate the left, the right was interested primarily in increasing its power and resisted further compromises. Despite the legalism of the CEDA, its youth group experienced the vertigo of fascism and adopted part of the fascist style, minus the key ingredient of violence, which was much more typical of the left.

The center-right government failed to enact a positive socioeconomic program, and its very positive record on education was not enough to compensate. The trough of the economic depression in Spain had come in 1934, and the government thus gave the impression that it did not care and was even willing to make things worse, although that was not exactly the case. While the repression went on, its dragnet swept up ordinary anarchists, who had not participated in the insurrection. Though the center-right government was not able or willing to conduct a thorough repression, it was also unable or unwilling to do anything to conciliate the more moderate sectors of the left. Since it ended up largely rehabilitating the revolutionaries, it would have been better advised to make a greater virtue of this policy, possibly conducting an official investigation into the initial excesses of the repression in Asturias. Failure to do the one or the other, together with the rightist-orientated alteration of some of the earlier socioeconomic reforms, presented the image (rather more than the practice) of a government system totally hostile to the left, though unwilling to repress it consistently. The result of government policy, despite its relative leniency, was thus not to conciliate the left or to achieve any constitutionalist consensus, but to continue to stimulate a broadly based hostility on the left, which therefore formally refused to repudiate the revolutionary violence of 1934. The left was ultimately responsible for its own program and actions, but the center-right government was nonetheless responsible for failing to institute a resolute policy that moved firmly in one direction or the other.

The Change in Communist Tactics: Toward the Popular Front
By the end of the summer of 1934 the Comintern in both France and Spain was beginning to change its tactics considerably. Joint action with Socialists in France and entry into the Worker Alliance in Spain marked only the first step in an evolution that would not be completed until the Seventh Congress met in Moscow a year later, but the movement toward formation of a broader antifascist alliance of the left was now under way and had begun to supersede the tactics of the Third Period, which were now seen to have been too narrow.

News of the insurrection was received with enthusiasm at Comintern headquarters, but the Soviet press insisted that the Spanish revolt was merely a defensive struggle against fascism. Only after final defeat did *Izvestia* declare that it had been a major step toward the complete revolutionary liberation of the Spanish proletariat. While the fighting continued, the political commission of the Comintern told PCE leaders that their struggle must be conducted on two fronts: the armed combat of the Worker Alliance and the creation of a broad antifascist front with the left Republican parties. Hence the position taken by the ECCI in mid-September was altered further to direct that the new government to be established by the revolt should not be a provisional revolutionary government per se but an "antifascist concentration of the left" that would include the left Republicans—for the first time placing Comintern policy slightly to the right of that of the Spanish Socialists. Such a new government, however, would carry out a sectarian leftist policy, legally dissolving all conservative parties, purging the army and the police, and holding a referendum on the confiscation of large estates.[43]

The new tactics reflected the fact that general Soviet policy was undergoing significant change. During 1934 it had become clear that Soviet efforts to maintain a positive relationship with Nazi Germany had been a complete failure. Though Stalin would never cease to signal the Hitler regime that he was interested in friendly relations, he began to move to reduce Soviet isolation and develop a broader framework of security, which later would be called the policy of "collective security." On the one hand, the Soviet peace policy was continued in the Far East, as by 1935 the USSR sold its interest in the Chinese Eastern Railway to placate the Japanese in Manchuria. On the other, the Soviet Union joined the League of Nations for the first time in September 1934, at the same time that the Comintern was encouraging insurrection in Spain. As recently as 1930 Stalin had publicly called "present-day bourgeois France . . . the most aggressive and militarist of all aggressive and militarist countries in the world," but by February 1935 the Soviet foreign minister, Maksim Litvinov, informed his British counterpart that the government understood that Hitler now intended to attack only on Germany's eastern front, and so in May 1935 the Soviet regime signed bilateral mutual defense pacts with both France and Czechoslovakia, in the event that either signatory suffered aggression as defined by the League of Nations.[44]

Meanwhile Comintern policy continued to evolve, a process that had been expedited by the return to Moscow of Georgy Dimitrov in February 1934. The Bulgarian Dimitrov had been head of the West European bureau of the Comintern, based in Berlin. Arrested and put on trial after the Reichstag fire, he engaged in a clever and assertive defense that managed to humiliate Hermann Göring and made Dimitrov an international Communist hero. Eventually released, after two months of recuperation he was able to return to full-time work and argued strongly for cooperation with social democrats against fascism. At that point he had greater prestige than any other Comintern figure and, even more important, enjoyed the personal respect of Stalin, who soon appointed him secretary of the Comintern.[45] In May 1934 Dimitrov had summoned Maurice Thorez, the French secretary, to Moscow and insisted that he work immediately to overcome the breach with French Socialists, an innovative approach that the apparatchik Thorez at first resisted.[46] Dimitrov got his way, but as negotiations between French Communists and Socialists went forward, an internal struggle had to be fought out at the Comintern headquarters in Moscow, with Dimitrov, assisted by Manuilsky and the Finn Otto Kuusinen, facing down the old guard. On the first of July Dimitrov penned a memo that very delicately questioned the priority of the united front from below and the "social fascism" approach, and suggested the need for a united front from above with the Socialists as well as with "different strata of the petite bourgeoisie."[47] During the past year certain sectors of the German, French, and Czech parties had all suggested some sort of change in this direction, but Stalin remained unconvinced. Only days before the signing of the pact between the French Communists and Socialists on July 27, 1934, he repeated his opinion that social democrats were basically social fascists.

Dimitrov's new approach nonetheless began to gain strength, and the leaders of the French party pushed ahead with it. On October 9 Thorez gave a speech calling on the Communists and Socialists to negotiate with the democratic "middle classes," and he quickly moved to extend the initiative to the French Radical Party. Since he had not specifically been authorized to go that far, a Comintern delegation hurried to France to try to cancel his speech at the Radical Party conference on October 24, but arrived too late. Though the meaning of the speech was made appropriately ambiguous, by November the central committee of the PCF approved extension of any broader front as far as the democratic Radicals. So extensive an alliance strategy was not yet part of Comintern policy, but Stalin decided to give his approval. The meeting of the ECCI presidium in mid-December then ratified the tactic of a broader Popular Front, though its character and extent remained relatively undefined.[48]

Explaining it became the task of the Seventh Congress of the Comintern, which met in Moscow from July 25 to August 21, 1935. There Dimitrov officially announced the need for "a broad people's anti-fascist front," which was facilitated to some extent by presentation of a new definition of fascism as "the open terrorist dictatorship of the most reactionary, chauvinistic and most imperialist elements of finance capital." This definition was narrower than the one that had prevailed during the past seven years of the Third Period, and thus logically exempted social democrats and democratic middle-class groups, with whom it might conceivably be possible to cooperate. Dimitrov held that fascism should not be considered the same form of domination as bourgeois democracy; it was distinctly worse. The problem was made more serious by fascism's ability to generate mass support among broad sectors of the petite bourgeoisie and even among some workers.[49]

Hence "a broad people's anti-fascist front" was needed, though its formation was held to require no change in fundamental Comintern strategy. The basis of any new alliance would still be "the proletarian united front," which must be adjusted to conditions in any given country. The language remained ambiguous; it referred to Lenin's stress on the need to investigate "forms of transition or approach to the proletarian revolution," and at one point seemed to suggest that Communists would join a Popular Front only in conditions of prerevolutionary crisis. Thus Dimitrov stressed that it would be quite wrong to view a Popular Front government as "a special democratic intermediate stage lying between the dictatorship of the bourgeoisie and the dictatorship of the proletariat," which it might delay. Such a coalition could be no more than temporary, a tactic for the defeat of fascism and to advance "the revolutionary training of the masses."

In the current situation of crisis in various countries, Dimitrov explained, a Popular Front coalition would be desirable and could even lead to a Popular Front government. He posited three prerequisites for the formation of such a coalition government: willingness to reject the policies and functionaries of the bourgeoisie, commitment of the masses to vigorous struggle against fascism and reaction, and the willingness of at least a sizable part of the social democrats to support severe measures against fascists and other reactionary elements. In practice it would develop that not all of these prerequisites were met, so Communist parties would not participate in Popular Front governments, but would lend them strong support.

A Popular Front government would be a "democracy of a new type," going beyond bourgeois democracy and pointing toward a soviet democracy. It was the indirect path to socialism first essayed in Outer Mongolia, but that was not a precedent that could be usefully cited. Such a "new type" of democracy would not introduce socialism but would begin the nationalization of selected parts of the economy and distribute land to poor peasants. It was a type of government that would be formed "on the eve of and before the victory of the proletariat," and was "in no way" to restrict the activity of the Communist Party. The goal remained the insurrectionary seizure of power and the dictatorship of the proletariat.

Hence the proletarian revolution remained very much on the agenda. Dimitrov emphasized: "We state frankly to the masses: Final salvation this [Popular Front] government cannot bring. . . . Consequently it is necessary to prepare for the socialist revolution! Soviet power and only soviet power can bring such salvation!" The top Italian Comintern official, Palmiro Togliatti, delivered the second most important speech at the congress, tying the Popular

Front tactic to the Soviet government's new collective security policy, emphasizing that defense of the Soviet Union must be the top priority of all member parties.

Another resolution that was approved directed that "as a rule" the Comintern should henceforth "avoid direct intervention" in the internal affairs of member parties. The Comintern bureaucracy was further centralized and rationalized. Togliatti stressed that Communist parties had to have an appropriate degree of autonomy to follow the necessary national forms of the proletarian revolution. Direct Comintern advisers therefore would remain regularly in place to advise the three key West European parties of France, Spain, and Belgium.

The congress also ratified the important goal of "organic unity" with Socialist parties, Aesopian language for their fusion with and takeover by the Communists. Thorez announced that the French party was working for unity with the Socialists to "prepare for armed insurrection, for the dictatorship of the proletariat, for Soviet power as the form of the workers' government." He added that a Popular Front government would have the task of "leading the masses to the dictatorship of the proletariat, to the soviet republic."[50]

Much remained vague, but the Trojan horse aspect of the new tactic, what Elorza and Bizcarrondo have called its "Janus face," was made perfectly clear. There was no vagueness about that whatsoever. Or, as McDermott and Agnew accurately put it, the Popular Front involved a change in immediate tactics, but no change in revolutionary strategy.[51]

Developing the Tactical Change in Spain
The defeat of the insurrection had left the Comintern leaders not depressed but enthusiastic about the prospects for future revolutionary action in Spain. The initial Comintern line was that the defeat had been due to the failure of Socialist organization, the general lack of support from the CNT, and the failure to adopt the full Communist program, especially the prior formation of factory and worker committees. The ECCI, however, blew hot and cold about applying the new Comintern tactic to Spain. During the course of the insurrection, it had introduced the tactic of a broader new "antifascist concentration of the left" with some, at least, of the left Republican forces. Afterward, however, it drew back, restraining the Spanish leadership from going as far as the French Communists in seeking a broader alliance, warning them against "opportunist deformation" and making it clear that bourgeois parties should not participate in the antifascist front, which should not consist merely of parties but should be organized as much as possible from the base. The PCE was ordered to

maintain the united front with the Spanish Socialists, but to reinforce criticism of the Socialists' earlier democratic collaboration with the bourgeois Republican parties and avoid any relaxation in the revolutionary struggle against capitalism, while actively developing organs of military self-defense.[52]

On November 26, 1934, the PCE leadership first proposed the formation of an organic *comité de enlace* (liaison committee) with the Socialists. During the first nine months of 1935 it sent more than ten official communications to the PSOE, proposing a variety of joint groups and activities and complaining about the Socialists' failure to respond. A special issue of *Bandera roja* in January 1935 was titled "The revolutionary unity of the proletariat" and emphasized the need to achieve organic unity between the two parties for "the overthrow of the dictatorship of the bourgeois-landlord bloc by popular armed insurrection and the establishment of the revolutionary power of the workers and peasants, in the form of soviets." Liaison committees were created in a few provinces where the local Socialists were willing to cooperate, and in such cases these organs were considered more important than the local Worker Alliances. At the same time, a seemingly contradictory proposal was drawn up to make local Worker Alliances sovereign over local member parties, forming their own assemblies and electing local leaders. This plan was conceived as the ultimate consummation of the united front from below and as the instrument that could prepare the way for revolutionary soviets, operating in conjunction with the Socialists.[53]

All such continued machinations, even after suppression of the bloody insurrection, were possible because Spain was of course ruled not by any "dictatorship of the bourgeois-landlord bloc" but by a liberal democracy that showed extraordinary tolerance toward groups attempting its violent overthrow. All the revolutionary parties disclaimed any official responsibility for October and hence were not completely suppressed, though many publications were shut down and many leaders and militants arrested.

Identifying themselves more completely with the insurrection and conducting their largest propaganda campaign to date, the Communists were able to take advantage of the aftermath of the revolt to gain new followers on the extreme left and to provide assistance to prisoners, their family members, and refugees. A key entity in this activity was the Comité Nacional de Ayuda a las Víctimas (National Committee of Aid to Victims), set up by the Comintern in Paris under the nominal leadership of Julio Alvarez del Vayo, a Socialist luminary closely connected to the PCE. A commission composed of three Communists and three Socialists initially was to supervise a fund of 3 million francs that had been collected in the Soviet Union, but the Socialists insisted on separate accounts. Such assistance was important to the Socialists, who received little financial support from a Second International that frowned on their revolutionary activities. In addition, about one-fourth of the Spanish refugees allowed into the Soviet Union were Socialists, though when they returned over a year later many complained of poor treatment.[54] The Communists rapidly developed a series of new fronts stemming from the insurrection, such as the Committee in Support of an Amnesty, which included major Socialists and fellow travelers; the Committee of Women against War and Fascism; and the Association to Aid Workers' Children.

The tactical reorientation of the Comintern was first clearly reflected in Spain in a special issue of *Bandera roja* in December 1934, which announced a new policy—formation of a Concentración Popular Antifascista (CPA; People's Antifascist Association) to "fight against the parties that have betrayed the Republic of the People." Its goal would be to achieve the dissolution of all the nonleftist parties and to initiate the program of a people's republic, such as distribution of land to the peasants and liberation of national minorities. Terminology for the new tactic in Spain would remain multiple and confusing until the spring of 1936, but before the end of 1934 the basic Popular Front plan had been introduced under the rubric of the CPA. At this point the term "Popular Front" was used in Spain only by the Spanish Section of the World Committee for the Struggle against War and Fascism, which in the standard tactic of front organizations was seeking a broad alignment with noncommunist leftist intellectuals and left Republican parties in support of its own propaganda.[55] The CPA was officially formed five months later, in May 1935, with the membership of all the Communist organizations and various fellow-traveling groups such as the Izquierda Radical Socialista (Radical Socialist Left), the Juventud de Izquierda Federal (Federal Left Youth) and the Unión Republicana Femenina, the most important being the Juventud de Izquierda Republicana (the youth group of Azaña's party). Despite the continued use of inflammatory revolutionary language, the emphasis now lay on political struggle, and immediate insurrectionism was condemned. Thus when the Catalan Communist *Lluita* came out in April 1935 for the complete destruction of the bourgeois regime, it created confusion and had to be toned down.

By the middle of 1935 the PCE was promoting three parallel alliance tactics. The first was "organic unity" and eventual fusion with the Socialists (which the Comintern felt confident would soon bring the much larger socialist movement under Communist domination); the second was the CPA (whose name

was changed by June to Bloque Popular) as a broad alliance of the left that included certain sympathetic forces of the lower-middle-class left as a sort of
Popular Front to work for broad political goals; and the third was the development and tightening of the Worker Alliances (AOs) into effective joint revolutionary instruments of the worker left to prepare the transition to revolutionary
soviets. Yet another new concept developed in this year of conceptual and tactical realignment was the *pueblo laborioso,* which might be translated as the
"community of labor," a vague and ambiguous but broader concept that could
be used in conjunction with the CPA to bring the leftist sectors of the lower
middle classes into union with workers and peasants. All this involved the
usual Communist combination of two-phase tactics, one for the short term
(which required broader support) and another for the ultimate revolutionary
phase, which was being developed at the same time.[56]

May also brought announcement of a joint program by the French, Spanish,
and Italian Communist parties, as arranged by the Romansky Lendersekretariat
of the Comintern, which proclaimed the need to combine democratic and revolutionary programs. This plan merely restated the CPA program in a broader
context, specifying that in Spain a "broad antifascist front" was to lead to a
"Revolutionary Provisional Government," theoretically democratic, which
would confiscate large landholdings, nationalize industry, dissolve the armed
forces, arm workers and peasants, and liberate national minorities.

In Spain the revolutionary core of the CPA would still be a properly organized Worker Alliance. A manifesto was therefore launched the same month to
all "anarchist, syndicalist, Socialist, and Communist" workers, which lamented
that, according to Communist definition, "the leadership of the Socialist Party
has never seriously addressed the problem of politically preparing the masses
for insurrection" because it was afraid of a real worker revolution. The manifesto
therefore called for a complete reorganization of the Worker Alliances (naturally
under Communist hegemony, though this was not spelled out) on the basis
of a thirteen-point program, whose most important features were:

1. Confiscation without compensation of all the land of large landholders,
   the church, and the government for free distribution to farmworkers
   either individually or collectively, "according to their own decisions."
5. Confiscation and nationalization of large industry, finance, transportation,
   and communications.
8. Recognition of full autonomy for Catalonia, the Basque Country, and
   Galicia, even as independent states.

9. Immediate unconditional liberation of northern Morocco and all other Spanish colonies.

11. Dissolution of the armed forces and the arming of workers and peasants. Purge of "enemies of the people" (the standard Stalinist purge term) throughout the government.

12. Creation of a "Worker-Peasant Red Guard," with election of officers.

13. "Proletarian solidarity with the oppressed of the earth and fraternal alliance with the USSR."

Preparation of the text was apparently supervised in Moscow by Togliatti, who rejected a draft that had hailed "the flag of the soviets" raised in Asturias and had hewed more closely to the Soviet model.[57] The new-style Worker Alliance would cooperate with a broader Bloque Popular Antifascista (the confusing alternate nomenclature for the CPA) to establish the Provisional Revolutionary Government. These somewhat confusing and overlapping revolutionary proposals were then reprised by the party secretary, Díaz, on June 2 at a mass rally at Madrid's Cine Monumental, the largest Communist meeting since the insurrection. Only eight months after the bloodshed, he was free to boast grandiloquently and falsely that "we are responsible for the revolutionary movement of October," emphasizing that "the Communist Party of Spain claims for itself all the political responsibility for the movement and victorious [sic] insurrection of Asturias." He also stressed the need for a democratic program based on the Bloque or Concentración Popular Antifascista that would serve as a banner for new elections "that will have clear antifascist and revolutionary significance." Such elections would soon lead to a "Provisional Revolutionary Government."[58]

Representatives of the PCE at the Seventh Comintern Congress in August reported that they had not planned or sought the October insurrection, but then claimed that after they had joined it they had assumed the leadership in Asturias, where they had fought for the creation of soviets and a worker-peasant government. In Asturias they had defeated "fascism" and had created a "Red army." This had become the Spanish party's standard line, propounded in a pamphlet published by its politburo, Los combates de octubre, and in many other documents. After the Seventh Congress, however, the party adopted a tone of increasing cordiality to other leftist groups. It even toned down the ECCI's label of "traitors" for the anarchists in Catalonia; now they merely had "a position contrary to the movement."[59]

In France the initial agreement for the Rassemblement Populaire of Communists, Socialists, and Radicals had been signed on July 14, some weeks before the Comintern had made the Popular Front tactic official. The shifts in the PCE's tactical line between December 1934 and May 1935 indicate a process of adjustment by the Spanish party, as well, but the course was much slower and more erratic in Spain, in part because the party was so small and had so little influence.

The kinds of nuance employed by the PCF with regard to the government of France would not be found in the discourse of the PCE, which changed comparatively little during much of 1935. Members of the cabinets of the center-right governments that year came and went rapidly, primarily because of the interference and manipulation by the Republican president, Niceto Alcalá Zamora, but to PCE spokesmen they were all the same—each new Republican administration was simply defined as a "fascist dictatorship," as though the Comintern line of the Weimar Republic had never changed.

The PCE scored its first significant propaganda success in 1935. The party claimed to be putting out a total of forty-two publications in Spain—most of them legal, a few illegal—and this expenditure was testimony to the importance Spain now held for the Comintern. Thanks to Soviet funding and vigorous publicizing, the party was able to make itself much better known than ever before, and thanks to the practical assistance it offered and the aura of Soviet revolutionism it exuded, it was more attractive to Socialists than ever before. Support was increasing so significantly that 1935 can be called the first year of the party's rise; probably most of the new members who joined a Marxist party in Spain that year joined the PCE. And though the Communists did not convince the left that they were the main force behind the insurrection, they certainly managed to convince the right. From that time forward, the Spanish right would generally see the Communist Party as stronger and more influential than it actually was.

Division within the Socialists

The partial moderation of Comintern tactics raised the possibility that the PCE would now be positioned to the right of an insurrectionary Socialist party for the first time. Though the disaster of October convinced the sector of the Socialists led by Indalecio Prieto that revolutionary tactics were generally a mistake, the outcome had the opposite effect on the Socialist Youth and on the *caballeristas* in the UGT and in the party itself.[60] The FJS leader, Carlos Hernández Zancajo, published a booklet titled *Octubre: Segunda etapa* (October: The second phase). Hernández denied that the PSOE had ever had the characteristics of a typical West European social democratic party; "our party has always advocated revolutionary violence and has used it on various occasions, most recently in October." Socialist revolutionaries now called for what they termed the "Bolshevization of the Socialist Party." Hernández demanded the "revolutionary purification" of the party, withdrawal from the social democratic Second International, "the reconstruction of the international worker movement on the basis of the Russian Revolution!" and the achievement of the "dictatorship of the proletariat" in Spain.

To challenge the "Bolshevizing" trend in their party, the small group of Marxist moderates who supported the philosophy professor and veteran leader Julián Besteiro began publication in June of a new weekly called *Democracia*. Besteiro pointed out that Lenin was able to seize power in 1917 because the choice lay between Bolshevik dictatorship and seeming chaos. The situation in Spain was totally different, for the country still possessed functioning institutions, a regular army, a democratic political system with adult suffrage for both sexes, and until recently a rising standard of living. But telling the truth in Spain in 1935 did little good, and democracy lost supporters on both left and right with each passing month.

Much more influential was *Claridad,* the new caballerista daily started in July to support the Bolshevizers, directed by Luis Araquistain, the leading caballerista theorist, or at least what passed for one. During the summer Araquistain carried on a debate (using the pages of his monthly *Leviatán*) with Vicente Uribe of the PCE's politburo, writing in *Pueblo,* a Comintern-subsidized newspaper. Araquistain trumpeted the need to introduce the Soviet model in Spain immediately through violent revolution, whereas the Communist leader Uribe, following the new Comintern line, urged a more restrained and channeled policy.

The great majority of the Bolshevizers in the Socialist Party were not crypto-Communists, but considered themselves loyal Socialists. Only a very few of their leaders, such as Alvarez del Vayo, could be described as eventual crypto-Communists, though the leaning toward communism was even stronger in the FJS, most of which was taken over by the Communists by April 1936. Closer relations with the Communist Party were facilitated during 1935 by the fact that in the aftermath of the insurrection the Socialist apparatus fell into the hands of Del Vayo and the ex-Communist Ramón Lamoneda, who promoted more active association with his former party and brought in Communist leaders and propagandists to speak to Socialist groups.

Founding of the POUM

The only new challenge to the PCE among the worker left emerged in July 1935, on the eve of the Seventh Congress in Moscow, when Maurín's BOC and the Trotskyist ICE merged to become a new-style independent Spanish communist party, the Partido Obrero de Unificación Marxista (POUM; Worker Party of Marxist Unification). The POUM would become famous two years later not because of its achievements but because of the manner of its suppression by Soviet power in the Republican zone during the Civil War. George Orwell praised its revolutionary ardor and purity in his widely read memoir *Homage to Catalonia.*

Maurín's analysis of the insurrection and its aftermath appeared in his book *Hacia la segunda revolución* (Toward the second revolution), published in April 1935. Maurín had not initially supported the idea of a Worker Alliance revolutionary insurrection—at least at that time—and had participated in it only out of solidarity. In the new book he repeated his evaluation of it as premature. True revolutionary conditions still had not been fully developed in Spain, the positive role of the bourgeoisie having not been fully completed. When full revolutionary conditions developed—Maurín was convinced they would not be long in coming—Spain would supposedly find itself in a better situation than Russia in 1917, for Spanish workers had a much greater democratic tradition and could bring democracy with them into the revolution; further, there was infinitely more revolutionary consciousness among the rural population in Spain (at least in the southern half) than in Russia. Thus while Lenin had had to renounce any possibility of maintaining a democratic type of dictatorship and had had to prosecute the Russian revolution under very onerous conditions, the Spanish proletariat was proportionately more numerous and more mature. In Spain the proletariat would have the task of rapidly completing the final phase of the democratic revolution and of carrying it almost immediately into the socialist revolution, so that it would be a "democratic-socialist revolution." In a West European and increasingly democratic Spain this second revolution could not be carried out by a single party alone but would need support from "the immense majority of the population."

Maurín's minimum program for completing the democratic revolution —rather similar to the PCE's formula for the "democratic republic of a new type" for its Provisional Republican Government—called for creation of an Iberian Union of Socialist Republics, with the right of complete secession. It included nationalization and redistribution of land, the nationalization of major industry, banks, mines, transport, and foreign commerce, the six-hour day, and the arming of workers, all of which was supposed to result in a gigantic increase in production. "Organs of power" were to be "elected democratically by the workers," but, he warned ominously, the socialist state, unlike the "fascist" state, "will lack rights. It will have duties." What is striking to the observer is how near Maurín's doctrines were to those of the Comintern as the latter were being reformulated in 1935. To Communists, however, Maurín was not distinguishing the two revolutions clearly enough. They regarded his thesis as a heterodox blurring of distinctions, inadequately and improperly formulated in terms of a dangerous "Trotskyite" adventurism, above all lacking the tutelage of the Comintern.

Maurín also developed further his theory of fascism, defined in standard Marxist fashion as the final desperate paroxysm of capitalism in decline. He observed that fascism depended on a number of factors, such as the division of the worker movement, the defeat of "petit bourgeois democracy," a climate threatening international war, and an ever more threatening state of internal conflict. Yet fascism faced a difficult future in Spain, he concluded, where the continuing memory of the recent dictatorship had created an aversion to overt authoritarianism. Moreover, in Spain the petite bourgeoisie was still oriented toward democracy, while fascism had no support among workers (as it did in Italy and Germany) and did not even have the backing of the small industrial bourgeoisie. The small fascist movement was itself divided and lacked a significant leader. The Catholic CEDA, though large, could not really become a fascist party because its chieftain, Gil Robles, in fact "was afraid of fascism." Hence the only real basis for counterrevolutionary power would be the military, as in Portugal, Eastern Europe, Latin America, and Asia. Finally, a successful fascism depended on the existence of a defeated leftist revolution, which fascism could purport to transcend. The only thing that had failed in Spain, according to Maurín, was the purely "petit bourgeois" democratic revolution, whereas the "democratic-socialist revolution" was gaining more and more support. Despite certain inaccuracies, this was a more reasonable assessment of the prospects for a Spanish fascism than was normal among Spanish Marxists.

Just as some Socialists in 1931 had seen the Spanish Republic as the start of a broader democratization in Europe that would initiate the downfall of fascism, Maurín was certain that the growth of the "democratic-socialist revolution" in Spain would serve as a catalyst for the downfall of fascism in Italy, Germany, Poland, and Portugal. He fantasized that the resulting socialist states might join the Soviet Union to form the United States of Europe. Maurín admitted that any attempt to introduce such a revolution in a West European country, with more advanced institutions and a larger middle class, would at first bring civil war, but he assured his readers that such a civil war in a West European country would be much briefer than the one in Russia (1918–21), primarily because at the present time it could count on international proletarian support and would be shielded from counterrevolutionary intervention by the terms of international imperialist rivalry and the danger of world war. Araquistain was also developing this last point in *Claridad*, but they were both dead wrong, as would become clearer in Spain a little over a year later, when international factors would predominantly favor counterrevolutionary intervention.

Worker Alliance groups were still important, according to Maurín, because they could still play the role of soviets, but they needed to be "democratized." In Spain they should function as united fronts for the existing worker organizations, a "superorganization formed from the top," rather than new creations, as in Russia in 1905 and 1917. In fact, as soon as the insurrection had failed, the Socialists in their disarray had lost interest in the AOs, most of which quickly disappeared. Soon outside of Catalonia the BOC was participating in an AO only in Palma de Mallorca. Though by 1935 some sectors of the Juventudes Libertarias (Anarchist Youth) were interested in joining the AOs, most of the new functioning ones that were set up in the course of the year were started by the PCE as part of its new pre–Popular Front strategy of building the Bloques Populares Antifascistas, and thus were seen correctly by other groups as little more than a Soviet maneuver. The BOC leaders were particularly bitter over the special relationship developing between the PCE and some sectors of the PSOE. Within the AOs in Catalonia so much quarreling developed over the economic relief provided by the Comintern's Socorro Rojo Internacional (International Red Relief) that AOs continued to function only at the lowest levels and possessed vitality perhaps only in Valencia, where the dissident treintista anarchosyndicalists participated actively.[61]

The Comintern maneuver to bring the PSOE and PCE together underscored the importance of a larger new united Marxist-Leninist party free of Soviet machinations that could lead the way to victory for the democratic-socialist revolution in Spain. On February 3, 1935, there was a meeting of representatives of the BOC, USC, the Catalan federation of the PSOE, the PCC (the pseudo-independent Catalan Communists), and the Trotskyist ICE. The Communists still hoped to win over the members of the BOC, though they considered Maurín a "Trotskyist renegade" and their rival on the Marxist left. Thus the PCE proposed the formation of the same kind of liaison committee *(comité de enlace)* they were proposing to the Socialists, but the BOC categorically refused.[62]

The closest prospective allies of the BOC were indeed the Trotskyists of the ICE. The ICE was vigorous in intellectual and theoretical activity but otherwise very weak, with no more than eight hundred members, primarily in Madrid, Extremadura, and the north. It had begun to distance itself from Trotsky as early as 1932, however, when it had rejected Trotsky's request that it join his newly created International Left Opposition, which for another year had claimed to be a "fraction" of official international communism before forming its own International Communist League (ICL). The ICE from its inception had broken with the Comintern and never pretended to be part of international Sovietism. When in 1934 Trotsky pushed the tactic of "entryism," encouraging dissident communists to enter the Second International Socialist parties and win them over to revolutionism, the ICE had also rejected that idea in favor of an appeal for the union of all true communist groups.

By 1935 Andreu Nin, the ICE's main leader, had come to the conclusion that the latter tactic could function effectively only vis-à-vis the BOC in Catalonia. In April the ICE leadership proposed that its members form a new party with the BOC in Catalonia and join the Socialists elsewhere, as Trotsky had recommended a year earlier, but most members refused, saying that they were too few to influence the Socialists from within. Trotsky had blasted Nin the preceding year for failing to adopt the Trotskyist line in every detail, and now his ICL denounced any potential union with the BOC as "centerism," warning that if the ICE failed to join the PSOE, the true revolutionary Bolsheviks in the PSOE would end up dominated by Stalinists. Agreement between the BOC and POUM was thus not reached until July. Only a few members of the ICE joined the Socialists instead, while Trotsky pronounced himself willing to accept the new party if it would join his ICL (also known as the Fourth International). This the leaders of the new party refused to do.[63]

The official founding of the POUM took place in Barcelona on September 29. With a membership of six thousand at the very most, the new revolutionary party was officially structured on the basis of Leninist democratic centralism and formally accepted Maurín's doctrine of the democratic-socialist revolution. There is little doubt that it was internally more democratic than the PCE. Though the POUM contained a significant small core of intellectuals and theorists, it was made up primarily of blue-collar and service workers, most of whom spoke Catalan as their native language. In a generous gesture toward the former ICE, the POUM gave its leaders twelve of the forty-one seats on the new central committee, a substantial overrepresentation.

In his new book Maurín declared that the Comintern had failed as a center of world revolution and functioned merely as "an instrument in the service of the Soviet state," which was of course true. Though the POUM rejected "Trotskyism," it would remain friendly to Trotsky—the BOC had called the constant and ferocious Soviet attacks on Trotsky an "incitement to assassination" (which proved to be exactly the case)—and occasionally publish his articles.

Maurín and the POUM leaders denounced the new Comintern tactic of the Popular Front, claiming that there was no inherent conflict between fascism and bourgeois democracy because both were essentially capitalist, so that this tactic merely reflected the opportunism of the Soviet state, alarmed about the danger from Nazi Germany. They held the mere defense of bourgeois democracy to be Menshevik (ironically, the Comintern had expelled Maurín four years earlier as a "Menshevik"), whereas the correct position was that of Lenin, who in 1917 had defended the bourgeois democratic republic represented by the Provisional Government under Aleksandr Kerensky against Lavr Kornilov's attempt to impose a military dictatorship but nonetheless refused to join Kerensky. Thus the Popular Front supposedly represented postponement of the class struggle, having been designed primarily for the defense of the USSR. Maurín did agree with the Comintern on the importance of winning over the petite bourgeoisie, but he insisted that their support should be enlisted on behalf of the socialist revolution; they had to be convinced that only the socialist revolution would solve the economic problems of the entire society. The POUM accepted the need for some sort of broader alliance for the next general Spanish elections, which would inevitably have a "markedly revolutionary character," but any alliance would have to be carefully delimited.

Forming the Spanish Popular Front

After the Seventh Congress in Moscow the PCE forged ahead with the effort to create its own version of the Worker Alliances. They found the task more difficult than they had anticipated. Whereas the party had claimed to be participating in sixteen provincial AOs in April, many of them proved phantasmal and two months later the number was down to eight. The party claimed to have absolute hegemony in the AOs in the provinces of Seville, Jaén, Málaga, Navarre, and Valladolid (though the last three also seem soon to have disappeared) and to exercise considerable initiative in Vizcaya, Huelva, Almería, Segovia, Pontevedra, and the Canaries. The guidelines in October stressed the importance of setting up AOs even in the workplace. The party claimed that 207 AOs existed on the local level, 75 percent of them led by Communists "more or less directly." Workplace AOs took form, however, only in

Vizcaya, where there were said to be forty-nine, and in Seville, where there were four.[64]

By the autumn complete civil liberties had been restored and Spain was full of political meetings, some of them very large. The left was eager to seize the initiative and rallies became frequent. At the largest of the Communist meetings in Madrid, on November 2, the keynote speech by José Díaz, reporting on the recent Seventh Congress, revealed little new Popular Front moderation. After calling for formation of a broad new Bloque Popular of antifascist democracy to "conquer fascism definitively," he stressed the importance of moving to a worker-peasant government en route to the dictatorship of the proletariat. "We are fighting for the dictatorship of the proletariat, for the soviets. We announce this clearly because, as the party of the proletariat, we never renounce our objectives. But at the present time we understand that the struggle is taking place not on the basis of the dictatorship of the proletariat but on that of the struggle of democracy against fascism as the immediate objective." The Communist front for that battle was the Bloque Popular Antifascista (BPA; People's Antifascist Bloc), and by December the party claimed to have organized BPA committees in fifteen cities, though only five of them were provincial capitals. For the first time there was progress in Barcelona, where the Partit Comunista de Catalunya was outflanking the POUM in its relations with the other small Catalan Marxist parties. On January 12, 1936, the PCC entered into an agreement to form a special liaison committee with the Unió Socialista de Catalunya and the Partit Català Proletari, and sought to extend this agreement to the Catalan federation of the Socialist Party and to Estat Català.[65]

Ever since April the left Republicans and the semimoderates currently in control of the Socialist Party had made it clear that they intended to reverse the failure of 1933 and establish a firm alliance in the next elections. The Comintern was perfectly happy to join a pact somewhat along the lines of the three-party Rassemblement Populaire announced in France in July. Even in France Léon Blum, the relatively moderate leader of the French Socialist Party, saw the new alliance as a historical initiative that would regenerate the French left, France itself, and all of Europe. Though Blum had been the leader most responsible for reestablishing the Socialist Party in the 1920s, after the Communists had taken most of its following, he now was beginning to swallow the Comintern line about a new "organic unity" between the two parties, though Blum fantasized that once unity was achieved, the French Communists could be persuaded to break with Moscow.

The Comintern was hoping for much more from the partially "Bolshevized"

Spanish Socialists. Largo Caballero, who had steadfastly refused in court to admit the slightest connection with the insurrection he had planned for nine months, was temporarily released from prison in November to visit his sick wife. During this brief liberty he met with Vittorio Codovilla, the chief Comintern representative in Spain, who quickly telegrammed Manuilsky in Moscow that Largo "agrees with the essence of the decisions of the Congress and with their application to Spain." Largo accepted the proposal for the small Communist CGTU to enter the UGT (a process begun soon afterward), but did insist that the redevelopment of the Worker Alliance should be controlled from above, by the parties themselves, and not by fusing party membership from the base.[66]

In Spain the Communists were more immediately concerned with unity with the Socialists and a broad worker Bloque Popular than with a French-style Popular Front with middle-class parties, even though that sort of front was readily accepted—and even sought—as an electoral tactic. In December the Spanish-speaking Jacques Duclos, a top Comintern operative and French party leader, was sent to Madrid to hold extensive conversations with Largo Caballero in his prison cell over a period of three days—itself eloquent testimony to the extreme liberalism and broad extension of civil liberties provided by what Communists called the "fascist dictatorship" in power. By that time the French parties had converted the Rassemblement Populaire into what the Communists called the Popular Front, a firm electoral alliance for the balloting that would take place in France in the following year. All the Spanish left was hoping for new elections as well, and the Comintern now gave priority to forming a similar Popular Front pact in Spain. Largo Caballero, however, who was remarkably inept at practical politics, had just weakened his own position in the Socialist Party by resigning from the PSOE's national committee over a minor conflict with his rivals. Moreover, he tended now to take a position to the left of the Comintern. In an article that appeared in *Claridad* on November 23 the still-imprisoned Socialist leader called for Bolshevization and the dictatorship of the proletariat without the distinctions and nuances that the Popular Front tactic had introduced into Communist discourse. Such rhetoric was typical of caballeristas and their publications generally.

After the split in the leadership of the Socialist Party in December had left the semimoderate Indalecio Prieto in control, the *prietistas* moved rapidly to solidify arrangements with the left Republican parties for an electoral alliance, since it had become clear that a new round of balloting would not be long delayed. The Socialist and left Republican leaders had little interest in including the extreme revolutionary left, but full participation by the divided Socialists was vital. Despite his revolutionary extremism, even Largo Caballero had admitted for some time that at least a limited electoral alliance with the left Republicans would be necessary, and by early January the caballeristas had formed their own negotiating committee on the basis of an ad hoc alliance with representatives of the PCE and several other small extreme left groups. Largo Caballero accepted the idea of a broad electoral pact, which in Spain would be generally known as the Frente Popular, with the left Republicans and the Socialist Party leadership, though he insisted on and gained acceptance of the inclusion of the PCE and the smaller revolutionary parties.[67]

All the spokesmen of the worker left emphasized the tactical nature of the new electoral alliance. In his first major campaign speech, Largo Caballero, now free from jail, emphasized that the function of the Popular Front was simply to free the thousands of leftist prisoners and restore the political hegemony of the left generally, and involved no renunciation of the goal of socialist revolution. In essence, this was the Comintern's position, but Largo had no interest in introducing the short-term tactical qualifications that the Communists acknowledged. Nor was the position of the prietista leadership of the party as moderate as it usually has been presented, for on the following day El Socialista also declared: "It is appropriate, then, that we say: 1936, a revolutionary year. Once the left is victorious, nothing will prevent 1936 from marking the beginning of the revolution that did not take place with the crumbling of the monarchy and the dawn of the Republic."

Initially the Communists and caballeristas had prepared an electoral program that called for confiscation of all large landholdings without indemnity (contradicting the legislation of 1933 by the earlier leftist governing alliance), a purge of the army and the administration, expulsion of all religious orders, and new legislation that would in effect outlaw all conservative and rightist parties, thus achieving the "republic of a new type" called for at the Seventh Congress.[68] The official Popular Front program, released on January 15, however, had been developed by the left Republicans and prietistas, and was more moderate. It called for vigorous prosecution of agrarian reform, an extension of social and labor reforms, and a purging of the bureaucracy, but rejected confiscation of land without compensation, a political purge of the army, or the outlawing of the political opposition. On the night of the 14th, just before the program was issued, Felipe Sánchez Román, the most intelligent, most responsible, and most moderate of the left Republican leaders, withdrew his very small party from the Popular Front. He had made a major contribution to drawing up the program, and his withdrawal has usually been attributed to opposition to the recent inclusion of the PCE. That was doubtless a factor, but the withdrawal seems to have stemmed from a broader reconsideration of the entire Popular Front tactic by which nominal Republican democrats were joining forces with violent revolutionaries, of whom the Communists were only a small minority.

By that time Codovilla, Díaz, and other PCE leaders had left for Moscow to receive last-minute instructions. There the Spanish delegation was reprimanded for its failure to bring Largo Caballero more fully into line, since the basic goal was fusion with the Socialist Party and Socialist Youth. Manuilsky explained once more that the Seventh Congress had mandated a merely temporary acceptance of the Bloque Popular (i.e., Popular Front) for electoral and short-term political purposes, but the basic goal remained the same: "That is, the dictatorship of the proletariat, the smashing of the bourgeoisie through violence, the rupture of class collaboration," and the establishment of the Soviet model. It was important that Largo be made to understand the importance of the role of revolutionary soviets, or their direct functional analogues, in Spain's revolutionary process. Therefore, even during the forthcoming electoral campaign, the PCE must go beyond the Bloque Popular itself and vigorously promote its program to complete the full bourgeois-democratic revolution as soon as possible, since the fundamental goal was the "democratic dictatorship of the proletariat" (Lenin's slogan in November 1917). Expansion of Worker Alliance groups was indispensable, for they could subsequently play the revolutionary role of soviets as the alternative to and subversion of even the "republic of a new type." The conclusion of the discussions was that in the short term the party must advance a "program of democratic-bourgeois revolution" that maintained democratic liberties (up to a point) but would go beyond the official Popular Front program by demanding the confiscation of large landholdings and the purging of the army.[69] Meanwhile, in a large joint Socialist-Communist rally on January 22 in Madrid, Largo Caballero spoke and Jesús Hernández announced that they were working toward a united revolutionary Marxist party to establish the dictatorship of the proletariat.

The Spanish leaders faithfully implemented the Comintern guidelines during the four-week electoral campaign, which enjoyed a large infusion of Comintern funds.[70] Writing in *Mundo obrero* on February 3, Díaz called for "the complete liberty of the Catalan, Basque, and Galician peoples," and insisted that "it is necessary to dissolve the monarchist and fascist organizations," thus outlawing all the right. At a large meeting on February 11, five days before the balloting, Díaz emphasized that the function of the Popular Front was simply to complete the bourgeois-democratic revolution, while preparations were afoot to move on to the dictatorship of the proletariat. "The decisive blow" would come through "insurrection," as in October, the ultimate model.[71] On the same day he published an article in *Mundo obrero* to stress that the forthcoming elections were not merely "elections of a normal type," as in a bourgeois democracy such as the United States, Great Britain, or Switzerland. They would serve as a plebiscite, to make it possible to carry out the Popular Front program first and then to go on to the socialist program. On February 14, two days before the balloting, *Mundo obrero* called attention once more to the ultimate goal of a "worker-peasant government," whose revolutionary program was presented and then soon repeated in an official party pamphlet. In this outline the soviets were called Worker Alliance groups and a three-step program was detailed: first, a victorious Popular Front; after completion of its program it would be replaced by a worker-peasant government, which would prepare for establishment of the dictatorship of the proletariat.[72]

Altogether, the attempt to paint the French and Spanish Popular Fronts as equivalent enterprises is misleading.[73] Though the French Communist Party had the same Comintern-imposed goals as the PCE, the much more stable French political environment and democratic consensus made it impossible for them to be presented in the aggressive terms used in Spain. Nor could a parallel be drawn between the two Socialist parties, since only a very small left wing of the French party was interested in Bolshevism. The goal of the French Socialists in their relations with the Communists was to convert them to social democracy. Finally, the Spanish left Republicans were scarcely the equivalent of the French Radicals, a large, established middle-class party that scrupulously respected constitutionalism and generally supported conservative economic principles. In the French Popular Front there was no support for violence or attempted revolution, whereas in Spain even the left Republicans ran on a platform of justification of the 1934 insurrection. Despite the widespread fears of French conservatives, the Popular Front in France lacked the prerevolutionary thrust of its Spanish counterpart. At the slightest whiff of a real revolutionary program, the French Radicals would have pulled out, as they eventually did anyway. The only Spanish left Republican leader who sustained equivalent principles was Sánchez Román, who abandoned the Popular Front early on.

The Elections of February 1936

In the negotiations for individual party candidacies in the Spanish electoral bloc system, the left Republican parties were given priority, because the Popular Front pact was only an electoral alliance and not a program for a broad Popular Front coalition government. The left Republican parties would form the government alone, and though they were inevitably a minority, they were given a disproportionate number of candidacies in order to have some sort of base from which to govern. Unlike the French Popular Front, which provided a governing coalition of Socialists and Radicals with a broad base, the Spanish Popular Front planned a narrowly minority government from the start—only one of several fatal flaws.

The Socialists accepted a degree of underrepresentation in support of this scheme, and the only other party to be systematically overrepresented was the Communist. That this should be the case was absurd and has never been adequately explained. Communist ambition alone could not possibly have sufficed, and the most obvious explanation is strong support from the Socialists. Conversely, the POUM was underrepresented and given only one candidacy. By contrast, the pro-Soviet Unió Socialista de Catalunya was given three slots in Catalonia, while the Catalan Communists, the Catalan Socialists, and the Partit Català Proletari (each weaker than the POUM) all received one candidacy each.

The POUM leaders had never been happy with the Spanish Popular Front formula, which they considered confused and weak, but they had to avoid total isolation and took what was offered. The POUM was the only Popular Front party that ran on an immediate revolutionary platform. It accepted the need for a general electoral victory to gain an amnesty and restore Catalan autonomy, but its own twenty-five-point program emphasized the insurrectionary goals of Worker Alliance groups and its plan to "outflank" *(desbordar)* a Popular Front government as soon as possible, replacing the Popular Front with an exclusively worker front and worker government. Maurín pledged that he would immediately present this program as a deputy in the new Cortes to "unleash the social revolution."[74]

The Communists did do more than any other party to encourage the concept of broad Popular Front unity and urged the creation of Popular Front committees at all levels, from small towns up, a goal that remained far from realization. One week before the elections, Diego Martínez Barrio, the most moderate of the left Republican leaders, tried to maintain that the Popular Front was a "conservative enterprise," but *El Socialista* thundered on the same day: "We are decided to do in Spain what has been done in Russia. The plan of Spanish socialism and Russian communism is the same. Certain details of the plan may change, but not the fundamental features."

The elections indeed had the air of a plebiscite, and some voters abandoned the center in order not to waste their vote, casting it for left or right depending on which side they considered the lesser evil. Commentators have frequently pointed out, however, that it was the most moderate candidates on each side who drew the most votes. Six people were killed on election day, but in the vast majority of districts voting was relatively peaceful and generally fair. The Popular Front list drew 43 percent of the popular vote, while Popular Front candidates also picked up votes on other coalition lists, though not enough to claim an absolute majority of the popular vote, which was not necessary under the Spanish large-district list system. Altogether the Popular Front gained 60 percent of the parliamentary seats, a potentially dominant majority, which it subsequently increased to approximately 67 percent through manipulation of the results by the electoral commission of the new parliament.[75] Ultimately seventeen of the twenty-two Communist candidates were elected, a remarkable breakthrough due not to any mass popularity of the party at that time but to the privileged number and position of their candidates on the alliance list. It was not necessary for voters in a given district to vote for all the names on a given alliance list, and the Communist candidates consistently drew fewer votes even in winning districts than did left Republicans and Socialists. At the conclusion, however, all the left was delighted; the Popular Front had won its first major victory. The victorious left totally ignored the fact that they had won only about 2 percent more of the popular vote than the right and right-center combined. They were firmly convinced that they had received an absolute historical mandate to work their will on Spain.

CHAPTER FIVE

Communism and the Implosion of the Republic

February–July 1936

THE IMPLOSION OF the Spanish Republic between the winter and summer of 1936 constituted a degenerative process without precedent. The nearest equivalents might be found in Italy, Germany, and Hungary in the immediate aftermath of World War I, but the comparability of such cases is limited, because the Central European countries were profoundly affected by the war and had not enjoyed five years of peacetime life as democratic polities, as Spain had done. The Austrian crisis of 1933–34 did take place in an established democratic republic, but, in addition to the basic left/right deadlock in internal politics (somewhat similar to the Spanish case), it was profoundly influenced by German pressure and the rise of a powerful Nazi movement within Austria. The breakdown of the Weimar Republic in Germany provides some parallel, because of fragmentation so extreme that the Republic could not function normally, but the German system was under the direct assault of a nationalist movement that eventually seized power. Such a force was lacking in Spain.

The Spanish Republic was an established regime that had conducted three democratic elections over a period of five years and, despite numerous shortcomings, had maintained a basically constitutional polity. It was not directly affected by war or international threats, or by the rise of a strong fascist movement, which existed only in the rhetoric of the left. There was a strong force of the authoritarian right in the CEDA, but only on one occasion—in the immediate aftermath of the 1936 elections—did it propose an authoritarian intervention in the democratic process, and thus its record on that score was much cleaner than that of the left in general. Although from 1933 Republican politics were increasingly influenced by foreign examples, there was never any significant foreign or international intervention; the breakdown of the Republic was an exclusively domestic process.

It is customary for commentators to cast a sort of solomonic blame on both left and right for the breakdown, concluding that powerful forces on both sides ultimately rejected the democratic constitutional state, and there is an undeniable truth to that assessment, but the conclusion that both extremes were therefore equivalent actors in the Spanish tragedy is too categorical and does not altogether correspond to the facts. The main source of breakdown in the Republican polity stemmed from the revolutionary process that paralleled the establishment of the Republic, at various times sought to overthrow the system, and first presented a major though unsuccessful challenge in October 1934. To this must be added the destructive machinations of a president who, though liberal in sympathies, intervened in the political process in inappropriate ways of dubious legality, as well as the fixed Kerenskyist orientation of the middle-class left Republicans, who insisted on an exclusively leftist regime despite all opposition and therefore felt they must always rely on and support the worker left, no matter how destructive its actions.

Most Spanish political forces treated the elections of 1936 as a plebiscite on the insurrection—the left as its validation, the right as its repudiation. This plebiscite was won by the left with a clear if narrow plurality of votes and, thanks to the bloc representation system, a clear majority of seats. That outcome may have doomed the democratic Republic, for its new government was committed not to maintaining full Republican democracy and constitutionalism, the rules of the game, and equal government for all, but to a sectarian interpretation of the constitution and the elimination of the political and legal influence of the right, whether by fair means or foul. An electoral victory by the CEDA would probably also have led to the end of Republican democracy, though probably in less catastrophic form.

The Popular Front largely ceased to exist as an organized coalition once the elections were over, and was divided between the Republican or "bourgeois" left and the worker left, most of which was now oriented toward revolution. This situation, rather than weakening the revolutionary process, in some respects enhanced it. The Republican left had burned all bridges with the center and right, and could remain in power only by ceding more and more to the worker parties. Rather than being restrained by the Republican left, those parties consistently blackmailed it, with ever-increasing effectiveness. Diego

Martínez Barrio, the most moderate of the left Republican leaders, lamented in a book published in 1943 that "certain Socialists, and all the Communists, suffered from the mirage of what had taken place during the Russian revolution of 1917, and handed to us Republicans the sad role of Kerensky. According to them, our mission was reduced to smoothing their road to power, since the phase of the democratic revolution had already ended in the history of Spain."[1] This observation was fully correct, but it was something that revolutionary Socialists and Communists had made perfectly clear since 1934, and it never stopped the left Republicans from staking their entire policy on alliance with the Socialists. The Marxist left indeed assigned the role of Kerensky to the left Republicans, but it was a role they were to some extent willing to assume. During the spring of 1936 the center and right reminded the left Republicans of this fact with increasing frequency, but the latter found it impossible to avoid a fate on which, in a sense, they had deliberately staked their whole policy. Their refusal to compromise with the center or right left them no alternative; complete leftist sectarianism inevitably led to Kerenskyism.[2] The left Republican utopia of a petit bourgeois anticlerical republic purged of all conservative and Catholic influence was a fantasy of nineteenth-century petit bourgeois radicalism that not only denied democracy but also had no chance of being enacted in Spain. Vain and self-absorbed politicians with little sense of or interest in the commonweal, the left Republicans clung, however unhappily, to their self-appointed if ultimately Kerenskyist role in the revolutionary process, as indeed the left wings of their own parties and their youth groups engaged in more direct collaboration with the revolutionaries.

The second most important role was played by the Socialists. Well before the elections, they had become divided between the Bolshevized caballeristas, in control of the UGT, and the more moderate sector led by Prieto, in control of most of the party apparatus. The internal political dynamics of the Socialists mirrored that of the left in general. Just as the left Republican government was leveraged by the worker parties, the more moderate Socialists would be effectively frustrated and to some extent leveraged by the caballeristas. On the other hand, the differences between the two sectors of Socialists have sometimes been exaggerated. The prietista Socialists were not always moderate in their tactics, and were equally agreed on a complete leftist takeover of Republican institutions. The prietistas' respect for constitutional niceties was sometimes only marginally greater than that of the caballeristas, but they had a more realistic sense of the limitations and requirements of leftist power, and they lacked the arrogance, blindness, and hubris of the caballeristas.

The new Azaña government moved rapidly not merely to cancel what remained of the repression but also to reverse its terms. All revolutionary criminals were released irrespective of the character or extent of their crimes, while military and police leaders of the repression—that is, the nominal defenders of the constitutional state—were in some cases themselves thrown into jail. Their imprisonment foreshadowed the Francoists' policy of prosecuting as criminals people who had merely tried to uphold the legal order. The revolutionaries were not only released from prison but required by law to be restored to their former jobs and positions. Thus employees were reestablished in hundreds of firms they had sought to overturn, and apparently one employee had to be rehired by a shop whose owner he had murdered. Police officers guilty of treason to the constitutional order were restored to their positions.

There is neither space nor need to narrate details of the progressive decline of public order and constitutional process. Arbitrary actions and violence took many forms: arbitrary arrests of centrists and rightists while the left usually enjoyed impunity; falsification of electoral results and processes; widespread confiscation of property, particularly urban church buildings and property in the southern countryside, and considerable destruction of other property; the greatest strike wave in Spanish history, often aimed not at improving wages and conditions but at worker dominance; subversion of normal police functions, first by reincorporation of policemen and officers who had subverted constitutional order in 1934 and then by employment of Socialist militants as auxiliary police; and a mounting spiral of political violence. All this reached a climax on the night of July 12, when one of the leading spokesmen of the rightist parliamentary opposition, the monarchist José Calvo Sotelo (who himself endorsed a violent and authoritarian political solution), was illegally arrested by government police and immediately murdered by a Socialist auxiliary who accompanied them. This was the Spanish equivalent of the Matteotti affair in Italy twelve years earlier: the murder of Giacomo Matteotti, leader of the United Socialist Party who led the campaign against Mussolini in the Chamber of Deputies, provoked antifascist demonstrations, but King Victor Emmanuel III refused to sack Mussolini. In each case the murder was carried out by the sector primarily responsible for political violence: in Italy by Fascists, in Spain by Socialists. With the exception of Italy in 1924, this was a crime without precedent in the history of European parliamentary government, but by 1924 the Mussolini government was ceasing to be parliamentary, and by July 1936 the Spanish Republic had ceased in practice to be a democratic constitutional state.[3]

Communist Policy and the Marxist Revolutionary Left in the Aftermath of the Electoral Victory

The Comintern leaders were naturally pleased with the electoral results, and immediately afterward a PCE delegation departed for Moscow. There Manuilsky prepared a new document for the Romansky Lendersekretariat to guide the Spanish party in what he termed the "REVOLUTION being developed." Even though the new Azaña government was not a true Popular Front government but simply a "bourgeois government of the left," it should be both supported and pressured in the right direction. "It is necessary to present a platform of demands with the goal of isolating Acción Popular [CEDA] and the other reactionary parties from their base and undermining their economic support," leading to large-scale confiscations. It was equally or more important "to develop a mass movement outside parliament," make the Worker Alliance groups "genuine collective mass organs of a worker-peasant democracy," and gain recognition for them as "legally recognized government organs."[4] Or, as Elorza and Bizcarrondo put it, "that is to say, under the cover of supporting the Popular Front, what Manuilsky proposes is a new scheme for preparing the Soviet revolution." Manuilsky also prepared a letter to Díaz, who had remained in Madrid, to stress that "the very first coming weeks have paramount, even decisive significance" for "the ultimate fate . . . of the democratic revolution in Spain," requiring mass mobilization, aggressive action, and establishing unification with the Socialists.[5]

Mundo obrero had declared two days after the elections that "we must follow the path of completing the democratic-bourgeois revolution until it takes us to the point where the proletariat and the peasantry assume responsibility for making the Spanish people as happy and free as the Soviet people through the victorious completion of socialism under the dictatorship of the proletariat." (These words, written less than three years after the mass famine and destruction wrought by Soviet collectivization and on the eve of the Great Terror, read today almost as a macabre exercise in black humor.) The party newspaper then came out with the new demands on February 25:

- Confiscation of all lands not yet in the hands of the peasants, which the latter may work individually or collectively.
- Cancellation of all peasant debt, increase in wages, and reduction of the workday.
- Nationalization of enterprises, banks, and railroads.
- Liberation of oppressed people: Catalonia, Vizcaya, Galicia, and Morocco.

- Suppression of the Civil Guard and Assault Guard.
- Arming of the people.
- Suppression of the regular army and liquidation of officers; democratic election of commanders by soldiers.
- Fraternal alliance with the Soviet Union.

The Communist line was thus brutally frank. There was no "Trojan horse" pretense of supporting bourgeois democracy. The minority left Republican government should be pressed to complete the Popular Front program; then the left should quickly move to the more radical program being advanced by the PCE, carrying out large-scale confiscation of land, basic nationalization of industry, destruction of the existing police and armed forces, and the political elimination of the conservative parties (if they still existed) and the mass arrest of their most active elements. Codovilla opined that the weakness of the minority left Republican government would turn out to be a great advantage, enabling it to be moved along rapidly and then be replaced.[6] After the left was broadened and the right eliminated, the left Republican government must give way, as indicated in a *Mundo obrero* editorial of February 24, to a "worker-peasant government." This program obeyed the classic Marxist-Leninist scheme in which a worker-peasant government, once the final phase of the democratic revolution had been completed, would initiate the direct transition to socialism, though it would not itself constitute the dictatorship of the proletariat and the full construction of socialism. In a joint PCE-PSOE meeting just before the elections, Díaz had emphasized the difference between a socialist government and the initial worker-peasant government.[7] Though the PCE wanted to move rapidly toward a worker-peasant government, it continually reproached the caballeristas for premature references to the dictatorship of the proletariat.

Contrary to the prevailing notion that the Communists occupied a moderate position in the Popular Front, PCE spokesmen were normally the most vigorous and most coherent of all sectors in demanding completion of the Popular Front program immediately so as to move rapidly beyond it. By this point Dolores Ibárruri (La Pasionaria) had emerged as a major figure in the party, one of the most outspoken and extreme spokespersons. At a major meeting on behalf of Socorro Rojo Internacional (International Red Relief), she declared with dramatic insistence, "The ministries and state organs must be completely cleaned out. We live in a revolutionary period and no one must come to us with complaints about legality, about which we have been fed up since the fourteenth of April [1931]. Legality is imposed by the people, who on the sixteenth of February called for the execution of their murderers. The Republic must satisfy the needs of the people, for if it does not, the people will take over and impose their will." She concluded: "Against the legality of assassins is that of the people. We will win it through our revolutionary zeal. Long live the revolution!" In her maiden speech before a parliamentary body on the first of March, she repeated: "We live in a revolutionary situation that cannot be delayed by legal obstacles, of which we have already had too many since the fourteenth of April. The people impose their own legality and on the sixteenth of February asked for the execution of their murderers. The Republic must satisfy the people's needs. If it does not, the people will overthrow it and impose their will."[8] In this and many other meetings Communist spokesmen demanded not merely the arrest of everyone in a position of authority in October 1934 but the official outlawing of conservative and rightist parties, a major step toward the consolidation of the people's republic "of a new type."[9] The other revolutionary groups made similar demands, though not in such consistently orchestrated style. In mid-March the Azaña government outlawed the Falange, Spain's only fascist party, and arrested many of its leaders, alleging illegal activities. By that standard, of course, nearly all the worker parties ought to have been outlawed.

Outside of parliament, it was the POUM and left Socialist spokesmen who made the most sweepingly extreme statements, declaring that Spain would soon be ready for the dictatorship of the proletariat without making the distinctions and qualifications of the PCE about all the necessarily more limited preliminary steps. Perhaps the most categorical once more was Luis Araquistain, editor of *Claridad,* the intellectual leader of the Bolshevizers in the Socialist Party (who in only one more year would find himself in violent opposition to the Communists). During the election campaign, Araquistain had delivered a lecture in Madrid on "the historical parallel between the Russian and Spanish revolutions," a perception he continued to elaborate during the months that followed. He flatly denied Besteiro's contention that only the historically unparalleled disintegration of civic institutions had made the Bolshevik takeover possible in Russia. He similarly derided Besteiro's analysis (which repeated the earlier Menshevik analysis regarding Russia) that Spain had not yet completed the course of development toward socialism outlined by Marx. According to Araquistain, "history, like biology, is full of leaps." The present backwardness of Spain was supposedly equivalent to that of Russia in 1917, making Spain ripe for revolution. The events of 1931 to 1934, particularly the latter year, constituted "Spain's revolution of 1905." Its middle classes and conservatives were weak, and the Republic itself had done no more than create "a weak state" that could no longer resist revolution. "These undeniable objective facts incline me to believe that Spain could very well be the second country where the proletarian revolution triumphs and is consolidated, without having to worry excessively about counterrevolutionary dangers from abroad. Neighboring great powers are fully preoccupied with their own problems. . . . In the end the Soviet Union would not permit other European states to intervene in a socialist Spain." Hence "the historical dilemma is fascism or socialism, and only violence will decide the issue," but given the weakness of "fascism" in Spain, socialism would win.[10]

Araquistain returned to the same theme in the March issue of his monthly *Leviatán:*

> Historical conditions found in Spain are extremely analogous to those of Russia at the end of the nineteenth and beginning of the twentieth centuries: a capitalism already in its financial phase without an effective haute bourgeoisie, and with a petite bourgeoisie lacking political parties, thus having to end up coming over to the Socialists; a weak state and a proletariat eager for power, conscious of its historical mission and with a revolutionary potential like no other in the world outside Russia, having been cured, again like no other, of all illusions about democracy under a capitalist regime.[11]

Meanwhile the leaders of the PCE, following Comintern instructions, gave special priority to the "triple unification" with the Socialists, meaning unification of the parties, the trade unions, and the youth organizations. In mid-November 1935 the executive commission of the UGT had officially accepted the entry of the small Communist CGTU into the Socialist trade union organization, but months were required to go through this process, which still had not been completed by March 1936. More promising was the keen interest of the FJS (Socialist Youth) leaders in promoting rapid unification of their group. The Comintern bosses were somewhat concerned about the extremism and possible Trotskyism of the FJS activists, and underlined the need for a unified youth organization to accept direction from the Comintern and to recognize the USSR as the homeland of true socialism and accept the leadership of Stalin, but as early as February 21 Codovilla was able to telegram that the FJS leaders accepted all these requirements. A small delegation led by the FJS leader Santiago Carrillo then went immediately to Moscow, where the combination of prudence, firmness, and revolutionary zeal exhibited by Carrillo evidently made a good impression.[12] Carrillo and the other Young Socialists were even more impressed by the center of Soviet power, and by Manuilsky's advice about the way to adjust the revolutionary process to the situation in Spain: the Spanish party, he told them, had to proceed with the hammer and sickle in one hand and the cross in the other.[13]

On March 4 the PCE's central committee sent a long letter to the executive commission of the PSOE, proposing formation of Worker Alliance groups, led by the Socialists and Communists but "freely and democratically constituted" at every level.[14] So far the AOs had generally languished, but they remained high on the Comintern agenda, and could become the instrument for the joint action of the two principal Marxist parties, the goal being "rapid execution of the pact of the Popular Front and struggle for our own program of a worker-peasant government." That government would involve the frequently mentioned large-scale land confiscations; nationalization of large industry, banks, railroads, and other transportation; major social reforms; "national liberation" of Catalonia, the Basque Country, and Galicia; immediate unrestricted liberation of the Moroccan protectorate; dissolution of the army, Civil Guard, and Assault Guard; and "proletarian solidarity with the oppressed of the entire earth and fraternal alliance with the Soviet Union." This twelve-point program was almost identical to the party's earlier thirteen-point program, save for elimination of the point calling for financial aid to smallholders. The worker-peasant government was thus to establish an economic structure similar to that of the Soviet Union under the NEP of 1921–28.

Moreover, the central committee proposed the formation of liaison committees at all levels to begin the merger of the two organizations into "the single Marxist-Leninist party of the proletariat," on the programmatic basis of "complete independence from the bourgeoisie and complete rupture of the social democratic bloc with the bourgeoisie; immediate achievement of unity of action; recognition of the need for the revolutionary overthrow of the domination of the bourgeoisie and the establishment of the dictatorship of the proletariat in the form of soviets; renunciation of support for the bourgeoisie in the event of an imperialist war; building of the party on the basis of democratic centralism to ensure unity of will and deed, tempered by the experience of the Russian Bolsheviks."

With the executive commission of the PSOE controlled by semimoderates, there was no immediate response, for the prietistas (or so-called centrists) regarded unification with the Communists as suicide. On the following day (March 5), the executive committee of the caballerista UGT proposed to the party apparatus and the FJS that a new joint committee be formed of two representatives from each of the worker parties in the Popular Front, to join forces to carry out the Popular Front program. Nothing came of this proposal.

Meanwhile, in new balloting for the leadership of the party's Agrupación Madrileña, the caballeristas, who seemed to enjoy increasing momentum, gained control of the key Madrid section of the party. On March 16 the Madrid section adopted a new statement declaring that "there is no alternative to the establishment of revolutionary socialism" through the "dictatorship of the proletariat. . . . The organ of that transitory dictatorship will be the Socialist Party." It would seek the unity of all the proletariat and would propose a program roughly similar to that announced by the PCE for a worker-peasant government, in the hope of gaining complete victory at the next party congress. On the one hand, the Communist leaders were gratified by the pro-communism and radicalism of the caballeristas, but on the other, the Comintern remained very critical of the continued independent course of the Socialists, of the caballeristas' insistence on ignoring the more complex and measured formulation of tactics and strategy by the Comintern, and of the lack of any concrete new progress toward party unification.[15]

The tiny sector of the Socialist Party led by Julián Besteiro was in despair. That same month the *besteirista* Gabriel Mario de Coca completed the manuscript of a short book denouncing the "Bolshevization of the party." It concluded:

> I close my work with the impression of the triumph of Bolshevization at every level of the party. The parliamentary minority in the new Cortes will be impregnated with a strong Leninist tone. Prieto will have few deputies by his side and Besteiro will be completely isolated as a dissenting Marxist. . . . And the impression all this leaves for the future of the workers and the nation could not be worse. The Bolshevik centipede will be sole sovereign of the proletarian horizon and my Marxism can but imagine that it will be seeking one of its greatest victories. If in October 1934 it only managed to have Gil Robles govern for a black phase with exceptional powers and the Constitution suspended, with the most sterile outpouring of workers' blood, in the future it can be expected to complete its definitive work.[16]

Throughout the spring and early summer of 1936 the likely consequences of the revolutionary process in Spain were frequently pointed out by commentators, normally in the center and on the right. Their prognostications, though fully accurate, were almost universally ignored on the left.

The Shift in Comintern Policy

At this point Comintern policy was about to undergo another shift, completely unrelated to developments in Spain. Hitler's successful remilitarization of the Rhineland on March 7 rang alarm bells in the Kremlin. Germany's first major violation of Versailles was completed with no more than verbal protests from the Western European powers. It made the new Soviet policy of collective security more important than ever, though it also placed the success of that policy in greater doubt. *Izvestia* was careful to avoid commentary for a full week, until the French senate completed ratification of the recently negotiated French-Soviet defense pact. Dimitrov was much quicker to telegram new instructions to the PCE leaders, emphasizing the importance of organizing the mass mobilization of Spanish workers in opposition to Hitler's policy.[17] The worsening strategic situation made Spain more important to Moscow than before, but also implied greater caution, a point that does not at first seem to have been grasped by Codovilla, much less by the PCE leaders.

Codovilla had just sent a long report to Moscow on March 4 declaring that the Azaña government was moving rapidly toward completion of the Popular Front program and was even going beyond it. He was essentially correct. He went on to say that "the revolutionary situation is developing rapidly. Solution of the land problem through revolutionary means will soon have to be faced and, with the development of the struggle, the problem of power. Hence the question of the Alliances plays a decisive role. In order to organize them and to popularize the program of the worker-peasant government, the party is taking measures to reinforce its work in the agricultural regions. The influence and organization of the PCE grow continuously."[18]

During March and early April the PCE continued to emphasize the development of Worker Alliance groups. A plenum of the central committee meeting in Madrid from March 28 to 30 concluded that the present "government, because of its bourgeois character, cannot lead the democratic revolution to its conclusion." Hence the party must prepare to go beyond it to install a worker-peasant government. Díaz continued to call for expansion of Worker Alliance groups as "future organs of power," and Codovilla seemed convinced that the pressure from the left would soon lead to the breakdown of the present structure of the Spanish state. He reported on April 4: "The present situation of conflict cannot long endure, making great battles foreseeable in the near future."[19]

The Comintern leadership now became seriously concerned that the situation in Spain was moving too far too fast and might soon get out of hand.

With the international situation deteriorating and the development of the French Popular Front, much more moderate in tone than its Spanish counterpart, proceeding nicely and about to face general elections, a major blow-up in Spain could be counterproductive. Dimitrov and Manuilsky replied on April 9 that any danger of a breakup in the Spanish Popular Front or the Azaña government should be avoided, and the same was true with regard to any threat of a new anarchist insurrection. Excessive strike demands by either the CNT or the UGT should be vigorously resisted. "Do not allow yourselves to be provoked and do not precipitate events that at the present time might be harmful for the revolution and only assist the triumph of the counterrevolution. . . . In all the party's activity it must be kept in mind that in the present situation the creation of soviet power is not the order of the day, but that, for the time being, the aim is only to create the kind of democratic regime that shuts the door to fascism and to counterrevolution and generally strengthens the position of the proletariat and its allies."[20] The Comintern line and previous statements of the PCE had made it clear that this "kind of democratic regime" would of course have nothing in common with liberal democracy. Though it would use the facade of democratic legitimacy to strengthen its position, it would employ democratic institutions to begin the process of building a people's republic that would exclude all nonleftist elements and constitute the first major phase of the revolution.

In practice, the Comintern's shift toward a more moderate tactical line proved confusing to the PCE leadership, which throughout March and the first part of April continued to promote the formation of Alianzas Obreras throughout Spain; as late as April 11 Díaz referred to them in a speech as "future organs of power."[21] In a major parliamentary debate on April 15 he did not disguise the fact that the party's ultimate goal remained the dictatorship of the proletariat. Only after that point did the shift in the Comintern line begin to be fully implemented. Public calls for the expansion of a new Popular Front gave way to fervent support of the one that existed, at least in theory. In *La Correspondencia internacional*, the party's international bulletin, on April 17 Díaz denounced "exaggerated impatience" and emphasized the importance of maintaining the Popular Front, which still had "a long road" to follow.[22] The party even began to discourage strikes with such goals as the thirty-six-hour week, declaring that the current forty hours were acceptable. It insisted on major changes in the status of labor only through formal Republican legislation and finally withdrew its perpetual opposition to compensation for land confiscated. Whereas before it had opposed the existing system of Republican autonomy statutes in favor of breaking Spain up into a series of nominally independent states, it now supported the existing territorial structure of the Republican state. The goal now was a strong, united, exclusively leftist Republican state that could eliminate the right by harassing or legislating it out of existence. Similarly, the Communist position emphasized strong Spanish support for the Soviet Union—with which the Republic still had not established formal diplomatic relations—and the League of Nations; Dimitrov repeated at this time that the top priority of the Comintern was the defense of the Soviet Union.[23] Even so, the adoption of a more moderate temporary line did not involve any fundamental disguise. On May 27 *Mundo obrero* endorsed once more the ultimate formula of a worker-peasant government, which it called in standard terminology the "democratic dictatorship of the workers and peasants."

May Day, 1936, in Madrid produced the biggest Communist demonstration in Spanish history to that point, with thousands of party members marching in formation and the uniformed Juventud Socialista Unificada (JSU; United Socialist Youth), now generally (though not entirely) under Communist control, parading in the paramilitary style of the era. Party membership was increasing rapidly, rising from 9,200 in May 1934 to 11,275 on the eve of the insurrection before dropping in 1935 under the weight of the repression. During the latter part of 1935 and the electoral campaign membership rebounded, reaching at least 14,000 by February 1936, and the party officially declared twice as many. During the spring and summer membership doubled and tripled. The party claimed to have 100,000 members by July, though the real affiliation may have been no more than half that figure.[24]

This growth was impressive but the party was still not a full-fledged mass movement. Nonetheless, many Spanish conservatives seemed fully convinced amid the prerevolutionary turmoil of the spring and early summer that communism was growing by leaps and bounds. The military rebels and their allies who initiated the Civil War proper on July 18 would soon forge documents in an effort to prove that a Communist takeover of the Republic was scheduled for August—a complete fabrication. Yet it remains a fact that conservatives were genuinely convinced that Communist and hence Soviet power in Spain had become very great. It should be kept in mind that the PCE did everything it could to foster this impression, presenting an image of rapidly growing power, inevitability, and triumphalism. Communists in fact made up but a small minority of the immense leftist march on May Day, but, like their Bolshevik predecessors in 1917, they focused on the capital and did everything possible to magnify their presence in Madrid. Certain aspects of the revolutionary style particularly impressed middle-class onlookers, such as the gigantic hammers and sickles, the massed clenched-first salutes, the huge banners of Lenin and Stalin, and the sight of hundreds of young Socialist and Communist women chanting "Hijos sí, maridos no!" (Children yes, husbands no!). Perhaps even more important was the embracing of Bolshevization by many Socialists, since they were a large movement that had already led one major revolutionary insurrection.

The POUM in the Spring of 1936

By the spring of 1936 the most consistently revolutionary position in Spain was held by the POUM, whose executive committee had declared the preceding December that it was "the true communist party of Catalonia and of Spain." In the sense of being a native Spanish communist party not controlled from abroad, this was undoubtedly correct. Andreu Nin, its number two leader, held that the electoral victory of the Popular Front had been made possible only by the earlier violent insurrection, which he declared the only secure road to power. When the Cortes opened on April 15, Maurín was the only Popular Front deputy who vehemently criticized the Azaña government directly, denouncing the prime minister's opening speech, in which he attempted, albeit feebly, to calm the country. Even more than the caballeristas, the POUM had become the party of civil war, though in its arrogance it assumed that the right was so weak that civil war could not last long. The official POUM position was that the Azaña government should immediately give way to a more radical Popular Front transition administration, which would prepare for a worker government much more quickly than the Comintern was willing to countenance at that time.[25]

In its revolutionary maximalism, the POUM inveighed against pacifism and the League of Nations as mere bourgeois formulas. Both the POUM and the anarchist FAI denounced the Popular Front tactic in general and also criticized the Socialists' support for League sanctions against Italy. The Socialists, they said, seemed to assume it was possible to work with capitalist powers and that there was a difference between capitalism and fascism. However, the POUM's earlier attempt to convene its own National Conference against War in October 1935, which had sought to expand interest in anti-imperialist bellicosity into revolutionary civil war, had failed completely.[26]

The POUM still sought to further the objective of creating "a great revolutionary party." It agreed with the PCE's concern to expand the currently uncertain Worker Alliance groups and in May proposed formation of a liaison committee with the PCE and PSOE. POUM leaders termed rejection of this proposal further proof that their party was "the only defender of the socialist revolution within the ranks of our proletariat."[27] Largo Caballero proposed that the POUM merge with the Socialists, an invitation that was indignantly rejected, though some of the local Socialist Youth sections declared that they would not go through with the current JSU merger unless the POUM youth were also included.

Communist Policy toward the Other Marxist Parties

To the dismay of the POUM, the other Marxist parties in Catalonia were drawing closer together. The consequences of the October revolution had radicalized the once somewhat moderate Unió Socialista de Catalunya, which in June 1935 had asked to be admitted to the Comintern as a "sympathizing section." At that time a liaison committee was formed between the USC and the Partit Català Proletari, and it was joined in December by the Catalan Communists (PCC) and a few months later by the Catalan Socialists. By June 23 the committee had reached agreement on seven points: joint identity as a class party of workers and peasants, democratic centralism, support for the Comintern, the defense of the USSR against imperialist war, national liberation, the revolutionary conquest of power by armed insurrection, and the imposition of the dictatorship of the proletariat. It looked as though the Comintern goal of a unified revolutionary Marxist party in Catalonia was about to be realized, but it would be very small, with only 2,000 members, compared with 5,000 for the POUM in all Catalonia, though the allied parties were slightly larger than the POUM in Barcelona. Based on the Catalan section of the UGT, they also represented a combined syndical membership of 80,000, larger than that of the POUM.[28]

The POUM also accepted the responsibility to "defend the USSR," but its leaders asserted that the best way to do so was through outright revolution in Spain, while control of a new Catalan Marxist party by the Comintern would mean that its components could not be "objectively revolutionary" and would even place themselves "to the right of social democracy."[29] Similarly, when the merged JSU began to set up a Youth Front with left Republican youth, the POUM also denounced this step as a move to the right.

Comintern unification tactics vis-à-vis the main sector of the Socialist Party were less successful. The main achievement was formation of the JSU, which went ahead rapidly in the spring. With the conversion of Santiago Carrillo, Communists dominated the JSU from the start, though in the slow unification of the two syndical systems the Communist unions were easily overshadowed. The caballeristas had some interest in unification of the two parties as long as they believed that the Socialists could absorb the Communists, but after the experience of the JSU, that seemed much less likely. Neither major sector of the Socialists had a clear position concerning a new expansion of the Worker Alliance.

The caballeristas of the UGT had much more interest in some sort of revolutionary alliance with the CNT, which held a reunification congress at Zaragoza during the first ten days of May. The anarchosyndicalist movement had suffered a severe loss of membership as well as internal division as a consequence of the mass strike-and-insurrection policies of 1932–33. Congressional delegates represented only 550,595 workers, but at that moment the CNT was probably growing more rapidly than any other worker group. The congress proposed a revolutionary alliance with the UGT, but only on the basis of complete renunciation of collaboration with any Republican government, an agreement to "completely destroy the political and social regime," and the support of 75 percent of the membership in a subsequent referendum. The congress endorsed once more "the insurrectional method for the conquest of social wealth," with the goal of the abolition of private property, building of libertarian communism, and the formation of autonomous communes to form the Confederación Ibérica de Comunas Autónomas Libertarias.[30]

As a result of the Asturian insurrection, the repression, and the Popular Front campaign, some progress had been made in relations between the two syndical organizations, but all the differences remained. On May 24 Largo Caballero publicly embraced a CNT leader in Cádiz, but more common was a kind of competitive radicalization between the two movements. Since the CNT was not part of the Popular Front, the government was sometimes willing to take action against CNT excesses. After labor conflict resulted in the killing by CNT gunmen of both a Socialist official and a Communist official in Málaga in early June, the authorities closed all CNT centers in that province.

The most intense intergroup conflict among the revolutionary left was nonetheless the Comintern's campaign against "Trotskyism" in Spain—meaning the POUM—which was intensified in the latter part of April. The PCE advanced the line that the POUM "was paid with fascist gold," and by June Mundo obrero insisted that Maurín was "a renegade in the service of reaction." Whereas Carrillo and young JSU radicals had once been the sector of Spanish Marxism most sympathetic to the former BOC, with Bolshevization Carrillo and the JSU spokesmen now spearheaded the attack, seconded not merely by the entire apparatus of the PCE but also by ultra pro-Communist elements of the Socialists, such as Margarita Nelken and Julio Alvarez del Vayo. By late spring POUM spokesmen were complaining of assaults on and attempted sabotage of some of their meetings, and even some local JSU figures in Catalonia also protested the attacks, while PCE leaders sought to persuade Largo Caballero that the POUM should be eliminated from the Worker Alliance or any other alliance mechanism.[31]

As indicated earlier, the old Izquierda Comunista de España had been categorically Trotskyist, at least until 1934, and the BOC generally sympathetic to Trotsky, though never formally Trotskyist. But formation of the POUM had marked a final break with formal Trotskyism, even on the part of Nin, since it was based on categorical rejection of Trotsky's tactic of "entryism" into existing Socialist parties. For his part, Trotsky had not reciprocated Maurín's admiration, denouncing the latter's concept of the "democratic-socialist revolution" as pure nonsense, since in Russia in 1917 the proponents of democratic revolution and of socialist revolution had been on opposite sides of the barricades. From Trotsky's point of view, the democratic revolution had been completed in Spain, and the Popular Front as led by petit bourgeois left Republicans was merely recapitulating it. While denouncing what he called "the treachery of the POUM," he insisted that in Spain a revolutionary struggle had to be waged against the Popular Front.[32] Maurín himself declared in La Batalla on the symbolic first of May that "I am not a Trotskyist . . . but . . . ," making clear that none of the POUM leaders considered themselves insulted by the term, for Trotsky had "one of the best organized minds of the socialist movement" and was "the greatest Bolshevik leader after Lenin."[33]

The POUM is usually said to have had about 10,000 members when the Civil War began, but that figure may be doubted, since, as Andrew Durgan points out, in December 1936 Nin stated that it had been no more than 6,000. The party was growing, like the left generally, and outside Catalonia was strongest in other parts of the northeast, such as Valencia, Castellón, and eastern Aragon, with small nuclei scattered throughout Spain.[34]

The POUM leaders told their small number of syndical followers in most of Spain to work within the UGT. A POUM syndical conference in Barcelona on May 2 transformed the POUM syndicates proper into the Federación Obrera de Unidad Sindical (FOUS; Worker Federation of Syndical Unity), with almost 50,000 members, most notably in Lérida. By contrast, by June the CNT had a minimum of 133,000 members in Barcelona province alone and the Socialist/Communist UGT/UGSOC 86,000 members in all Catalonia but mainly concentrated in Barcelona province. This was further indication of the POUM's failure to break out of its isolation. Though POUM leaders judged the largest CNT strike in Barcelona that spring to have been mistaken in its narrowness and extremism, they generally applauded CNT tactics and called for more and bigger strikes.[35]

The POUM sharply protested Socialist and Communist support for the new left Republican government of Santiago Casares Quiroga, formed in Madrid in mid-May after the elevation of Azaña to the Republican presidency. The two larger Marxist parties had now withdrawn earlier demands for the dissolution of the Civil Guard and a drastic purge of the army. As early as November 1935 Maurín had called for the armed reorganization of the Worker Alliance militia of 1934 and he repeated this point more and more insistently during the spring of 1936. PCE spokesmen denounced this position as "a Trotskyist provocation," while the POUM claimed that the Milicias Antifascistas Obreras y Campesinas (MAOC), of which the PCE proudly boasted, "did not exist." That charge was incorrect, for the MAOC, though numbering only a few thousand (mainly in Madrid), did receive paramilitary training by politically affiliated army and police officers and several Communist militia leaders who had themselves been trained in Moscow. The POUM made at least some effort to give its youth group, Juventud Comunista Ibérica (Iberian Communist Youth, or JCI), a little paramilitary training, and increasingly turned to direct action in strikes and agitation.[36]

The reorganization and expansion of Worker Alliance groups largely failed to materialize. The POUM continued to call for it but got little response. Only the PCE had given the matter equal attention, but as Comintern tactics became increasingly moderate, the party talked of the AO less and less, while the caballeristas, as usual, were interested in the AOs simply as an expansion of the Socialist organization. Therefore with the opening of the Cortes in April the POUM adopted the new tactic of calling for formation of an all–Popular Front government to pursue a more radical policy, but once more generated little support. When, by mid-June, approximately 110,000 workers were on strike in Madrid, party spokesmen hailed the action as the possible beginning of the worker revolution, but strike activity in some parts of the country subsequently declined.[37] On the worker left only Communists and some of the prietistas had anything approaching a realistic sense of the potential strength of the right, and thus three days after the assassination of the rightist Calvo Sotelo in July—which would be the final catalyst to civil war—Maurín said to a friend in Madrid that nothing was likely to happen for the time being and left for a meeting of the POUM regional committee in Galicia. At that point his participation in the Spanish revolution that he so ardently desired came to a sudden end, as the outbreak of the fighting left him trapped behind insurgent lines.

The Popular Front Victory in France

May was a time of euphoria for the Comintern in southwestern Europe, with everything looking more and more positive in Spain and a clear-cut electoral triumph of the Popular Front being consummated in France only two months after the French Senate had finally ratified the French-Soviet defense pact. Victory in France seemed to provide further evidence of the utility of the Popular Front tactic. Altogether the three main Popular Front parties increased their combined vote totals by only 1.5 percent over the preceding elections but as a bloc scored a decisive victory. The Radicals, as the right wing of the alliance, in fact declined, their share of the total vote dropping from 20.07 to 16.57 percent. The Socialists held about the same position, drawing votes away from the left wing of the Radicals but losing slightly more to the Communists and in toto holding fewer seats than in the preceding parliament. The big winners were the French Communists, who jumped from twelve seats and only 8.4 percent of the vote in 1932 to seventy-two seats and 15.3 percent in 1936. The Parti Communiste de France (PCF; Communist Party of France) was now by far the largest Communist party in Western Europe and entered the second of its three major phases of growth, shooting upward from 87,000 members in 1935 to 326,500 by 1937, at which point it had a larger membership than the Socialist Party. Trade union support grew equally rapidly.[38] Moreover, the victory of the French Popular Front touched off an enormous strike wave—largest in French history to that point—much more quickly than did the elections in Spain, though the disparity may have been partly due to timing: the French elections were held in the spring, the Spanish in winter.

France was not Spain, however, and the French Popular Front was not the Spanish Popular Front. Their programs were in some respects superficially similar, but the French program was more moderate, aimed at the defeat of fascism but not at the elimination of all conservative forces in French politics and institutions. In France as in Spain, the Communists did not enter the government, but in France the large Socialist Party was relatively united, contained only a small revolutionary wing in no way equivalent to the *bolchevizantes* in Spain, and now assumed government responsibility for the first time. The Socialist leader, Léon Blum, who stood to the right of all the Spanish Socialist leaders save Besteiro, presided over a governing coalition made up primarily of Socialists and Radicals. The new French government was thus more broadly based than its Spanish counterpart and was both stronger and more moderate, and hence not subject to strong Kerenskyist leveraging from the extreme left, which in any case was very weak in France. Blum negotiated a quick end to the strike wave that brought major gains for labor, life returned to normal, and the government enacted a much more coherent and moderate legislative program than its counterpart in Madrid. There was little violence and little in the way of direct action.[39]

Moreover, by this time the lower-middle-class liberal democratic Radical Party differed considerably from the left Republicans in Spain; it was more solidly established and more democratic. It absolutely refused to play a Kerenskyist role vis-à-vis the worker left and exercised a considerable moderating influence on the government. Instead of moving ever farther left, like the left Republicans, who had adopted a semisocialist economic program and whose youth group had formed an alliance with the Communists, it was frightened by the postelectoral strike wave and soon began to move farther toward the right.

The Final Phase of the Parliamentary Republic

Amid this euphoria Codovilla and Hernández appeared again in Moscow to report to the Comintern on May 22, presenting a glowing account that clearly impressed their superiors. According to Elorza and Bizcarrondo, when they reported that Communist municipal councilmen were exercising considerable power and influence in a number of towns and even determining which opponents should be thrown into jail, Dimitrov enthused, "That is a real democracy!"[40] When, however, Codovilla and Hernández raised the question whether such favorable conditions should rapidly lead to the development of the "democratic dictatorship of the workers and peasants," Dimitrov quickly quashed such speculations, emphasizing that the current priorities were simply the strengthening of the Popular Front and decisive victory over fascism.[41] The subsequent resolution of the Romansky Lendersekretariat on Spain remained cautious, reaffirming established goals:

Continued agitation and completion of the triple alliance (labor, youth, and party) with the Socialists, while being sure to gain the support of moderate Socialists as well. Farmland should continue to be confiscated, but in an orderly way according to the formal legislation of the agrarian reform. Strikes should be used "rationally" and there should be no general strikes. Communist syndicates should strive for worker control in industry but for the time being the party should promote nationalization only of the Bank of Spain and of the railroads, measures supported by some bourgeois progressives. Agitation should particularly target the youth and the

armed forces and should give priority to expansion of the MAOC.
All "monarchist" organizations—meaning apparently all conservative groups—should be officially outlawed, their property confiscated and their leaders arrested, the Catholic Gil Robles and the
liberal democrat Lerroux being specified by name. The "democratic
revolution" should first be carried to full completion, creating
a new form of leftist people's republic with all non-leftist forces
eliminated.[42]

In the first draft of this resolution, some elements of the earlier more directly revolutionary program surfaced, with instructions to try to expand the
Worker Alliance groups as "organs of the struggle for power" of the revolutionary
masses, but were soon dropped. The final draft merely emphasized supporting
the Popular Front, with Alliance groups functioning as democratically elected
committees to deal with concrete issues under the aegis of the Popular Front.
Codovilla and the Spanish leaders, so long trained to revolutionary maximalism,
seem not to have fully grasped the more moderate tactical line being imposed
by Dimitrov and his chief assistant for southwestern Europe, Palmiro Togliatti.
It was hard for them to avoid falling back into the earlier terminology, particularly
given the ambiguity of many Communist terms.[43]

While caballeristas publicly called from time to time for creation of a "revolutionary militia," they did very little in practice. Communists, though many
fewer, were much better organized. A Comintern adviser on paramilitary and
other subversive activities, Vittorio Vidali (who went by the pseudonym Carlos
Contreras), arrived in May, and was assisted by Enrique Líster and several other
young leaders who had undergone training at the Frunze Academy in Moscow.
By mid-June the party announced that its MAOC forces in Madrid numbered
2,000, with the goal of becoming a "broad mass organization with a semi-
military character," thus constituting "the organizational basis for the future
worker-peasant red army."[44] Terrorist sections were split off from the MAOC
proper so as not to compromise the parent organization. They carried on urban
guerrilla warfare against Falangists in Madrid but tried to avoid killing policemen, so as not to arouse greater alarm among the middle classes. Communists
were also influential in the formation of the Unión Militar Republicana Antifascista (UMRA; Republican Antifascist Military Union), a small organization
of leftist officers who sought to counter rightist organizations within the armed
forces. They would later claim that the UMRA was an outgrowth of the tiny
Unión Militar Antifascista that the party had set up in 1934.[45] In addition,

Líster directed a secret "antimilitarist section" that collected information and sought to sow revolutionary subversion among Spanish soldiers.

There was no specific agreement among the left concerning a people's or democratic "republic of a new type," but in practice both the left Republican government and the Socialists often acted as if there were. While the Communists continued to demand that the conservative parties simply be outlawed through legislation, the government had already outlawed the fascist Falange by decree in mid-March and some two months later closed the principal non-leftist syndical organization, the Federación Nacional de Uniones de Trabajadores (National Federation of Workers' Unions, or FNUT), with nearly 300,000 members, because of alleged "provocations." The much greater provocations of the leftist syndicates were largely ignored, particularly in the case of the UGT.

Conditions demanded by hotel employees in Barcelona, spurred on by the POUM, would have ruined the industry. When owners offered the workers profit sharing, the CNT refused. After fierce strikes, the streetcar company of Valencia and a railway in Andalusia had to dissolve and hand their activities over to the government. Hundreds of smaller companies were being ruined. Even major leaders of the worker groups, including the Communists, warned of the danger of polarizing the society prematurely. After the builders' association of Seville gave in to exorbitant demands by CNT strikers, the secretary of the CNT national committee, Horacio Prieto, said that for the time being workers must moderate their demands; otherwise they would prematurely and unnecessarily provoke employers to move to the extreme right in reaction. On May 26 El Sol quoted Prieto as saying that the massive seamen's strike was out of control and would ruin Spanish maritime activity, creating a national crisis.

Tax collection had dropped considerably and capital was fleeing the country. The left Republican government had failed to complete a national budget, as it became harder and harder to fund the national debt and issue government bonds. By June the decline in the balance of payments threatened a major devaluation of the peseta, but this was the least of Spain's economic problems. Employers called upon the government to take constructive action, as its French counterpart was doing, but Casares Quiroga was not a constructive statesman like Blum and did little. On June 7 La Veu de Catalunya published a manifesto by no fewer than 126 economic associations, declaring their willingness to accept most of the initial economic program of the Popular Front but asking for quick government action to avoid economic anarchy, and proposing a temporary freeze on salary increases and a reform of the labor tribunals to make them less partisan. Two days later El Sol calculated that a million workers were currently on strike. On June 26 and July 5 it reported resolutions similar to those in *La Veu* that had been passed by an extraordinary national assembly of the Chambers of Commerce and Industry. Both Besteiro in the Cortes and an agrarian expert writing in *El Sol* on July 15 and 17 warned that all the rural strikes and land occupations were destroying the structure of the agrarian economy, and in their present form could benefit neither smallholders nor farmworkers in the long term.

On May 25 Felipe Sánchez Román, the only significant left-liberal leader to have abandoned the Popular Front, whose polarizing and destructive consequences he had quickly grasped, convened a meeting of representatives of his Partido Nacional Republicano. It approved his proposal for formation of a national unity government of all the constitutionalist parties (placing the left Republicans in that category) to crack down on violence and disorder and to enforce the laws. The Socialists would be invited to participate if they would accept such a program. They ignored the proposal. Nearly a month later the centrist liberal Miguel Maura published a series of articles in *El Sol* warning that Spain was headed toward either complete anarchy or·civil war, either of which would be a disaster. He also proposed a national unity constitutional government, which he called a temporary "national Republican dictatorship," to enforce the constitution and save the polity.[46] The left Republicans once more showed little interest; their leftist sectarianism and de facto Kerenskyism made it impossible for them to break with the worker left.

Communist spokesmen continued to push steadily for constitutional means of eliminating the rightist forces, in consonance with their long-time program of consolidating a "people's republic of a new type." On July 1 the PCE delegation in the Cortes submitted to the representatives of other Popular Front parties a legislative proposal that would mandate arrest and prosecution of all those in positions of authority in the government during the October insurrection and the subsequent repression, from Prime Minister Lerroux on down, and subject them to confiscation of property, even though that sanction was illegal under the Republican Constitution. The fundamental concept was that the criminals would arrest and prosecute those who upheld the law, just as the military rebels in the civil war soon to break out would prosecute and execute those who had failed to rebel as culpable of "illegal rebellion." The left Republican government had shown that it was more than willing to bend the constitution, but on this occasion it rejected a proposal that would have directly violated a specific article of it. Later, on July 9, the Communists did obtain agreement from other Popular Front parties that the summer adjournment of parliament would be delayed until the issue of "responsibilities" for the repression had been fully decided.[47]

The climax came on the night of July 12–13, when a Republican police detachment illegally arrested and then killed José Calvo Sotelo, a leader of the far-right parliamentary opposition. This murder, carried out in retaliation for the killing some hours earlier of a leftist Assault Guard officer, was neither planned nor ordered by the government but was nonetheless a direct consequence of left Republican state policy. First, illegal arrests had been formally authorized by the minister of the interior. Second, the Azaña/Casares Quiroga administrations had officially pardoned and returned to duty revolutionary police officers guilty of treason. Third, since early May it had become a practice on certain occasions to include Socialist Party activists in police units, sometimes officially deputized for service and at other times simply incorporated ad hoc. A major figure in implementing these last two policies was the left Republican Bibiano Ossorio Tafall, undersecretary of the interior, who had been carefully cultivated by the Communists and was one of the more radical, pro-Communist young second-rank leaders of the petit bourgeois left. It was not a policeman but a prietista Socialist illegally participating in the arrest who in a vengeful instant shot the monarchist leader in the back of the head.[48]

The government issued a vague statement of concern but took no action to reassure the opposition and made no serious effort to arrest and prosecute the murderers. Its principal response was to close two monarchist centers, suspend two leading conservative newspapers, and arrest some two hundred more rightists to add to the thousands of rightists already imprisoned, as though the monarchists had been responsible for murdering their own leader. Despite the limited importance of the Communist Party, the extent to which the government was willing to cooperate in carrying out the short-term Communist program was remarkable. To try to give a modest appearance of impartiality, it arrested a few anarchosyndicalists and closed the main CNT headquarters in Madrid, although the CNT also had nothing to do with the killing.

Only the Communists had a coherent short-term program—unless one considers the POUM project of proceeding directly to the first steps of revolutionary socialism a coherent program. The afternoon after the murder, the Communist deputies submitted the following legislative draft, which appeared immediately in *Mundo obrero*, to the other Popular Front groups:

Article 1: All organizations of a fascist or reactionary nature, such as Falange Española, Renovación Española, CEDA, Derecha Regional

Valenciana and others with similar characteristics, will be dissolved and their properties confiscated, as well as those of their leaders and inspirers.

Article 2: All persons known for their fascist, reactionary, or anti-republican activities will be arrested and prosecuted without bond.

Article 3: The newspapers *El Debate, Ya, Informaciones,* and *ABC* and all the reactionary provincial press will be confiscated by the government.

This sweeping, totally unconstitutional proposal was a major feature of the plan to introduce the "new type" of all-leftist republic—something sought, mutatis mutandis, by all the Spanish left in varying degrees and ways—but postponement of the next parliamentary session made its formal presentation impossible before the fighting began; its provisions then were carried out in a violent and revolutionary manner largely without benefit of legislation.

It was generally recognized after the murder of Calvo Sotelo—the killing of a leader of the parliamentary opposition by the government's own police, a deed unprecedented in a modern West European government—that the Spanish polity had collapsed and that some sort of direct civil armed confrontation, however short or long, was inevitable. The destruction of public order and progressive elimination of property and constitutional rights would have resulted in civil revolt in almost any country; revolutionary processes, if carried far enough, always end in civil war, unless the revolutionaries possess overwhelming force from the outset.

One of the leading advocates of civil war was Luis Araquistain, editor of the revolutionary Socialist *Claridad.* Like Maurín, he had earlier opined that the left could easily win a revolutionary conflict and that the tense international situation precluded counterrevolutionary foreign intervention. After the killing of Calvo Sotelo, he wrote to his wife that an attempted armed revolt by the right was now likely, and as a result "a dictatorship will be imposed either by us or by the other side."[49] He was correct. The democratic Republic had ceased to exist.

On July 17, only a few hours before the military revolt would begin in the Moroccan protectorate, Dimitrov and Manuilsky sent an urgent telegram to the politburo of the PCE, insisting on immediate exceptional measures to thwart the "fascist conspiracy" and avoid civil war. They urged the leaders in Spain to encourage maximum unity of the Popular Front and press ahead vigorously with their program of using legal governmental means to arrest rightists, purge the army, police, and administration, and suppress the rightist press. In addition, they should press for introduction of a special *tribunal de urgencia* with revolutionary plenary powers to apply the maximum penalties to rightists and confiscate their property, while the party should press forward with the formation and expansion of Worker-Peasant Alliance groups as active liaison units of the Popular Front.[50] To this date little had been accomplished on that score. Most of these injunctions were not new, but the Comintern leaders stressed them with the greatest urgency because of the obvious and imminent danger of armed rightist revolt and civil war. From the Soviet viewpoint the situation in Spain was for the moment close to optimal, though it should be moved steadily to the left through official government rather than revolutionary action. The Comintern sought to avoid civil war, which would place everything at risk and create potential international complications as well.

CHAPTER SIX

Communism and the Spanish Revolution

July–August 1936

THE MILITARY REBELLION that began the Spanish Civil War was a pre-emptive strike by approximately half of the army, led by a diverse cadre of officers, primarily of middle and junior rank. It initially sought a new, more conservative and authoritarian republic that would put an end to the growing anarchy, the pervasive misgovernment or lack of government by the left Republicans, and the mounting threat from a profoundly disunified but ever-expanding and violent revolutionary left. Later, after the rebellion had begun, the insurgents would release forged documentation in an effort to show that the Comintern planned to take over the government no later than August.[1] Though some individual Communists may have engaged in loose talk of that sort, the evidence is clear that the Comintern intended to continue the Popular Front formula indefinitely and had no such immediate plan or timetable in mind. Nor is it even likely that most of the rebel leaders believed it did, for they well knew that the great bulk of the prerevolutionary agitation and activity stemmed from Socialists and anarchosyndicalists. At the same time, it should be kept in mind that "communism" had come to serve the right as a catchall term for the entire revolutionary left, just as the left called all the right "fascist." The greatly increased presence, propaganda, and activism of the PCE in Madrid during the spring and early summer of 1936 only heightened this tendency.

The more moderate sectors of the Popular Front had called time and again for patience, moderation, and discipline, failing to grasp that the prerevolutionary violence was less a tactic than a fundamental attitude on the worker left that could not readily be restrained—not that the government ever took any serious measures to restrain it. Thus Indalecio Prieto lamented privately, "Only one thing is clear: that we are going to deserve a catastrophe because of our stupidity."[2] His final warning appeared in his Bilbao newspaper, *El Liberal*, on July 17, only hours before the rebellion began: "The citizens of a civilized country have the right to tranquility, and the state has the duty to assure it. For some time—why should we deceive ourselves?—Spanish citizens have seen themselves dispossessed of that right because the state cannot fulfill the duty of guaranteeing it to them. . . . In the same way that history comes to justify peasant revolutions, it can approve military insurrections when the one and the other put an end to regimes that, for whatever reason, have become incompatible with the political, economic, or social progress required by peoples."

President Azaña made an effort to form a compromise government only on the night of July 18–19, after the revolt had begun, and by that time it was too late. The caballeristas, for that matter, vetoed any compromise by mounting a loud demonstration early on the morning of the 19th, so that the government formed later that day under the pharmacy professor José Giral was based on another all–left Republican cabinet, which constituted a mere reprise of the failed and inept Casares Quiroga administration. Though at that point less than half the army had rebelled and most of the paramilitary police forces (Civil Guard and Assault Guard) had remained loyal, the Giral government turned immediately to "arming the people," the people armed being the organized leftist worker groups; the Republican government had already suppressed nonleftist worker groups. Once armed power in what would soon be called the Republican zone passed into the hands of many thousands of ad hoc revolutionary militias, whatever authority remained in the hands of the Republican government began to disappear. The revolutionary groups in turn would soon require the disbanding of what remained of the regular army, on the grounds that no regular military units could be trusted.

Though the Giral government remained in session in Madrid, its authority was increasingly ignored even in the capital, where a kind of dual authority developed between the feeble government and the revolutionary groups somewhat similar to the unstable dyarchy of the Provisional Government and the Soviets in Russia in 1917. In many other regions, Republican government authority disappeared almost altogether, falling into the hands of the largest worker party in each district, or in most cases of an ad hoc worker party alliance. In Catalonia there reigned a peculiar dualism between what was left of the authority of the Catalan government and the de facto power of the CNT and other groups. Much the same alliance that had produced the October insurrection took control of most of Asturias. The Giral administration sent a special commission to take charge of government in Valencia, but at the end of July its dwindling functions were taken over by a "regional executive committee" of the worker parties, which was later melded with residues of the government commission. The only exception to revolutionary domination lay in the Basque provinces of Guipuzcoa and Vizcaya (especially the latter), where Basque nationalists governed in conjunction with the three main revolutionary movements. Within a very few weeks what little remained of Republican government in the so-called Republican zone had largely given way to what Carlos Rama has called the "Revolutionary Republican Confederation of 1936–37."[3] Several nominal leftist strongholds nonetheless fell at the beginning. In Zaragoza the CNT was victim of its own disorganization, and much of the province immediately fell under rightist military control. The same thing occurred in "Red Seville," seized by General Gonzalo Queipo de Llano in an audacious coup de main, the greatest initial achievement by any of the rebel leaders.

The Spanish revolution was the last in the twenty-year revolutionary chain stretching from 1917 to 1936–37. All the preceding revolutions had been touched off by World War I or its turbulent aftermath. There had also been a revolutionary upsurge in Spain, as was seen in Chapter 2, during the latter part of World War I and the years immediately following, even encouraged as in Russia by German money (though the amount employed in Spain was tiny by comparison), and led primarily by the CNT. The first leaders of the Comintern had looked longingly at the revolutionary spirit of Spanish anarchosyndicalists but could find no way to attract them to their own party. After World War I the revolutionary upsurge in Spain was contained, not without difficulty, for two reasons: the organizational capacity of the revolutionary Spanish worker groups was limited by the prevailing political and social system and the underdevelopment of the economy, while Spain's neutrality had enabled the established institutions to weather the war years better than those of many other European countries.

For that reason especially, the democratization experienced by many lands in the aftermath of World War I was delayed in the Spanish case until 1931. The great acceleration of economic, social, and cultural development experienced by Spain during the 1920s had fundamentally altered society and drastically raised expectations, producing psychologically one of the most fundamental of revolutions—the revolution of rising expectations. Spanish development in the 1920s, however, managed only the first takeoff of modernization; the initiative was still far from completed. Though growing dynamically, Spain had remained less developed than the rest of Western Europe. Then suddenly much more was expected and demanded of the Second Republic than of any other regime in Spanish history—more, for example, than would be demanded of the democratic monarchy in 1976–77, which was asked only to introduce basic democracy and civil rights. Between 1931 and 1936 the combination of full democracy and organizational freedom, combined with enormously increased expectations, produced an outburst of leftist enthusiasm. Soon, as the new economic frustrations of the Depression and domestic political confrontation mounted, radicalization without precedent produced a unique revolutionary situation that at that moment existed in no other country in the world.

All the revolutionary organizations (though not exactly the Comintern leaders) were certain that the overwhelming force of historical change was on their side and that the right could be crushed rapidly—at most with a few weeks of civil war. This was a disastrous miscalculation, for the Spanish middle classes, though relatively weak and only a minority of the population, were proportionately a larger minority than their counterparts in Russia in 1917. Indeed, one of the fundamental functions of the Popular Front was theoretically to try to win over much of the Spanish lower middle class. As it turned out, under iron military leadership—with General Francisco Franco playing the role of a sort of counterrevolutionary Lenin—the conservative and Catholic sectors of the population would demonstrate greater unity, determination, and efficiency in civil war. When to this development was added a relative preponderance of foreign intervention in their favor (exactly contrary to the confident predictions of revolutionaries such as Araquistain and Maurín), the fate of the Spanish revolution would be sealed.

With the outbreak of the revolution, all the leftist groups grew rapidly, led by the two main syndical organizations, the CNT and UGT, each of which claimed to have two million affiliates in the Republican zone by the end of 1936. During the first months the CNT expanded more rapidly, for the loose and flexible anarchosyndicalist structure was less demanding and more attractive than the UGT's.[4] Moreover, some of the rural areas in the southwest in which the UGT was stronger were soon lost to the rebels, while at first the main centers of anarchist power were rather less affected. In Catalonia the anarchists quickly armed 40,000 militiamen and enjoyed de facto power. There, however, the four very small pro-Comintern Marxist parties ignored the wishes of Codovilla and the PCE leaders in Madrid and on July 25 officially created the new Partit Socialist Unificat de Catalunya (PSUC; United Socialist Party of Catalonia). Though it would never be as fully subservient as the PCE, it became in effect the new Soviet Communist party of Catalonia, but in the first few weeks its power was less than the anarchists'.

On July 22 the president of the Catalan Generalitat, Lluis Companys, embarked on an explicit system of revolutionary dualism, recognizing alongside his own regional government a new Comité Central de Milicias Antifascistas and even deferring to it. The Comité, which held power to wage the military struggle and also to control much of the internal affairs of Catalonia, represented above all the CNT and the FAI, but also Esquerra Catalana and the smaller revolutionary parties. A revolutionary rivalry and antagonism soon developed between the FAI-CNT and the pro-Soviet PSUC, the former vetoing participation of the latter in the first new Catalan government formed at the beginning of August exclusively by left Catalanists. CNT leaders declared that their organization was perfectly capable of taking over the full government of Catalonia, but that they accepted the continuation of a limited Generalitat administration with circumscribed powers because of the military crisis and also in order not to frighten foreign powers. The CNT's main ally was the POUM, from the beginning even more committed to revolution à l'outrance than the anarchists. In turn the Butlletí de la Generalitat announced that real power lay in the hands of the Comité de Milicias, which had established a revolutionary new order that all the leftist parties had to respect. As in nearly all violent revolutions, the new order was thoroughly authoritarian, little regulated by law, tempered only by the limited interaction of the various leftist parties. Horacio Prieto, secretary of the CNT's national committee, was later explicit: "We went straight to dictatorship; even the Bolsheviks themselves, in their first historical opportunity, were not so quick to implant absolute power as the anarchists in Spain."[5]

The political and military revolution was accompanied by a social and economic revolution in most of the Republican zone, the only major exception being part of the Basque Country. The caballerista Claridad declared on August 1: "We are, as a result of the military revolt, involved in a profound revolutionary process. . . . Every instrument of state, and especially the army, must also be revolutionary." On the 22nd it added that "the people are no longer fighting for the Spain of the 16th of July, which was still a Spain socially dominated by the traditional classes, but for a Spain from which these classes have been definitely eliminated. The most powerful support for the war is the economic and total uprooting of fascism, and that is revolution." Claridad called it a "social war more than a civil war." Yet, with the exception of the POUM, even most of the revolutionaries agreed that it was still useful to maintain the shell of a Republican government, even if only for propaganda and foreign policy. This did not keep certain leaders of the two massive syndical organizations from mutual conversation about an all-syndical revolutionary government, and by the end of August rumors flew around Madrid that a UGT-CNT "National Revolutionary Junta" might soon replace what was left of the Republican government.

In industry and agriculture, the revolution took the form first of worker control and then of collectivization. In a report to the central committee of the French Communist Party on October 16, André Marty reported that in the Republican zone some 18,000 enterprises had been "taken in hand. . . . The great bulk of Spanish industry is now controlled by the workers."[6] At first no formal collectivization or nationalization was announced; the syndicates simply took control. Only in Catalonia, where Companys and the Generalitat sought to channel the revolution and begin to restore legality, was a legal structure of industrial collectivization developed. In August the Catalan government created a Consell d'Economia de Catalunya with representation of all the leftist parties, which soon produced its own "Pla de Transformació Socialista del País," though this plan was never directly implemented. The CNT entered the Catalan government in September, and on October 24 the new CNT councilor of economics, Juan Fábregas, issued a collectivization decree. It formalized collectivization of all industrial plants employing more than 100 workers and provided for the collectivization of units that employed between 50 and 100 workers, provided that 75 percent of the workers in a given enterprise approved. Units employing fewer than 50 workers would be collectivized only with the owners' consent, though otherwise de facto worker control would usually reign.[7] In addition, in Catalonia smaller firms and shops formed a sizeable number of *agrupaciones* (associations) or *concentraciones* that served as an intermediate form of collective. Neither the Socialist nor the Communist party approved the expropriation of smaller properties, though the extent of such expropriation varied greatly from district to district. The mining and industrial firms of Asturias were not formally collectivized but brought under complete control of the syndicates.

Both the Republican and Catalan governments recognized the need for state supervision of key military and related industries, though achieving it would prove a long and arduous task. The Generalitat established a War Industries Commission, though at first with little control. Eventually, by October 1937 the Commission would be supervising fifty arms factories employing 50,000 workers, plus 30,000 more in auxiliary production—though this was probably too little and too late.

The grand design of the CNT to achieve "libertarian communism" was "socialization" (as distinct from, for example, Soviet state nationalization) under the syndicates of entire national branches of production.[8] The idea was that socialization would provide syndical representation and autonomy while avoiding state domination. This concept did not conform to Socialist notions, and hence in urban industry the UGT frequently would not collaborate. Socialization in fact never went beyond a single entire industry in any given city.

CNT leaders were aware of the need to modernize and boost production. When possible, a certain amount of new equipment was purchased, but under the CNT there was no centralization or overall plan. Factories often continued to produce consumer goods, which were more profitable, and CNT-run or collectivized enterprises would later be charged with "syndical capitalism" and "syndical egotism" in Barcelona. Financial support services were never developed, and on the shop level there was eventually a lessening of worker discipline, increased absenteeism, and occasionally even sabotage.[9]

The creation of collectives was most widespread in agriculture. Though in many provinces smallholdings were respected, this was not always the case, as anarchosyndicalist and Socialist farmworker syndicates occupied all the larger and most of the medium properties. Edward Malefakis, author of the principal study on the prewar agrarian reform, has concluded that in the fourteen provinces that made up the core of the Republican zone, 41 percent of all the land was expropriated. This amounted to well over half of all the arable land. Of the amount expropriated, approximately 54 percent was organized into collectives, the remainder being reassigned for individual farming. As Malefakis has pointed out, proportionately more than twice as much land was expropriated in Republican Spain as in the Russian Revolution, and very much more was reorganized into new collectives.[10]

Collectives normally had one of three political colorings, as either CNT, UGT, or mixed CNT-UGT collectives, with the POUM participating in a few areas. The size and functioning of the collectives varied considerably. Purely CNT collectives tended to be the most radical, with total social inclusion, family salaries, and more than a few attempts to ban the use of money. Some UGT collectives were much more moderate, functioning more as cooperatives for private property owners. Blessed by favorable weather conditions, agricultural production increased slightly in some parts of the Republican zone, only to fall disastrously, together with that of industry, in 1938.[11]

It will never be possible to say exactly how many agrarian collectives were formed. During the latter part of the Civil War, after many anarchist collectives had been broken up, the Republic's Instituto de Reforma Agraria (IRA; Institute of Agrarian Reform), directed by the Communist Vincente Uribe, announced that it had officially recognized 2,213 collectives. This figure, however, did not include Catalonia, Aragon, or the Levant. Of the total, 823 had been formed by the UGT, 284 by the CNT, and 1,106 by both. The CNT claimed that altogether they alone had formed more than 3,000 collectives, the bulk of which had never been recognized by the IRA. The CNT's figure is almost undoubtedly an exaggeration, and may have been arrived at by counting each semi-autonomous collective subsection as a collective in itself. One of the few comprehensive studies suggests that even the IRA indulged in this practice, so that the total number of individual collectives formed may not in fact have been greatly in excess of 1,500.[12]

To leaders and spokesmen of the revolutionary left, the uprising of workers in the Republican zone constituted a proletarian revolution more profound, authentic, and spontaneous than that of Russia in 1917. The initial Russian revolution of 1917, in February (according to the Gregorian calendar), was a popular protest uprising by the people of St. Petersburg and other cities against the existing government. A worker revolution per se did not arise at first, though the situation steadily developed in that direction during the spring and summer. The Bolshevik October Revolution (November, in the Western calendar) was simply a violent coup d'état by one organized party. Thus Andreu Nin would declare that what was happening in Spain was "a more profound proletarian revolution than the Russian revolution itself," declaring with typical POUMist hyperbole on August 1 that "the government does not exist." On September 7 he announced that the dictatorship of the proletariat already existed in Catalonia, while the POUM's JCI called for the formation of revolutionary soviets throughout the Republican zone. Despite the hyperbole of the extreme revolutionary left, there is little doubt that there was much more immediate, direct, spontaneous, and also organized revolutionary activity by workers in the more advanced and self-conscious Spanish society of 1936 than in the Russia of 1917, and in the countryside the difference was much greater yet. Not only was proportionately more land seized in Spain than in Russia, but the rural population was more revolutionary by far. In Russia the great bulk of the rural population did not participate in new revolutionary collectivizations but merely seized landowners' property and added it to the traditional peasant village communes.

George Orwell made the atmosphere of revolutionary Barcelona famous through his wartime memoir, but similar conditions existed in many other cities. The former Radical deputy Clara Campoamor wrote: "The appearance of Madrid was incredible: the bourgeoisie giving the clenched-fist salute. . . . Men in overalls and rope sandals, imitating the uniform adopted by the militia; women bareheaded; clothes, old and threadbare; an absolute invasion of ugliness and squalor, more apparent than real, of people who humbly begged permission to remain alive."[13]

The first business of the worker revolution was the Red Terror—organized mass executions in most parts of the Republican zone; again, the main, if only partial, exception was the Basque province of Vizcaya. In Russia there were many random murders, particularly of military and naval officers, from the very beginning of the February Revolution, but not organized mass killings, as in Spain. Even after the Bolshevik dictatorship was imposed, Lenin did not at first enact general terror; he officially adopted the policy of Red Terror only in the summer of 1918. In Spain, almost as if by prearrangement, mass executions also began in the opposing zone. The immediate outbreak of political mass murder on both sides stemmed from years of extreme tension, previous attempts at violent revolutionary insurrection, the most virulent forms of mass propaganda, and extreme dehumanizing and demonizing of the enemy by both left and right. The PCE had contributed proportionately as much or more to the terror than had any other revolutionary organization, and it played an active role in the killings in Madrid and several other provinces.

Massive executions have characterized most of the revolutionary/counter-revolutionary civil wars of the twentieth century, from Russia and Finland in the early years to Afghanistan in the final years of the century. The blood lust derives in considerable measure from the apocalyptic nature of such conflicts and the attempt to create a new society purged of antagonistic elements, combined with the widespread perception that the enemy is not merely wrong but the metaphysical incarnation of evil and must be eradicated before he imposes the same terror against one's own side. A revolutionary civil war is not just a political conflict but a contest of ultimates demanding an uncompromising solution.

During the war, both sides widely publicized (and indeed greatly exaggerated) the atrocities of their enemies, publicizing the most inflated statistics, normally involving claims of a total of up to half a million killings by each side, in each case an exaggeration of somewhere between 800 and 1,200 percent. Subsequent demographic studies would indicate a total of approximately 100,000 executions by both sides combined—less than one-half of 1 percent of the total population of the country, but nonetheless a high figure. It is probably somewhat greater than the equivalent figure for Russia, though somewhat exceeded by the statistics for Finland, where a three-month civil war produced more than 20,000 victims of the repression by both sides combined, a figure amounting to slightly more than two-thirds of 1 percent of the population.[14]

Publicity and media coverage had expanded greatly between 1917 and 1936. During the first months especially the eyes of most foreign correspondents, news services, and cameramen were fixed on Spain, and particularly on the large cities in the Republican zone, which inevitably drew the most attention. Thus during the first part of the war the Republican zone generated the greater share of the atrocity stories eagerly distributed throughout the Western world. "What the nonsympathizing external world saw in Red Spain was above all Bolshevik terror and chaos: badly dressed masses armed with rifles filling the streets; the *paseos* in which they executed enemies; the undisciplined mob of anarchists; the mummies of nuns dragged out of their tombs and placed on display in the streets; violent expropriations; forced collectivizations."[15]

The Comintern had been more concerned than most of the worker parties to avoid a major military revolt and the danger of civil war. For most of its history, the Comintern had demonstrated ignorance and misjudgment concerning Spain, but by the early summer of 1936 the broadening of Soviet policy in Western Europe had lifted it somewhat above the myopic tunnel vision common to the rest of the revolutionary left in Spain. From the Comintern's viewpoint, the country's present situation of an increasingly powerful if fragmented left, a weak right, and a decomposing polity neared the optimum. Any overtly revolutionary measures would probably be counterproductive. Victory in the elections had given the left complete control of national institutions— with the partial exception of the armed forces—and this domination of a legitimate constitutional polity should be the vehicle for advancing the program of the left. Parliamentary legislation could advance agrarian reform and all other social programs, and could further be used to give a veneer of democratic legitimacy to the basic goal of outlawing the right and converting the Republic into an all-leftist regime—a people's republic, in the Soviet language employed since 1924. This basic policy position had been repeated over and over, not merely in Comintern instructions but also in the public proposals of the PCE.

When the rebellion began, the Comintern was still seeking to expand the Workers' Alliance groups, hoping to integrate them with the Popular Front, with the very small but growing MAOC serving as a paramilitary shield. There was of course not the slightest pretension that the Spanish Popular Front would function like the French Popular Front. Unlike France, Spain was undergoing decomposition, and Republican legality could be used as cover for establishing total leftist domination. One worry for Moscow was the danger of another abortive CNT insurrection, which could be enormously counterproductive. Though in fact there was for the moment no such danger, Moscow could not be sure of that and urged PCE leaders to try to work with the CNT to bring it within the Popular Front, where presumably it would be easier to influence and control. By the same token, new legislation and government policy should do everything possible to expand and strengthen the UGT and establish its dominance.

The relative ease of the suppression of the initial revolt in Madrid and the left's dominance in all but one of the major cities induced a mood of euphoria in Codovilla and the PCE leaders during the first days of the Civil War. As early as July 20 Codovilla reported to Moscow that not only had the revolt been crushed in Madrid but everything was being brought under control in a radically new situation that was offering "enormously" increased opportunities to the PCE.[16] On the same day *Mundo obrero* declared inaccurately that "the traitors have been defeated throughout Spain," and one day later that "the revolt can be considered crushed." Codovilla repeated these judgments on each of the two following days.[17] On July 23 he and Díaz reported that since "the army is virtually dissolved" and worker militias were being formed all over, the party would push to replace the army with the militias, though they asked for confirmation of the correctness of such a policy. The only problem was burning and pillaging by anarchists. In a second message on the 23rd they even opined that since the present situation "transports even the most timid to justify any kind of revolutionary measure," the new policies would soon require the Communists to enter the Republican government, "in the conditions of a huge development of the bourgeois democratic revolution," and asked for advice on such a move.[18]

Orders from Moscow, first dispatched on July 20, were much more cautious, stipulating that the only slogan must be defense of the democratic republic and that top priority must be given the military struggle. Popular Front defense committees should be set up all over, but the worker parties should not enter the government unless the Giral administration proved ineffective and a major crisis developed. Moreover, the Moscow bosses had access to both the foreign intelligence gathered by the NKVD (secret police) and the West European press and quickly realized that the situation was much more complicated than Codovilla and the Spanish leaders seemed to realize. On July 23 a discussion took place in the ECCI Secretariat. Dimitrov recognized that in this situation "the Spanish comrades have a lot of temptations," and even speculated, contrary to the standard line, that with the army virtually "smashed," it might have been possible for the revolutionaries to seize control of Madrid, "overthrow the Azaña government," and create "a real republican democratic government," meaning a complete new-style people's republic; but as it was, the situation was too complicated. A revolutionary militia would be inadequate, so that "it is necessary now to create a people's republican army"—so far as is known, the first serious recommendation of such a policy. Under these circumstances, there would be no question of "creating soviets" or "trying to establish a dictatorship of the proletariat," which would be "a fatal mistake." Once the conflict had been won, Communist policy could go forward. In Spain as in "France, Belgium, and so on . . . , when our positions have been strengthened, then we can go further." At the present time the only slogan must be defense of the democratic Republic on the basis of a broad Popular Front that would also attract the lower middle class.[19]

That same day Dimitrov informed Codovilla and Díaz that their information was "insufficient, not concrete enough, and sentimental."[20] The Comintern adviser was warned to send more serious and precise information, to stop exaggerating and expressing inflated optimism, and to cease speculating about grand political designs. There would no question of entering the Republican government unless it became absolutely necessary for winning the war. Above all, they must form a new regular people's army supported by, but in no way replaced by, a worker militia. The Communists should try to attract loyal officers to their own ranks and seek ways of winning over the rebel officers. Then, on the 31st, the Moscow bosses added that the Spanish party must make it clear not only that it was fighting for the democratic Republic, but that any current property confiscations "are not directed against private property but against those taking part in the rebellion." Foreign property must be respected and persecution of Catholicism should not be carried too far, especially in view of the extreme anticlerical atrocities of the anarchists. The Spanish leaders were urged to try to get all the Popular Front parties to make similar announcements endorsing these points.[21]

Thus on July 22 *Mundo obrero* headlined "Discipline, Hierarchy, and Organization," and one day later adopted the slogan "the Republic of the people," but that was quickly deemed too radical and the slogan "the democratic Republic" was soon restored. Increasingly Communist propaganda made a broader cross-class patriotic appeal to support the war effort. On July 29 La Pasionaria read over the radio a public announcement by the party's central committee refuting charges being made abroad and in the opposing zone that the Republic was falling into the hands of the Communists. "We, the Communists, defend a regime of liberty and democracy." All of Spain was being made the national victim of international fascism, she said, and she compared the rebel leaders to "Don Opas and Count Julián," who allegedly had invited the Muslim invaders into Spain in 711, necessitating the Reconquest. This was the beginning of the party's new national patriotic line, which it would never relinquish. Ibárruri declared that Spanish fascists had mobilized "the most ferocious Kabyles of the Riff" with promises of "booty"—"rape, murder, robbery, everything is permitted them." She inveighed against national "traitors" to Spain, and assured the world that the Republicans would have no trouble winning so long as foreign intervention did not become too severe.[22] On August 11 the central committee issued a major announcement that repeated the reference to eighth-century traitors and declared that because of the "imperialist powers," "the independence of Spain is in danger."[23] On August 18 *Mundo obrero* declared that the "struggle between democracy and fascism" had "become transformed into a holy, into a national war, into a defensive war of the people." This became the standard line for the remainder of the conflict.

Each side fully believed its own propaganda in this regard. Fears of some sort of foreign control or takeover could become the more real not simply because of the inherent paranoia of full-scale civil war but also because of the legacy of Spain's weak and disappointing international history during the late nineteenth and early twentieth centuries. Spain not only had been despoiled of the remnants of its great historic empire but had found itself virtually ignored and nearly isolated in the power politics of Europe before World War I, as France and Germany, each in its own way, had endeavored—in the case of France, with some success—to dominate interests that still lay within Spain's radius of action.

In the confusion of those first days, however, it was impossible to keep all the pieces together even within the Communist camp itself. By July 30 Codovilla and Díaz had to report that their "instructions" to Communist leaders in Barcelona had been ignored and the new PSUC had been created, though "we consider this action to have been a serious mistake." From the viewpoint of Communist leaders in Madrid, it was an undesirable complication, but the move had been completed and now they must make the most of it.[24] In fact, this would turn out to be a useful new organization for Communist policy in Spain.

The situation had become paradoxical in the extreme. For fifteen years the Comintern had desperately sought to provoke or exploit revolutionary situations. It had involved itself in multiple violent initiatives in Germany, an insurrection in Estonia, and even an attempt to blow up the entire Bulgarian government. After 1928, with the declaration of the Third Period, Comintern leaders were certain that the hour would soon be at hand. This policy had backfired disastrously in Germany, and the increasingly dangerous international situation had encouraged the abrupt change to collective security and the Popular Front. So long as the Comintern had promoted standard Third Period revolutionary tactics, the PCE had done little better than stagnate. The switch to the Popular Front had coincided with the total polarization of Spanish society. The revolutionary process in Spain developed from 1934 on pari passu with the moderation of short-term Communist tactics. By the spring of 1936, the bulk of the worker left in Spain was tactically positioned to the left of the PCE.

Nonetheless, over a decade and a half the Comintern had worked out relatively flexible tactics and strategy that were calculated to maximize the revolutionary possibilities in a given country over the long term. Yet in China, where the indirect approach had been given its best shot, it had ended in disaster in 1927 when Chiang Kai-shek had turned out to be Kornilov rather than Kerensky. The totally fragmented left in Spain provided a more propitious environment, and in retrospect there seems little doubt that the policy conceived by the Comintern for the PCE by the spring of 1936 was the most astute policy being followed by any revolutionary party in Spain. Only the Communists had a concrete policy designed to minimize radicalization in the short term, thereby keeping the present situation under control, while maximizing a clear potential revolutionary policy in the long term. Nearly all other leftist parties in Spain lacked a specific strategy, reeling from one circumstance to the next. The only exception was the totally doctrinaire POUM, which always had a strategy that was almost always ineffective.

The Comintern had made an effort to keep the situation in Spain from blowing up during the spring and early summer of 1936, realizing that such an eruption would probably be counterproductive. Yet even the Communists contributed, particularly through their hyperactive propaganda and agitation and partly through their specific policies, to the radicalization of the Spanish situation. Even the Comintern could not restrain itself from seeking an active advance of leftist power, simply because the situation seemed so favorable. Communist moves to advance leftist social policies and eliminate the right were calculated in terms of legality and parliamentary action, but their main effect was simply to help consummate the polarization, and thus were in a sense too clever even for the good of the left. The Comintern operated on the basis of a clear strategy of stages, from the Popular Front to the people's republic to the worker-peasant government, but it lacked power to control the left as a whole or, for that matter, to force conservative forces to sit still while the left carried out its program.

While most of the revolutionary left hailed the beginning of the Civil War, from the Comintern's viewpoint it was an undesirable complication. Though the PCE leaders quickly concluded that the outbreak of the revolution might bring them great new opportunities, for the Comintern the revolution quickly became a major problem. A revolution of infantile leftism out of control ran the risk of destroying itself, making it impossible to concentrate on waging the military struggle and stimulating countervailing foreign intervention, while alienating democratic opinion in France and Britain. The Popular Front enjoyed the great advantage of controlling whatever was left of Republican institutions, a system of legitimate and democratic origins. Rather than waste this advantage in a revolutionary orgy, Soviet policy urged all the leftist forces to wrap themselves in the banner of legality and democracy, maximizing social support at home and abroad. The revolution should not be overturned, but it needed the firmest channeling, which would be a tall order. A channeled revolution and a powerful new people's army would constitute the platform for further evolution of the Popular Front program, laying the basis for a new people's republic even while the war was being waged. This strategy would require a bilevel policy once more: international propaganda and diplomacy would emphasize democracy, while within the Republican zone the revolution needed to be channeled on behalf of the war effort and the "democratic republic of a new type."

By August 1936 the immediate problem was whether or not there would be an adequate opportunity to pursue such a bilevel policy. On the one hand, the Republican zone had become the scene of the most intense and spontaneous proletarian revolution in history, which might be too intense and too fragmented to channel. On the other, after the first days, the leftist militia had proved a spectacular military failure. The revolution and all the left thus might meet rapid military defeat, which would cancel all political calculations, whether Soviet or hyperrevolutionary.

CHAPTER SEVEN

The Soviet Decision to Intervene Militarily

July–October 1936

THE USSR WAS the only power that had been intervening systematically in Spanish affairs before the beginning of the Civil War, operating its own political party within the country and at long last achieving some success. By comparison, Nazi Germany limited itself to small-scale propaganda funding, and Fascist Italy, while engaging in more extensive cultural and propaganda activity, otherwise did no more than pay a small subsidy to the Falangist party from May 1935 to January 1936.[1] Rome and Berlin were both taken by surprise at the outbreak of the conflict; the surprise was slightly less in Moscow, where Comintern bosses had labored for months to discipline their own party in particular and the Spanish left in general en route to the building of a people's republic.[2] Agents of General Francisco Franco, commander of the rebel army of the south, contacted both Hitler and Mussolini on July 25–26, and both quickly decided independently to send a small number of airplanes and other weapons and ammunition to the insurgents. Two of the initial squadron of twelve Savoia-Marchetti medium bombers had to crash-land in French Algeria on the 30th, providing the first news abroad of such assistance, at least on the part of Italy.

The beginning of the war was initially of greater concern in Moscow than in Berlin or Rome, for Moscow had a good deal of political capital invested in Spain, not merely in the PCE but as one of the two bastions of the Popular Front; furthermore, a much more radicalized situation offered the USSR a greater long-term opportunity in Spain than in France. Despite occasional references in memoirs, there is no reliable evidence of any immediate Soviet reaction that involved military assistance.[3] Since there were still no formal diplomatic relations between Moscow and Madrid, Spanish affairs were nominally in the hands of the Comintern.

The new Giral government in Madrid, its powers rapidly dwindling, began to seek arms abroad on July 20, its first full day of existence. The Franco-Spanish commercial treaty of 1935 contained a provision for regular Spanish arms purchases, France having become the principal foreign supplier. Blum's Popular Front government in Paris quickly responded in the affirmative and began to ready planes and other arms for shipment. Much of the cabinet was opposed, however, and few French arms were dispatched. It had already been planned for Blum to be in London on July 23–24 for talks with France's chief ally, where he apparently received a sharp warning. Britain's Conservative leaders had no desire to see themselves or the French involved in Spain or to bolster a revolutionary regime in Madrid. Moreover, when Blum got back to Paris on the night of the 24th, he was met by leaders of the Radical Party, the conservative wing of the French Popular Front, who declared themselves shocked and dismayed by the decision to send arms. In the cabinet meeting the following day, even a majority of the Socialist ministers advised caution. French Socialists were well aware of how much the Spanish Popular Front differed from their own and were not eager at that point to be involved in the Spanish revolution, which differed so radically from the style and tactics of French Socialism.[4] It was therefore agreed to adopt a policy of non-intervention, though it was not announced until July 31. (Mussolini apparently learned of it before the announcement, however, and proceeded to send the first Italian arms.) Only a portion of the initial French arms shipment was allowed to proceed to Spain. Final reconfirmation of the decision not to intervene and to seek an international non-intervention agreement was made in Paris on August 8. The French Socialists had little choice, for overt intervention would have broken the French Popular Front, brought the right center to power in Paris, and possibly wrecked the British alliance on which France was depending.[5]

Meanwhile the Giral government, though unable to enforce most of its decisions in the Republican zone, generated a series of initiatives to purchase arms abroad. With the sizable Spanish gold reserve, fourth largest in the world, money would not be lacking. Over several months multiple initiatives, official and unofficial, both by the government and by individual parties and regional governments, would be launched, primarily in France, but also in Britain and other countries.[6]

In connection with these efforts, Giral turned to the Soviet Union. Diplomatic relations still had not been established, in itself a measure of the extent to which the left Republican government had ignored international relations.[7] On March 3, little more than a fortnight after the elections, *El Socialista* had announced that formal diplomatic relations with the Soviet Union were a priority. Los Amigos de la Unión Soviética had enjoyed their most active year in 1936, with committees in no fewer than forty-five Spanish cities and Azaña himself on their national committee. On April 23, the eve of Azaña's elevation to the Republican presidency, *Pravda* had published an interview conducted by the noted Soviet journalist Ilya Ehrenburg, in which Azaña also declared establishment of relations with the Soviet Union to be a priority. Azaña claimed that he had wanted to visit the Soviet Union during the summer of 1935 and that Stalin's regime constituted a "guarantee for peace," demonstrating that his perceptions were no keener in foreign than in domestic affairs. Yet nothing had been done, so on July 25 Giral had to direct his letter to the Soviet ambassador in Paris as the nearest Soviet envoy, asking the Soviet government for "a great quantity of weapons and all categories of military supplies."[8]

Foreign diplomats reported that Moscow's initial response to outbreak of civil war in Spain was uncertainty. The conflict was a negative development from the Soviet viewpoint, since otherwise things had been moving along so well in Spain, and civil war could complicate all of Moscow's West European policy. The Soviet Union was already committed to developing a program of collective security, particularly with regard to France and Czechoslovakia, but also potentially on a broader front. It was directed against the expansion of Nazi Germany, yet in a different dimension Soviet policy also labored to achieve rapprochement with Germany, always potentially desirable from Stalin's point of view.[9] There had been no response from Berlin, and after July 30 it became clear that Italy was providing military supplies to the Spanish insurgents.

Soviet press commentary on the conflict in Spain was somewhat guarded during the first two weeks. The Nazi press soon began to charge the Soviet Union with being the real instigator of the conflict, and Soviet newspapers first reported German and Italian aid to the rebels on July 26, even before there was any proof. The first *Pravda* editorial on the Spanish war, on August 1, was headed "Fascism means war; socialism means peace." Several other editorials then appeared in *Pravda* and *Izvestia,* then no further editorial on the subject in *Pravda* until September 22. From approximately the first of August, however, the Soviet press published daily reports accusing international fascism, meaning Germany and Italy, of fomenting and sustaining the war. One study has found that from 10 to 15 percent of all the news space in *Izvestia* was devoted to Spain from the beginning of the war in July 1936 until mid-October 1937, when the coverage finally began to decline.[10]

Meanwhile the Soviet leadership had to evaluate the situation in much more precise terms than the euphoria of initial reports from Madrid, to determine whether the leftist forces in Spain were sufficiently committed and organized to have a serious chance for victory and whether they were genuinely in great need of outside assistance. As the former NKVD agent Walter Krivitsky wrote in 1939, Stalin "made haste slowly, as he always does. There was a period of watchful waiting, of furtive exploration. Stalin wanted to be sure first that there would be no quick and easy Franco victory."[11] A second consideration was whether or not the outbreak of the revolution had carried the situation too far to be really useful to Soviet policy. Other concerns would be the form that assistance, military or otherwise, might take and how to overcome the technical and logistical problems involved, in a period in which the Soviet navy was weak. (According to the research of Milan Hauner, not yet published, Stalin proposed to remedy this situation with his plan to build a *bolshoi flot* [great fleet]—an ambition rather similar to Hitler's later "Z-Plan"—which he had initially begun to develop in December 1935.) A final consideration was simply whether it was too bold and risky for the Soviet Union to be significantly involved both politically and militarily at the opposite end of Europe at a time of mounting international tension.

It is clear that during August and September Stalin and the top Soviet leaders underwent a process of reaction, calculation, and planning that ultimately produced a scheme for significant military intervention in the Spanish Civil War. This decision was reached incrementally, beginning with a public economic assistance campaign inside the Soviet Union on August 3 and culminating in the Politburo's official approval of a detailed plan for military intervention on September 29.

Ever since that time there has been much speculation about the character and extent of the Soviet intervention and its fundamental goals and motivations. Soviet intervention was carried out with greater secrecy than Italian and German intervention, and no news of it was published officially inside the Soviet Union until well after the end of World War II. The extreme complexity of Soviet policy produced much misunderstanding at the time and has continued to bedevil historians ever since. Soviet historiography and participant memoirs, which began in the 1950s and continued at a varying but impressive rate for many years, have assigned the Soviet regime nothing but the highest motives for the intervention in Spain: defense of the Spanish people and resistance to fascist aggression. Conversely, the extensive historiography of Franco's Spain attributed only the most sinister intentions to Soviet policy, whose fundamental aim was allegedly to establish a tyrannical Soviet-controlled Communist regime.[12] Western scholarly analysis has generally fallen between these two extremes, but no consensus has been reached.

The standard position of both Western and Soviet scholars has been that Soviet intervention was intended to implement the announced Soviet strategy of collective security, the official policy of the Soviet Union from the winter of 1935 to the winter of 1939. Thus, in a lengthy history of the Soviet Union that was translated into Russian and published in Moscow, the Italian historian Giuseppe Boffa has written that "the Spanish question was for Soviet diplomacy the soil which Moscow could exploit for imposing on Britain and France strict obligations concerning opposition to Fascism and consequently getting from them solid security guarantees."[13] Some variant of this interpretation has frequently been found in the literature.[14]

Yet the question has been raised as to whether major intervention in Spain was truly calculated to achieve such ends. That is, did an effort to achieve victory for the Spanish revolution really seem likely to encourage the bourgeois democratic governments of France and Britain to line up on the same side? Some analysts have raised serious doubts.[15] There is no doubt that Stalin would have been delighted if Britain and France were to intervene on the side of the Republic, but by the end of September he clearly was willing to take such a stand himself, however devious the implementation of this policy became. There is evidence that Maksim Litvinov, the chief spokesman for the collective security policy, opposed the intervention, and Jonathan Haslam has observed that the Spanish war "in fact complicated rather than facilitated [Litvinov's] larger aim of building a collective security interest in Europe."[16] As will be seen, Soviet diplomacy was willing to challenge British and French non-intervention policy, even at the cost of political confrontation with the Western powers. Soviet policy showed undeniable determination to take a stand against fascism.

It is generally held that by the mid-1930s Stalin had largely lost interest in the Comintern and turned his back on the idea of igniting international revolution. This judgment is doubtless correct up to a point, but it overlooks the extent to which revolutionary policy remained part of the fundamental Soviet revolutionary-imperial paradigm, as the precise terms of Popular Front policy made clear. Communist parties abroad and Soviet citizens and officials alike naturally expected the Soviet Union to provide support to the only country where a workers' revolution was in progress. As Krivitsky observed, the initial appearance of Soviet inaction was "giving rise to embarrassing questions in even the friendliest quarters."[17] Stalin was just beginning his great purge of the Soviet elite and of Soviet society generally, but for that very reason could not yet entirely ignore Soviet domestic attitudes.[18] Thus Kevin McDermott and Jeremy Agnew observe that "the Soviet Union's tardy response to the outbreak of the Spanish Civil War served to strengthen dissident voices," while Michael Alpert has claimed that the concern to assist the Spanish left momentarily "crystallized the internal Russian opposition to Stalin's international policy."[19] Jonathan Haslam notes that Litvinov "found himself in a direct line of fire from revolutionary internationalists in the Comintern and outside," while Gerald Howson concludes that the Soviet Union had to act "as the leader of the world movement and it was probably this consideration which outweighed the rest."[20] Indeed, as "a responsible Soviet official" told Loy Henderson, the American chargé in Moscow, on August 3, the "Soviet leaders" believed "that if the Soviet Union is to continue to maintain hegemony over the international revolutionary movement it must not hesitate in periods of crisis to assume the leadership of that movement," though Henderson added that he had been assured this would not go beyond "financial assistance."[21] The Soviet domestic press did not hide the revolutionary character of the struggle in Spain, nor did Stalin in at least one of his public pronouncements, which avowed that Soviet assistance could not be denied "to the revolutionary masses of Spain."[22]

Conversely, numerous historians conclude that Stalin's principal motivation was simply Soviet geostrategic self-interest, whether or not a collective security agreement could be achieved.[23] Nothing was in fact more important to Stalin than what he conceived to be geostrategic self-interest, but these diverse motives are not by any means mutually exclusive. In varying ways and to varying degrees they all obtained, and Soviet policy made an effort to combine them all. The Popular Front tactic had provided a means of managing revolution politically and screening it with political semipluralism and democratic forms, while collective security and geostrategic self-interest presumably went hand in hand. Support for the Spanish Republic would take a stand against fascism, while public denial and extreme secrecy might avoid alienating Britain and France. Ideology remained important, but Soviet policy sought to combine it with pragmatic politics. If communism became increasingly influential within the Republic, that was all to the good.[24]

The policy of intervention took at least two and half months to work out, however, and developed only incrementally. During the first weeks the only tangible support provided was the massive campaign for humanitarian aid for the Republic that began officially on August 3, when *Pravda* announced that workers in a number of Moscow factories had agreed to donate 0.5 percent of their monthly salaries and a whole series of mass rallies on behalf of the Republican cause were organized in the largest Soviet cities. On August 4 both *Pravda* and the Foreign Ministry's *Journal de Moscou* came out in favor of humanitarian assistance, while Karl Radek declared in *Pravda* that "the German and Italian Fascists are preparing to intervene against the Spanish revolution in order to place in their hands the important trump-cards for the preparation of a world war and the new territorial distribution of the world."[25] A day later it was announced that contributions already exceeded 12 million rubles. Another campaign began on September 12 and went on for most of the autumn, the total reaching 47 million rubles by October 27. A third campaign would be organized by the beginning of 1937 and a fourth in mid-1937. During the Great Terror, periodic campaigns on behalf of the Spanish Republic became a regular feature of Soviet life. Some citizens seem to have participated in them with genuine enthusiasm. Amid one of the grimmest periods of Soviet history, the regime found that they provided a new, more positive form of mass mobilization that identified popular sympathies with an attractive cause.

Antifascism was a dominant theme, but mobilization on behalf of the worker revolution in Spain also played a major role, as *Pravda* announced in September that Spanish workers had taken over 18,000 industrial enterprises. This news made it possible psychologically to break out of a sense of Soviet isolation and identify with the advance of the revolutionary cause abroad. Soviet totals for the Spanish relief campaign altogether came to 115 million rubles for 1936, 102 million for 1937, 45 million for 1938, and 9 million for 1939—a total of 271 million rubles, or approximately £1,416,000 sterling, which took the form of large amounts of Soviet foodstuffs and other civilian goods shipped to Republican Spain. Since there is no means of verifying these figures, what they really amounted to is anyone's guess, yet there seems no doubt that there was substantial Soviet humanitarian relief during the course of the war.[26] Support from the Comintern relief campaigns mounted in other countries as well. The first Soviet ships carrying civilian goods departed in September and enjoyed an enthusiastic reception on the Spanish coast. Even members of the CNT turned out en masse on October 13 to greet the *Zirianin*, the first Soviet relief vessel to arrive in Barcelona.[27]

Meanwhile, as negotiations proceeded for the establishment of formal diplomatic relations between Moscow and Madrid, they coincided chronologically with the development of negotiations by the representatives of Britain and

France for the adherence of European states to their proposed non-intervention agreement on the Spanish war. At this point Stalin was hoping for effective implementation of the recently ratified Franco-Soviet defense pact, and thus when his erstwhile French ally proposed through its Moscow embassy on August 5 that the Soviet regime join in a five-power non-intervention agreement that in this version would include Italy and Germany as well, he had little alternative but to reply positively. The Soviet regime had invested enormous propaganda resources in peace campaigns ever since 1917—this was part of its basic stock in trade—and at that point no doubt hoped that the agreement might restrain German and Italian intervention. Since it was clear, however, that the Portuguese government was doing all it could to help the insurgent Spanish Nationalists and was also becoming a conduit for German supplies, the Soviet government at first announced that it would adhere to the agreement only if Portugal did so. Since Lisbon did not refuse and Berlin joined the agreement on the 17th and Rome on the 22nd, Moscow had little alternative but to do the same on August 23, and five days later announced an official ban on weaponry in Soviet shipping bound for Spain. The international Non-Intervention Committee then began its formal meetings in London in mid-September.[28] Throughout these weeks, nonetheless, the Soviet press continued to insist that the Republic's struggle against "fascism" was absolutely in the interest of the entire international community, and especially of the democratic countries.

Since July 21 the Comintern had been whipping up support for the Republic in more than a dozen countries. Existing front organizations swung into action and new ones sprang up. The World Committee against War and Fascism was founded on the first day of the campaign, followed on July 23 by International Worker Aid. The most active parties were those in France, Britain, Poland, and the United States. The World Committee against War and Fascism convened a general European conference in Paris on August 13 to generate support, and on the last day of that month International Red Relief spun off a new International Committee to Aid the Spanish People, also centered in Paris. Later no fewer than fifteen front organizations supporting the Popular Front and the Republic would be identified as operating within the United States.[29] Communist newspapers in several countries had gotten off on the wrong foot by hailing the revolutionary advances of Spanish workers, but the Comintern brought them to heel on the Popular Front line.

By far the most important party abroad was the French Communist Party, which had always served as a kind of big brother to the PCE. It now played the leading role in the Comintern, first as the model Popular Front Communist

organization in the larger Popular Front country, second as the source of special tutelage and assistance to the PCE, and third as a source of information
on the PCE for Moscow. The French Socialist prime minister, Léon Blum, recognizing the importance of the Comintern and Soviet nexus, established direct
personal relations with the Soviet embassy and even with the Comintern office
in Paris.[30] In August the Comintern dispatched such top PCF leaders as André
Marty and the Spanish-speaking Jacques Duclos to Madrid, while the veteran
Hungarian Erno Gero was sent to Barcelona (where he would be known as
Pedro) as adviser to the new Catalan PSUC.

The French Communist press played a leading role in presenting the Soviet international (as distinct from Soviet or Spanish Republican domestic)
line on the character of the struggle in Spain. On August 3 L'Humanité featured
a banner statement from the PCF central committee that assured French readers that the goal of the Republican war effort in Spain was "THE DEFENSE OF
REPUBLICAN ORDER AND RESPECT FOR PROPERTY," which would certainly have
been original news to those living in the Republican zone. Marty reiterated
that the conflict was not between "capitalism and democracy" but between
"fascism and democracy," insisting that "the only possible task" was "not to bring
about the socialist revolution, but to defend, consolidate and develop the bourgeois democratic revolution."[31] During August PCE spokesmen in Madrid reiterated such claims to the international press.

To implement the campaign on behalf of the Spanish left, the PCF attempted to tie the cause of the Republic to French security and patriotism. On
July 30 L'Humanité announced that the Spanish Republic was fighting "for the
security of both republics," "for the security of France." This assurance quickly
produced a PCF initiative for a broader French patriotic alliance, a sort of left-
liberal union sacrée known as the Front Français. This effort, which began on
August 6 and continued for more than a month, failed to draw much support
even from the French Socialists, who found it artificial and pseudochauvinist.[32]

Though the French Popular Front government continued to do what it
could unofficially to assist the Republican cause, with France serving as a somewhat sub rosa conduit for military supplies under what Blum himself called
non-intervention relachée (relaxed non-intervention), France had begun to polar-
ize over the Spanish situation even before the fighting began.[33] Pressure from
the right remained very strong throughout the life span of the Popular Front
government, and by August 1936 Blum already feared that his country was
"on the eve of a military coup d'état."[34] Later, in 1942, he wrote to his wife that
"before any foreign war, France would have had civil war, with precious little

chance for a victory for the Republic." Nonetheless, the Blum government continued its peculiar form of "relaxed non-intervention," allowing the passage of contraband and granting other facilities. As Blum put it in 1945, "We supplied arms without saying so."[35]

The Spanish war divided not merely France generally but also the French Socialists particularly, though the full hardening of lines between left and right in that party did not crystallize until 1938. French Socialist leaders were uncertain as to whether what was going on in the Republican zone was defense of a bourgeois democratic system or a socialist revolution. The party's left wing was inspired by the Spanish revolution and wanted mass action against Blum's policy. Marceau Pivert, a chief leader of the ultraleft, and a few others followed the POUMist line: avoid defeat by promoting revolution. His sector rallied around the *tendance* called the Gauche Révolutionnaire. In a report from Barcelona, published in France on August 24, 1936, Pivert shrilled: "Now the revolutionary forces are on the march: a new humanity is being born—a new invincible proletarian consciousness is being formed. . . . At the center of this new wave of world socialist revolution, Red Barcelona, we can perceive this new world. . . . *Révolution d'abord!* The Spanish proletarian revolution is going to be an impregnable bastion of the world revolution."[36]

Paul Faure, the influential secretary of the party and a chief leader of Socialist moderates, strongly supported Popular Front reforms in France but thought that his country was not yet ready for socialism. In foreign affairs he was more pacifist than Blum, believing that France was permanently weaker than Germany and thus needed to be very cautious. His subsequent memoir, *De Munich à la Cinquième République* (1948), strongly supported non-intervention. He was always very suspicious of the Soviet Union, with his eye on the icebreaker doctrine, and thought that the Soviets wanted to provoke war either to spread revolution or to protect themselves from Germany. Though he could not say so publicly while the Spanish conflict lasted, on October 13, 1939, after Stalin had allied himself with Hitler and France was at war with Germany, Faure declared that the PCF "did everything possible—on command of its masters in Moscow—to push France into war over Spain, then over Czechoslovakia, and now over Poland."[37] Despite its relationship with the PCF, the Blum government would never be amenable to Soviet policy.

After formal relations with Madrid had been established, the Soviet Politburo met on August 21 to determine the first diplomatic appointments to the Republic. Well before this point Stalin had taken a keen interest in policy toward Spain and as early as July 22 his Politburo had directed that Soviet oil be sold to Republican Spain at below-market prices.[38] For the next year or so he would make the Civil War a prime focus of his attention. The leading Soviet scholar on this topic has written that "practically not one document on the Spanish question escaped his attention."[39] Thus the Soviet personnel assigned to Spain were chosen with care. The choice for ambassador fell on Marcel Rosenberg, one of the most veteran Soviet diplomats, former delegate to the League of Nations. Vladimir Antonov-Ovseenko, an Old Bolshevik and putative leader of the storming of the Winter Palace in 1917, would be consul general in Barcelona. The military attachés were also carefully selected, for they were intended to play a special role in helping to advise in the development of Republican military forces. The military staff dispatched to Spain consisted of experienced high-level personnel, led by the Latvian Old Bolshevik General Jan Berzin (pseudonym of Peteris Kjusis), a veteran of both the 1905 and 1917 revolutions. Berzin had created and long administered the GRU, the Soviet military intelligence system, and was posted to Spain (where he would be known as Grishin) as head of the military mission. It may also have been at the meeting of August 21 that the decision was made to send a very limited number of Soviet pilots and other air force specialists to Spain immediately; the Republican government needed crews for the planes it had obtained from France and elsewhere.[40] In this manner Stalin moved incrementally toward greater intervention, even though as of late August no decision had been made to send significant numbers of either Soviet military equipment or personnel.

From the Soviet point of view no selection was more important than that of the NKVD intelligence chief and security control. The person selected for this role was the veteran Aleksandr Orlov (pseudonym of Leiba Feldbin), a top foreign intelligence officer. Orlov had been NKVD *rezident* in Britain a few years earlier at the time of the initial recruitment of the subsequently infamous "Cambridge five." After being recalled to Moscow, he continued to monitor the activities of British agents and also gave lectures at the NKVD training school for espionage. His expertise had been recognized just a few months earlier, in the spring of 1936, when he had been made a member of the elite six-member committee that advised the Politburo and Foreign Ministry on foreign intelligence. There he came to the personal attention of Stalin, who may have fingered him for the Spanish assignment. Orlov may first have been placed in charge of coordinating intelligence on Spain as early as July 20, and was finally ordered to the new Madrid embassy on August 26 under the cover of political attaché.[41] In addition to overseeing security, intelligence, and counterintelligence, Orlov, who had gained experience in guerrilla warfare during the

Russian Civil War, would be placed in charge of supervising the development of Republican guerrilla activities in the Nationalist zone. In 1936 he held the rank of major in the NKVD, equivalent to that of general in the regular army, and years later would boast in exile that he had been the most important Soviet official in Spain. Whereas Rosenberg arrived in Madrid by August 28, with most of his staff soon following, Orlov did not appear in Spain until mid-September. The first Soviet pilots arrived no later than the beginning of September, with others to follow by the middle of the month.[42]

The importance of propaganda and image in the Spanish war was reflected in the fact that the first noted Soviet figures to arrive in Spain were neither diplomats nor military personnel, but journalists and filmmakers. The prominent journalist Mikhail Koltsov appeared either on or shortly after August 8 and remained in Spain for months, dispatching a lengthy series of reports to *Pravda*. He later produced a journalistic memoir in installments. In addition, Koltsov, who enjoyed a personal relationship with Stalin, apparently sent reports directly to the Soviet dictator and even played a limited role as a political adviser in Madrid.[43] Another top Soviet journalist, Ilya Ehrenburg, who had written a sardonic book on his observations in Spain during the drafting of the Republican constitution in 1931, was apparently held back at first because he was so closely identified with extremist antifascist propaganda that it was feared that his presence in Spain might be counterproductive. Since Ehrenburg was already in Paris, however, he managed to wangle his way to Spain before the end of August.[44]

In the meantime, two Soviet documentary filmmakers, Roman Karmen and Boris Makaseev, had been ordered to Spain in mid-August and arrived on the 23rd. They began filming one day later and sent their first footage back to Moscow as early as August 25. Within less than two weeks the first Soviet newsreel from Spain, *Events in Spain*, was being shown in Moscow, and soon circulated throughout the Soviet empire. The two filmmakers would remain in Spain for nearly a year, producing at least nineteen newsreels and two feature-length documentaries, *Madrid Defends Itself* (1936) and *Spain* (1938). Material from Spain would play a major role in Soviet newsreels and film propaganda at least through 1938.[45]

As of late August, however, the Soviet Union had not intervened militarily. The few Soviet military personnel in Spain could be readily identified as part of the new embassy staff or, in the case of the pilots, dismissed as a handful of "volunteers." Foreign diplomats in Moscow picked up indirect reports of heated discussion at the highest level of Soviet government. The French embassy relayed word of a conflict between "moderates," such as Litvinov and Stalin, who wanted to avoid heavy involvement, and hard-liners, such as Molotov and the ultraleft, who sought to challenge fascism directly and provide major assistance to the Republic.[46]

Many years later the American historian Stephen Cohen picked up rumors that in a series of meetings at the end of August or the beginning of September, Old Bolshevik leaders gained agreement on some sort of military aid to the Republic and the dropping of charges against key targets of Stalin's malice, such as Aleksei Rykov and Nikolai Bukharin.[47] Something of this sort may have occurred, but, lacking Soviet documentation, it remains a matter of speculation.

By the latter part of August it had become abundantly clear that the disorganized revolutionaries were doing badly in the war. Though they had abundant manpower, they had no army. Even so, until the very end of the month the ultrarevolutionaries, from the POUM through the FAI-CNT to the caballeristas, rejected proposals to channel or moderate the revolution in favor of a more centralized government that would concentrate primarily on the war effort. As *Claridad* put it on August 22:

> Some say: "We must first smash fascism, let us end the war victoriously, and then there will be time to talk of revolution and to carry it out if necessary." Those who speak thus are still apparently not aware of the formidable dialectical movement that has swept us all up. War and revolution are the same thing, aspects of the same phenomenon. Not merely are they not exclusive and contradictory, but rather they are complementary and reinforce each other. The war needs revolution in order to triumph, in the same way that the revolution needed the war in order to break out.

Yet even Largo Caballero accepted at least part of the argument of the left Republicans and the Communists about the need for greater coordination, as well as the presentation of a moderate, democratic, and nonrevolutionary image abroad in order to gain some degree of foreign support. Thus in a letter of mid-August to Ben Tillett, the British trade union leader, he followed the standard line maintained abroad, that the Spanish left was merely fighting for political democracy and had no thought of introducing socialism.[48] The anarchist alternative to the present disorganization was formation of an all-syndicalist CNT-UGT national defense junta (not so dissimilar in terminology to that established by the insurgent General Emilio Mola in Burgos), but by the end of the month even the caballeristas saw the wisdom of creating a broad and inclusive Popular Front government, both for the propaganda argument of Republican "legitimacy" and for the even more important function of coordinating and developing the leftist forces.

From the Soviet point of view such a government should still be led by a left Republican such as the colorless Giral, but in addition to broad middle-class left Republican membership should include the Socialists and Basque and Catalan nationalists. PCE leaders were strongly in favor of Communist participation as well, but on the first of September Manuilsky wired them that "in view of the international situation" the Comintern leaders "consider your position erroneous and the participation of the Communist Party in the government inopportune."[49]

Comintern propagandists could present such a broad Popular Front government, with the propaganda advantage of participating bourgeois Catholic Basque nationalists (provided they agreed) and without the provocative participation of the Communists, as merely the advanced form of the "bourgeois democratic republic," with emphasis on "bourgeois," completely ignoring the fact that it had in practice already begun to go beyond even the "people's republic of a new type" hypothesized by Comintern doctrine in 1935–36. Though it bore no relation to liberal democracy, it would be incessantly presented as such not merely by the Comintern's propaganda but later by that of the reorganized Republican government and indeed by most of its partisans throughout the Civil War and for decades beyond. The myth of "republican democracy" would always lie at the core of the enduring myth of the Republic.

For the Soviet government, the Comintern, and the Spanish Communists, what was already being developed in the Republican zone was not the "bourgeois democracy" that they all proclaimed for international propaganda purposes but the highest stage of the "democratic revolution," the all-left "people's republic of a new type" proclaimed by Popular Front doctrine in 1935 and by Soviet policy on one level since 1924. The many historians and leftist writers who have castigated Communist policy during the war have failed to distinguish between international propaganda claims (almost identical to those of the Republican government) and the genuine position of the Comintern, the PCE, and Soviet policy generally concerning the wartime Republic, which was not at all that it was a bourgeois democracy but that it had become a people's republic that was not socialism but the antechamber to socialism. There is really no excuse for the way commentators have persistently misinterpreted and misrepresented the Communist position for so many years. The Communist position on the level of Comintern principles themselves—as distinct from the propaganda of Comintern front organizations—was always clear and consistent on this point, as were the public positions taken by the PCE inside Spanish politics from the autumn of 1935 to the end of the Civil War and beyond. The Communists played a double game rhetorically whenever they shifted levels, dimensions, or interlocutors, but that had been their standard procedure since 1917. A combination of mental laziness and political *parti pris* has long been responsible for the fact that virtually all noncommunist commentators from the right to the extreme left have tended to take the Comintern's international propaganda position for the real political Communist position during the Spanish Civil War, even though Communist spokesmen in the Republican zone insisted that their emphasis on channeling the revolution coherently was in no way "bourgeois" or "counterrevolutionary."[50] In fact, for nearly a year before the war began, PCE leaders had enunciated the nuanced position of a people's republic in the making with its advanced economic program and increasingly authoritarian political structure, even though it maintained a parliament of sorts.

In the Republican political crisis of the first week of September, the Soviet position was that a new all–Popular Front government should be led by Giral or some other left Republican as window dressing, and for the same reason preferably should not include Communist cabinet ministers. The main obstacle was the caballeristas, who disagreed on both counts. They insisted that a broader left-unity government should be led by Largo Caballero, the erstwhile "Spanish Lenin," and that Communist participation was indispensable. Otherwise, they allegedly warned, the Communists would "be held accountable for whatever happened."[51] In Moscow the Comintern leaders conducted an intense discussion of the Spanish situation on September 2, with Stalin participating intermittently by telephone. They reconfirmed that the goal was a broad "government of national defense" but moderated their position to permit two Communist ministers. They were also told that the Politburo would soon take up the matter of sending possibly significant military aid. On the following day, Dimitrov insisted to Díaz that Giral must remain prime minister (especially if there was to be Communist participation), and he also sent word to Duclos and Marty, the two French leaders working actively in the Republican zone, that they must make Spanish Socialists understand that a Socialist-led government would drive Britain to the other side and risk increased foreign intervention against the Republic.[52] This final attempt was in vain.

When the new government was formed on September 4 (to be announced the following day), Largo Caballero became prime minister of an all–Popular Front government that would soon include a Basque nationalist representative as well, nominally extending the coalition to the political center. PCE leaders reported to Moscow that they had managed to include as many left Republican ministers as possible, and that "everyone was intensely interested" in Communist participation, which became "impossible to avoid without creating a very dangerous situation."[53] Jesús Hernández, the bright young man of the party, took over the nonthreatening Ministry of Public Instruction, and the veteran Vicente Uribe became minister of agriculture, where it would become his responsibility to try to channel the process of agrarian collectivization. A quid pro quo exacted by the PCE was appointment of the leading Socialist fellow traveler, Alvarez del Vayo, as minister of foreign affairs. Here Largo exhibited some reluctance, correctly considering Vayo little more than a Communist agent, but Vayo was a nominal caballerista, and Largo's own choice for the job, the revolutionary guru Araquistain, urged acceptance and offered to take up the crucial ambassadorship in Paris.[54] At that time no one could have known that the new finance minister, the prietista Socialist Juan Negrín, would represent another almost automatic vote for the Communists. This was a unique government, for never before had Communist ministers participated in a coalition government outside the Soviet Union, with the exception of the short-lived Communist-Socialist Bela Kun regime in Hungary in 1919, yet this was not a normal parliamentary government but part of a political process that would be increasingly directed toward development of the "democratic republic of a new type." Its initial program, however, was only slightly more advanced than the nominal program of the feeble Giral administration. It announced emergency social and economic reforms, but only temporary administration of private property when the public interest required. The most revolutionary measure was legitimization of the previously announced *tribunales populares*, or people's courts, as a vehicle for revolutionary justice, though the intention in part was to regularize the Republican repression and bring the mass killings under greater control. There was no mention of parliament, for many opposition deputies had simply been murdered and the constitution in effect suspended, though Communist propaganda hailed the new government as "a continuation of the previous government."

From the Soviet point of view, it in fact represented a decisive step forward. News from the front had become increasingly negative for the left, as evidence of German and Italian assistance to the rebels mounted. The non-intervention agreement made normal sources of military supply unavailable to the Republic, leaving the Soviet Union as the sole remaining source of assistance. During the preceding month of August the Soviet Union had become the only state in the world to adopt a strongly pro-Republican position and had begun measures to supply significant humanitarian and economic assistance, as well as providing for a limited amount of military advice and the services of a small number of pilots. By September the issue facing Stalin was whether to send substantial military assistance to give the Spanish revolution an opportunity to prevail. The PCE itself remained a comparatively small minority party—even though it continued to grow rapidly—and the disunity among the leftist forces was great, but formation of the Largo Caballero government, despite certain shortcomings from the Soviet point of view, offered reasonable hope of overcoming that problem. Despite its modest initial program, the new government was generally agreed on the need to restore state authority and give priority to creation of a sort of Spanish Red Army.

Moreover, the Republican government had plenty of money to pay for arms, possessing the fourth largest state gold reserve in the world, and had already demonstrated that it was willing to spend this resource most freely. Nearly one-quarter of the gold reserve had already been transferred to Paris to facilitate arms purchases, though in view of the non-intervention agreement, it was not clear how useful this money would be. The new finance minister, Juan Negrín, a noted physiology professor and clinician, was, as indicated, from the prietista sector of the Socialist Party but also an admirer of the Soviet Union, a member of the front organization Amigos de la URSS, and a believer in vigorous administration and strong state action. He quickly hit it off well in personal terms with the experienced Artur Stashevsky, the new Soviet commercial attaché, and displayed strong interest in full economic cooperation with the Soviet Union in order to achieve major assistance.

It was clear that the forces of Franco's elite Army of Africa would be within striking distance of Madrid in just a few weeks, and Republican leaders were determined to continue the struggle even if the city fell. The gold reserve would be a major resource and it seemed highly imprudent to leave it all in the threatened capital. The Giral government had taken the first steps to plan to move the gold to a safer place, and thus on September 13 Negrín obtained a decree from President Azaña giving him carte blanche to move the gold whenever and wherever he wished. Almost immediately the finance minister began to move the gold to a secure site on the east coast near the port city of Cartagena, the major Republican naval base and also an area much more effectively under government control than Barcelona or even Valencia.[55]

According to the diary of Maksim Litvinov, the debate in Moscow had still not been resolved as late as September 10. For some time the Spanish case had been extensively discussed in the Politburo, and at its meeting on the tenth Stalin remained cautious, while Vyacheslav Molotov and Kliment Voroshilov urged direct military aid, even though the Largo Caballero government remained an uncertain entity. Litvinov agreed with Stalin, but was surprised by Stalin's continued vacillation on the issue.[56] The vacillation finally neared its end on September 14—the coincidence with the beginning of the removal of the Spanish gold reserve to Cartagena may not have been totally accidental—when Stalin appointed a high-level committee to work out feasible terms, amounts, and logistics for an "Operation X"—direct military assistance to the Republic.[57] Both the Comintern and Soviet agents in the West had already become active in the purchase of Republican arms, but the new plan was different, for it would involve large-scale direct Soviet assistance.[58] Soviet policy had been moving incrementally in this direction since about the third day of fighting, but any one or a combination of alternative developments might have obviated Stalin's ultimate decision: a rapid collapse of Republican resistance, a breakdown of the Nationalist insurgency, inability of the Spanish left to form a broader government, or more direct and powerful suasion by another major power. Yet none of these developments had occurred, and though the Soviet assistance would be financed by a series of state credits, by September 14 there was some indication that it might turn out to be fully reimbursed.[59]

The planning committee was convened on that date in the Lubianka by the head of the NKVD, Genrikh Yagoda (who within two weeks would be purged and replaced by Nikolai Yezhov, inaugurating the second phase of the Great Terror). The other participants were Semyon Uritsky, head of the GRU (Soviet military intelligence); Avram Slutsky, director of foreign intelligence operations for the NKVD; and General Mikhail Frinovsky, commander of NKVD military forces. Two days later the project that was code-named "Operation X" was formally organized, with "X" denoting the Spanish Republic, and a special "Section X" was created under Uritsky to coordinate the armed forces personnel, officers of the NKVD and GRU, financial supervisors, and transportation personnel who would participate. The ultimate commander of Operation X would be Stalin's old crony, General Kliment Voroshilov, the defense minister. All major details would apparently require Stalin's personal approval. The assistance would consist of sizable amounts of armaments—rifles, cannon, machine guns, and ammunition—part of which would be drawn from reserve stocks not of prime value, but it would also include significant amounts of late-model weaponry, especially warplanes and tanks.[60] The latter in turn would require some substantial numbers of Soviet pilots and tank crews. There is some indication that in the initial plan even Voroshilov proposed to send regular combat units of the Red Army, but top military commanders argued successfully that this would be too difficult and too risky.[61] Direct aid would continue to be augmented in other countries by the work of dummy companies and regular purchasing activities of Soviet agents and the Comintern parties, particularly the PCF.

While the plan for Operation X was being developed, a major meeting of the Comintern leadership took place in Moscow between September 17 and 21. Though discussion of the Spanish case was only the fourth item on the official agenda, it apparently occupied a great deal of attention. Codovilla presented a long report about the problems in Spain, which he blamed on all the other political forces. Dimitrov insisted that PCE leaders had followed false priorities, not recognizing that the chief tasks were strengthening the Popular Front and heading off a coup. It had been difficult for Spanish Communist leaders—encouraged for years to move more rapidly to "forming soviets"—to adjust fully to the policy shifts of 1935–36, and Codovilla admitted that they still thought too much in traditional terms. On the 18th the Comintern bosses decreed mobilization of a major new international propaganda campaign on behalf of the Republic, hopefully involving massive worker demonstrations in various key countries. More important was the decision taken on the following day, following a suggestion first advanced by French Communist leaders on August 28, to have the Comintern organize the recruitment of volunteers throughout the world, preferably "with military training," to be sent to serve in the Republican armed forces. This was the beginning of what would soon be called the International Brigades, for which the first organizational steps would be taken in Paris within a week.[62]

The Comintern leadership was much more explicit than either the Soviet government or the Spanish Communists about the nature of the political struggle in Spain on the international level. Dimitrov made it clear that—contrary to the international propaganda line—this was not a battle to preserve the original liberal democratic parliamentary republic. In his words, "The question of the democratic bourgeois state is no longer posed as before. . . . It will not be an old-style republic like, for example, the North American republic, nor will it be a republic in the French or Swiss manner. . . . It will be a specific type of republic with a genuine people's democracy. It will not yet be a Soviet state, but it will be an antifascist left-wing state, in which the genuine leftist elements of the bourgeoisie will also participate." It would be the "new type" of republic proclaimed with the introduction of the Popular Front tactic the preceding year, with all conservative influences removed and the economy

controlled by the workers, but not necessarily collectivized. Thus it would constitute "a special form of the democratic dictatorship of the working class and
peasantry" (Lenin's old formula); or, as Elorza and Bizcarrondo say, "an advance
version of what in 1945–1946 would be the People's Democracies."[63]

All this was explained more fully by Dimitrov's chief West European lieutenant, Palmiro Togliatti (who would later be on his way to Spain), in an article
published the following month under the title "Specific Features of the Spanish
Revolution." Here was presented, apparently for the first time, what would remain for more than half a century the standard Soviet and Communist definition
of the Spanish conflict as a "national-revolutionary war," a war both of Spanish
independence against the fascist states and domestically for a democracy of a
"new type." In this formula "national" stood not merely for Spain's independence
but also for the "liberation" of Catalonia, Galicia, and the Basque Country. The
definition of this "revolution" simply as socialism or the democratic dictatorship
of the proletariat and peasantry "would not explain its true nature," for it was
a particular form of democratic-bourgeois revolution. Nonetheless, it differed
from other bourgeois-democratic revolutions in not being led by the bourgeoisie
but instead representing a more advanced stage, carried forward by a special
Popular Front alliance of workers, peasants, the progressive petite bourgeoisie,
the most advanced sections of the liberal bourgeoisie, and the "oppressed"
"national groups." Within this alliance the working class, naturally led by the
PCE (whatever its minority status), was already in process of achieving hegemony, though this struggle was complicated by the size and influence of anarchosyndicalism and the existence of retrograde social democratic elements among
Spanish workers. Thus the result of the struggle would be not merely the final
completion of the bourgeois democratic revolution but the simultaneous construction of the "new type" of democratic people's republic, which would eliminate all "fascism" (meaning all nonleftist elements). Thus "this new type democracy will not . . . cease to be the enemy of every form of the conservative spirit,"
while "offering a guarantee of further economic and political conquests by the
workers of Spain."[64] There was in fact nothing new here but simply a detailed
recapitulation of the standard Comintern position on the evolution of Spanish
affairs as enunciated time and again over the past fourteen months. There
would be no deviation from this basic doctrine regarding the Spanish revolution
of 1936–39 down to the time of the dissolution of the Soviet Union more than
half a century later, and it would still be echoed by party-line post-Soviet Russian
historians even after that.

While the final planning for Operation X went forward, on September 20

a Politburo resolution reaffirmed collective security as the basis of Soviet policy.[65] The reality would soon be more than ever a two-track policy, and indeed
Litvinov seems to have feared that greater Soviet involvement in the Spanish
revolution would ultimately be counterproductive. Most Western governments
were well aware of the longer-term Soviet icebreaker strategy of interimperialist
war, and the new Spanish policy might only heighten fears of Comintern and
Soviet expansion. Litvinov was correct, for almost from the beginning of the
new involvement in Spain many Western leaders feared that Soviet policy
sought to incite war between Western powers. The determination to go through
with intervention would be yet another example of the Soviet policy of playing
both ends against the middle, an exercise in which the Soviets sometimes tried
to be too clever; policy might be so devious that it canceled itself out. The first
Spanish ship loaded with Soviet arms, the *Campeche*, was ready to leave Odessa
on the 26th, and that afternoon Stalin personally telephoned the order for it
to depart.[66] Three days later a special meeting of the Politburo, chaired by Molotov and Kaganovich in Stalin's absence, approved the final plan for Operation X,
which henceforth would proceed relatively rapidly.[67] It was now becoming a
race against time, as Franco got nearer and nearer Madrid. That very day Koltsov's dispatch in *Pravda* was headed "Madrid Prepares to Defend Itself," and
its text judged that "it is hard to predict what will become of the struggle: will
Madrid be a Spanish Verdun or will it share the fate of the Paris Commune?"
Soon afterward Kaganovich wrote to his fellow Politburo member Sergo Ordzho-
nikidze, "The Spanish affair is not going well." Sending sizable military assistance all the way to Spain "is very difficult for us technically and, secondly, on
their part they have little order and organization—our party is still weak and
the anarchists remain true to their own ideals."[68]

With a major military assistance program decided on, the question now
was the goals. What could Stalin hope to achieve? As Geoffrey Roberts observes,
Soviet policy was not always merely devious, and stated ideology and goals
were first of all simply what they were declared to be, to assist the Republic to
victory and advance the cause of the left generally.[69] As Soviet activities in Spain
broadened during the next year, a set of interrelated goals emerged: military
and political victory in Spain; geostrategic advancement of Soviet interests in
Western Europe; and collateral benefits in a variety of areas, such as propaganda,
political mobilization, intelligence, and military testing and improvement.

With regard to the first goal, available evidence indicates that at least
through the summer of 1937 the Soviet intention was to enable the Republic
to win a military victory, even though major intervention was delayed so long

that the initial concern was simply to avoid defeat. Intervention as late as October–November 1936 might come too late, but Stalin was clearly willing to undertake what was for him an uncharacteristic gamble. What made the risk seem worth taking was that the Soviet intervention would take place on a larger scale than anything Germany and Italy had done so far, and the two fascist powers were unlikely to counter the Soviet escalation with escalation of their own. Unfortunately for the Republic and the Soviets, however, they would soon do so. A related direct benefit of the intervention would be to strengthen Spanish communism. The stronger Soviet and Spanish Communist influence became, the greater the possibility of channeling the Spanish revolution along the announced lines of the new type of people's republic proclaimed in the Comintern's Popular Front strategy.

As indicated earlier, the second goal—geostrategic advancement—was less clearly charted, for major intervention on behalf of the Spanish revolution was unlikely to alter the policy of the capitalist democracies. Yet, however contradictory, such remained a basic goal of Soviet policy down to the spring of 1939. The Soviet representatives remained active in the Non-Intervention Committee and Soviet and Comintern propaganda never ceased to appeal to Western public opinion. So much energy was expended in this endeavor that it could not have been mere window dressing or misinformation. The emphasis on utmost secrecy in Operation X was designed to disguise or hide it as much as possible from the Western countries, despite the naiveté of such pretensions. The effort was doomed to failure, and the Spanish intervention had the effect of discouraging Western adherence to the Soviet scheme of collective security, but the evidence is clear that in this respect as in others, Stalin hoped to play both ends against the middle. Even if broader agreement with the capitalist democracies were not achieved, protraction of the Spanish conflict might divert, distract, or bog down the fascist powers, to that extent enhancing Soviet security, while a Republican victory under Soviet tutelage could only enhance Moscow's strategic position.

Soviet achievements would in some ways be greatest in the third set of objectives. The Popular Front banner of antifascism provided a strong magnet to draw political support even among Western left-liberals who had previously tended to be anti-Soviet. At the time when totalitarianism was at its most extreme and naked within the Soviet Union, antifascism restored the appearance of progressivism and created much stronger moral standing for the Soviet Union, at least in left-liberal quarters, than it had enjoyed a few years earlier. Indeed, except for the brief period of the Nazi-Soviet Pact (1939–41), antifascism would remain the perpetual banner of the Soviet Union until its demise in 1991, and help to give it a greater standing than it would otherwise have ever enjoyed.

The Soviet Union already had a formidable intelligence network in Western Europe, but the broad scope of new Comintern activities in various countries and of Orlov's NKVD operations in the Republican zone would provide opportunity to widen that network further. The windfall of foreign passports provided by the members of the International Brigades would provide documentation to penetrate new countries, particularly the United States, where the Soviet network, despite the energetic efforts of the Communist Party of the USA, had heretofore been relatively weak. A few years later these new opportunities would make an important contribution to the success of Soviet espionage in gaining the secrets of the development of the atomic bomb.

The Spanish war would also provide the first opportunities to test the new advanced-model Soviet weaponry, especially in tanks and aircraft, developed under the five-year plans since 1928. It would also provide the first direct new battlefield experience for some of the elite new cadres and officers of the Red Army. The experience gained would help to improve the next generation of Soviet weapons, though the conclusions drawn by the Red Army regarding tactics and operations would sometimes prove very faulty.

In summary, from September 1936 the Soviet regime was becoming committed, more or less as Roberts has indicated, to a four-track approach to the Spanish war: major internal participation and manipulation through the Comintern and the PCE; major direct military assistance and participation through Red Army weapons and personnel; major collateral political, propaganda, and material assistance to the Republic through the Comintern, its parties and front organizations, as well as through the provision of food and other non-military supplies from the Soviet Union, with other Soviet collateral assistance from a variety of dummy companies; and active diplomatic support for the Republic, particularly in the Non-Intervention Committee (NIC), as well as through various channels and efforts of bilateral diplomacy, to discourage German and Italian assistance to the other side, as well as to encourage Britain and France to adopt policies more favorable to the Republic.[70]

During October, as sizable Soviet military shipments made their way to Spain, Soviet representatives began to take an increasingly assertive stance in the Non-Intervention Committee in London. This shift was designed both to put pressure on the other leading participants in the committee and also to provide potential justification if and when evidence of Soviet intervention began to leak out. Adopting the only confrontational posture of any of the delegations in the early weeks of the committee, Soviet representatives declared on October 7 that if Italy, Portugal, and Germany did not cease to intervene, the Soviet Union would consider itself free of obligations incurred under the agreement. This had no effect. Italian and German duplicity was approximately equal to that of the Soviets, but the two major democratic allies had no intention of seriously challenging any of the powers that were intervening so long as they continued to participate regularly in the NIC. This was the sort of thing that earned the NIC the reputation of diplomatic fraud of the century, even though it has much competition for this dubious honor. The viewpoint of London and Paris was that even a hypocritical and duplicitous participation in the NIC was better than none at all. Soviet diplomats at first brought their most concrete charges against Italy and Portugal, because charges of their intervention were most strongly supported by evidence. On October 12 and 23 they repeated that the Soviet government would consider itself bound to non-intervention only to the degree that other signatories did, and on the 28th proposed that the NIC establish control of Spanish ports to guarantee compliance.[71] This strong stand drew counterblasts from German and Italian diplomats, and on October 23 the British representative cited three violations of non-intervention by the Soviet Union and only one by Italy. Three days later the French representative wrote a letter to his Soviet counterpart insisting that the aggressive Soviet stance, with its repeated threats to pull out, placed the entire work of the committee in jeopardy. Privately the Soviet ambassador to Britain, Ivan Maisky, would admit to Foreign Secretary Anthony Eden that the Soviet Union had begun to intervene, but insisted that it had done so merely to prevent Germany and Italy from gaining a stronger international position.[72]

Soviet diplomacy continued to take a stern and aggressive posture in support of the Republic throughout the life of the NIC, as well as at the League of Nations in Geneva, and in London and Paris, engaging in scathing denunciations both publicly and privately. None of the other participants—not even Germany and Italy—denounced Soviet duplicity as strongly as the Soviets proclaimed the misdeeds of others, but such lack of symmetry was common in Soviet relations. Soviet representatives were also active in helping develop details of the NIC's first plan to attempt to monitor non-intervention in March 1937, though this effort also came to naught. The Socialist International and the International Federation of Trade Unions were also severely critical of the NIC, but rejected all proposals for joint action with their Soviet colleagues of the Comintern.

While publicly admitting no more than humanitarian assistance, Stalin made clear the Soviet Union's firm support of the Republic in a personal telegram to the central committee of the PCE on October 15, which did not hide the revolutionary character of the struggle in Spain: "The workers of the USSR are doing no more than their duty in giving the help they are able to give to the Spanish revolutionary masses. They are well aware that the liberation of Spain from the oppression of the Spanish reactionaries is not merely the private business of the Spaniards, but the common cause of all advanced and progressive mankind."[73] This last clause would become the most famous and oft-cited of all Soviet statements on the Spanish war.[74] *Izvestia* published Stalin's message the next day. Two of its phrases—"revolutionary masses" and "cause of all advanced and progressive mankind"—were frequently repeated in Soviet commentary and propaganda on the Spanish war. Similarly, *Pravda* reiterated that month that victory over fascism and the triumph of the bourgeois-democratic revolution in Spain were but necessary prerequisites for the final goal of the socialist revolution.

Meanwhile, in one of the most extraordinary financial operations of the century, the Republican government was arranging for payment in full in advance for shipments of Soviet arms. It readily obtained permission from Stalin to move most of the remainder of the gold reserve of the Banco de España to the Soviet Union, where it could find both security and effective use. The origins of this maneuver have never been fully clarified. In mid-September 10,000 boxes of fine gold (503 tons of it, nearly all in coins whose total weight was slightly greater) had been moved to Cartagena, together with all the silver reserves, some paper money, and other financial assets. Nearly a quarter of the total gold had already been shipped to France for commercial use, and later even more was sent, amounting to 9.6 tons of fine gold during the second half of September and 52 more tons during October. Other small shipments continued during the late autumn and early winter, until by February 1937 a grand total of 174 tons of fine gold, or 27.4 percent of the total original reserves, had been shipped to France.[75]

By October, however, the Republican government was finding ever-increasing difficulty in making effective use of its gold and credit in Western Europe. An effort had been made to coordinate the multiple purchasing commissions that had been dispatched to Paris, London, and elsewhere, one of which had been described by an observer at a London airport as composed of "little men in black suits . . . on the tarmac with bags of gold buying any aircraft they could."[76] Though the chaos of the first months was being reduced, facilities were severely limited, while the new Nationalist government of Franco was actively attempting to block use of Republican reserves in the West. Conversely, the first boatload of Soviet arms had already arrived on the fourth, with the promise of much more to follow. Although there is no documentary evidence, it is more than likely that Negrín and Largo Caballero would have promised subsequent gold transfers to pay for Soviet arms.[77] Since mid-September *Mundo obrero*, undoubtedly on Comintern instructions, had been full of an unusual amount of publicity concerning the Soviet Union, and the demarche in the Non-Intervention Committee on October 7 could be read as a signal of the new Soviet policy.

Sending gold reserves abroad for deposit during wartime had ample precedent. France did it in World War I and again on the eve of World War II, as Negrín was undoubtedly aware. To send gold to the world's leading revolutionary state rather than to a bastion of world capitalism, as France had done, was quite a different matter, but then the Spanish Republic had become the world's number two left revolutionary state. Negrín himself was developing ever closer Communist connections. His personal secretary, Benigno Martínez, with whom he was on intimate terms, was a Communist Party member, and he quickly developed a close personal relationship with his chief counterpart in the Soviet embassy, Artur Stashevsky, the commercial attaché; they frequently lunched together.[78] The sometime NKVD *rezident* Walter Krivitsky would later claim that Stashevsky persuaded Negrín to send most of the remaining gold to the Soviet Union for safekeeping, though Aleksandr Orlov, the NKVD boss in Spain who supervised the transfer, concluded that the initiative simply lay with Negrín himself, who came across to Orlov as a typical Western left-wing intellectual, "opposed to communism in theory, yet vaguely sympathetic to the 'great experiment' in Russia," characterized by "political naiveté"—a classic example of Lenin's "useful idiot."[79] Negrín was no idiot, but he looked very favorably on the Soviet Union, which he considered a benign force and probably the Republic's only hope.

What is clearly known is that Largo Caballero signed a letter in French (probably drafted by Negrín), which was handed to Ambassador Rosenberg in the name of the Republican prime minister on October 15, asking for permission to send a large amount of gold for safekeeping to the Soviet Union. Two days later a second letter indicated that the Republican government would want to use the gold with Soviet assistance for international payments.[80]

The Soviet Politburo dispatched the two proposals on October 17 and 19.[81] Orlov has testified that on the 20th he received a telegram from the NKVD chief in Moscow, Nikolai Yezhov, who transmitted a direct message from "Ivan

Vasilievich" (the personal pseudonym Stalin used for special communications) that ordered Orlov to take charge of shipping the gold from Cartagena to Odessa in Soviet vessels. The Russian military historian Lieutenant Colonel Yury Rybalkin has concluded from the speed and firmness of the Soviet response that the whole operation had already been negotiated informally and secretly in advance of the official communications, though the rapidity alone is not necessarily conclusive on this point.[82] Stalin specifically forbade Orlov to offer the Spanish authorities any kind of receipt, which would be arranged once the gold was in the Soviet Union. Orlov has testified that he made the arrangements with Negrín two days later, on the 22nd. He has also written that when he asked a high treasury official how much of the gold was to be transported, the latter replied, "Oh, more than half, I suppose." The NKVD chief added, "It would be, I said mentally, a lot more."[83] Altogether 7,800 cases of gold, involving 510 metric tons, of which 460 tons were fine gold, were transported. Orlov used Soviet tank crewmen, who had arrived in Cartagena but were still waiting for their tanks, to drive the trucks that ferried the gold to four Soviet ships in Cartagena harbor during the next fortnight. Accompanied by three minor officials of the Banco de España, all the gold arrived safely in the Soviet Union in early November, though one of the vessels was delayed by mechanical trouble.[84] The Soviet authorities eventually provided a receipt for 7,800 cases on February 7, 1937. If the numismatic value of the coins that made up nearly all the gold is not considered (only 13 of 7,800 cases contained ingots), the market value of the pure gold alone would have amounted to $518 million at the price level of the times. Though the gold was technically sent to the Soviet Union initially for safe deposit without any specific agreement concerning quantities for commercial use or payment to the Soviet government, Orlov claimed to have learned that Stalin announced privately that the Spaniards would never see their gold again "any more than they can see their own ears."[85] At any rate, Stalin was sufficiently pleased that in January Orlov was awarded the Order of Lenin, the highest Soviet decoration.

Though there is no indication of any dispute in the Republican government over shipping the gold to the USSR, the decision later became extremely controversial. The initial decision was apparently made by Negrín with the approval of the prime minister; Largo Caballero wrote years later in his memoirs that there was no other choice.[86] Apparently neither Azaña nor the cabinet in general was consulted, although Prieto, as minister of the navy, had to be informed in order to provide full naval protection for the shipment. Prieto later even denied having provided naval protection, but this is not credible. It must be remembered that Negrín to that point had been a strongly committed member of the prietista faction of the Socialist Party and that in the autumn of 1936 he and Prieto remained in close contact. There is no evidence that Prieto was part of the original decision, but he was soon brought into the plan and did provide considerable Republican naval protection.[87] Azaña never refers to the gold in his diary and probably was not informed of the transfer at that time. Years later Prieto claimed that the Republican president became enraged when he learned of it and threatened to resign, whereas Ambassador Marcelino Pascua claimed that his good friend Negrín had told him "repeatedly" that Azaña in fact never objected.[88]

Given the difficulties that the Republican purchasing agents were encountering in Western Europe and the importance of the current arms shipments from the Soviet Union, it was perfectly understandable that a certain portion of the gold reserve might be sent to the Soviet Union, but sending nearly all of it was a different matter. There is no indication that Negrín made any serious attempt to establish commercial terms for the arms being supplied or to negotiate a long-term credit arrangement. To have ignored all other alternatives and suddenly to have placed nearly all the Republican eggs in the Soviet basket represented a desperate, probably reckless effort to solidify Soviet support and to rely almost exclusively on Soviet assistance. Henceforth the Republic would become both financially and militarily dependent on the Soviet Union, since only a minor amount of gold was retained in Spain. As Angel Viñas, author of the only scholarly study of the gold operation, has written, by sending nearly all the gold to Soviet coffers, "the Republic lost a negotiating tool" and inevitably encouraged "the growing Soviet influence in the decisions of certain Republican leaders."[89] Cartagena, where the gold had been stored, was the chief Republican naval base and in no danger whatsoever in October 1936. For any normal government to have done what the Republican authorities chose to do would have been insane, but for a revolutionary polity fighting for its life to send most of its reserves to the bulwark of the world revolution had a certain logic to it. Even from a revolutionary viewpoint, however, the Republican government might have retained greater leverage by keeping much of the gold in Spain. Its choice represented a desperate embrace of the Soviet Union as the only means of sustaining the struggle, and probably was not needed to obtain Soviet military assistance.

Though the Republican government did become almost exclusively dependent on the Soviet Union for military supplies and assistance, many supplies—primarily but by no means exclusively civilian goods—continued to be purchased through Western channels. Even in the West, however, the Soviet Union participated actively through the facilities of its Western banks, the Banque Commerciale pour l'Europe du Nord in Paris and also to some extent the Narodny Bank in London. In Paris the PCF played a major role. It founded its own company, France-Navigation, to assist the Republic, and within eight months the company owned at least sixteen vessels totaling 310,000 tons. At the end of the Civil War these assets remained in the hands of the PCF, which had also drawn heavily on Spanish funding to found a new daily newspaper, *Ce soir*, which was soon publishing half a million copies and was very active in the propaganda war.[90] The Soviet Union and the Comintern provided crucial assistance, but the wartime Republic paid its own way, and both the Soviet Union and the French Communist Party probably turned a profit on their activities on its behalf, an ironic circumstance for revolutionary anticapitalists.

Soviet Military Participation

1936–1939

INTERVENTION IN the Spanish Civil War in some ways constituted the most extensive Soviet military action since the close of the Russian Civil War in 1921–22.[1] Many more troops had been involved in the domestic campaigns against Muslim rebels, who had finally been subdued by 1936, and more had also been used in the conquest of Outer Mongolia in 1921 and in the Manchurian operation of 1929, but other actions such as those in Iran and Sinkiang had involved no more than a handful of troops. Altogether, the number of military personnel was limited, and Soviet sources recognize little more than 3,000 in all, of whom 200, or 6.67 percent, were killed.[2] This rate of loss was about average for the two contending armies (which averaged approximately 7 percent fatalities) and was exceeded only by that of certain special units, such as the International Brigades, about 15 percent of whose effectives were killed, or by the Navarrese forces on Franco's side, whose proportion of loss was higher yet. The extent of Soviet involvement was exceeded only in the sizable operations against Japan in 1938 and 1939, but that confrontation involved direct defense of the USSR homeland. Even so, the Soviet manpower involved in Spain was far exceeded by the approximately 16,000 Germans and 70,000 Italians who at one time or another served in Spain; even if the 42,000–51,000 members of the International Brigades are included, the Soviet participation still lags behind that of the Axis. Offsetting the small numbers, however, was the skill level of the Soviet personnel. Not a single one was an ordinary infantryman. The largest contingent was made up of the nearly 800 air crewmen who flew in the Republican air force, followed by several hundred tank crewmen. Many of the rest were officers, some of fairly senior rank; the remainder consisted of technical support personnel, nearly all of them commissioned or noncommissioned officers.

By 1936 the Soviet Union was much better positioned for sizable intervention in Spain than it would have been only a few years earlier. Industrial and military expansion had now been under way for eight years, and sizable amounts of up-to-date new equipment were rolling off Soviet assembly lines. Since 1934 major emphasis had been placed on military preparedness of the general population. Paramilitary instruction was increased, and the Soviet Union became the only country in the world where a certain proportion of young women were systematically taught to fire weapons. Preparedness for the next war and its proximity had become an important theme in Soviet popular culture.

The shipment of arms to the Republic was carefully organized by Operation X, its secrecy and security guaranteed by a special "Section X" of the NKVD.[3] The largest shipments arrived in Spain during October and November; supplies then diminished, increasing in volume once more during a six-week period in the spring of 1937 when eight boatloads of arms arrived, followed by two more at the end of June. After this last spurt, shipments were fewer and even more intermittent, though at widely varying intervals they continued almost to the very end of the Civil War. The total volume of Soviet military supplies remains in dispute. Differing figures have been given by the two official Soviet publications that treated the problem, *International Solidarity with the Spanish Republic* and volume 2 of the official *Istoriia Vtoroi Mirovoi Voiny* (History of the Second World War), both of which were published in Moscow in 1974. The British scholar Gerald Howson reached somewhat different totals yet on the basis of Soviet documents available to him.[4]

In addition to the data listed in Table 1, Howson presents another set of totals based on documentation drawn from the Russian State Military Archives, with slightly lower overall figures. Some of the figures in *International Solidarity* are only approximations, while, as Howson suggests, its totals for airplanes may include planes obtained from non-Soviet sources by Soviet agents, or, as César Vidal suggests, the total number of planes shipped, not all of which were fully delivered.[5] One Communist source, for example, lists a grand total of 321 planes obtained by the Republic from other countries.[6] The totals for artillery also include from 240 to 340 grenade launchers, and so are less impressive than they may seem. Howson has also found that these figures include a small number of artillery pieces purchased outside the Soviet Union. When compared with the roughly known totals of arms supplied to the Nationalists by Italy and Germany, they amount to scarcely two-thirds the total number of airplanes and artillery, and enjoy a decided advantage only with regard to the late-model Soviet tanks.[7] One asset ignored in all such tabulations, however, is the approximately 300 Soviet-model fighter planes manufactured in Catalonia and Alicante on Soviet blueprints and with the assistance of Soviet technicians, which were incorporated into the Republican air force.[8] When these planes are included, the total number of Soviet-model planes received by the Republican air force would range from about 950 to 1,100, depending on which Soviet source is accepted. Jesús Salas Larrazábal, the only historian who has taken all these sources into account, arrived at a grand total of 1,008 Soviet planes from all sources in the service of the Republic.[9]

One advantage that the Soviet arms gave the Republican forces lay in their initial timing. The large shipments that arrived in Spain during October and November 1936 gave the Republicans temporary superiority in matériel on the central front during the last part of 1936, though this advantage began to dissipate during 1937 and had been substantially reversed by the end of the year. Though there were thus certain exceptions, Soviet supplies were sufficient to provide the Republicans with equality or superiority of arms for only a brief time.

There has been much debate concerning the quality of the Soviet arms as well. While the later Soviet sources stress quality, there have been abundant allegations from Republicans that part of the matériel was antiquated. Indeed, there is truth to both allegations, depending on which set of arms is being referred to. The Polikarpov I-15 biplane (known in Spain as the Chato for its thick snub nose), of which at least 161 were supplied to the Republicans during the first ten months of shipments, was fast and maneuverable, more than a match for the first Italian and German planes. Its successor, the monoplane Polikarpov I-16 (called the Mosca [fly] by the Republicans and the Rata [rat or sneak thief] by the Nationalists), which was delivered in increasing numbers during 1937 (at least 276 were shipped), was faster yet, with an extremely rapid rate of climb. The Nationalists did not achieve parity of matériel in quality of fighter planes until the new German ME-109 began to appear in 1937. Similarly, the Tupolev SB medium bomber, known as the Katyusha (pronounced "Katiuska" in Spain), was very fast and maneuverable and in late 1936 somewhat superior to its Italian and German counterparts. The fascists' bombers subsequently improved, however, while significant defensive weaknesses of the Tupolev bombers severely limited their utility.[10]

Table 1

Soviet arms shipped to Republican Spain, 1936–39, according to three sources

	INTERNATIONAL SOLIDARITY	ISTORIIA VTOROI MIROVOI VOINY	GERALD HOWSON
Aircraft	806	648	634
Tanks	362	347	331
Other armored vehicles	120	60	—
Artillery	1,895	1,186	1,044–1,144
Machine guns	15,113	20,486	17,780
Rifles	500,000	497,813	414,645
Bombs	110,000	—	—
Grenades	500,000	—	—
Ammunition (rounds)	3,400,000	—	—
Cartridges	862,000,000	—	—
Gunpowder (tons)	1,500	—	—

Sources: International Solidarity with the Spanish Republic (Moscow, 1974); *Istoriia Vtoroi Mirovoi Voiny* (Moscow, 1974), 2:54; G. Howson, *Arms for Spain: The Untold Story of the Spanish Civil War* (London, 1998), 302–3.

In tanks the superiority of Soviet matériel was yet more pronounced. As of 1936, Italy and Germany had produced no more than light tanks and tankettes. The Soviet T-26 (of which at least 106 arrived in the first two months of shipments) was more advanced. Weighing 9.5 tons, it mounted a 45 mm cannon as well as three machine guns. It had become the standard Red Army tank of its time. Altogether, some 12,000 T-26s were manufactured between 1931 and 1941, of which fewer than 2 percent were ever sent to Spain. The BT-5 (which began to arrive in 1937) was the earliest prototype for the subsequently world-famous T-34 of World War II. Larger and equally well armed, it was also very fast, traveling at up to 40 miles per hour. The light artillery and antitank guns sent by the Soviets were also generally quite good, and were similar to the models used by much of the Red Army during World War II. The Degtiarev light machine guns also compared favorably in quality with opposing weapons.

The other matériel varied greatly in quality, however, and part of it was inferior. Soviet suppliers saw the desperate condition of the Republican forces as an opportunity to eliminate obsolete Soviet stocks of World War I and even older equipment, so that particularly in the autumn of 1936 and the winter of 1937 the Republicans received a good deal of artillery, machine guns, and rifles of limited utility. Moreover, the Polish government sold off a sizable amount of antiquated equipment to the Republic at inflated prices, and used the proceeds to produce more modern matériel for its own forces.[11] Drawing in weapons from many countries, Republican infantrymen altogether employed approximately thirty brands of rifles using nine calibers of ammunition.

Aleksandr Orlov has written that the NKVD disinformation desk in Spain "was ordered to introduce into the channels of German military intelligence information that Soviet planes fighting in Spain were not of the latest design and that Russia had in her arsenal thousands of newer planes, of the second and third generation, possessing much greater speed and a higher ceiling. This was not true."[12] Orlov claimed the maneuver was successful, but there is no evidence that the Germans were impressed by it.

Though the Republican media always gave the impression that this weaponry was being supplied by the Soviet Union free of charge, payment had been guaranteed, largely in advance, by the transfer of gold, and the prices charged were in fact very steep. The Soviets told Republican authorities that these arms were being provided at discounted prices, when in fact the prices were inflated. The Soviets never gave the Republican government strict price quotations in rubles, and Howson has discovered that by arbitrarily manipulating the exchange rate, the Soviets in fact regularly charged 30 to 40 percent above the international market rate. The markup on certain arms was in fact considerably higher than that. As Howson demonstrates, Republican purchasing agents were regularly swindled by arms suppliers in many countries, but the financial premium imposed by their Soviet ally was by far the worst, because so much more money was at stake.[13]

In addition, the Soviets charged high prices for all manner of services and expenses involved in military assistance to the Republic and in the training of 600 Spanish pilots, tank crewmen, and other specialists in the USSR. The Republican government was billed for all salaries and expenses of Soviet personnel, their dependents, and their vacations back home in the Soviet Union, including those of military and intelligence personnel who never left the USSR. It was similarly charged with all salaries and expenses involved in transportation from the very first step in the Soviet Union. Billing for training of Republican personnel included every single cost conceivably connected with this activity, including the cost of constructing facilities subsequently incorporated into regular use by the Soviet armed forces.[14]

Thus the Soviet Union billed the Republic government more than $171 million for the first ten months of arms shipments, and all the rest of the Spanish gold was liquidated during the next ten months, either in payment for shipments that became increasingly expensive or in transfers to Soviet and Comintern agents making purchases and propaganda in Western countries, with special concern for the coffers of the PCF.[15] By mid-1938 Soviet authorities could therefore report that the Spanish gold supply had been completely exhausted and that henceforth the Republic would incur increasing debt to the Soviet Union for any further assistance.

The ultimate outlay of the Republicans for foreign military supplies must have been in the neighborhood of $800 million at then-current prices, all paid for immediately through the use of gold and other valuables. By comparison, the cost of German equipment and related expenses to the Nationalists amounted to somewhat more than $225 million and that of an even larger amount of Italian arms and other Italian assistance to more than $410 million—nearly all of it provided by Germany and Italy through generous terms of credit. Whereas the Republicans had paid the Soviet Union and other suppliers for nearly all goods and services even before the end of the war, Hitler and Mussolini reduced the lavish credit extended to Franco by 25 and 33 percent, respectively, after the war ended. Most of the debt to Germany was retired through exports during World War II, while Franco paid the remaining Italian debt to Rome in increasingly inflated and inexpensive lire until the debt was retired in 1961. Other terms of credit were also extended to Franco by foreign suppliers, most notably American oil companies. Altogether Franco received nearly $700 million of goods and services from foreign sources on credit—nearly as much as the Republic paid out in gold and other valuables—and through that credit received in toto a larger volume of military supplies and support and, in the final analysis, generally higher-quality matériel and assistance.

Stalin also became increasingly parsimonious in the use of Soviet shipping. During the first year of the war some eighty-seven Soviet ships were intercepted by the Nationalist navy, while approximately twenty-five vessels bearing arms got through unchallenged, thanks to the strictest Soviet and Republican security. Of the intercepted vessels, three were sunk and another eight declared prizes of war because they contained at least some contraband. The only Soviet vessel that was sunk carrying arms is thought to have been the *Komsomol,* destroyed on its second voyage by the Nationalist cruiser *Canarias* on December 14, 1936, though Soviet sources have always denied that it was carrying arms.[16] The Nationalist navy was inferior in size and strength to the Republican forces in the early weeks, but soon became much more effectively operational and aggressive than its foe, a situation due in part to the frenzied slaughter of a large proportion of the officers on Republican warships in the revolutionary orgy of the initial days of fighting. Operational defensiveness bordering on quiescence reflected the cautious policy of the Republican command, concerned not to appear provocative to other powers, and the primarily defensive operational scheme developed by the chief Soviet adviser, the naval attaché Captain Nikolai Kuznetsov.[17] After the *Komsomol* was sunk, Stalin stopped using Soviet ships on the Mediterranean route, partly to avoid losses but also to avoid political complications. Soviet agents in turn were given orders to try to sabotage shipments from other European countries to the Nationalists.[18]

By the end of November 1936 the total number of Soviet military personnel in the Republican zone probably amounted to at least 700, composed principally of senior officer advisers, pilots, tank crewmen, and support staff, but also including a small but significant NKVD contingent. The senior military adviser was Jan Berzin, formerly head of the GRU, followed by the military attaché, Vladimir Gorev, chief adviser to the Republican central front. There were also specialist advisers for aviation, artillery, and armor on the central front, and advisers were sent to certain other regions as well. Some were assigned to the training and development of the cadres of the new Republican People's Army. The training site of the new International Brigades had already been established at Albacete the month before.

The Soviet advisers were not encouraged by the situation. The security chief dispatched his first report on October 15 in pessimistic terms, lamenting that "there is no unified security service" and that "in the present Government there are many former policemen with pro-Fascist sentiments. Our help is accepted politely, but the vital work that is so necessary for the country's security is sabotaged."[19] Decades later, in the flood of Spanish Civil War memoirs penned by surviving Soviet participants during the 1960s and 1970s, relations with the Republicans were usually painted in glowing terms.[20] The tendency then would be to look back on the Civil War nostalgically as the brightest area of Soviet activity in the otherwise grim and deadly 1930s. The attitude of the Republicans toward Soviet advisers was generally positive and cooperative, but establishing completely smooth working relations was more difficult. Almost none of the Soviet personnel knew Spanish, and they were accustomed to the totalitarian methods and enforced obedience of the Soviet system—something entirely lacking in the revolutionary Republican zone.[21]

The official position of the Soviet government was that any Soviet citizen who appeared with Republican forces had volunteered, though in fact all Soviet personnel were carefully selected and in most cases received at least a little special training. Not a few ordinary Soviet citizens did seek to volunteer to assist the Republicans, even applying directly to the new Republican embassy in Moscow, but there is no evidence that any of these genuine volunteers were accepted.[22]

The distribution by professional category of nearly 2,100 Soviet personnel, more than 90 percent of them military, who served in Republican Spain, as listed in Soviet military documents, is shown in Table 2. Other Soviet sources have given a figure of 3,000 for the total number of Soviet personnel in Spain, which is probably more accurate as a global statistic. The data in Table 2 are nonetheless the most precise available, though probably incomplete.[23]

Whereas total fatalities among Soviet personnel reached nearly 7 percent, in the two main combat categories of pilots and tank crewmen it reached 13.5 percent, almost as high as in the International Brigades. The famous phrase attributed to Stalin by Walter Krivitsky—"Stay out of the artillery fire!"—may have applied to the advisers, but certainly not to the combat personnel.[24] More troublesome for the Soviet government than the death of any of its military personnel in Spain was their potential capture by the Spanish Nationalists, which might lead to political embarrassment and other complications. This did occasionally happen, particularly during the collapse of the Republican northern front in 1937. Whenever possible an intense effort would be made to exchange such prisoners for captured Germans or Italians.[25]

The two priorities for the Soviet advisers and their subordinates were to help organize the defense of Madrid during October and November, and to help plan the organization of the new "Ejército Popular," the Republican People's Army, with which the new Largo Caballero government had replaced the short-lived "Ejército Voluntario" (Volunteer Army) created by the Giral government. It marked a 180-degree shift in the caballerista position, for as recently as August 20 *Claridad* had blustered: "To think about any other kind of army to replace our existing militia and in some fashion control its revolutionary action is to think in a counterrevolutionary way." A week later Largo himself had complained that "the military caste" was "being resuscitated," and criticized the Communists for thinking that the Soviet experience gave them the right to take charge of such things, declaring that the original Leninist principle had been "the people in arms"[26]—a polemical device that especially annoyed the Soviets. After becoming prime minister, however, Largo underwent a rapid conversion. He ordered establishment of a new central general staff on the

Table 2

Soviet personnel in Spain during the Civil War, by category (incomplete)

CATEGORY	TOTAL NUMBER	KILLED AND MISSING IN ACTION
Pilots	770	99
Tank crewmen	351	53
General military advisers and instructors	222	6
Interpreters	204	3
Engineers and specialists	131	1
Signals operators	111	—
Sailors	77	—
Artillery advisers and instructors	64	—
Coders	56	—
Anti-aircraft specialists	36	—
Other advisers and instructors	27	3
Field engineers	10	—
Medical specialists	10	—
Political workers	9	1
Fuel and chemical specialists	4	—
All categories	**2,082**	**166**

Source: Russian State Military Archives, in D. L. Kowalsky, "The Soviet Union and the Spanish Republic, 1936–1939: Diplomatic, Military, and Cultural Relations" (Ph.D. diss., University of Wisconsin–Madison, 2001), 408.

very day his government took office (September 5) and eleven days later a unified central command for all Republican forces. On September 30 he announced the incorporation of all militia officers into the new regular army and established terms for bringing the 150,000 or more militiamen under the code of military justice no later than October 20.[27]

General recruitment had already been decreed by the Giral government at the end of July and now it began to be put into effect. With its official insignia of the red star, its clenched-fist *Rot Front* salute borrowed from the German Communists, and on October 16 the installation by decree of the institution of political commissars, it became formally a Spanish variant of the Red Army.[28]

On October 18 Largo further decreed the beginning of the organization of the first six regular Mixed Brigades, the new combined-arms group that was to become the basic unit of the People's Army. Both Soviet and Spanish Republican officers subsequently took credit for originating the Mixed Brigade, which was also later criticized for overly complex combinations of arms within a comparatively small unit.[29]

The Spanish Communists had been reluctant to press the Giral government too hard for centralized militarization, for fear of playing into the hands of the ultrarevolutionaries. The PCE thus emphasized that the revolutionary militia would form the basis of the new army, though of course once the army was organized, the militia would cease to exist as such.[30] After Largo had taken charge of the government and assumed responsibility for the new military policy, the Communist leadership pressured him severely. *Mundo obrero* published a steady drumbeat of articles on the need for unity, organization, centralized militarization, and the purging of traitors in the rear guard. Virtually every single one of Largo's new measures beginning the organization of the People's Army had earlier been strongly urged by the PCE.

Despite its small size, the PCE was proportionately better prepared for civil war than any other leftist party. Only the PCE had a fully organized paramilitary force, the MAOC (mainly in Madrid), even though it numbered only a few thousand. Only the PCE had a handful of young leaders, such as Enrique Líster and Juan Modesto (prewar head of the MAOC), with genuine military training—short courses in the Frunze Academy in Moscow, with a Comintern veteran from Trieste, Vittorio Vidali ("Carlos Contreras"), already in place before the beginning of the war to supervise and coordinate its military activities.[31] Moreover, only the PCE was operated and controlled by a highly militarized and militaristic power, the Soviet Union, which would give it all manner of military advice, training, and support. Thus the Bukovina native Manfred Shtern ("General Kléber"), one of the first Soviet army officers to arrive in September, initially reported to the central committee of the PCE and to its own forces, rather than to the Republican ministry of war.[32]

All the leftist parties operated their own militia recruitment centers during the chaotic first weeks of the Civil War, but the PCE came nearer than any of the others to achieving genuine coherence. Its efforts were, as usual, concentrated especially in Madrid, though it was active in other areas as well. The existing MAOC sections in Madrid were used as an organizational cadre, which soon became known as the Quinto Regimiento (Fifth Regiment), so named because it was intended to serve as the "people's regiment" to replace the four regular army regiments that had previously formed Madrid's garrison. The Quinto Regimiento organized thousands of volunteers and set up cadre sections in other provinces to feed its recruitment. By 1937, when its efforts had been fully incorporated into the People's Army, it had organized at least 50,000 volunteers, though of course Communist propagandists claimed even more.[33] Moreover, though they insisted that all recruiting by political parties be immediately superseded by the direct draft of the People's Army, the Communists themselves maintained their own separate recruiting centers for some time.

Communist influence and participation in the key new units of the People's Army being organized in the central zone were very great from the start. As Shtern later reported, "At that time, the party had succeeded in having Largo Caballero appoint five comrades, from a list drawn up by the party, to work on the general staff, in order to have their own eyes and ears in the central leadership of the army. I was on that list as General Kléber for work in the operations department. . . . "[34] Three of the first six brigade commanders were Communist-affiliated officers. Two of the most important positions on the new general staff also went to Communist officers. Alejandro García Val was given the number two position, and he and Antonio Cordón (always rendered "Karton" in the Soviet documents) were given control of the operations section. Cordón also became head of the technical secretariat of the Undersecretariat (Subsecretaría) of War, which controlled army personnel, matériel, and supply. In addition, the Communist Major Eleuterio Díaz Tendero was made director of the army's information and control department. As head of the leftist UMRA before the war, he had kept a file on the political sympathies of army officers, and his new post gave him power to approve or reject all officers in the new army on the basis of political reliability. The party's assiduous effort before the war to enroll left-wing army officers began to pay big dividends soon after the fighting began.

In addition, Communists quickly dominated the central command of the new system of political commissars. The fellow-traveling foreign minister, Alvarez del Vayo, was soon also made director of the Political Commissariat, where the secretary general was Felipe Pretel, another Socialist of similar persuasion. Antonio Mije of the PCE's politburo became head of the organizational subcommissariat. José Laín, a young leader of the Juventud Socialista Unificada (JSU; United Socialist Youth) who had recently converted to communism, was made director of the new school for commissars, and another Communist, Pablo Clavego, quickly whipped out the first commissar's guidebook, *Algunas normas para el trabajo de los comisarios políticos* (Some rules for the work of political commissars).

An important responsibility of the three top Soviet advisers assigned to the central front—Vladimir Gorev, Kirill Meretskov, and B. M. Simonov—was to help supervise and coordinate the development of the key People's Army cadres. By late October they submitted to the Republican general staff their "Plan of First Priority Measures for the Organization of the People's Army," outlining the development of a full cadre structure with a reserve system, the training of a complete new officer corps, guerrilla units, intelligence and counter-intelligence, basic political indoctrination, development of national military industry, and building the defense of Madrid.[35] Not all of these guidelines were followed, by any means, but the plan provided a general organizational blueprint for a new Spanish revolutionary regular army, much of it modeled on the Red Army.[36]

As key adviser to the central front, Berzin and other Soviet sources gave Gorev a great deal of credit for organizing the defense of the capital. He was hardworking, relatively unobtrusive, and generally popular with the Republican military. Spanish sources generally do not give the Soviet advisers as much credit for leading the organization and planning the People's Army as do the Soviets, but there is no doubt as to the ubiquity of their role. They may not always have been able to impose their point of view, but as more of them arrived, they began to be assigned in varying strength to almost all of the far-flung Republican fronts, though they played an effective role in Catalonia only after the middle of 1937.

Soon after the beginning of the battle of Madrid, at the beginning of November, the first of the new Comintern-recruited International Brigades entered combat. This Comintern initiative, officially adopted only in mid-September, had been implemented rapidly and vigorously. Within no more than a month the first volunteers were being trained at a new base in Albacete. The chief Comintern adviser was the PCF leader André Marty, seconded by the Italian Luigi Longo.

The saga of the International Brigades created one of the most enduring myths of the Spanish war. The spectacle of these supposed "volunteers for freedom" forming an international volunteer army to combat "fascism" created a legend irresistible to left-liberal opinion around the world, echoes of which linger today. In 1995 the Spanish Socialists carried a vote in the Cortes to grant Spanish citizenship to the surviving Comintern volunteers.[37]

Soviet citizens were not themselves allowed to volunteer, but hundreds of young foreign Communists currently living in the Soviet Union were sent to Albacete. The largest single national contingent was recruited by the PCF in France, through which most of the volunteers passed on the way to Albacete. Altogether volunteers from more than a score of countries participated, and the 2,800 Americans who served almost equaled the number of Soviets who were present in Spain.

A very high percentage of volunteers were Communists, but a small minority were not, for some were simply young left-wing idealists eager to combat fascism.[38] Some really did think that they were fighting for democracy, but most were in Spain in support of the Comintern to help impose a "new type" of republic on Spain. As the American writer and International Brigades veteran William Herrick has put it, "Yes, we went to Spain to fight fascism, but democracy was not our aim."[39] Discipline was strict and further political indoctrination intensive, leading to a fairly large number of disciplinary executions.[40] The Comintern also required that volunteers entering Spain give up their passports. Some never got them back, for genuine foreign passports were extremely useful to the NKVD, particularly in the case of the new-style American passports, which were very difficult to counterfeit.[41] In addition, non-Russian Red Army officers on active duty, disguised as foreign volunteers, were placed in charge of nearly all the original brigades. They included the Bukovinan Red Army officer Manfred Shtern ("Kléber," first commander of the 11th Brigade); the Hungarian Red Army officer Mate Zalka ("Lukacs," commander of the 12th Brigade); a second Hungarian Red Army officer, Janos Galucz ("Gall," commander of the 15th Brigade); and the Polish Soviet officer Karol Swierczewski ("Sverchevsky," a veteran of both the Bolshevik Revolution and the Russian Civil War, and in Spain "Walter" or "Volter," commander of the 35th Brigade).

The total number of volunteers has been a guessing game for years. An early Soviet study reported only 31,237, while estimates by Spanish Nationalist commentators have ranged as high as 100,000. A later Soviet version cites Swierczewski as giving a total of 42,000, while the most precise Soviet study came up with the figure of 51,000.[42] The latter is the most accurate calculation, though it may include thousands of wounded who were reorganized at the Albacete base and then returned to the front, in which case the total number of foreign volunteers would have been no more than perhaps 42,000. Volunteering was not always easy. Some of the new recruits suffered considerable hardship and even imprisonment en route to Spain. Moreover, one Soviet document has reported that 300 died when the steamer *Ciutat de Barcelona* was torpedoed by an Italian submarine in May 1937.[43]

The brigades became a terrific propaganda device, but how effective were they militarily? Communist propagandists have often credited them with turning the tide in the initial defense of Madrid, but most Spanish experts in military history find this claim dubious. Franco's first assault had already been defeated before the first *brigadistas* arrived on the front. In November 1936 they never amounted to more than about 10 percent of the defenders, and it is doubtful that their role was decisive. Nonetheless, they fought bravely and made a notable contribution. For the first eight months the brigades were frequently used as shock troops. Often they fought well and suffered unusually heavy casualties, though occasionally there were breakdowns and routs. By the summer of 1937 Red Army reports on their combat effectiveness had become universally negative. They had suffered heavy casualties and the brigades were increasingly filled with Spanish draftees. By the end of 1937 they had become "international" in name only. Altogether their total combat deaths of nearly 7,000 were unusually heavy—among the most severe of any group in the war. If captured, they were likely to be treated much more harshly by the Nationalists than were Spanish Republican soldiers.[44] Between November 1936 and the summer of 1937, the period of their most intense combat, they made an important contribution to the new People's Army. Nonetheless, for nearly a year they were not under the regular command structure of the People's Army but constituted a semi-autonomous Comintern force, directed by their advisers and the Soviets. Only in September 1937 were the brigades finally brought directly under the Republican command structure, and even then did not entirely lose their special status as Comintern units.

The first notable impact of Soviet participation was felt in the air war on the crucial central front. Though the Republic had maintained control of about two-thirds of the small, obsolescent Spanish air force, that initial advantage had been lost within six weeks as the tiny Nationalist air force was reinforced by Italian and German planes, which gave the Nationalists air superiority in their rather slow drive on Madrid during September and October. The first Soviet bombers arrived by ship in mid-October and the first Polikarpov I-15s before the end of the month. All these planes, difficult for inexperienced pilots to handle, were flown by Soviet pilots. The first bombing raid by the new SB medium bombers on October 28 was indecisive, but the appearance of the fast Polikarpov fighters in combat after the first of November rapidly altered the equation of aerial combat. Nationalist planes suffered significant losses—though not nearly as great as those claimed in Soviet military reports—and Republican squadrons gained control of the skies over Madrid. As Soviet deliveries declined during the first half of 1937, the Republic lost its air superiority and had only 222 functional warplanes as of July 1. Command of the air was a major factor in the Nationalist victories that altered the balance of power between June and October of that year.

The nearly 800 Soviet pilots who flew in Spain performed important services but their utility declined during 1937 as shipments dwindled. They were often overworked, like the German and Italian pilots on the other side, and their counterpart Spanish flyers were often inadequately trained. The Soviets also suffered a high rate of mishaps, losing fourteen planes to pilot error in December 1936 alone. Altogether more than one-third of all Republican aircraft losses from October to December 15, 1938, were due to accidents.[45]

Soviet pilots declined in number during 1937 and were finally withdrawn altogether by September 1938, as Stalin became more cautious. They performed important service for the Republic, though they lacked the means to maintain air superiority for long. Overall, they were not as skilled as their German and Italian opponents and they sustained comparatively high losses. The casualty rate accelerated in 1937, when 47 of 276 Soviet pilots were killed, a fatality rate of 17 percent. The almost exact rate of loss was sustained the following year, when 31 of 183 flyers were lost. Ultimately, of the fifty-nine Soviet servicemen in Spain who were later decorated as "Heroes of the Soviet Union," the highest Soviet medal, thirty-five were airmen.[46]

The other key Soviet combat participants were the tank crewmen, who entered battle on October 29 in a mobile assault against advancing Nationalist troops at Seseña, southwest of Madrid. There the Soviet T-26s rolled through the small Nationalist units and penetrated deep into their rear, but ultimately had to be withdrawn for lack of support.[47] Though Spanish crewmen were included in the tank units from the very beginning, the number of Soviet tank crews that remained in combat declined well into 1938. Since Soviet tanks were superior to those on the opposing side, the weak Nationalist antitank guns could not readily check them at first, but those guns later improved in quality. Concentrated Soviet/Republican tank attacks could usually pierce the enemy lines, as notably in the battle of Guadalajara in March 1937, at Brunete in the following July, and in the first phase of the battle of Teruel in December 1937, but the People's Army commanders were never able to develop effective combined-arms operations, so that successful tank attacks were poorly supported and never sustained.

Though Soviet military doctrine had earlier stressed massed armor and "deep penetration,"[48] there was scant opportunity under the limited Spanish conditions to apply Soviet grand theory, which began to change with the great purge of the Red Army in 1937. Little or no effort was made to combine armor and aerial assaults. Conversely, tanks were employed effectively on the defense and in counterattacks. Committed in small numbers and sometimes piecemeal, Soviet armor was never able to contribute to a successful offensive, with the partial exception of Teruel. Franco's infantry early began to find means of coping with the enemy, and quickly developed the rudimentary flammable antitank device that would later be baptized the "Molotov cocktail" when it was used by Finnish soldiers against Soviet tanks in the Winter War of 1939–40. Thus the People's Army never managed to make any decisive use of its only continuing advantage in matériel. Soviet crewmen nonetheless continued to serve in diminishing numbers until at least the spring of 1938, fought courageously and sometimes skillfully, and had some local successes, though they won no major battles. One in every seven was killed, a fatality rate slightly higher even than that of Soviet airmen.[49] When Semyon Krivoshein, the first Soviet armor commander, was recalled after less than two months in action in December 1936, he was replaced by Dmitry Pavlov, who was so highly regarded that upon his recall to the Soviet Union in 1938 he became the Red Army's ranking tank commander.[50]

Soviet advisers and personnel played a smaller role in the Republican navy, but because of the navy's severe command deficiencies they were important there as well. Oleg Sarin and Lev Dvoretsky found evidence in the Soviet archives that "in some cases Soviet personnel commanded and manned submarines and motor torpedo boats in offensive and defensive actions," but such actions were generally limited.[51] Nikolai Kuznetsov served as chief adviser and de facto supervisor of the Republican navy for almost the entire war and was promoted upon his return to Moscow, ending World War II as commander in chief of the Soviet navy.[52] The initially superior Republican navy was increasingly kept on the defensive and rarely struck a telling blow. From late 1936 on, the somewhat smaller but much more combat-worthy Nationalist fleet seized the offensive and became ever more aggressive during the main part of the war. In this area the Soviet contribution was less important, but still had some significance in giving slightly greater cohesion to the Republican navy.

Soviet supervision played a more important role yet in Republican guerrilla operations, for these were directed by Aleksandr Orlov and his NKVD agents. Orlov has claimed that by July 1937 he was training 1,600 guerrilleros in six schools and that 14,000 were already operating behind Nationalist lines; all these claims are probably exaggerated. It is interesting to reflect that if the Robert Jordan of Ernest Hemingway's For Whom the Bell Tolls had ever existed, he would have been working for Orlov and the NKVD. Nationalist intelligence calculated that about 3,600 Republican guerrilleros were active in the final phase of the war.[53] Despite the glowing but meretricious reports that Orlov sent back to Moscow and an occasional real success behind Nationalist lines, Republican guerrilla operations were in general not very effective and rarely caused serious complications behind Franco's lines. One limiting factor that was not present in either the Russian Civil War or the Soviet campaigns in World War II was the generally firm control the Nationalists enjoyed in most sectors of their rear guard. Barton Whealey's conclusion is convincing: "The Loyalist government's guerrillas constituted only ancillary . . . forces" and "at most . . . achieved marginal success." He notes further that such operations were of less use to the Spanish Republicans than for the Soviets themselves "as a laboratory for limited testings of new equipment and some minor tactics."[54] Leonid Eitingon, Orlov's deputy in charge of guerrilla operations, was also deputy chief of such operations for the Soviet Union during World War II, and sometimes employed Spanish Communists in this work.

The three hundred or more Soviet military engineers in the Republican zone had three major tasks: maintenance of the Soviet equipment, training and supervision of Republican maintenance staff, and development of the Republican military industry. The Soviet government made available a number of key patents to the Republican arms industry, which managed to complete production of approximately three hundred Polikarpov I-15s and I-16s during the final year of the war. Catalan and Levantine industry also produced other airplanes, motors, trucks, artillery, machine guns, and a wide variety of ammunition, but the production totals remained limited. Mobilization and development of war industry never enjoyed more than minor successes and were a chief target of Soviet complaints. Ambassador Pascua reported that when he personally asked Stalin for more matériel in February 1938, Stalin complained that the Republicans did not "have a deep interest in your own production. You could be doing much more."[55]

Soviet advisers, limited by their numbers and by their general ignorance of Spanish, seem to have played a relatively small role in the training of new recruits and officers of the People's Army. Though they helped to develop the training facilities and programs of the new mass army, they were not present in numbers equivalent to those of their German counterparts in Franco's training programs, which were more professional and generally superior to those of the Republicans. It is sometimes difficult to evaluate just how important and influential the Soviet personnel were in the Republican war effort. The senior advisers sometimes suffered from attempts by Voroshilov and other commanders in Moscow to micromanage operations and strategy in a war the Soviet military bosses did not understand as well as they thought they did. Moreover, many advisers were called upon to undertake extremely complex tasks for which they were simply not adequately prepared. In addition, the massive purge of Red Army commanders in the Soviet Union inevitably had at least some effect on the morale and initiative of the Soviet personnel in Spain.[56] The key contributions of airmen and tank crewmen are clear enough, but what is harder to determine is whether or not the advisers were as dominant in the development and direction of the People's Army as they claimed in their reports to Moscow. Altogether 584 Soviet advisers served in Spain, 100 being sent in 1936, 150 in 1937, 250 in 1938, and possibly as many as 84 in the first months of 1939, though each served a comparatively brief tour of duty.[57] They played a role in some of the training programs and certainly they enjoyed an advisory status on all the main fronts. Conversely, Colonel Vicente Rojo, the Catholic professional officer who soon became Republican chief of staff, may have been the most able strategist on either side in the Civil War. He was no puppet of the Soviets, though he listened very carefully to their advice. Soviet advisory assistance definitely played its part in enabling the Republic to create as much of a regular army as it did, and was probably most important on the central front late in 1936 and early in 1937.

Several Republican brigades were directly commanded for months by Soviet officers, and since Spanish Communist officers came to command many of the best Republican units, and indeed a significant proportion of all Republican units during 1937–38, there developed a concentration of Communist command in large parts of the Republican army. The nature of its strategy and performance cannot be understood if the large Communist presence is not taken into account. Yet many Republican units were not commanded by Communists, and in much of the People's Army the Soviet role was merely advisory. The result was a complex set of arrangements in which both Soviets and Spanish Communist commanders were of major importance, but did not produce an army merely controlled by Communists *tout court*. In addition, the Communist identity of some of the Republican officers who joined the PCE was not merely newfound but also shallow, as the events of March 1939 would demonstrate. The semipluralism that existed in Republican Spain generally also existed within the People's Army, despite the undeniable Communist hegemony over the best-equipped and most combat-worthy units during 1937 and 1938.

One of several ways in which the Soviet advisers constituted a problem rather than a solution lay in the autonomous control they exercised over key sections, such as the armor, the most important air units, and the International Brigades. This control gave them predominant influence in the most important aspects of Republican strategy and helped to determine the way the war was fought. As Michael Alpert concludes, "Russian control of Soviet tanks and planes was, of course, another matter and there is abundant proof that aviation was not controlled by the Spanish and that planes were often unavailable when needed."[58]

There is no doubt that the Soviet advisers were often overweening and controlling, even though their efforts to dominate were often not completely successful. Even Comintern advisers occasionally complained about the insistence of Red Army officers on trying to control the Spanish Communist and other Republican military, pointing out that the Spanish Communist officers could not be expected to develop fully without greater autonomy. A major goal of Soviet advisers was to overcome the internal division that plagued the Republicans, but their tendency toward domination, particularly on the central front, added to internal tensions and produced a negative political reaction in the long run.

To this problem must be added the strictly military limitations and failures of Soviet advisers, some of whom even Voroshilov admitted were not well prepared for their roles.[59] Potentially fruitful proposals were sometimes vetoed because they stemmed from noncommunist sources. In this regard it is sometimes difficult to distinguish the limitations of the Soviet advisers from the many limitations of the People's Army in general. Operations remained relatively simplistic and lacked coordination, sometimes relying on Soviet-style frontal charges en masse. Conversely, aerial and naval activity became almost exclusively defensive. The Soviets inevitably contributed to the climate of paranoia in military affairs, but suspicion was already at a high level because of the extreme polarization and fragmentation of Republican politics.

The Soviet advisers also had their full share of personal failings. In the Soviet reports one finds complaints of drunkenness and of slovenly dress and behavior. The highest ranking Soviet commanders were well aware that smooth working relations were often not established with the Spanish military, and Soviet reports contained many complaints about the lack of tact shown by Soviet officers in their dealings with their Spanish counterparts, even to the point of "rudely interfering with operation instructions of commanders." Clashes with the wide-ranging security and intelligence activities of the NKVD were not unknown, and the NKVD managed to have at least five advisers sent back to the Soviet Union for political reasons.[60] Cultural differences between the spontaneous and egalitarian Spaniards and the disciplined and hierarchical Soviets could be profound, but here the personality of individual Soviet officers might make a crucial difference. Most Soviet personnel's ignorance of Spanish significantly hampered relations. Nearly 10 percent of Soviet personnel came to be translators—a high percentage, but one that considerably ameliorated the problem. Typically, an individual adviser would not remain in Spain more than five to six months, and such a short tour of duty made it difficult to build experience.[61]

Many of the older advisers soon suffered a dire fate in the purges, beginning with the GRU and NKVD supervisors in Moscow, Semyon Uritsky and Avram Slutsky. Senior advisers such as Jan Berzin, Vladimir Gorev, Manfred Shtern, the senior aviation adviser Yakov Smushkevich, and a fair number of others perished, as did the three top Soviet civilian diplomats in Spain and the leading correspondent, Stalin's personal friend Mikhail Koltsov. The bulk of the younger officers and ordinary personnel survived and normally rose in rank during World War II. Some, such as I. S. Konev, Nikolai Kuznetsov, Rodion Malinovsky, and Dmitry Pavlov, eventually reached the summit of the Soviet military command structure.

The Spanish Republican People's Army never became a fully cohesive skilled army, though it sometimes fought well enough. After the first months, the armies on both sides were made up of conscripts, and it is not surprising if many of these recruits participated in the fratricide with less than full enthusiasm. The Soviet advisers did not award high marks to Franco's infantry even during the early phases, judging that only the Legionnaires and Moroccans fought really well. The Republican *milicianos* were even worse, however, and the People's Army never managed to overcome manifold limitations, only a part of which were due to limited weaponry. Thus the Nationalist general José Solchaga might well confide to his diary, "Fortunately for us, the Reds are even worse!"[62]

Militarily the Spanish Civil War was overall a low-intensity war punctuated by occasional battles of high intensity. There is no question, however, that despite significant limitations and even some counterproductive effects, the Soviet assistance postponed the Republicans' defeat, though at no time was it of sufficient magnitude to give them a major chance for victory. Hitler's position was not much more decisive. The difference for Franco was that Mussolini, unlike the other two dictators, made a major commitment to victory in Spain, and the technical quality of the Germans' assistance, while often of no greater volume than the Soviets' and sometimes smaller, was very distinctly higher.

Overall, the German and Italian counterescalation of November and December 1936 raised the stakes to a point where Stalin was not willing to make a direct bid for victory, but sought only to maintain Republican resistance in the hope of more favorable geostrategic conditions in the future.

CHAPTER NINE

The Policy Struggle under the Largo Caballero Government

September 1936–May 1937

SOVIET POLICY MAKERS were dissatisfied with the Largo Caballero government from the beginning, but accepted it as a reasonable start toward a viable Popular Front government. The development and comparatively rapid growth of the People's Army were gratifying; September and October were a time of frenzied activity, both in military mobilization and in Communist expansion. The new prime minister tried to follow the official line, declaring that his government was merely fighting for the "democratic Republic" and sought to uphold the "Republican constitution."[1] Within less than a month he even called the first rump session of the Cortes since the fighting began. As Burnett Bolloten has observed, it was a strange parliament because so many of the opposition deputies had either fled or been executed. Nonetheless, the left Republican *Política* would declare on December 2 that "the Republic confirms the existence of a flourishing and vigorous constitutional life," even though mass arbitrary executions had not yet come to an end. The same claim was repeated energetically by Republican diplomatic representatives abroad. Largo declared to the foreign press that the People's Army was merely fighting for "the parliamentary regime of the Republic," and he assured a delegation of visiting British MPs that "the Spanish government is not fighting for socialism but for democracy and constitutional rule."[2]

In this connection the largely impotent presidency of Manuel Azaña filled a dual role: for foreign consumption he provided the best symbol of the putative survival of a democratic republic, while internally he was the chief of state whom the disparate members of the Popular Front found least divisive.[3] He had few illusions about what was really going on in the Republican zone and believed that military defeat was probably inevitable. His only hope was to carry on resistance long enough to elicit intervention or mediation by the Western democracies, though he realized that neither was likely. Moreover, he fully understood that the revolution had more than marginalized the middle-class Republican left, who in fact faced no future if the People's Army should win a clear-cut victory. Later, in mid-1937, he remarked to his coreligionist the distinguished medievalist Claudio Sánchez Albornoz: "The war is lost, absolutely lost, and, if by a miracle it were won, we Republicans would have to embark on the first boat that left Spain—if they allowed us to"—the typical lament of a Kerenskyist.[4] Nonetheless, though he moved out of Madrid to Valencia on October 19, Azaña firmly maintained the camouflage of Republican democracy and constitutionalism.

Growth of the PCE

The Communist Party grew rapidly, though its numbers could not match the mass worker following of the CNT and UGT. Whereas membership had totaled 50,000–60,000 on the eve of the Civil War, eight months later, in a report of March 1937, Díaz would claim a membership of 249,140, of whom purportedly 87,660 (35.2 percent) were industrial workers, 62,250 (25 percent) were farmworkers, 76,700 (30.7 percent) were landowners or tenant farmers, 15,485 (6.2 percent) belonged to the urban middle classes, and 7,045 (2.9 percent) were from the professional classes and the intelligentsia.[5] The second line of Communist organization was the Juventud Socialista Unificada (JSU), for whom Santiago Carrillo claimed a (doubtless inflated) membership of 150,000 at the beginning of the war and 300,000 by April 1937,[6] while the PSUC claimed to have grown rapidly to 45,000 members.

The PCE was governed by a secretariat and a politburo of eight members, and the Central Committee now had forty-five members. The administrative structure was divided into eight sections,[7] and the party was organized on four levels: the local cell (theoretically of five members), local sections called *radios,* district *(comarca)* sections, and provincial sections. All but the first level were administered by their own committees, with their own secretariats, and by 1937 the system was broadly organized throughout the Republican zone.

The party grew paradoxically first as a party of revolution but second as a party of order. In addressing the only revolution to have appeared anywhere in Western and Central Europe for nearly two decades—and certainly the greatest direct revolution of workers to have ever occurred anywhere—Communists could present themselves as the only movement with a successful experience and understanding of revolution. Amid the continued crisis of civil war and revolution this claim attracted a significant number on the left and among the lower classes who had been unaffiliated. At the same time, the PCE grew as a leftist party of order, albeit of revolutionary order, which—unlike the anarchists, POUM, or even the Socialists—concentrated on formal unity, discipline, organization, military priorities, and the maintenance of an advanced mixed economy protected at least in part from direct collectivization. Available evidence indicates that the PCE attracted some of the most radical new affiliates, but also those who were seeking a more coherent and disciplined leftist party to prosecute the war, as well as lower-middle-class members—according to PCE data, 76,700 of them—who owned or operated their own farms. More regular army officers who served in the People's Army joined the PCE than any other party because of its emphasis on unity, discipline, and priority for the war, while lower-middle-class property owners sometimes joined it as protection against indiscriminate collectivization. Similarly, the party continued to take care to attract intellectuals, offering them special facilities. Finally, thousands of people seem to have joined the party during the second half of 1936 and the first part of 1937 simply because it was getting stronger and stronger, and appeared to have the most coherent policy for dealing with power.

The Comintern advisers were gratified by the sudden growth of the PCE into a mass party, larger in total members than the Socialist Party though totally lacking the Socialists' very large trade-union following. Eventually, however, they became concerned over the fact that no more than 35 percent of the membership consisted of workers and were stung by the anarchist charge that the PCE was "the political party of the petite bourgeoisie." Thus a report to Moscow at the end of March 1937 insisted that the party must "radically expand" its worker base.[8]

With the possible exception of the POUM, the PCE was much more centralized, unified, and clearly organized than any of the other worker parties, though not to the extent indicated by the formal Comintern organization chart. A succession of dramatic events, coupled with rapid growth in membership and serious problems in communications as well as internal alterations in the party, produced more than a little confusion. The chaos of the first weeks of the Civil War to some extent disrupted intraparty coordination. Local sections sometimes had to be left momentarily autonomous. Though local leaders generally sought to follow Comintern guidelines, local sections in a few instances exceeded them by participating more extensively in social and economic revolution than was theoretically allowed.[9] The most egregious case developed in Vizcaya, where the Basque Communist leadership followed autonomous, even nationalist policies until the provincial party leader was eventually expelled.

The Comintern advisers complained throughout the war about the shortcomings in the party organization and much of the party leadership. They emphasized with pride the party's achievements in military development but lamented that they had not been accompanied by equivalent development of the party organizational structure. An evaluation of October 14, 1936, declared the functioning of the PCE's politburo to be "shockingly primitive," with too much disoriented talk, while another of March 28, 1937, stressed that structural weaknesses persisted and many organizational problems had not been overcome. Even at the latter date Ibárruri was said to have no full-time assistant and had to type the drafts of her own press material, while Díaz had only two technical assistants.[10]

After years of constant prodding by Moscow to be more revolutionary and "form soviets," even the national leaders of the party had difficulty in fully adjusting to the much more nuanced and complex tactic of the Popular Front. The Popular Front had been fully operational for only a month or two when the Civil War further changed the equation. Even Comintern advisers sometimes had to scramble to keep up. Codovilla had been caught badly off base during the first days of fighting, and two other high-level advisers, Boris Stepanov and Erno Gero, were soon dispatched to Madrid and Barcelona respectively to provide firmer guidance. They were followed by the top Hispanophone PCF leaders, André Marty and Jacques Duclos, and by others. While the Comintern bosses continued to try to micromanage as best they could from Moscow, the top advisers on the scene in Spain did not always agree among themselves. As a leader of a West European party, Marty was disgusted by the "intolerable" arrogance of the often obtuse Codovilla, complaining to Moscow that "Codovilla views the party as his own property." Since Codovilla also proved sometimes inept in transmitting Comintern guidelines effectively, Marty sneered that he ought simply to become a leader of the PCE itself and leave the advising to someone better qualified. In several of his reports Soviet ambassador Rosenberg echoed these criticisms.

Creation of the PSUC had only compounded the problem, creating a completely separate organizational structure and a new set of leaders to deal with, and requiring a regular Comintern adviser in Barcelona. Gero, not surprisingly, drew criticism from his Comintern colleagues in Madrid, though the PSUC quickly proved itself to be a political success.[11]

War and Revolution

All the worker parties were in favor of pursuing war and revolution at the same time, but they differed very substantially in the weight to be given each side of the equation. During August the PCE had been partly on the defensive, unable to challenge directly all the centrifugal excesses of the extreme left. Formation of the Largo Caballero government made it possible to begin the restoration of a more centralized Republican state and to press more directly for the main points of the Communist program, just as it had made it more appropriate to send sizable Soviet military assistance.

Though Largo Caballero, partly with Communist assistance, began the organization of a mass, disciplined, and organized People's Army, his honeymoon with the Communists lasted no more than a few weeks. What caballeristas and Communists meant by unity and priority for the war effort seemed to differ more than a little. The new prime minister was willing to defer the collectivist revolution only to a limited degree. On October 2 he declared in *Claridad* that at the close of the war "the structure of the country" would have to "change completely" in the social and economic order and become "a true republic of workers."

The Comintern advisers reported to Moscow that although the party was rapidly growing stronger and achieving success in military organization, it was not getting adequate cooperation from the prime minister. He protected the interests of the anarchists and extreme revolutionaries, and did not implement policies that would build maximal strength and unity, showing little interest in purging incompetents, "traitors," and "saboteurs." He had insisted on combining the Ministry of War with the presidency of the government, but lacked the leadership skill and administrative ability for such power. PCE leaders worked hard to persuade Largo to create a general defense committee that would bring in representatives from all the parties but also enable the Communists to have a more direct voice in military policy. Largo refused, and soon became increasingly resistant to further extension of the Communists' influence at the senior command level, seeking to reduce the extensive influence they had already acquired.

The PCE also pressed for government control of industry and finance, with nationalization of certain key industries but avoidance of general collectivization. Thus its spokesmen had hailed the few categorical economic actions of the Giral government, such as its extension of state control over all electrical power companies in decrees of August 14 and 20 and September 1, as major "revolutionary achievements" that began creation of a new "state capitalism" appropriate for the Popular Front's semipluralist phase of economic transformation.[12] Full collectivization was rejected as wasteful, centrifugal, and harmful to the lower middle classes without providing any commensurate economic or political advantages.

The only area in which the Communists conceded the legitimacy of partial collectivization lay in agriculture, and then only on carefully defined terms. A great deal of de facto collectivization in agriculture had already been carried out, primarily by the CNT and the UGT, during the first two months of the war, and the pressure here was great. Although it has its own distinct character, it was somewhat reminiscent of the pressure that Lenin had had to face in Russia during the Russian Civil War and also during the subsequent compromise period of the New Economic Policy (NEP) from 1921 to 1928. Agriculture was one of the two portfolios held by the party in the new government, having been placed in the veteran hands of the Politburo member Vicente Uribe. He in turn appointed the key party troubleshooter Enrique Castro Delgado as head of the Instituto de Reforma Agraria (IRA), from which to channel the agrarian revolution. The Comintern considered it very important to guarantee the property and support of the lower middle and even middle middle classes in the countryside so long as they had not already rallied to the insurgents. Collectivization should be restricted to the properties of the latter elements and to the latifundists. Thus in a key decree of October 7 Uribe declared the official confiscation without indemnity of all agrarian property belonging to all those who were involved either directly or indirectly in the rebellion against the left. It stated that large units would pass into the hands of collectives, except that all those who were already renters of small operations on such properties would continue to have permanent use of such lands (together with the stipulation that each such unit not exceed thirty hectares of unirrigated land, five hectares in irrigated areas, or three hectares of fruit trees). This latter provision was intended once more to protect the lower middle class while legalizing the expropriation of a large amount of land. That same day *Frente rojo* enthused that it "is the most profoundly revolutionary action carried out since the military rising. . . . More than 40 percent of private property in the countryside has been annulled." In fact, as Bolloten has pointed out, nearly all—if indeed not every bit of—such property in the Republican zone had already been seized by the

CNT, UGT, or POUM, but now a Communist minister would claim official credit for the confiscation.

Both the CNT and the spokesmen of the farm laborers of the Socialist FNTT declared that the measure was inadequate and should be extended across the board to all capitalist landed property, and especially to all landowners, no matter the size of their property, who had ever at any time in the past opposed the left. But many of those landowners were exactly those whom this measure was designed to protect, and the ministry proposed to spare small and medium owners, particularly, who might be conservative in their attitudes but had not overtly supported the rightist revolt. Uribe's position was that henceforth any further collectivization beyond the terms of the decree should be strictly voluntary, and thus in the following months tension with the two great syndical confederations was extreme. Their leaders insisted that the agrarian reform remained altogether incomplete because some farm laborers still remained without land or a place in a collective. One of the most tense situations lay in the Levant, where anarchists denounced the fact that prosperous fruit-tree owners of the old Partido Autonomista had been allowed into the UGT, and this conflict continued into 1937.[13]

Uribe insisted that all violence and disorder in the countryside must end because it was alienating supporters of the Republic and, equally important, because it was dislocating vital production. He was of course supported by other spokesmen of the movement, Santiago Carrillo insisting to doubters in the JSU that even the Soviet Union had waited nine years to collectivize agriculture.[14]

The Defense of Madrid

The military crisis began to reach a climax at the beginning of November, when Franco's small columns finally neared Madrid. The Largo Caballero government had no confidence that the capital could be held but was determined to continue the struggle even if it fell. On the evening of November 6 Largo and his colleagues fled to Valencia, after breaking open the safe deposit boxes in the Banco de España and carrying off all the contents.[15] Command of the capital was left in the hands of a new military leader, General José Miaja, together with a newly appointed Junta de Defensa de Madrid. The first of the International Brigades arrived just after Franco's initial weak assault had been beaten off.

The Communist leadership realized that a major opportunity had opened for them: the possibility of seizing the leadership and reaping the propaganda advantages of a successful defense of the capital, abandoned by the regular government. Their emphasis on military strength now paid political dividends. Of the ten members of the junta, only two were officially Communists, but two others were pro-Communist Socialists, such as Carrillo (who would soon formally join the party), and Miaja himself would also join the party, assuring the Communists half of the votes on the junta. Half did not guarantee full control, and considerable conflict developed with the CNT members of the junta, but it provided determined leadership for a city under assault.[16]

The junta imposed a ruthless policy of public order and security. More than two thousand political prisoners (and possibly as many as three thousand) were removed from the city's jails and executed en masse at Paracuellos del Jarama and other sites east of the capital. Since many of those executed were army officers, the operation became a sort of Spanish Katyn, a preview of the grisly operation in Belarus in 1940 in which Stalin liquidated 20,000 members of the former Polish army's officer corps. It also foreshadowed Soviet policy in the summer of 1941 when Soviet police executed tens of thousands of political prisoners in the cities of western Russia as their forces retreated before the German advance. Since the JSU leader Santiago Carrillo was the junta's head of security, in charge of police, he has usually been assigned the principal responsibility for the mass liquidation.[17]

During the defense of Madrid the comparison with the Russian Revolution and the defense of Petrograd in 1919 came heavily to the fore, pressed vigorously by Communist propagandists. This campaign was to some extent inaugurated by the Soviet journalist A. Golubev with his article "Madrid in 1936 and Petrograd in 1919," which appeared in *Izvestia* on October 24. At one point Soviet planes flew over the Spanish capital trailing a banner reading "Imitate Petrograd!" The evidence suggests that some of the defenders of Madrid did indeed take courage from the Russian example, but if they did, the boost to their morale may have been attributable less to the popularity of the PCE—itself only relative—than to the power of the Russo-Soviet myth of successful revolution, which had always exerted a certain psychological appeal on the Spanish left. This battle was also the part of the Spanish war in which the role of Soviet assistance was most obvious and dramatic, even though the immense majority of the city's defenders were native Spaniards. The commander, Miaja, was a circumspect political moderate willing to cooperate fully with the Soviets. He benefited greatly from having the best chief of staff in the People's Army, Colonel Vicente Rojo, who, though Catholic, tended toward the political left and also worked very well with the Soviets. The defense of Madrid was designed by the shrewd and erudite Rojo, together with Vladimir Gorev, the Soviet military attaché, assigned as chief adviser to the Madrid front. The newly arrived Soviet matériel was indispensable and the Soviet air and tank crews played important roles, while the first International Brigades participated in some of the most intense fighting. The stimulus in prestige and power that their presence gave the PCE, together with the party's key role in the Madrid Defense Junta, was very great.

Soon after the Madrid front stabilized, around the beginning of December, the Spanish capital was apparently visited by Avram Slutsky, the NKVD chief of foreign intelligence and Orlov's supervisor. On his return to Paris, Slutsky is reported to have been favorably impressed, even though he was not unaware of Republican weaknesses, which "must be firmed up." Krivitsky quotes him as concluding: "After all, it is our Spain now, part of the Soviet front. We must make it solid for us."[18]

The Communist Victory Plan

The Communist leadership now felt strong enough to launch a major manifesto, released by the central committee on December 18 and known as *Las ocho condiciones de la victoria* (The eight conditions of victory). It restated in detail all the basic Communist theses about unity, discipline, and prioritizing the war. The Communist position on social and economic issues was firmly stated:

> The accusations made against us from time to time, saying that we are sacrificing the goals of the revolution in order to win the war, are, aside from being perfidious, puerile. The struggle to win the war is inseparably united to the development of the revolution. But if we do not win the war, the revolution will fail. This idea must penetrate deeply within the masses if we are to avoid stifling the war effort. We fight to create a better society in which it will be impossible to repeat such criminal and monstrous deeds as this rebellious subversion. But all the dreamers and irresponsible elements who seek to carry out in their own town or province projects of 'socialism' or 'libertarian communism' or of any other kind must be made to see that all such efforts will come crashing down like a castle of cards if the fascists are not annihilated. . . .
>
> Our Party—a responsibly revolutionary party that does not toy with the interests of the working masses, but struggles and labors without rest to unify the masses in the battle—does not want to sacrifice them in vain, does not want to attempt premature revolu-

tionary experiments at the expense of the workers, but to create the necessary conditions for their triumph. And today the necessary conditions for the triumph of the working masses are summed up in just one: combine every effort toward a single objective: winning the war.

The manifesto then summarized the Communist program in eight basic points. The four economic points were: (1) nationalization and reorganization of the "basic industries, and above all of war industries"; (2) creation of a "Coordinating Council of industry and the economy in general, in which are represented all the technicians and specialists of the Popular Front, so that this high state organism can orient and direct production and have everyone observe and apply their decisions"; (3) establishment of worker control over production, "with the organs charged with applying it acting in accord with the plan prepared by the Coordinating Council"; (4) agricultural production of "what is needed for the front and the rear guard on the basis of a plan established by representatives of farm organizations and the parties and organizations of the Popular Front, including respect for the product of the agrarian masses' labor, whether individual or collective, and a guarantee to agrarian producers of a remunerative price for their products, as well as national and international markets."[19] This was a practical presocialist plan essentially similar to Lenin's New Economic Policy of 1921, which had been introduced at a time when Russian Communist leaders had recognized major obstacles to the immediate establishment of socialism in Russia.

At this point the Communist leadership seemed to be entering a period of euphoria, reflecting the growth in military and political strength in recent months. A long report by Codovilla on December 24 made extravagant claims, declaring that support was rising on almost every side, that Communists held 80 percent of the command positions in the army and a "majority" of the important posts in the Republican police, and were receiving bountiful assistance from other groups. The left Republicans and the Masonic elements led by Diego Martínez Barrio were said to be cooperating fully, while broad support existed among the Socialists for fusion with the PCE.[20] The report contained more than a little hyperbole, as was customary with Codovilla, but was accurate in drawing attention to the surprising expansion of Communist influence.

The main internal political problem was how to deal with the anarchosyndicalists and their libertarian revolution. The Soviet military attaché, Vladimir Gorev, had reported to Moscow on September 25 that the anarchists' support was indispensable for victory, but that this would be only the end of the first round, for "a struggle against the anarchists is absolutely inevitable after victory over the Whites. This struggle will be very harsh." André Marty presented the same conclusion in more detail to the ECCI Secretariat on October 10, saying the anarchists' support was needed at present, but that "after the war we will get even with them, all the more since at that point we will have a strong army."[21]

The CNT and the POUM

For its part, the CNT had never had any policy for taking power, nor for that matter did its leaders have any intention of trying to do so at the present time. Thus in Catalonia the CNT controlled only part of a dual power structure, enjoying untrammeled direct rule only in the newly established Council of Aragon, which governed eastern Aragon.[22] The CNT's war policy was to build some kind of revolutionary confederation with other worker groups to prosecute the revolution and wage the war at the same time, an amorphous formula that lacked concreteness and practicality. The earlier proposal for a CNT-UGT national defense junta having been thwarted by formation of the Largo Caballero government, the CNT's leaders then negotiated with the prime minister intermittently for two months before finally swallowing their anarchist principles on November 3 to enter a reorganized Largo Caballero government in which they held four ministries. This settlement finally realized the goal of a coalition government representing all the major leftist forces, but it was an unwieldy one that now consisted of no fewer than eighteen ministries and remained strongly divided.

The nearest thing to a clear-cut revolutionary ally of the CNT was the POUM, which had also expanded with the revolution, but since it started from a very small base, it never developed on the scale of the larger movements. By December POUM spokesmen claimed that party membership had grown in five months from 6,000 to 30,000, however, and its revolutionary line was even more clear and conclusive than that of the anarchists.[23] With the disappearance of Maurín, the secretary general, the ultradoctrinaire Nin became acting head of the party as political secretary (since a new secretary general could be chosen only by a full party congress). Nin insisted that after the first days of combat in Barcelona the workers must keep their arms, so that they could eliminate the bourgeoisie at home even as they made their way to the front. Capitalism in Spain had definitely collapsed and the Cortes belonged "in a museum of antiquities." POUM leaders invited the FAI-CNT to join them in a real "worker democracy," which would constitute the dictatorship of the proletariat. In a major speech in Barcelona's Teatro Gran Price on September 6, Nin trivialized the war, whose principal consequence had been to speed up "the revolutionary process, provoking a proletarian revolution more profound than the Russian revolution itself." The revolutionary militia would all alone become the new Spanish Red Army and win the war directly. He fulminated: "The struggle in Spain is not for the democratic Republic. A new dawn rises in the skies of our country. This new dawn is the socialist Republic."[24] POUM publicists denounced the Popular Front as a bourgeois compromise, which they argued had been responsible for the Civil War, holding implausibly that if the worker left had moved directly to creation of a worker regime in the spring of 1936, there would have been no such conflict.

The party's central committee had voted to foster the establishment of a Soviet-style regime in Spain. Its "Resolution," published on September 18, declared the need to "transform radically the entire political and social structure of the Republic." This task "requires the formation of a worker government, which, abandoning altogether the preceding republican-bourgeois legality, will immediately convene a new Constituent Cortes, elected by Committees of Workers, Peasants, and Combatants, to establish the constitution of the new regime produced by the revolution. Any attempt to restrict the current magnificent uprising to the limits of the democratic-bourgeois Republic must be combated implacably as counterrevolutionary."[25] The FAI-CNT naturally rejected as too statist this demand to apply an immediate ultra-Leninist formula to the Spanish revolution—that is, the Leninist formula of 1917–18 as contrasted to his economic policy of 1921—exposing once more the deep Leninist/anarchist fissure that divided the extreme revolutionary left.

One measure that the Barcelona left did agree upon was the immediate extension of the revolution across the straits of Gibraltar to northern Morocco. Until 1935 the independence of Morocco had been a standard demand of both the PCF and PCE, but adoption of the Popular Front had brought a change in the Comintern line. CNT leaders began negotiations with Moroccan nationalists in August about the possibility of granting the protectorate full autonomy, if not independence, in return for a nationalist revolt, supported by the Republic, which would overwhelm the rebels' rear guard and recruitment base in Morocco and threaten to change the balance of power in the war. Negotiations finally led to signature of a pact on September 20 between the nationalist leaders and the forces represented in the Comité Central de Milicias Antifascistas. It promised full autonomy for the protectorate on these terms and pledged the signatories to work for a similar arrangement for French Morocco. A delegation composed of representatives of the FAI-CNT, Esquerra, UGT-PSUC, and POUM then went to Madrid on the 26th to try to persuade the new Largo Caballero government to accept the pact. After several days of negotiations, this effort failed. The Republican government still sought France's good will, and the proposal also contradicted the legalitarian line of the Comintern. In Paris the PCF maintained its posture of a *front français* and proclaimed support for French foreign and colonial policy as part of French defensive patriotism. The failure of the attempted revolutionary démarche in colonial policy marked the first total defeat for the revolutionary extreme left.[26] As usual, the PCE tried to square the circle by making an independent propaganda appeal to the Moroccans to rise up against Franco.

Barcelona continued to lead in the institutionalization of the revolutionary process and had produced an all-left government five weeks earlier than Madrid. There the CNT became increasingly frustrated in its efforts to turn the Comité Central de Milicias into a ruling syndical defense junta and also failed in its independent efforts to import arms. When it had finally become clear during the course of September that the main source of military procurement would have to be a regular government, the CNT leaders had been told again and again that they would not receive assistance until they entered a regular government in Catalonia. Thus on September 26 the young Esquerra leader Josep Tarradellas succeeded in forming a new government of the Generalitat that was even more complete than the second Largo Caballero administration because it included not merely three ministries for the CNT but also that of Justice for Nin, out of a total of twelve portfolios in the government. To that extent the realities of civil war had forced an abrupt change of policy on both the CNT and the POUM in Catalonia.

The CNT controlled the Ministry of Defense and still retained its local *patrullas de control*, whereas in Madrid (at least theoretically), the local patrols and death squads had been nominally incorporated into a rear-guard Milicia de Vigilancia on September 28. Conversely, the CNT nominally accepted a decree of the Tarradellas government on October 9 that ordered dissolution of all local revolutionary committees in Catalonia, the first clear-cut counterrevolutionary measure in the region.

The Comintern had supported formation of a broader government in Catalonia that included the anarchists, but the Moscow bosses were enraged by the inclusion of the "Trotskyist" POUM. Erno Gero had to send back contrite messages, reporting on October 19 that this step had been necessary to win the adhesion of the anarchists, and more correctly characterizing the POUM as "half-Trotskyist." In Madrid, Codovilla was still unhappy about the creation of the PSUC, declaring that its actions in joining such a government showed that within it "there are elements with a Trotskyizing mentality," and warning on October 13 that the PSUC showed signs of wanting to "emancipate itself from the political assistance of the Communist Party of Spain" and that it harbored "nationalist and socialist elements . . . whom our comrades have not been able to dominate."[27]

From this time on Communist pressure against the POUM mounted, on direct orders from Moscow. At a time when so-called Trotskyism had been made a centerpiece of the show trials in Moscow, it was deemed intolerable that an anti-Stalinist "Trotskyism" of any sort flourished in Spain. Trotsky himself was currently living in Norway, which was under heavy pressure from Moscow to expel him. Though *La Batalla* in fact engaged in harsh criticism of Trotsky, Nin still had great personal regard for his former mentor and by early August persuaded the POUM central committee to invite him to come to live in Barcelona. Trotsky apparently wrote a letter declaring his acceptance, but it was intercepted by the Italian political police, and Companys forbade the invitation, knowing that the anarchists also hated the "butcher" Trotsky, who had participated in the liquidation of libertarians in Russia.

For that matter, Trotsky had sharply criticized the POUM ever since its founding for being inadequately revolutionary. On July 16, as the war was about to begin, he had denounced Maurín's entire policy as "nationalistic-provincial and petit-bourgeois; reactionary in its entire essence," and called Nin "a completely passive dilettante." On July 30 he had similarly denounced "the reactionary cowardice of the Popular Front" in toto. Nonetheless, during the early weeks of the Civil War there had been little difference between his own prescriptions for the Spanish revolution and those of the POUM, while he reserved his greatest ire for all the other Popular Front parties. He then denounced the POUM for having entered the Catalan government, as well as for having merged its syndical organization, the FOUS, with the Catalan UGT (a policy that Trotsky himself had once urged), which he said showed a complete lack of revolutionary resolve. His latest demand was that the POUM merge with the CNT.[28] It refused to do so, calculating that it would be swamped in an anarchosyndicalist movement that was approaching a membership of two million. As it turned out, the POUM quickly lost all influence in the UGT as well.

The real Trotskyists, meanwhile, were insignificant. After the Civil War began, a tiny handful of diehard Trotskyists from the old Izquierda Comunista formed a new "Sección Bolchevique-Leninista" (SB-L; Bolshevik-Lenin Section).

When the SB-L and its leader, "G. Munis" (Manuel Fernández Grandizo), asked to join the POUM in November, Nin replied that they would be accepted only if they dissolved their entire group or if those who joined broke all ties with it. This they refused to do.[29]

Growth of the PSUC

The new PSUC was enjoying explosive growth. For the first time in Catalonia, where, as its leader, Joan Comorera, said, "There is no Marxist tradition," a strong Marxist party developed. The PSUC quickly established itself as the main leftist alternative to anarchosyndicalism and by the spring of 1937 claimed to have nearly 50,000 members, 60 percent of them industrial workers and 20 percent farm laborers.[30] Key leaders of the former Partit Comunista de Catalunya took over the crucial positions in the new party organization, party press, syndical system, and internal security. The PSUC proved particularly effective in implementing the Comintern policy of attracting the lower middle class. It spoke out more boldly than did the Esquerra against the attempted revolutionary expropriation of rural smallholders, and welcomed GEPCI (Gremios y Entidades de Pequeños Comerciantes e Industriales, or Guilds and Small Business and Industrial Entities), the Catalan small businessmen's organization, into the Catalan UGT. During the course of the Civil War the Catalan UGT would enroll nearly half a million members and for the first time offer a major Marxist labor alternative to the CNT, though its membership leaned somewhat toward the lower middle class.[31]

Erno Gero (or "Pedro," as he was known) revealed greater skill and dexterity as Comintern adviser in Barcelona than did Codovilla in Madrid, and has been described by Bolloten as displaying "extraordinary energy, tact and efficiency." Gero had been a militant of the Bela Kun revolution of 1919 and later served as Kun's secretary in the Comintern; he also assisted in the purge of the Hungarian Communist Party in the Soviet Union. He had been in Barcelona off and on since the early 1930s and spoke Catalan. He was particularly skillful in managing Comorera, convincing him that he had a great future in communism provided that he abate his Catalanism, and was effective in reducing the Catalanist currents within the PSUC. Gero became the dominant Soviet authority in Barcelona, charged with monitoring the new Soviet consul, Vladimir Antonov-Ovseenko, and even entrusted by Aleksandr Orlov with the initial supervision of the NKVD structure in Barcelona.[32]

The Republican Mission to Moscow
Diplomatic relations with the Soviet Union during the Civil War, which might
be presumed to have been an important aspect of Republican government,
were conducted in an altogether anomalous way. Such relations took place almost exclusively in the successive Republican capitals, with little use made of
the new Republican embassy in Moscow. Marcel Rosenberg was a very active
ambassador in Spain, sometimes making daily visits to Largo Caballero, often
accompanied by Soviet military advisers, with the strongly pro-Communist
foreign minister, Julio Alvarez del Vayo, sometimes serving as translator. In
the initial presentation of credentials, Rosenberg made a ritual promise not
to interfere in domestic affairs, but he quickly proved arrogant and overweening
in his insistence on Soviet proposals for military strategy and administration.
Largo Caballero soon learned to loathe Rosenberg and, according to Araquistain,
at one point peremptorily ordered the Soviet ambassador out of his presence,
shouting that whatever the weakness of the Republican government, it remained
a sovereign state and its prime minister would not be dictated to by a foreign
ambassador in his own office. Though there is no confirmation that such an
incident took place, it is not improbable. All the evidence indicates that Rosenberg considered himself more as a Soviet proconsul than merely an ambassador,
and there is further evidence that his arrogance and attempts to control as
much as possible made him unpopular with other senior Soviet personnel
and were not approved by Moscow.[33]

The experience of Marcelino Pascua, the new Republican ambassador to
Moscow, was quite different. Like his good friend Juan Negrín, Pascua was a
Socialist physician of semimoderate political background who had made a professional trip to the Soviet Union in earlier years and had a smattering of Russian. With the bulk of Spain's professional diplomats having defected to the
insurgents, Pascua's political credentials and professional background were
deemed sufficient to merit assignment to what some would have called the
Republic's most important ambassadorship, though Araquistain has written
that his selection was due above all to Negrín's personal influence. Negrín was
undoubtedly a factor, but other concerns were the paucity of the Republic's
diplomatic resources and the insularity of most Spanish political parties. Though
Rosenberg had arrived in Madrid before the end of August, the Republican
prime minister did not officially authorize a Spanish embassy in Moscow until
September 16. Pascua was appointed five days later and given a massive sendoff
when he departed by train toward the end of the month.

Pascua's reception in the Soviet Union was lavish beyond his wildest dreams, first in Leningrad and then even more so in Moscow. His brief arrival speech —delivered in both Spanish and Russian—was broadcast throughout the Soviet Union, hardly a common diplomatic gesture. Social invitations were lavished on Pascua, and since the new embassy's budget was meager in the extreme, the Soviet government awarded it a large automobile for its private use. Initially Pascua was given a suite of rooms free of charge in the National Hotel and before long was granted free use of the eight-bedroom house occupied by the mission of the Belorussian SSR only eight blocks from the Kremlin, the Belorussians being summarily evicted.

Pascua apparently had no specific instructions other than to establish close relations and to maximize military assistance. His embassy staff consisted of no more than a commercial attaché and his budget remained exiguous. The Republican government was deficient in communications facilities and lacked an adequate code system, so Pascua enjoyed the most limited contact with Madrid/Valencia/Barcelona, as the seat of government shifted about. Conversely, he enjoyed more direct access to high Soviet officials than any other ambassador in Moscow, but even so, given the poor communications with Spain, it may be doubted that he fully understood the nature and scale of the Soviet intervention in the Civil War.

On his first day in Moscow he telegrammed Madrid asking that his secretary and the sole attaché both be sent at once, and also that he receive four copies of the *libro blanco*—the Spanish diplomatic code book—since he had left without any. Once more, it was the Soviet government that had to provide him with a full-time interpreter and a secretarial staff. Eventually the Republican government sent him an inexperienced secretary who he complained knew neither shorthand nor typing. Under these circumstances the commercial attaché had to serve as assistant to the ambassador and thus had no time to do his own work.

The state of abandonment in which the Republican government left its Moscow embassy can be described only as irresponsible. The neglect might be seen as part of the increasingly anti-Soviet stance adopted by Largo Caballero, but even the ultra-pro-Soviet Negrín, one of whose sons came to live at the embassy and study Russian, did nothing to remedy the situation the following year. Initially the government had explicitly refused to send any military attachés to the capital of the power on which it was becoming militarily dependent for its life. In the absence of either a military attaché or conditions in which the commercial attaché could do his own work, it was almost impossible for the embassy to make any contribution to negotiating greater military aid or to monitor payments from the gold deposit, which were being debited by the Soviet government at an artificially high exchange rate that cost the Republic many tens of millions of dollars. When he did try to negotiate about arms shipments, Pascua was embarrassed by his ignorance of the current situation in Spain and of the most recent intentions of the Republican government. He and the attaché received the standard salaries of the diplomatic corps, but the embassy's meager expense budget was cut further in 1938. Despite all the attention initially showered upon him by the Soviets, Pascua soon felt increasingly isolated and abandoned. The first Russian winter came as a deeply depressing shock and the ambassador experienced the common frustrations of the Western student of Russian as he endeavored to improve his skimpy knowledge of the language—"This is the devil's language!" he exclaimed in a letter to his counterpart Socialist ambassador in Prague, Luis Jiménez de Asúa. After ten months he returned to Spain for consultation and spent little more time in Moscow. Pascua was highly regarded, however, and in 1938 he was made ambassador to France, exchanging his barren post for the lavishly supported embassy in Paris. The Moscow post was left in the hands of a chargé d'affaires. Soviet authorities were amazed and dismayed by the state of abandonment in which the Republican government left the Moscow embassy, probably the least important of several factors that cooled relations by 1938.[34]

The virtual abandonment of the Moscow embassy is difficult to account for. Given the high-level Soviet presence in Spain, the top Republican leaders may have assumed that the only important relations were those conducted with Soviet officials in Spain, yet such an explanation seems inadequate. Rivalry in the Republican government may have played a role, but so pro-Soviet a foreign minister as Alvarez del Vayo had every reason to support the embassy in Moscow. The whole episode is another example of the failure of Republican leadership.

Stalin's Letter to Largo Caballero

In the third month of Pascua's mission, Stalin took the unprecedented step of sending a personal letter (also signed by Molotov and Voroshilov) to the Republican prime minister. Its primary concern was to impress upon Largo Caballero the need to follow Soviet recommendations for the channeling of the revolution in Spain and to give it an appearance of democratic constitutionalism —rather than, for example, try to follow Lenin's course of 1918, which for that matter had ended in economic collapse and was not mentioned. Stalin emphasized that "the Spanish revolution is carving out its own path, different in many aspects from the one followed in Russia. This is due not only to different social, historical, and geographical conditions, but also to the necessities of the international situation. . . . It is quite possible that the parliamentary path may be a more effective means of revolutionary development in Spain than in Russia. . . . The Republican leaders should not be rejected but should be attracted and brought nearer to the government." Above all, it was necessary to ensure the support of Azaña and his group for the government and to do "everything possible to overcome their vacillations. This is necessary to prevent the enemies of Spain from considering it a Communist republic and to impede their open intervention, which constitutes the greatest danger for Republican Spain." At the time this letter was prepared, the extent of the new military counterescalation by Italy and Germany was not fully clear, but it had become increasingly menacing. Hence the importance of making the role of the left Republicans more prominent, to influence opinion in the West.

The Soviet leaders specifically recommended:

One must pay attention to the peasants, who are of great importance in an agrarian country like Spain. It would be advisable to formulate decrees on agrarian questions and taxes, which are the main peasant concerns.

It is necessary to attract the urban petite and medium bourgeoisie to the side of the government or, in any case, to offer them the possibility of adopting a neutral posture that is favorable to the government, protecting them from attempts at confiscation and assuring them, as far as possible, of freedom of commerce; otherwise, these groups will follow fascism.[35]

Largo Caballero took his time before replying on January 12:

You are right to point out that appreciable differences exist between the development of the Russian revolution and our own. In fact, as you yourselves indicate, the circumstances are different. . . . But in response to your allusion it is appropriate to point out that, independently of the fate that the future may reserve for parliamentary institutions, they have no enthusiastic supporters among us, not even among the Republicans. . . . I am in absolute agreement with you in what you say concerning the Republican parties.

He assured the Soviet leaders that his government always sought to work with the left Republicans, who "participate in large measure in all the local, provincial, and national political organs. The fact of the matter is that they themselves scarcely do anything to affirm their own political personality."[36] In this regard Largo Caballero seems to have been telling the truth. Azaña's critics on the right had long accused him of "Kerenskyism," but that is not fair to Kerensky. Azaña and his left Republicans remained supine throughout the revolution.

Stalin also queried Largo Caballero as to whether Rosenberg and the other top Soviet personnel were performing well, having received reports on the Soviet ambassador's strident behavior. Though Largo Caballero replied diplomatically in the affirmative, Stalin, as usual, had his doubts. Later, on February 2, when Stalin received Ambassador Pascua in the Kremlin, he denounced the chief Soviet diplomatic representatives in Spain as inadequate. Rosenberg was to be replaced with someone "less enfant terrible" who would be more diplomatic with the Republican government, and it would be prudent to replace Antonov-Ovseenko as consul in Barcelona with someone "less revolutionary and conspicuous."[37] One week later, the Politburo recalled Rosenberg (to his execution, as it would later turn out), replacing him as ambassador in Valencia with Ivan Gaikis, the counselor of embassy. Three months later, Gaikis was also withdrawn (and also shortly executed), and the Soviet embassy was left in the hands of the chargé d'affaires.[38] No regular ambassador was ever appointed again.

The recall of the two ambassadors may simply have stemmed from the desire to purge them, along with the millions of others being executed or imprisoned at that time in the Soviet Union, but it probably also reflected the larger designs of Soviet policy in 1937. In his meeting with Stalin on February 2, Pascua presented President Azaña's new proposal for a treaty of friendship between Republican Spain and the Soviet Union, which Azaña apparently sought to draw closer together to enhance the Republic's security. It was typical of Azaña's insularity and lack of political understanding that he apparently did not understand that such a treaty threatened his most basic goal, which was to end the Civil War not by military victory with the Soviet Union's help but with a more peaceful intervention and mediation by Britain and France. Stalin, with his broader grasp of international politics, immediately saw how counterproductive such a gesture might be and replied: "On the contrary. Perhaps it would be useful to declare that there are no special ties between the USSR and Spain. Yes, sympathy between the masses, but no secret treaty. . . . There are those in the English government who will come out in favor of aid if the USSR backs off. . . . Let me stress that Spain must distance herself somewhat from the USSR in order to obtain aid from England."[39] Stalin added that consequently it would be prudent for him to withdraw two diplomats with such ultra-Bolshevik, hyperrevolutionary images as Rosenberg and Antonov-Ovseenko. These remarks are further testimony to Stalin's genuine belief that he could make his policy of careful but major intervention in Spain compatible with the goal of collective security with the Western democracies or at least with encouraging them to change their policy toward the Republic. Given the polarization in France and the general timidity of French policy, he correctly perceived that the initiative in the West lay with Britain, but seemed unwilling to accept the fundamental conclusion—which all the Civil War bore out—that Soviet military support of the Spanish revolution, no matter how disguised and whether or not it was directed secondarily or primarily against Nazi Germany, in fact had the opposite effect of encouraging the British government to maintain a non-intervention policy whose consequences were beneficial primarily to Franco.

Communist Policy in Catalonia

By the close of 1936, Comintern advisers and Spanish Communist leaders had developed considerable confidence in their political prospects, buoyed by the defeat of Franco's assaults on Madrid during November and December. Codovilla, ever overoptimistic, reported to Moscow on December 24: "As you see, the power of the enemy is beginning to decline."[40]

In internal affairs, the Communists were proceeding on four main fronts: *(a)* pressuring the Largo Caballero government to accept its priorities in military and economic policy; *(b)* pressuring the Socialists to proceed with plans for unification of the two parties that had been partially shelved since April; *(c)* urging the CNT to cooperate more fully with the Republican government and the Communist program; and *(d)* beginning the process of excluding and isolating the POUM until, they hoped, the small alternative communist party could be driven into liquidation. All these policies were pursued simultaneously, with considerable success being achieved on *a* and *c*, though very little on *b*. By December the Comintern felt strong enough to take more vigorous action than ever before on *d*.

This task required a harder line in Barcelona, where Antonov-Ovseenko's political style had been more moderate and cajoling than Rosenberg's in Madrid, and had been successful in gaining greater political and military cooperation from the CNT.[41] It turned out that the Soviet consul was an Old Bolshevik acquaintance of Andreu Nin from the latter's long sojourn in Moscow during the 1920s, but his position regarding the POUM had been brisk and categorical, making it clear that greater Soviet assistance of any kind for Catalonia would depend on dropping "Trotskyists" from the Catalan government. The POUM had counterattacked by publishing a pamphlet authored by the consul during the early phase of the Russian revolution which insisted that a revolutionary militia was better than a regular army, while Gero, who was too intelligent to consider the POUMists Trotskyists *tout court*, had reported that the operation was going to be the more difficult "because the POUM militia fight well" at the front.[42]

Antonov-Ovseenko also found the Catalanist Esquerra leaders somewhat disconcerting, not for their radicalism but for their Catalan *seny* (common sense) and objectivity. He was taken aback to be lectured by Jaume Miravitlles about the falseness of the standard Popular Front antifascist theme. As Miravitlles told him quite accurately, "In Catalonia there is no fascism." "Here the war is with Spanish militarists and clericalism." Moreover, the anarchists were too bloodthirsty. "It was enough to shoot 500, and they had shot 8,000 in Barcelona alone" (a slight exaggeration, but in general accurate), while Italian Fascism was "a characteristic of youth and national consciousness." Even worse was the fact that "yesterday Companys expressed . . . the exact same opinion about the lack of fascist elements in the Franco uprising, adding," to the Soviet consul's astonishment, "that they might try to agree with Italy on a cessation of assistance to General Franco."

Antonov-Ovseenko concluded that "M. and C.'s scheme shows the great confusion of the ruling petit bourgeois Catalan democrats," though they were much more reasonable and easier to deal with than were POUMists and anarchists. He patiently explained that their Italian strategy was illusory and, according to the consul, would only strengthen Italian designs on the Balearics. Instead, he stressed the importance of the Catalan government's mounting a big propaganda campaign to paint Franco as planning to hand over the Balearics to Mussolini, which might frighten London and Paris. Even so, Companys came back to the same definition of "the nature of the 'generals' rebellion' in Spain," and his hopes of making a deal with Italy. He ended, however, by more or less agreeing that it was "too late." Even though Catalanist leaders also liked to dream of a benign French protectorate over an autonomous Catalonia, Antonov-Ovseenko concluded that they were coming around to accepting his position.[43]

The Soviet representatives in Barcelona and the PSUC could generally count on the support of the Esquerra for developing stronger government in Catalonia, as they sought greater centralization, tighter administration, intense concentration on the war effort, and the eviction of the POUM from the

Generalitat. The success of the defense of Madrid and the growth of Soviet and Communist power made it possible to take more direct action on all these issues, as the Communists began to show, in the words of E. H. Carr, "an excess of over-confidence."[44] They first saw to it that the small POUM affiliate in Madrid was excluded from the new Junta de Defensa,[45] and on November 24 the PSUC leadership had proposed to the CNT that the POUM be eliminated from the Catalan government in order to form a new government "with full power." The CNT refused, and when on December 8 Companys also called for "a government with full power," the CNT replied harshly that that would mean dictatorship.

While *Pravda* editorialized that in Catalonia the "cleaning up of Trotskyist and anarchosyndicalist elements will be carried out with the same energy as in the USSR," on December 11 the Comintern leadership telegrammed Codovilla, Gero, and Díaz: "It is necessary to move toward the political liquidation of Trotskyists, as counterrevolutionaries and agents of the Gestapo." POUMists were to be evicted from all interparty committees and from any participation in government, and their publications entirely suppressed.[46] Instructions were also issued to break up relations between the POUM and the CNT, and to persuade the CNT to join in an anti-Trotskyite campaign.

On December 12 Joan Comorera publicly demanded the ouster of Nin as minister of justice in the Catalan government, because of his supposed disloyalty and his repeated attacks on the great Soviet ally. Comorera also demanded an end to the special Catalan Secretariat of Defense and to the internal Junta de Seguridad, both dominated by the CNT. Though the anarchist leaders in Barcelona were sometimes pleased with the strongly revolutionary position of the POUM, they did not at all agree with its ultra-Leninist line, which sought to repeat as exactly as possible the Russian Revolution of 1917. Moreover, Antonov-Ovseenko continued to make it perfectly clear to Companys and to the anarchist leaders that Catalonia could not expect to get further support from the Soviet Union unless the POUM were expelled from the government.[47] Both the Esquerra and the CNT therefore agreed to eject Nin, the CNT took over the Defense portfolio, and the PSUC received Nin's old post in Justice. Then, to help the CNT rationalize the situation, the PSUC announced that it too as a political party was leaving the government, though in fact it now dominated the Catalan UGT and through it would still control three portfolios, including Justice. The CNT, however, had not increased its representation and thus was left in a weaker position in Barcelona than before. It was typical of the anarchists' approach to political reality that they tended to categorize these maneuvers as mere "quarrels among Marxists," lumping them all together and concluding that it was not inappropriate for the Marxists to decide what sort of participation in government they should have.[48] Indeed, an uninstructed Soviet citizen arriving in Barcelona at that time would have been hard put to find any iconographic difference between a typical meeting of the POUM—replete with giant red banners, hammer-and-sickle emblems, and great portraits of Lenin—and meetings of the Communist Party anywhere else, except for the one missing element: no banners of Stalin.

On January 18, 1937, with the second Moscow show trial about to begin, the Comintern wired the PCE leadership to prepare to "use the trial of Piatakov and conspirators to liquidate the POUM politically by attempting to obtain from the working-class elements of that organization a declaration condemning Trotsky's terrorist gang."[49] This was easier said than done. The POUM had been the only Popular Front party to protest the death sentences in the first Moscow show trial the preceding August, while La Batalla charged that the Communists did not desire a true workers' revolution in Spain because they would be unable to control it. When the second Moscow show trial opened in January, the POUM newspaper announced that the defendants were innocent and that the accusers were betraying the revolution, brandishing in Moscow the same charges of being "agents of the Gestapo" that were being used against the POUM in Barcelona. It also insisted that the only reason the Soviet Union had sent arms to the Republic was to defend the Soviet Union against Germany, not to defend the workers' revolution in Spain. A ferocious polemic was launched against Antonov-Ovseenko personally, as the representative of counterrevolutionary Stalinism.

The POUM's press, though limited, was thus active and provocative. In English the party intermittently published a bulletin titled The Spanish Revolution and distributed it in Great Britain and North America. It recapitulated the basic line of La Batalla: the only choice was total worker revolution or fascism, and the CNT was criticized as well for having created economic "syndicalization" rather than "socialism" in Catalonia, though the POUM had generally supported the collectivization decree of the preceding October. It also supported a new army but insisted that it must be a revolutionary "Red Army of the Spanish Workers," similar to what Trotsky had developed in Russia in 1918. Though the bulletin at first welcomed Soviet aid, by November 11 it had begun to denounce "the reactionary role that is being played by the Stalinists in Spain." On November 18 it hailed the anniversary of the Russian Revolution and Civil War, with which the POUM felt so totally identified, but confidently predicted:

"We are convinced that the present Spanish revolution will be able to establish itself in a much shorter time" and "that its international significance will be no less," for "the Spanish revolution with its international outlook will not serve to establish another 'Socialism in one country' but will be a step forward toward the world revolution." On December 9 the POUM leadership did recognize that there had been a failure in strategy at the beginning of the conflict in not preparing for a longer civil war. By January 6 it compared the slanders against the POUM with the charges during the Russian Revolution that Lenin was a German agent. One concession that had been made to the CNT during the autumn, however, had been eventually to drop the slogan "dictatorship of the proletariat" and replace it with "worker democracy," though that term was still accompanied on occasion by "worker-peasant government," so long a standard PCE term before April 1936.

The difference between POUMism and the bureaucratic degeneration of Sovietism was declared to be the difference between a true "worker democracy" and a "dictatorship of the party." By February 6, after the second show trial, Stalinism was denounced as "Thermidorean," and the party's executive committee endorsed the call for an international commission of inquiry to consider the slanderous accusations being made against the POUM.[50]

The Failure of International Alternatives

By midwinter the Communist drive against the POUM had stalled, basically because the party and its Soviet allies had not yet developed as strong a position in the Republican government and politics as they had recently hoped. With both the military situation and internal Republican politics stalemated, at this point the Soviet government became momentarily interested in playing the Moroccan card in order to gain British and French assistance. In keeping with the general Soviet line, this move could not be a quasi-revolutionary reversal of the status quo, as the forces in Catalonia had tried to arrange the preceding September, but a straight old-fashioned deal among the colonial powers themselves. Near the close of January Gero returned to Barcelona from a brief trip to Moscow and told the PSUC leaders that the Republican government must be willing to consider giving up not only Morocco but even the Canary Islands, for Russian Communists had ceded to Germany far more than that in the spring of 1918 to safeguard their own victory.[51] By the end of that month the Soviets strove to persuade Alvarez del Vayo that it might be useful to cede the Moroccan protectorate to Britain and France in return for their action to end the German and Italian intervention.[52] Alvarez had already rejected as unrealistic a scheme that Araquistain had presented during a trip to Madrid on January 12, to seek to buy Hitler off with a large Spanish loan, but he followed up the Soviet suggestion. During February Republican diplomats in London and Paris attempted to broker a deal over the Spanish protectorate.[53] The concept was rather extreme, since Britain and France would have had to go to war with Nationalist Spain to take possession of the territory, but it obeyed the priorities of the Soviet doctrine of capitalist imperialism, which held that colonial powers were aggressively eager to seize ever more territory. News of the offer eventually leaked out and appeared in the Nationalist zone in *El Adelanto* (Salamanca) on March 17. Negotiations were extended in the direction of Rome as well, and the Republicans are said to have learned that Italian intervention could be ended only at the price of draconian concessions that would have virtually given Italy control of the Balearics as well as other Spanish territory. In desperation, by March the Republican government finally inquired in Paris as to whether France would be willing to accept benignly a Moroccan nationalist rebellion that was carefully confined to the Spanish protectorate, but the French government was understandably not enthusiastic.[54]

Renewed Pressure on the Socialists and Anarchists

During the winter of 1937 the Communists redoubled their efforts to sway the Largo Caballero government and to influence the CNT as well. A major radio address by Ibárruri in January recapitulated the core of the preceding month's *ocho condiciones de la victoria*, stressing that "the principal branches of industry, and primarily the munitions industry, must be nationalized and reorganized to meet the needs of the front and the rear." She called for a special interparty Council of Coordination to "administer and regulate production."[55] The Communists had no difficulty finding allies to defeat a proposal presented by the new cenetista minister of industry, Juan Peiró, which would have extended the Catalan-style legislation on the collectivization of industry over the entire Republican zone. Conversely, however, the Largo Caballero government made little progress on any sort of general scheme for industrial transformation and development of industry, to the frustration of the Soviets.

Communist representatives negotiated, flattered, and cajoled in an intense effort to win over the CNT leadership. Federica Montseny, one of the four anarchist ministers, later recalled: "The advice they gave us was always the same: it was necessary to establish in Spain a 'controlled democracy' (euphemistic term for a dictatorship); it was not advisable to create the impression abroad that a profound revolution was being carried out; we should avoid awakening the suspicion of the democratic powers."[56] The CNT had already made numerous concessions in practice, but it refused to concede anything in principle. Its *Boletín de información* declared again on January 19: "The thousands of proletarian combatants at the front are not fighting for a 'democratic republic.' They are proletarian revolutionaries who have taken up arms to carry out the revolution." Anything else was "reformist *counterrevolution*."

Communist discourse had to proceed on two fronts, for on the one hand it had to convince the anarchosyndicalists and others on the revolutionary extreme left that it was not counterrevolutionary, as POUMists and cenetistas said, while on the other it had to convince skeptics and extremists, among Socialists as well as anarchists, that the Communist concept of a "democratic republic" was at present the only practical goal. Thus, when the JSU (whose leaders had now officially affiliated themselves with the PCE) held its first and only national conference in Valencia during January, Santiago Carrillo dutifully presented the party line:

> There are those who say that in this phase we must fight for the socialist revolution, and there are even those who say that when we declare that we defend the democratic republic we are engaged in a deceptive maneuver, in a maneuver to hide our true policy. The fact is, comrades, we are fighting for a democratic republic and, moreover, for a democratic and parliamentary republic. And we say this not as a tactic or as a maneuver to deceive Spanish public opinion, or in order to deceive universal democracy. We are sincerely fighting for a democratic republic because we know that if we committed the error of fighting for the socialist revolution in our country at the present time—and even for a long time after victory—we would have awarded the victory to fascism, we would have guaranteed not only that our country would fall under the feet of fascist conquerors, but also that at the side of these invaders would fall the boot of the democratic-bourgeois governments of the entire world, who have already made it explicit that in Europe's present circumstances they will not tolerate a dictatorship of the proletariat in our land.[57]

The official line sometimes made Communists uneasy, and indeed some JSU militants at the front sent in letters protesting the speech. For that matter, soon after his arrival André Marty had expressed concern as to whether the official slogans of antifascism and victory over fascism were too negative and lacked positive content, while in Barcelona the PSUC, having to compete every day with the FAI-CNT and the POUM, used much more explicitly revolutionary language. At a meeting in Barcelona on December 20, held by the PSUC to explain the recent change forced on the Catalan government, Antonio Sesé, one of the new party's leaders, declared that the current support for the petite bourgeoisie would only be temporary. "The time for the liquidation of the petite bourgeoisie will come" once the war had been won, and Comorera concluded the meeting with the promise that the Catalans "will also be, on the day after victory, the first Iberian nationality to install the complete socialist republic." Nor was this frank explanation restricted to a single meeting, for these remarks were all immediately distributed in a published pamphlet.[58]

In daily affairs, the Communists naturally recognized the fact of the revolution, since they were participating in it and had their own ideas about it. Carrillo himself recognized much more frankly many years later: "At that time we called it popular revolution. We all knew that it meant the establishment of socialism in Spain. That was clear. Where were the great capitalists, the landlords, the apparatus of the bourgeois state? They had disappeared. Therefore, all the discussion seemed to me absurd and Byzantine."[59] But this "absurd and Byzantine" pretension was loyally maintained throughout by the PCE apparatus—and on most occasions by that of the PSUC as well—because Stalin refused to run what he saw as the risk of undercutting the collective security policy or of having no chance to change the policy of the British and French governments. Thus a month after the meeting in Barcelona on December 20, Comorera informed the PSUC central committee that "the most essential thing at this time is to seek the collaboration of the European democracies, and in particular that of England."[60] Comorera repeated two days later that Britain was the key conservative capitalist country and that for victory in the struggle it would be necessary to make a better impression on London.[61]

In their public discussions within the Republican zone, Communists were often reasonably explicit about what they meant by a "democratic republic." In an ongoing polemic with the newspaper CNT, Mundo obrero insisted on March 3 that the anarchosyndicalists had no reason to be confused about the meaning and nature of such a regime, in which, as in the wartime republic, the left had a monopoly on armed force, the old army had been replaced by a people's army, the peasants had most of the land, worker control reigned in the factories, there had been large-scale expropriations of land and industry, and the "democratic republic" was being led primarily by the working class. Mundo obrero went on:

Our republic is thus of a special type. A democratic and parliamentary republic with a social content such as has never existed before. And this cannot be considered the same as the classic democratic republic; that is, like those that have existed and still exist where democracy is a fiction based on the reactionary domination of the great exploiters. Having made this clear, we have to say to our colleagues of CNT that we do not reject or contradict the doctrines of revolutionary Marxism in defending democracy and the Republic. It was Lenin who taught us that the most revolutionary position is always to confront the concrete reality of a given country in order to apply the most appropriate revolutionary tactic, the one that will lead reliably to the final goal.

In other words, anarchosyndicalists, POUMists, and some left Socialists continued to complain falsely that the Communists defended capitalist liberal democracy, since that was indeed the propaganda line on the international level. But on the domestic level, within Republican Spain, "democratic republic" referred exclusively to the "new type" of left monopoly regime reintroduced into Comintern discourse in 1935 (and, they might have added, first introduced by the Red Army into Outer Mongolia in 1921). The term "democratic republic" therefore referred purely to a limited political semipluralism that naturally excluded all the center and right, or about 50 percent of the population, and embraced a NEP-style temporary acceptance of a certain degree of private property, while embracing nationalization of major industry. Its content in no way resembled that of a capitalist liberal democracy, though some of the superficial forms might be the same.

In a Soviet-length marathon speech to the PCE central committee on March 5, Díaz tried to be precise: "We fight for a democratic republic, for a democratic and parliamentary republic of a new type and with a profound social content. The struggle going on in Spain does not have as its objective the establishment of a democratic republic like that of France or of any other capitalist country. No, the democratic republic for which we fight is different. We fight to destroy the material basis on which fascism and reaction rest, for without the destruction of this basis a true political democracy cannot exist." In such a republic "the great landlords no longer exist; the Church, as a dominant force, also does not exist; militarism has similarly disappeared, not to return; nor do the great bankers and industrialists any longer exist. . . . The weapons are in the hands of the people," and therefore it was important in such a complex struggle not to lose one's head about "libertarian communism" or "socialization."[62] One might paraphrase Díaz and other Communist spokesmen by saying that for them the purpose of the fierce conflict being waged in Spain was to render Spanish citizens as felicitous as those of Outer Mongolia.

CNT publicists replied that they remained unconvinced, insisting that a revolution could never be carried out with the approval of the international bourgeoisie. The Communists' double game was too subtle for them and simply did not fit into the simplistic and categorical anarchosyndicalist doctrine. Conversely, soon afterward José Giral delivered a speech declaring that Izquierda Republicana and the Communist Party were almost entirely in agreement on current policy—though he did not engage in speculation about the political future of this "new type" of republic. Praise of Communist policy was not unusual among left Republicans at this time, based on perceived common interests in restoring a stronger Republican state and moderating the excesses of the revolution.

One basic Comintern goal in the "new type" of republic was to establish a great united Marxist party with the Socialists that would be primarily under Communist control. This project required continuation of the seemingly contradictory policy that the PCE had followed toward the PSOE ever since 1934—on the one hand sharply criticizing the Socialists for their divergences from the Communist line and seeking to divide them further to facilitate Communist penetration and takeover, while on the other proclaiming the utmost in fraternal feelings in order to achieve the fusion as soon as possible. Concerning the first tactic, Jesús Hernández has explained how his colleagues played on the rivalries and divisions within the Socialists: "From their suicidal antagonisms we were able to benefit in advancing our cause. Today we supported this one in his fight against that one, tomorrow we would reverse the roles and support the latter, while today, tomorrow, and always we pushed some against others to their mutual destruction, a game that we practiced openly with considerable success."[63] In this game they were assisted by the leading fellow travelers, beginning with the foreign minister, Alvarez del Vayo, who also served as commissar in chief of the People's Army and happened to be vice president of the Madrid section of the PSOE. Others included Edmundo Domínguez, head of the UGT's national federation of construction workers; Amaro del Rosal, head of the UGT's National Federation of Bank Employees and a member of the UGT executive committee; Felipe Pretel, treasurer of the UGT; and the Cortes deputies Francisco Montiel and Margarita Nelken. On the eve of the Civil War Nelken had hidden in her apartment the leader of the police detachment that murdered Calvo Sotelo and after the fighting began had asked repeatedly to join the PCE. Montiel was permitted to join and soon became a central committeeman, but Nelken was told that she was more valuable burrowing from within the PSOE.

The great success thus far had been the fusion of the JSU in March–April 1936, with the nominally Socialist leaders of the new movement, headed by Santiago Carrillo, formally affiliating with the PCE by the end of 1936. Since it had never been possible to hold the official national unification congress, Carrillo substituted for it a special national conference, convened in Valencia in January 1937 and carefully filled with picked representatives to ratify the JSU's line. Though the young people generally stood to the left of the regular Socialist Party members, a good many were not altogether in sympathy with the new alignment, which openly announced the Communist affiliation of the JSU in March 1937. Only after this did some young Socialists begin to protest publicly, during the spring and summer of 1937.

The unified party that the Communists sought was to be called the Partido Socialista Unificado de España (PSUE; United Socialist Party of Spain), similar to what a decade later would be termed the Sozialistische Einheitspartei Deutschlands (SED; Socialist Unity Party of Germany) in East Germany and to other formations in the post–World War II people's republics. Largo Caballero's interest in fusion had decreased sharply during the spring of 1936 when he saw what was happening with the JSU. After he formed his first government the Communist pressure had increased; Codovilla insisted in September 1936 that since Largo Caballero was now prime minister, he could simply carry out the fusion by fiat. Later, when Ambassador Pascua made his first trip back to Valencia from Moscow, he bore a special request "in the name of Stalin" urging Largo to proceed to the fusion.[64] It was much too late. By the autumn of 1936 Largo Caballero was already merely accepting the Communists as a necessary evil and from there his attitude became even more negative. Later, after he had been forced from power, he publicly taunted the Communists with their old demand that the basic requirement of a unified movement was a "complete rupture" with the bourgeois Republican parties, demanding to know if they still maintained that position.

Other than the small pro-Communist minority, whatever support there was for fusion within the PSOE came from the so-called center or prietista sector of the party. Not that the prietistas were eager for fusion per se, but they hoped to use the new "joint action" committees being set up with the PCE during the first months of 1937 as a means of strengthening themselves and using Communist power to discipline the caballeristas.[65] These joint committees never became effective vehicles for fusion, however, because of the strong opposition from the Socialist left and from the UGT (within which the former Communist syndicates still maintained their separate identity), and because the prietistas did not really support it that heartily, either.

The NKVD in Spain

An important part of the increased Soviet/Communist power in Republican Spain pertained to the extensive and complicated security and intelligence NKVD network operated by Major Aleksandr Orlov. During the first phases of the Civil War, other leftist parties, including the PCE, sometimes temporarily maintained their own jails of one sort or another,[66] but the prison system developed by Orlov—albeit partly with Spanish personnel—was a special extraterritorial affair, a partial totalitarian equivalent of the extraterritorial systems maintained by the Western colonial powers in China during the nineteenth and early twentieth centuries, with the crucial difference that it could not be acknowledged publicly. This system began to operate before the end of 1936 and would reach its apogee under the Negrín governments during 1937–38. Its prisons contained and provided for the execution of foreigners and the members of the International Brigades whom the Soviets wished to discipline or liquidate, as well as of a growing number of dissident Spaniards, though the number of native Spaniards executed there probably did not become significant until mid-1937.[67] By that time Orlov would be maintaining his own crematorium to dispose of the corpses, supervised by a key NKVD officer, Stanislav Vaupshasov.[68] By the overall standards of the Spanish war (or those of the Soviet Union), the total number of victims was not particularly great. Even when the executions in the International Brigades are combined with those of civilians by the NKVD in Spain and their Spanish agents, the total probably did not reach the nearly 3,000 executions in a few weeks east of Madrid at Paracuellos del Jarama and other sites in November 1936.

Orlov's reports would claim that by mid-1937 he was directing thousands of Republican guerrilleros in operations behind Franco's lines and maintaining six guerrilla training schools. On occasion some of his Soviet lieutenants, such as Vaupshasov, personally led a few of these operations, though Orlov exaggerated the scope and significance of all these activities in his reports to Moscow.[69]

More significant than the guerrilla operations was the intelligence network that Orlov rapidly built up in the Republican zone. Alvarez del Vayo gave him full access to the communications of the Republican foreign ministry, so that, as Orlov reported on May 23, 1937, "the good relations between us and the Ministry of Foreign Affairs make it possible to read all cryptograms being sent and received by the foreign legations in Spain." Not merely were initiatives by anti-Communist Republican diplomats such as Araquistain in Paris known almost as quickly in Moscow as in the Republican government, but the diplomatic correspondence of the representatives of other countries was being directly handed over to Soviet code breakers, as well. According to NKVD/KGB records, Orlov was so successful in his intelligence operations that "he was given an unusual degree of independence" and extended his networks into France and the Moroccan protectorate. It was Orlov's henchmen who collected the passports of dead International Brigade soldiers, and even of some of the living, particularly in the case of American passports.[70] The main target of intelligence activities was the Nationalist zone, where Orlov developed a sizable network of agents, using both civilian and military informers, as well as foreign journalists, such as Kim Philby, who had earlier been recruited at Cambridge under his supervision. This was one of Orlov's greatest successes, for his subsequent boast that he was soon able to inform the Republican general staff about all of Franco's offensives well in advance seems to have been generally correct. Such information helps in part to explain the nature of the People's Army's frequent preemptive offensives from Brunete to the Ebro.

Counterintelligence was equally important. The reports of Orlov, the Comintern advisers, and the Soviet military advisers and diplomats are all studded with vehement complaints about the numerous "traitors," "saboteurs," and "fascist agents" in the Republican zone. These persistent denunciations in part simply reflect the standard paranoid Soviet style, traitors and enemies lurking under every bed, but they also contain at least a kernel of truth. In a politico-ideological civil war such as that of Spain, many people were trapped on the side of those whom they opposed, resulting in many so-called *leales geográficos* in both zones and in both armies. Some of these "geographical loyalists" sympathized strongly with the other side and were willing to be recruited into its espionage activities. After the Red Terror was finally brought under control in December 1936, the initiative passed increasingly into the hands of police and organized special security forces. Orlov's agents were very active in sniffing out fifth columnists, periodically making arrests throughout 1937 and 1938, rounding up 270 alleged Nationalist agents in one big operation in the spring of 1937.[71] Nonetheless, in the multiparty, semipluralist atmosphere of the Republican zone it was never possible completely to eliminate the enemy's espionage activities, and the more tightly controlled Nationalist zone was no more successful in that regard.

Orlov is credited with having set up "the first NKVD extraterritorial spy school" in the Republican zone, which trained new agents for Soviet espionage abroad. The members of the International Brigades were carefully screened for good Soviet espionage material and provided many of Orlov's students, most of whom were eventually sent to espionage activities in Western Europe and North America. Moreover, because of his broad experience and expertise and because of the extent of his operations, by 1937 Orlov was even called upon to provide technical assistance for special NKVD kidnap and assassination teams who seized or liquidated White Russian leaders and Trotskyists in France.[72]

One of the chief NKVD centers was in Murcia, which had a Communist governor. There Orlov trained a six-man team to organize a revolt in the Moroccan protectorate. This mission, however, represented a new policy escalation, and Soviet authorities decided that the approval of the French government would be necessary if it were to continue. Not surprisingly, approval was not forthcoming. France was the target of Orlov's principal political disinformation effort, as he prepared false documents purporting to show that Hitler was establishing permanent German bases in Spain. This maneuver, however, was not well executed and had little effect.[73]

The other political parties in the Republican zone were also targets of Soviet espionage and all were penetrated to one degree or another. The major targets were the POUM and the FAI-CNT; both were successfully penetrated for purposes of intelligence and also in order to precipitate provocative gestures that would weaken their position and make it easier to take action against them. On October 15, 1936, having been in Spain for only a month, Orlov reported to Moscow that "the Trotskyist organization POUM, active in Catalonia, can be easily liquidated," and by March 1937 he claimed to have five agents in the POUM's Barcelona headquarters.[74]

In midwinter Orlov was involved in a serious automobile accident and suffered two crushed vertebrae. He was evacuated to Paris in February 1937 for a month's treatment and recuperation in a French hospital. There he is said to have been visited by his first cousin Zinovy Katsnelson, who was deputy head of the NKVD in Ukraine. Katsnelson is alleged to have tried to recruit him into a plot against Stalin by high-ranking NKVD officers, who for some time had been in possession of Okhrana (tsarist police) documents that revealed that Stalin had once been a police informer, and planned to move against the

Soviet dictator before he could liquidate a large part of the Soviet elite. Orlov was a loyal Bolshevik and refused; Katsnelson was soon arrested and subsequently executed.[75]

On February 27 Orlov returned an optimistic report to Moscow, declaring that "the Spanish Government possesses all the possibilities for waging a victorious war: they have modern weapons, an excellent air force, tanks, a navy and great resources," together with industrial and numerical superiority (which at that time was largely correct). But he denounced the "irresponsibility and sabotage" of Largo Caballero's "corrupt" government and strongly criticized the senior Soviet military advisers for their lack of practical military experience, insisting that in the supervision of combat activities Gorev was "a child," while Berzin was a military intelligence commander who was not an "expert" in serious military matters.[76]

At very nearly the same time, Berzin, who as former head of the GRU (military intelligence) probably felt a strong sense of rivalry with Orlov, was returning the compliment. By March he had dispatched a report to Voroshilov detailing the protests of high Soviet officials about the high-handed operations of Orlov and his agents. He claimed that they "were compromising Soviet authority by their excessive interference" and "were treating Spain like a colony." Berzin demanded that Orlov be recalled at once.[77] Avram Slutsky, chief of NKVD foreign intelligence, showed this report to Walter Krivitsky, NKVD *rezident* in The Hague. According to Krivitsky, Slutsky (who had visited Orlov in Spain) agreed with Berzin, saying that Soviet operatives were "treating even Spanish leaders as colonists handle natives." Orlov's ultimate supervisor, however, was the NKVD boss, Nikolai Yezhov, currently conducting mass arrests and executions in the Soviet Union. He ratified Orlov's policies and, according to Krivitsky, "himself looked upon Spain as a Russian province."[78] Berzin himself, however, was under Soviet criticism, and whether or not his criticism of the NKVD was a major factor, he would soon be recalled to Moscow, where he was eventually arrested and executed.[79]

The Communist Offensive against Largo Caballero

During the first weeks of 1937 the Republican government momentarily experienced a somewhat greater sense of harmony—however relative—than it had been accustomed to. By February the Soviet embassy even reported that the anarchists had become more cooperative. The Secretariat of the ECCI telegraphed Codovilla, Díaz, and Gero that their adversarial stance vis-à-vis the prime minister had been "an error," and that they must establish friendlier relations. They must also understand that for the moment the time was not ripe for unification of the two parties, and instead the recruitment of ordinary Socialists into the PCE should be encouraged, though fellow-traveling leaders such as Nelken should still remain in the PSOE.[80]

The fall of Málaga to Franco on February 10 initiated a big change. Up to that point, for three months the People's Army had enjoyed its first series of successful defensive operations around Madrid and during the second half of the month would register its best performance to date, for the first time stopping a major Nationalist offensive in open country, in the Jarama valley south of Madrid. A sizable number of mixed brigades had been formed, the beginning of a new officer corps had been created, matériel remained fairly plentiful (at least on the central front), and morale was generally high. The Jarama combat for the first time involved a major clash of sizable regular army formations on both sides, resulting in a defensive battle of distinctly higher intensity than those the Republicans had won earlier.

The collapse of Málaga, by contrast, had been an embarrassing rout. Even though one of the leading local officials responsible for this state of affairs in Málaga and the chief commissar there were Communists, Soviet representatives focused on Largo Caballero's administration of the War Ministry and especially the so-called traitor-officers in the Republican command; chief of these officers was allegedly Largo's undersecretary of war and favorite, Colonel José Asensio, who, unlike many of the other professional officers, was sometimes reluctant to cooperate overmuch with the Soviets. On February 14 the PCE leaders wired Moscow that the loss of Málaga had been due to "the tolerating of sabotage and treason organized by certain officers directing the Central General Staff at the side of the minister of war."[81] It may have been at this point that the final blowup between Rosenberg and Largo Caballero took place, at which the Soviet ambassador was expelled from the prime minister's office. At any rate, soon after the middle of February Rosenberg was recalled to Moscow.[82]

The top Soviet advisers nonetheless agreed with Rosenberg, and were reinforced during February with the arrival of the veteran Comintern official Boris Stepanov ("Moreno"), who at one time had headed the Romansky Lendersekretariat in Moscow and would now play a more senior role than Codovilla. He had earlier worked for two years in Stalin's personal secretariat and seems to have enjoyed the dictator's confidence. His reports on Largo Caballero would become increasingly negative, and on February 20 the deputy chief of the GRU in Spain, A. M. Nikonov, reported that "Franco's hand" could be seen in the breakdown in the Republican command, while some of the anarchists were guilty of "treason." Two days later Marchenko, the chargé currently in charge of the Soviet embassy in Valencia, gave the anarchists some credit for coopera- tion but reported that the "reactionary" Prieto, the naval and air minister, had attacked Soviet policy in a recent cabinet meeting, declaring that the USSR pursued separate goals of its own. Marchenko charged that Prieto was a "defeat- ist" who "sabotages" development of industrial and naval strength and that Prieto also accused Alvarez del Vayo of being no more than "a mouthpiece for Soviet diplomacy and subservient" to the Russians. That same day Berzin dis- patched a similar report to the GRU, stressing the need to eliminate what he called the "counterrevolutionary officer corps," by which he meant the small cadre of professional officers in the command structure of the People's Army who did not support the Communists. In an undated report Semyon Krivoshein, the first Soviet tank commander in Spain, even suggested that to achieve the "strong government" that the Republic needed "the Party ought to come to power even by force if necessary."[83]

Hugh Thomas judges that by this point the Communists had become "al- most the real executive power of the State," but such a conclusion is something of an exaggeration.[84] They had developed considerable power and influence within the recently restored Republican state, but that power had its limits, and Stalin had no intention of accepting Krivoshein's overly simplistic military recommendation, for both international and domestic Spanish reasons. A di- rectly Communist-controlled government was still politically unthinkable, and such an effort in the late winter of 1937 would have provoked so much internal conflict as to produce the collapse of the Republican cause.

Instead, from mid-February a steadily increasing Soviet and Communist campaign developed against Largo Caballero's administration of the War Min- istry. On March 13 Stalin, Molotov, Lazar Kaganovich, and Voroshilov and three of the principal Comintern chiefs (Dimitrov, Togliatti, and Marty) met in Mos- cow to discuss the situation in Spain. Stalin ruled that Largo Caballero would still be acceptable as prime minister but that he must be forced out as minister of war, while the unification of the PCE and PSOE must be given renewed pri- ority.[85] The goal was decisive new leadership of the war effort that would imple- ment the Communist military program more forcefully and fully while purg- ing the Republican command and officer corps of anticommunist elements.

Comintern advisers reported enormous satisfaction about the party's suc- cess in military mobilization and about the predominance of Communist officers, particularly on the central front. Of the approximately 245,000 party members, 143,000 were reported to have been mobilized in the People's Army by March 1937. Even earlier, in December 1936, Codovilla had reported with some exaggeration that 80 percent of the army "leadership" was already in Communist hands, while in the air force and navy thirty-nine of forty-two command positions were held by Communists. He had declared that whereas before the Civil War it had been hard to find a Communist officer, it was now hard to find an officer who was not Communist. By March Stepanov reported more moderately that "the great majority" of officers at the front were either Communists or Communist sympathizers, declaring that "this is an unprecedented political phenomenon." Later, on May 4, he reported the situation in more precise, less sweeping terms: "Communists or sympathizers make up nine-tenths of the officers of the central army," which may have been nearly correct.[86] Despite this success, at least on the central front, what lay beyond Communist control was the high command of the Ministry of War itself, under the nominal direction of Largo Caballero. Lack of Communists at the top was now limiting the appointment of Communist commissars, whose proportion, though high, was lower than that of Communist officers at the front.

During the autumn of 1936 the prime minister had already become concerned about the number of officer, command, and commissar appointments going to the Communists, and in November had issued a decree requiring the directors of the commissariat, the Socialist fellow travelers Alvarez del Vayo and Pretel, to submit all new commissar appointments to him for his personal approval. They had failed to do so, appointing many commissars "provisionally" exclusively on their own authority until finally Largo raged that 200 commissars had been appointed illegally and must be replaced. According to a Soviet report, by April 1937 125 of the 186 battalion commissars and 28 of the 62 brigade commissars on the central front were members of the party or the JSU.[87]

After Málaga fell, the Communists generated support among left Republicans and even to some extent among the CNT, forcing the ouster of Asensio. Largo Caballero nonetheless retained him in a different War Ministry post in Valencia, and quickly took revenge by dismissing the Communist major Eleuterio Díaz Tendero, in charge of new officer assignments in the army. Largo then seized the initiative in appointing a considerable number of noncommunist officers to higher command. For a brief period the Communists had difficulty in responding, but again were able to rouse support among the other parties and in March forced the ouster of General Toribio Martínez Cabrera, the noncommunist chief of the General Staff, and the controversy over military appointments and policy became even more acute.

Even more unsatisfactory from the Communist point of view was the political situation in Catalonia. There the drive against the POUM had temporarily stalled, despite Orlov's confident evaluation, and the POUM press continued to talk of preparing the workers for the revolutionary socialist conquest of power, despite the puny membership of the party. Though Antonov-Ovseenko had hoped to bring Companys and the Esquerra into a closer alliance with the PSUC on behalf of stronger government and state order, Companys remained cautious and still gave considerable priority to maintaining good relations with the CNT, even to the point of sometimes supporting it against the PSUC. The Communists were disgusted to observe a "bourgeois politician" like Companys tactically positioning himself to the left of the PSUC, declaring, as he had done at the close of December, that "the moment has come for the working classes when political power can pass into their hands."[88] The PSUC leaders did not quarrel publicly with this impeccably revolutionary declaration, but were, of course, not incorrect in judging that this was a somewhat cynical tactical maneuver to co-opt the loosely organized, increasingly confused CNT until the point was reached at which the left Catalan nationalists of the Esquerra might eventually regain power in Barcelona. The PSUC, on the other hand, had managed to outflank the Esquerra in its relations with the small-cultivator Unió de Rabassaires and the Catalanist white-collar Centre Autonomista de Dependents de Comerc i Industria (Autonomist Center of Commercial and Industrial Employees, or CADCI).

The Esquerra and the PSUC were nonetheless cooperating more and more within the Generalitat, as their ministers proceeded to dissolve the special food and supplies committees dominated by the CNT and then to appoint Eusebio Rodríguez Salas of the PSUC as the commissar general of public order. The CNT continued to resist efforts to merge all security forces in Catalonia into a single state police, but in March made further concessions on the extension of the military draft in Catalonia for the People's Army. This last initiative provoked a momentary desertion of the front by as many as a thousand or so CNT militiamen in Aragon, and the dispute over the centralization of police caused the CNT counselors to walk out of the Generalitat government on March 26, though a new government of much the same composition was reorganized on April 3. This dispute had produced a very sharp polemic between *Solidaridad obrera* and the PSUC press, with Antonov-Ovseenko playing a public role in pressuring the anarchists. The new acting ambassador in Valencia, Gaikis, was probably under orders to maintain more discretion than Rosenberg had done, and in a letter of March 27 Gaikis told the deputy Soviet foreign minister in Moscow that the Barcelona consul was causing "political harm" and "just affords support to our enemies." Soon afterward he was recalled, to suffer the same fate as Rosenberg.[89]

The commercial attaché Artur Stashevsky, who had become a personal friend of Negrín and generally enjoyed good relations with the Spanish, also returned to Moscow to report during April, and apparently seconded Berzin's recent critique of Orlov. As Krivitsky described it, "Though a rock-ribbed Stalinist, a rigidly orthodox party man, Stashevsky also felt that the conduct of the OGPU [NKVD] in the Loyalist areas was in error. Like General Berzin, he opposed the high-handed colonial methods used by Russians on Spanish soil." Stashevsky is said to have told Stalin that Orlov was doing a good job in counterintelligence against traitors "but he thought the OGPU should respect the regular Spanish political parties."[90] The courage and frankness of Berzin and Stashevsky are to be admired, and Stalin is said to have pretended at first to agree with Berzin, but there was nothing of which he approved more than highhanded police methods, and this was the beginning of the end for both highranking Soviet officials.

In fact, Stalin decided on the opposite course, encouraged by the increasingly paranoid ravings transmitted by Stepanov from Valencia. His reports repeatedly used the word "treason" to describe the military leadership surrounding Largo Caballero, which was characterized as being full of Trotskyists and agents of the Gestapo. In a typical Stalinist projection, he complained bitterly about an ongoing "anticommunist campaign" that he declared was being waged by all the extreme left, and concluded that Largo was directly conspiring with the British government to eject Soviet influence from Spain.[91] Similar judgments were expressed in a Comintern report from Spain of March 23 that Dimitrov sent on to Voroshilov. Acting Ambassador Gaikis followed it with a report in April that repeated that "the only revolutionary tendency of the Spanish worker movement is the Communist Party," while Largo Caballero was now "the largest obstacle in the path to victory." The "huge contribution" of the Soviets to the People's Army had been indispensable and the role of Soviet personnel should not be reduced.[92] Consequently on April 14 the Comintern bosses dispatched orders to the PCE to plan to precipitate a government crisis that would remove Largo Caballero as minister of war, though not necessarily as prime minister.

To do so the Communists would have to rely especially on the support of the "centrist" Socialists led by Prieto, and also on President Azaña and the left Republicans. Relations with the "reactionary" Prieto had already been mended, for he agreed with the Communist insistence on unity and more efficient centralized mobilization for the war through the Republican state. The cyclo-thymic Prieto blew hot and cold about the Communists. He was quite suspicious of them and resented their buildup of military and political power, but he tended to get along well with Soviet officials and agreed that Soviet help would remain indispensable for victory. Thus one Comintern report of March 28 had concluded that "the Socialists belonging to the 'centrist' faction have shown themselves significantly better than the 'left,'" and that the time had come to press ahead with fusion of the two parties, bypassing the caballeristas.[93]

Largo Caballero and his chief allies in the leadership of the national (as distinct from Catalan) UGT continued to drag their feet about participating in any national committee that would initiate fusion. The secretary of the PSOE party organization was Ramón Lamoneda, a onetime Communist from the 1920s who had become a prietista "centrist." In December the Socialist executive commission had proposed to the PCE politburo that a special national commit-tee be formed to coordinate the activity of the two principal Marxist parties, but this plan stemmed much more from concern to avoid the danger that the PCE might persuade some local Socialist sections to begin fusion directly, and was never implemented. Finally on March 29 the PCE politburo announced that it was establishing such a committee on its own initiative and during the following month Lamoneda appointed Socialist representatives to participate. For the first time in a year the Communists believed that real progress was being made, and now the policy of encouraging ordinary pro-Communist members of the PSOE to enter the PCE could be further expedited.[94]

At some point during March Díaz and Ibárruri held a personal meeting with President Azaña, who was said to have agreed that the Communist Party was "the most powerful," "the most disciplined," the most practical, and should have "more representation in the government." At the same time he recognized that because of "the international situation" the Communist Party should not be seen as too powerful. Azaña allegedly declared himself ready "to cooperate actively with the Communist Party in every condition."[95] Some details of this report may be taken with a grain of salt, but there is no doubt that Azaña found it useful to cooperate with the Communists in respect to order, central state power, and strong military organization.

Stepanov posed the political dilemma of the noncommunist left quite starkly:

> Caballero does not want defeat, but he is afraid of victory. . . . For Caba-llero and for the whole world a final military victory over the enemy means the political hegemony of the Communist Party in Spain.

This is a natural and indisputable thing. . . . This prospect inspires fear also in the anarchosyndicalists. And most of all, . . . a victory that guarantees a preeminent position for the party inspires fear also among the reactionary French bourgeoisie and especially in England. . . . A Republican Spain, raised from the ruins of fascism and led by Communists, a free Spain of a new Republican type, . . . will be a great economic and military power, carrying out a policy of solidarity and close connections with the Soviet Union.[96]

That prospect was indeed a growing dilemma for the noncommunist left by the spring of 1937, and it explains why Stalin was not likely to achieve his cherished goal of changing British policy.

The military controversy was raised to a new height on April 14, the very day the Comintern sent its instruction to drive Largo Caballero from the War Ministry, when Largo signed an order permanently curbing the autonomy of the Military Commissariat: henceforth all its personnel decisions would have to be approved by him, and all previous appointments that had not been ratified by him by May 15 would on that day be nullified. This order caused outrage among the Communist leaders and the top Soviet advisers, and it sparked a huge polemic between the caballerista press and that of the PCE. It also set a kind of deadline for the Communists to drive Largo from the ministry.

As tensions mounted, the Republican and Catalan governments undertook a series of measures to restore central authority, beginning in the final days of April. Historians do not agree as to whether these measures were simply part of general policy or whether they represented a concerted program of provocation to try to drive the revolutionary extreme left into an abortive outbreak that would enable the government to repress them more effectively. Robert J. Alexander, author of the most extensive study of the anarchists and the Spanish war, concludes that it is unclear whether these measures represented a planned provocation or not.[97] The Comintern report cited above concludes that "this means not passively waiting for a 'natural' unleashing of the hidden government crisis, but hastening it and, if necessary, provoking it." Krivitsky wrote two years later that "one of the leaders of the Russian anarchist group in Paris . . . was a secret agent of the OGPU" who was sent to Barcelona as a provocateur within the CNT, which he did his best to incite to violence against the Republican government. "He was sure there would be an outbreak in Barcelona."[98] That the CNT and POUM had been penetrated by outside agents does seem beyond doubt.[99]

The policy of reestablishing state authority had been ongoing ever since the formation of the Largo Caballero government, and to a lesser degree such a program had been implemented in Catalonia as well. One new measure of central government control was the occupation of the northern Catalan posts on the French border by Negrín's Carabineros in the final days of April. Armed police units had grown proportionately quite large in the Republican zone, surpassing their counterparts in the Nationalist zone, for the Guardia Civil had been reorganized and expanded as the Guardia Nacional Republicana and the Guardias de Asalto had grown to 40,000. As minister of the treasury Negrín had nearly tripled the Carabineros from 15,000 to 40,000, though they covered only half as much territory. By the end of 1937 they would be expanded even further, to 60,000, for an even smaller Republican zone. In the closing days of April they seized control of the French border posts, ejecting the anarchists previously in charge and killing several of them in the process. Though Largo Caballero had little interest in pressuring the anarchists at this point, it was an appropriate thing for Negrín to do, all the more so because he was thoroughly in sympathy with the Communist war program. The timing of this move obviously coincided with the Communists' determination to place maximum pressure on Largo Caballero and the extreme left. In addition, the expanded armed police forces in other parts of Catalonia dissolved several of the local anarchist revolutionary committees, which according to the decisions of the Generalitat should have ceased to exist several months earlier. By the end of April, a new climate of extreme tension had developed between the CNT and PSUC, and several anarchists and one PSUC leader were killed.

At this point the CNT was more divided than ever. Its leaders were mostly in favor of temporarily moderating the movement's position in order to win the war, while a militant minority was determined to make no concessions to Marxist "counterrevolution." Some of the most extreme had recently formed a new group of ultras called Los Amigos de Durruti, which may have had 5,000 members and frankly placed military effectiveness second to safeguarding and prosecuting the revolution. Partially protected by the strength of the CNT and the revolutionary ambience of Barcelona, the POUM remained as defiant as ever. Its press continued to talk of the need to form a new center of revolutionary power, often called a "revolutionary worker front," and at times urged the CNT leaders to join in establishing its dominance, at least in Catalonia, before the position of the PSUC and PCE became too strong. The main CNT leaders, however, were committed to cooperating with the Popular Front on the one hand and on the other simply did not agree with the Leninist strategy of the

POUM, which was oriented toward a centralized revolutionary power. Nin and his colleagues argued that the CNT position was weak and contradictory, lacking a clear strategy, but the dominant figures in the CNT did not accept the POUM's strategy, either.

The Fets de Maig: Abortive Revolt in Barcelona

The inflection point in Republican politics erupted around three o'clock on the afternoon of May 3, when truckloads of Assault Guards, under the orders of the PSUC security councilor in the Catalan government, attempted to wrest control of the telephone office in the center of Barcelona from the cenetistas who had controlled it since July 19. Individual PSUC leaders later conceded that this move had not been approved by the Catalan government but represented a Communist initiative. It was one more act in the policy of Communists and others to restore government authority, but very likely also part of the campaign to provoke a new crisis.

The result was the *fets de maig*, the May Days of 1937, three days of mini–civil war within the Civil War, which underscored once more the division within the left. This would be the first of two such internecine encounters, the second and more conclusive one being the struggle unleashed by the *casadazo* in Madrid in March 1939—the week of mini–civil war that virtually brought the conflict to an end. That was the defeat of communism, but the conflict in Barcelona was a victory that would soon introduce the mature phase of Soviet and Communist power in Spain.[100]

Fighting lasted from midafternoon on May 3 until the very early hours of May 6. The heads of all the extreme left groups (FAI, CNT, POUM, and Juventudes Libertarias) met on the first night of the conflict. The main leaders of the CNT preferred compromise and an end to the fighting, but there is evidence that Nin and most of the POUM leaders believed that the time had come for the ultimate revolutionary struggle for power.[101] Since the CNT did not agree, however, the POUMists refrained from officially advancing such a proposal. By the sixth a cease-fire was negotiated and soon after Barcelona was occupied by forces of the Republican government. That was the beginning of the end of Catalan autonomy and yet another defeat for the extreme left. Subsequently the official position of Nin and the POUM was that the CNT had been too timid but that the fighting had been inopportune and that the POUM had helped put an end to it. Only Los Amigos de Durruti remained intransigent, calling for formation of a *junta revolucionaria*, but they were altogether too few to continue the fighting by themselves. On the sixth *La Batalla* published a statement from the latter group demanding the death of those responsible for the counterrevolutionary provocation and the continuation of the struggle. The basic position of the POUM leadership remained unchanged; they still called for the development of a "revolutionary workers' front" that would permit "the working class to take power."[102]

Both *Pravda* and *Mundo obrero* immediately announced that the fighting in Barcelona had been initiated by Trotskyists and fascist agents, citing as proof praise from the Nationalist press for the anarchists' resistance. Soviet reports to the Comintern and to Voroshilov after the revolt ended claimed that there was evidence of "the connection of the Spanish Trotskyists with Franco" and that the Largo Caballero government had been very slow to take decisive action. One of the reports also stated that the extreme left was presenting the conflict as an attempt to resist the Communists' effort "to push aside all other political movements and establish their hegemony and dictatorship." The reports concluded that the moment had now arrived to "exterminate the POUM," as *Mundo obrero* announced daily, and to bring about decisive change through the crisis that now was inevitable in the Republican government.[103]

On May 9, the first Sunday after the fighting ended, the PCE held a series of meetings throughout the Republican zone to rally support. The main theme was the relationship of the party to the war and to the revolution, in order to refute the charges of the extreme left. The chief argument, as presented by Díaz in Valencia, was that the party was in fact already leading the most decisive aspects of the worker revolution in Spain, such as the final ratification of permanent changes in landownership through the Institute of Agrarian Reform. Even more decisive was said to be the role of the People's Army, which the PCE had played the predominant role in organizing, for this was called the truly revolutionary force par excellence—the army of the working class, whose military triumph would guarantee the definitive and permanent triumph of the political, social, and economic revolution. To win the war was to ensure the complete triumph of the revolution, and thus the Communist Party was the true leader of the worker revolution in Spain.[104] This totally contradicted the international line of the Comintern, but was an honest statement of the basic Soviet position concerning the future of the revolution in Spain.

A Comintern report dispatched from Spain on May 11 declared that the prietista leadership of the Socialist Party had taken the initiative of coming to the PCE central committee to propose close cooperation in the looming ministerial crisis. The prietistas, who claimed that they had gained the basic agreement of the left Republicans, proposed that Largo Caballero be eliminated from the government altogether (thus going further than the Communists) and replaced by the prietista Juan Negrín, who had taken a strong position in favor of maximalizing the war effort and was known to have the enthusiastic approbation of the Communists.[105] Prieto himself preferred to take the portfolio of a general ministry of national defense that would administer all the armed forces, thus achieving centralization of command. The overall representation of the parties would be only slightly modified.[106]

The same report also claimed that because of the profound internal division of the PSOE, work toward the unification of the two parties was moving rapidly. Close and friendly relations existed with the party's executive commission and also, allegedly, with the UGT leadership (though this last was something of an exaggeration). Indeed, rivalry between the two sectors of the Socialists was such that either one might try to steal a march on the other by going ahead on its own to negotiate the unification, or so the Comintern advisers liked to think. The Communists obviously preferred to proceed with the prietista leaders of the PSOE's executive commission, though they planned also to offer Largo "an honorable post in the future unified party."[107]

Matters finally came to a head in a six-hour cabinet meeting on May 13, two days after this report was dispatched. Hernández and Uribe demanded major policy changes and the immediate dissolution of the "fascist" POUM. This demand provoked a great controversy, with the prime minister denying that the POUM was "fascist" and insisting that the matter could be decided by the courts. Largo Caballero was especially angry because two of his most favored initiatives were being thwarted, primarily by the Communists. One was the long-debated notion of precipitating a revolt in the Moroccan protectorate, which contradicted Soviet foreign policy and was not favored by Republican moderates, either. The second was a planned offensive in Extremadura, to take Franco's army from the rear. The Soviets did not favor this idea because it was generated by noncommunist commanders, and it was vetoed from Moscow. Miaja would not release key units to participate and the Soviet advisers refused to provide necessary support by the air units that they controlled.[108] The two Communist ministers then stormed out of the meeting and were seconded by the prietistas, precipitating a full-scale government crisis.[109]

Largo Caballero now gave the final master demonstration of his truly appalling political incompetence. Though the prietistas were determined to be rid of him, neither President Azaña nor, at least officially, the Communists were taking that position yet. For his part, Azaña had long wanted a more effective government but feared an explosion from the UGT and CNT if Largo were ousted, so he asked Largo to try to form a new government. The minimal demand from the Communists was that Largo give up the War Ministry and relinquish all power over the "unconfirmed" political commissars.

The obtuse, narrow-minded Largo believed that he was still somehow in a relatively strong position. He returned to Azaña on May 17 not to reduce his own powers but to increase them, proposing that he not merely remain as president of government but expand his authority by taking over the broad ministry of national defense that had been talked of, with power over all branches of the military. Though he had not consulted with the CNT, leaders of both the UGT and CNT gave Largo their full support. Nonetheless, in his typically tactless fashion, Largo proposed to reduce the number of CNT ministries from four to two. This was too much for the embattled anarchosyndicalists, while the Communists, the executive commission of the Socialists, and the left Republican parties now stood firmly against Largo Caballero. Largo's de facto break with the CNT gave Azaña the opening he was looking for, and he turned formation of the new government over to the main candidate of the prietista Socialists and the Communists—Juan Negrín.

CHAPTER TEN

The Negrín Government

1937–1938

WITH THE FORMATION of the new government entrusted to Juan Negrín on May 17, the Communist strategy seemed to be crowned with success. As prime minister of the Republic from May 1937 to March 1939, Dr. Juan Negrín López would become the most controversial figure of the Spanish Civil War. By the winter of 1939 this Socialist politician, the principal war leader of the Republic and the champion of its policy of resistance, may also have become in some ways the single most hated personage in the Republican zone—even more than Franco. His fellow Socialist Luis Araquistain, the onetime maximal theorist of Leninist revolution in Spain, would eventually term him "the most disastrous and irresponsible statesman that Spain has had for many centuries."[1] Many thousands of Republicans would come to consider him a mere Soviet lackey, a treacherous politician who made himself a slave to Moscow, determined only to implement a cynical Stalinist policy of fighting to the last Spanish Republican, without seriously committing the Soviet Union.

Though by the first of March 1939 Negrín had relatively few supporters left in the Republican zone, his reputation more recently has grown among historians. Angel Viñas, a leading scholar of the Civil War, has called him "one of the most brilliant and extraordinary politicians of . . . all the Republican experience" and "the great statesman of the Republic."[2] Though the panegyrics of a partisan so extreme as Juan Marichal may be discounted, Negrín has also won the praise of major foreign scholars such as Hugh Thomas and Edward Malefakis.[3]

Juan Negrín was born of a prosperous middle-class family in Las Palmas in 1892, only months before the birth of his great rival, Francisco Franco, in El Ferrol. From the age of sixteen Negrín received his medical education in Germany, where he married a young music student of Russian Jewish background. In 1922 he won a chair in physiology at the Universidad Central (Complutense) and during his early years gained a reputation for research in physiological chemistry, though he published no scientific papers after 1926.[4] He opened a private clinic in Madrid but also remained active in university affairs, becoming secretary of the Facultad de Medicina in 1923 and later serving as technical adviser in the development of the Ciudad Universitaria. He also came to develop gross personal habits, such as extreme bulimia and orgiastic indulgence with prostitutes.[5]

Negrín joined the PSOE only in 1930, during the new wave of leftist enthusiasm that preceded the founding of the Republic. He had no interest in Marxist theory, allegedly referred to himself as "the only non-Marxist Socialist in the party," and naturally gravitated toward the moderate wing of the party, where his ability elevated him to a seat in the Cortes. Lacking the oratorical skill so prized in Spanish politics, he nonetheless achieved a position of some importance in technical parliamentary service, becoming president of the Comisión de Hacienda (the finance committee) of the Cortes. When a profound split developed in the PSOE in 1935, he remained with the prietistas, who controlled the party apparatus. Though known as a friend of the Soviet Union and an admirer of its great "experiment," he never promoted extreme revolutionism in Spain.

If he was no theoretical Marxist, neither was Negrín a democrat in either theory or practice. During the early phase of the Republic he was quoted as suggesting that the PSOE could achieve "a dictatorship under democratic forms and appearances."[6] By the beginning of the Civil War he had become a Socialist leader thoroughly dedicated to the imposition of a socialist regime in Spain, though not a socialist regime on the Soviet model. At no time was Negrín publicly associated with any explicit model of regime until he became prime minister of the "new type" of "democratic republic" in 1937. He had broken with the "Bolshevized" Socialists, as had all the prietistas, by the end of 1935 and was included in the Largo Caballero government as minister of finance at the insistence of Prieto, and as a result of his experience with finance in the first Republican Cortes.

He quickly established close ties with his counterpart in the new Soviet embassy, Artur Stashevsky, who seems to have been the most personable of the Soviet diplomats and the one who had the most sympathy and affection. Stashevsky and Negrín became good friends, and since Stashevsky had more experience in such matters and represented the Republic's only real ally, his influence on Negrín became considerable.[7] Stashevsky was able to promote the operation that relieved the Republican government of its gold and thus established Negrín as a man the Soviets could trust. Stashevsky became known in Soviet circles as "the richest man in the world" because of his special connections to the Republic's finances, while Negrín gave indication of his interest in the Soviet Union by sending his youngest son, Miguel, to live in Moscow with Ambassador Pascua, apparently to learn Russian and become well acquainted with the Republic's ally.[8] His work as minister of finance from September 1936 to May 1937 had dealt mainly with technical issues of using Republican funds for the purchase of arms and other necessities abroad. In this activity he initiated the process of making specific payments to the Soviet government of portions of the gold that it already held on deposit, either for Soviet arms already delivered or for indirect purchases of arms and other goods in third countries.[9] These payments apparently began on February 16, 1937, and continued for approximately a year.[10] In addition, Negrín reorganized and enormously expanded the ministry's Cuerpo de Carabineros, as indicated in Chapter 9, and used them at the close of April 1937 to begin to reestablish government control in Catalonia, a policy of the Communists but also of some of the other parties, and one to which Negrín was personally dedicated. There was general satisfaction among the Socialists, Communists, and left Republicans with his administration of the Ministry of Finance.

Negrín's political foes were later certain that he had been chosen and imposed as president of government by the Communists, while Azaña wrote in his diary that Negrín was his own choice.[11] Both concepts may be somewhat misleading. Both the Communists and Azaña favored the appointment of Negrín, but there is no indication that either of them initially pressed the issue. No later than March 1937, and probably earlier, Negrín was being spoken of among the Communists as a possible successor to Largo Caballero,[12] but as late as May 13 the Communists did not absolutely demand that Largo step down as prime minister, so long as the direction of the war effort passed to more capable hands. As Largo Caballero himself recognized, the candidacy of Negrín was initially pressed by the prietista Socialists, who had brought him into government in the first place.[13] They had discussed the matter well in advance with the Communists and left Republicans as the most desirable solution if Largo Caballero would not accept basic changes. Indeed, at first it seems to have been only the prietistas who absolutely insisted that Negrín become the next prime minister.[14]

There is little doubt, however, of Azaña's personal interest in offering the position to Negrín after Largo Caballero's egotism and arrogance had cost him the support of even the CNT. Negrín feigned reluctance but showed no surprise, and returned within a matter of hours with his new cabinet fully formed. He would maintain close contact for months with the Republican president, who as late as November would consider Negrín indispensable, though their relationship deteriorated very badly during 1938.[15] Negrín had become the most logical choice. He had kept a low profile amid the enormous factional infighting of the past year, and therefore was not subject to a veto by any of the major forces. As one of their own, he was the candidate of the prietistas, but he equally pleased Azaña and the left Republicans. No one could work better with the Communists and the Soviets, and he was also at least acceptable to the CNT. Prieto did not want to become prime minister, but he was willing to take over supervision of a new unified ministry of national defense and was happy to see his hitherto loyal associate become president of government. From the viewpoint of both Prieto and Azaña, the more suave manner of Negrín, what Azaña somewhat mistakenly called his "tranquil energy," would make him a better president of government than the mercurial and cyclothymic Prieto. Indeed, to Azaña Negrín probably resembled some of the more pro-Communist younger leaders in his own party, Izquierda Republicana, while the only disappointment for the Communists was Azaña's insistence that the former prime minister Giral replace Alvarez del Vayo as foreign minister.

Negrín's leadership was optimal from the Soviet viewpoint because he was a scientist of impeccable professional reputation, never a "Bolshevized" Socialist nor an extreme revolutionary and without any formal ties to the Soviet Union or the Communist Party. He could be presented as a moderate, European-style social democrat, however improbable this might seem to those who understood conditions in Republican Spain. Krivitsky put it well: "Though a professor, he was a man of affairs with the outlook of a businessman. . . . He would impress the outside world with the 'sanity' and 'propriety' of the Spanish Republican cause," and unlike Largo Caballero, he would "frighten nobody by revolutionary remarks."[16] Conversely, there is no evidence of any Communist conspiracy to groom Negrín for the office of prime minister. He had been mentioned in Stepanov's reports as one of the Socialist ministers most willing to cooperate with the Communists, but there was no indication that the Communists were necessarily preparing him for a higher role.[17] The choice of Negrín by the Socialists and by Azaña simply created an ideal convergence of interests that was fully acceptable to the Communists.

Negrín fully embraced his new position from the outset, being totally dedicated to Republican victory and to the concentration and development of state and military power necessary to that end. He had always admired strong leadership, and though he did not seek to Sovietize Spain, he clearly regarded the Soviet Union as the major progressive force in the world and was willing to collaborate completely with the Soviets to achieve military victory. This collaboration was only encouraged and facilitated by his Communist personal secretary, Benigno Martínez, who had been placed in this position at least in part by the initiative of the PCE leadership.[18] In economic terms Negrín agreed with the NEP-type policy of the Communists, which favored nationalization of industry but rejected general collectivization.[19] The new government would thus represent a moderation of the collectivist revolution but a radicalization of the war policy.[20]

His council of ministers was strikingly different from those of his predecessors, reduced from eighteen to nine, and was much more unified politically, excluding all the revolutionary extreme left, with no representative of either the UGT or caballeristas or the CNT (not, of course, to mention the POUM). Negrín would announce it as the fully democratic representation of all the regular political parties, from the PCE to the Basque nationalists. The CNT had withdrawn support from Largo Caballero after he had proposed increasing his own power while reducing their representation from four ministries to two, but their alienation from Largo left them with no candidate to oppose to Negrín, who would give them no ministry at all. Once more, the revolutionary extreme left had shown its practical ineptitude and its lack of any strategy for power. The response of the CNT national leadership to the new government was relatively conciliatory, though the CNT's heavily doctrinal press could only expostulate about the new "government of counterrevolution" and continue to denounce the PCE as "the party of counterrevolution," while declaring rhetorically that the revolution would continue. Within a matter of days the UGT agreed to withdraw its support from Largo Caballero and to support the new government, so that it began with comparatively good relations with the two great syndical movements, even though they had been excluded from power.

A telegram to the Comintern by Stepanov and Díaz on May 25 hailed the new government as a "true Popular Front government that takes up revolutionary war policy advocated by our work."[21] For the Communists, the time had arrived for what Stepanov termed a basic political "differentiation"[22]—

a differentiation between the Communists and the other forces willing to co-operate with their program (especially non-caballerist Socialists and left Republicans, but elements from other sectors as well) on the one hand, over against the extreme revolutionary left (caballeristas, part of the anarchists, and the POUM) on the other. For months the Communists had claimed to represent "the interests of the whole people" in the war effort,[23] echoing the terminology of the new Soviet constitution, which claimed to constitute a *gosudarstvo vsego naroda* ("a state of the whole people"). The time had come to press for a position of hegemony and dominance in the system, though not of formal leadership; Communists would still hold only two cabinet posts. Negrín could be expected to accelerate his predecessor's attempt to restore the central authority of the state and to centralize and energize military development. He was also willing to satisfy most of the Communist demands concerning internal security. From this point forward both the Comintern bosses and PCE leaders believed that the path was open to creation of what Díaz called the great "Partido Unico del Proletariado" (Sole Party of the Proletariat), though here they made their greatest mistake. Hernández admits that when his candidacy for the premiership was first discussed, Negrín had warned the Communists that he would not be a "straw man," and this independence, which would be scarcely discernible in military policy, was most marked with regard to the Socialist Party, whose underlying strength the Comintern underestimated.[24]

In the new government the Socialists retained control of the Ministry of the Interior, now headed by the prietistas Julián Zugazagoitia and Juan Simeón Vidarte as minister and undersecretary, respectively, but Vidarte embraced a policy of almost total cooperation with the PCE. Communists kept all the police positions that they already held and the party member Lieutenant Colonel Antonio Ortega was made director general of security, while Communist police chiefs were appointed for the three largest cities. From May 1937 the Republican security system became increasingly interconnected with Orlov's NKVD, and Vidarte would later admit that it was full of "nests of spies and confidants of the GPU."[25]

Control of security made it possible to launch immediately an offensive against two bastions of the extreme left: the agrarian collectives of the CNT and the POUM. The assault on the CNT had already begun in the early spring in the central zone, where Communists were strongest. Force had been used in Toledo province from late March and April even under the old government, apparently as part of the offensive of the Communists and certain sectors of the Republican government to regain direct control. Communist units of the

People's Army had broken up collectives by force. Even the moderate CNT leader Mariano Vázquez accused the Communists of murdering "dozens" of anarchosyndicalists, while the director of the newspaper *CNT* later wrote that sixty had been killed in Mora de Toledo alone. The true figure will never be known, but it is clear that the Communists had already begun an armed offensive against CNT collectives in the central zone.[26]

The offensive against the POUM began on the very day the government was formed, for to Negrín the party was a serious obstacle to the war effort. Since the May Days the POUM leaders had remained intransigent, insisting that nothing had changed. They planned to convene their party's second national congress in Barcelona, and Nin prepared the usual position paper, insisting on a "worker-peasant government" that would destroy the existing "reformist" Republican state. This change in the revolutionary correlation of power would supposedly affect not only Europe but the world, providing great stimulus to the world proletarian revolution.[27] Not all the POUM militants, however, agreed with this position of *révolution à l'outrance,* and some of the former *maurinistas* were said to be attempting to revive the BOC and install a more moderate line.[28]

Stalin had been demanding action for some time, and in the climate of the Great Terror he even harbored deep suspicion about the Comintern itself.[29] Orlov had already been concocting fake evidence with which to convict the POUM, which he explained on May 23.[30] In Madrid his agents had uncovered a new Falangist fifth-column group. Among its documents was a Madrid street map signed by the group's leader; on the opposite side of it Orlov forged a small text that would establish a connection between Nin and the Falangist, to which he added a set a numbers drawn from a Nationalist cipher code known as "Luci," already in possession of the Dirección General de Seguridad (DGS; General Security Administration).

La Batalla was shut down on May 27, and on June 16, three days before the opening of the POUM congress, agents of the chief of police of Barcelona, acting under four officers sent by the DGS, arrested Nin and the party's entire executive, closing its headquarters and remaining press facilities. All the top POUMists were sent to Madrid's Atocha prison, except for Nin, who was kept in a special NKVD jail in Alcalá de Henares. This news was withheld from Zugazagoitia, but *Mundo obrero* announced the arrest on June 18, kicking off a big PCE propaganda campaign against Trotskyists and fascist agents. Altogether, nearly a thousand party members were arrested and the 29th Division of the People's Army, made up of POUMist militias, was dissolved, its troops integrated into other units. On June 23 the government decreed establishment of a new Tribunal of Espionage and High Treason, composed of three civilian and two military judges.

These moves provoked a scandal both at home and abroad. The CNT protested the proposed new tribunal and the suppression of the POUM, and the other cabinet ministers quickly learned that the NKVD was behind the operation, though Negrín lent the prosecution his full support. Two very abrasive cabinet meetings followed. Zugazagoitia made two trips of inquiry to Madrid, though he does not seem to have pressed his investigation. Manuel de Irujo Ollo, the Basque nationalist minister of justice, made a sharp protest and, according to Prieto, later even charged that this scandal demonstrated that Carrillo should be prosecuted for the mass killings at Paracuellos del Jarama.[31] The only effective action, however, was Zugazagoitia's dismissal of Ortega as head of the DGS. He also ordered an inquiry and is said to have mandated a search of the headquarters of the PCE central committee, but Negrín intervened to block the inquiry and the PCE avoided the search by warning they would use armed force to defend their headquarters. Stepanov was furious, and labeled both Zugazagoitia and Irujo "fascists." Here the case rested. Ortega was replaced by Zugazagoitia's lieutenant, Gabriel Morón, but Morón found the DGS too thickly infested with Communists to make any major changes, and remained in the position only a few months.[32] Irujo did order a separate investigation by a judge in the Ministry of Justice, who arrested a few police agents but otherwise did not get very far. Negrín insisted on the Soviet version of the proceedings to Azaña, who was naturally skeptical.[33] Finally on August 14 Zugazagoitia issued a stern warning against further protest and indiscipline about the matter.[34]

Meanwhile Stalin issued a handwritten order, which remains in the KGB archives, that Nin be killed. Orlov first transferred Nin to a special NKVD *checa* in the basement of the Alcalá home of Ignacio Hidalgo de Cisneros, the Communist air force commander, where he was savagely tortured to make him "confess" and provide other information. After this effort failed, false documents were prepared first to legalize Nin's removal from the original jail and then to provide evidence that he had been "liberated" from the basement checa by foreign agents. German-speaking members of the International Brigades were used in the latter operation; they carefully left a wallet with German documentation as well as money from the Nationalist zone. On June 23 Nin was executed and buried about 100 meters from the highway midway on the road between Alcalá and Tajuña.[35]

Nin's disappearance became the principal cause célèbre in the Republican zone for the remainder of the war. He was the most prominent victim of the NKVD in the Republican zone. Most of the others were obscure Spaniards, but some of them were foreign figures of some note, such as the Austrian writer Kurt Landau, the journalist Marc Rhein (son of a prominent Russian Menshevik leader), the American José Robles (sometime secretary of the American writer John Dos Passos), and the British Labour leader Bob Smilie.

The official explanation, that Nin had been kidnapped by Gestapo agents, led to a propaganda war both official and clandestine. The PCE waged an enormous campaign to promote the official version, while the CNT and surviving POUMists replied with leaflets and other clandestine notices.

The Republic may have been well on its way to becoming a "democratic republic of a new type," but it was still a long way from being Outer Mongolia. The extension of NKVD power and of Communist police control that came with the Negrín government was considerable, yet it was far from being the total police control of the Soviet Union. On June 17, the first day after the arrests, surviving members set up a new POUM executive committee, which began to organize clandestine activity, was able to gain at least some support from the CNT, and succeeded in eliciting the interest of three international commissions to investigate the case. In addition to Nin, a number of other leaders and militants were killed in prison, but enough pressure was brought to bear that the executive committee members were moved from Madrid to Valencia. The major intellectual figures in the Republican zone, however, did little or nothing; only leftist intellectuals abroad spoke out clearly in support of legal process. The two leaders of the revolutionary left wing of the French Socialist Party, Marceau Pivert and Daniel Guérin, were particularly active. They charged that the Spanish revolution had been doubly betrayed, both by the Western powers and by the Communists. Pivert alleged that the Soviet Union was "oriented toward the hypothesis of a world war," and that it was crushing the Spanish revolution in an attempt to gain Britain and France as allies when a major new war broke out.[36] Meanwhile, a few members of the POUM remained members of municipal councils in Valencia and Castellón until the party was legally dissolved by official action on December 29, 1937.

Another Communist concern was to establish expedited court procedures to deal with dissidents and spies more swiftly. The justice minister, Irujo, was permitted to select the personnel for the new Tribunal of Espionage and High Treason that Negrín had set up by decree on June 22 and was successful in picking qualified personnel, so that the court functioned with some degree of responsibility. Thus Josep Rovira, commander of the POUM's Lenin Division, which had been dissolved, was prosecuted for high treason but absolved. There-fore—doubtless at the Communists' behest—Negrín tried again by introduc-ing a decree to create a new set of Tribunales Especiales de Guardia for treason. Irujo refused to sign the decree, declaring that the system was abusive. According to the notes of the new chief Comintern adviser, Palmiro Togliatti, he protested: "This is the checa, what Germans and Italians do"—he should, of course, have said Soviets even more—"there are no rights of defense," and later charged that the prime minister had asked Mariano Granados, a judge on the Tribunal Supremo, to create a draconian new court modeled on the treason tribunal of Fascist Italy. When Irujo protested that Nin was still "missing," the prime min-ister shrugged: "What does it matter? He is only one more."[37] Negrín promul-gated the decree without the minister's signature on December 1, and after President Azaña, who had been used to presiding over profound departures from the Republican constitution ever since February 1936, rubber-stamped the new law. Irujo resigned, insisting that the independence of the judiciary was crucial in a state of law and that justice could not be applied simply accord-ing to the whim of the government. He was replaced by his undersecretary, Negrín's confidant Mariano Ansó.[38]

The clandestine POUM provincial committee of Valencia began to issue a *Boletín de información* on April 23, 1938. It claimed to be following the standard POUM line but in fact modified and moderated it, now calling for "every effort for the war and for the unity of all antifascist forces, without exception." It de-nounced extremism and, though still opposing the Popular Front, now proposed an "antifascist bloc."[39] Togliatti lamented on January 28, 1938, "The POUM continues to be strong and is carrying on a very dangerous undermining activity in the factories."[40] The clandestine executive committee was not arrested until April 1938.

The show trial that Soviet policy sought proved to be impossible, for some residue of judicial integrity remained in Republican institutions and the Com-munists still lacked the power to override them. The trial of the top surviving POUM leaders took place in an open courtroom in Barcelona from October 11 to 22, 1938. Though there is some evidence that Negrín sought to placate the Soviets by intervening personally with the new court to obtain death sen-tences for at least some of the accused, the prosecution did not ask for capital punishment.[41] The accused had the right to counsel and defended themselves vigorously, with such figures as Largo Caballero, Araquistain, Irujo, Zugazagoitia, and the former anarchist minister Federica Montseny testifying for the defense. Charges of espionage and desertion from the front were dismissed, while testimony from two handwriting experts exposed Orlov's incriminating forgery as a hoax. The court concluded that the POUM leaders were definitely not fascist agents, as the Communists charged, but convicted them of undermining the war effort and of bearing considerable responsibility for the violence of the May Days in Barcelona. It decreed permanent dissolution of the party, sentenced four leaders to fifteen years' imprisonment and one to eleven years, and absolved two others.[42] Even under Negrín, Barcelona was not Moscow. Togliatti reported to the Soviet capital that the outcome was "scandalous," lamenting that (by Soviet standards) "no serious punishment" had been meted out.[43]

The other main target of Communist policy was the anarchist agrarian collectives. During the first weeks of the Negrín government action against them had been held in abeyance so as not to disrupt the harvest, which was bountiful in many parts of the Republican zone in 1937. As soon as the crops were in, the offensive commenced. On August 11 the government dissolved the anarchist-dominated Regional Defense Council of Aragon, which had originally been the only single-party provincial or regional government in the Republican zone, though other forces had later been admitted.[44] Líster's Eleventh Division served once more as the Communist shock force, and rolled into eastern Aragon even before the decree so as to take the anarchists by surprise. Its activity was expedited by the new Republican governor, José Ignacio Mantecón, like Bibiano Ossorio Tafall and others a fellow-traveling member of Izquierda Republicana. After the war he joined the PCE. On the grounds that the Aragonese collectives had been established by force, many were broken up and at least 600 cenetistas arrested. Anarchists later charged that "hundreds of collectivists were massacred."[45] While the number may be an exaggeration, some were undoubtedly killed. The action represented a concerted policy of the Republican government, Prieto having first issued orders to Líster on August 5.[46] A number of CNT collectives were also broken up in the Levant.[47] The national leadership of the CNT protested, a delegation telling Azaña on December 12 that if the CNT were to be destroyed, it would be better to let Franco win.[48]

Subsequently the two Communist members who had been members of the council admitted that the modus operandi had been unnecessarily harsh.[49] Other Communist officials later agreed. José Silva, the Communist general secretary of the IRA under Uribe, acknowledged that the breakup of collectives had been arbitrary and destructive; even functional, noncoercive collectives had been destroyed.[50] Antonio Rosel, one of the Communist members of the council, declared years later in an interview that "we went from an anarchist dictatorship to a communist one."[51] By October Communist officials of the IRA had to acknowledge that, as a result, agrarian conditions in eastern Aragon had gravely deteriorated. They even reestablished some of the collectives, though anarchists calculated that 60 percent had been permanently broken up.[52]

Stepanov was very pleased with Negrín's first weeks in power, describing him to Moscow as "energetic, bold and active, and without speaking very much [he] approves all the proposals of the PCE."[53] The PCE was now supporting a greater degree of formal "democratization" to open up the hegemony by other parties in certain districts and institutions that remained closed to them. Similarly, the Comintern judged that a more active process of political mobilization would be beneficial to the PCE. During the summer of 1937 the Communists used the term "popular revolution" to refer to the process under way in the Republican zone, though the term was of course deleted from any dispatches sent abroad. The extreme left responded to the new terminology by asking how there could be a genuine popular revolution without a concurrent social revolution. The Comintern advisers wanted to accent the political to the exclusion of the socioeconomic, which they believed could only favor them. As Togliatti put it in a report of August 30:

> The thing that is more striking than anything else is the lack of democratic forms that would permit the broad masses to participate. . . . The existing parliament does not represent almost anybody in present-day Spain. . . . The municipal councils and the provincial councils are created from above, by the governors. . . . Factory committees exist, but it is very difficult to determine if they are elected or appointed from above by the leadership of the syndicates: it seems to me that in the majority of the cases they are appointed from above. In these syndicates, which have become huge economic organizations, there is also very little democracy.[54]

What was sought, of course, was not any mass democratization but rather a broader mass mobilization that the PCE could use to advance its position.

The PCE continued to press for fusion with the Socialists. A letter of the PCE politburo to the executive committee of the PSOE on July 7 laid down the terms, stressing that the new unified party must achieve "a single will" and that all its decisions would have to be obeyed.[55] Ramón Lamoneda, chief representative of the PSOE on the liaison committee since April, continued to say that he supported fusion but emphasized that they needed to solve a series of practical problems first. Despite their internal divisions, the Socialists remained a large and indispensable force. Even the Comintern advisers were reluctant to press fusion too relentlessly, and toward the end of July instructed the PCE leaders not to force the issue too much. They were displeased that, contrary to instructions, Margarita Nelken had insisted on leaving the Socialist Party to join the PCE.

The basic goals by the summer of 1937 were to gain full control of the People's Army and the police structure, to achieve unity of action of the UGT and CNT under Communist hegemony, gain general support for the liquidation of the POUM, isolate Largo Caballero and the more extreme anarchists, and gain indirect control of the state. The Communists continued to encounter considerable opposition, however, and these goals were achieved very unevenly and incompletely.

The Nin scandal inevitably led to increased friction. The Comintern received a report on the cabinet meetings of July 14 and 15, in which there was a major fight over the dismissal of the Communist colonel Antonio Ortega as director general of security. The two Communist ministers took a hard line, threatening another crisis and an "appeal to the masses." This time Negrín did not support the PCE, insisting that Ortega would have to go. Prieto then launched into a tirade on Communist culpability, declaring that "the Communist is not a human being—he's a party, he's a line," though Negrín insisted ingenuously, "In the Nin affair, the Russians are absolutely without guilt; it is our police organs that are at fault." Hernández complained that the new government was now revealed to be as weak and uncertain as that of Largo Caballero.[56]

Two weeks earlier, on June 28, Prieto had issued a formal order as minister of national defense absolutely forbidding all political propagandizing and proselytizing within the armed forces. The slightest infraction was to be punished. Constancia de la Mora, the Communist wife of Hidalgo de Cisneros—in whose home in Alcalá the NKVD maintained a special "checa"—was chief censor of the Foreign Press Bureau and refused to allow the new order to be transmitted abroad. Prieto forced her resignation, but the PCE quickly obtained her reinstatement and the weak Giral then made her full chief of the Foreign Press Bureau. The PCE simply ignored the order, and Prieto found that he was unable to enforce it.[57] Nonetheless, the Comintern received a report that the Socialist chief naval commissar, the prietista Bruno Alonso, was attempting a similar policy in the navy and that the head of naval artillery at the big Cartagena naval base had told his officers that "the Soviet Union is nothing but a prison."[58]

Stepanov's report of July 30 was less sanguine concerning Negrín, who was being told by the PCE leaders that he must crack down on "pro-Trotskyist" ministers like Irujo and carry out a ruthless purge of both the army and the rear guard, and also cease to tolerate the publications that were constantly calumniating the USSR. With this government "the honeymoon is over." "It is true that with this government our party has more opportunities for work, for exerting pressure on government policy than . . . with the preceding government. But we are still far from the desirable minimum." The government had no united policy, but harbored several, "often diametrically opposed." In addition to the Communist policy, there was that of the prietistas, another of Irujo, another of the Catalan nationalist Jaime Ayguadé, plus the "additional policy of the counterbalancing Negrín," who was trying to hold them all together. "Negrín is full of good intentions, rushes around like the devil, almost always takes the party's advice, often turns to our comrades for advice, makes promises, takes it upon himself to carry out a number of matters, but does not carry them out, not even 50 percent," though he was "with conviction . . . seeking the closest collaboration with our party."[59]

The worst obstacles were Prieto, who now ran the armed forces, and his henchmen Zugazagoitia, Vidarte, and the naval commissar Alonso, while Irujo had been freeing "hundreds of fascists" and even wanted to arrest Santiago Carrillo for mass homicide. Stepanov concluded that Prieto's gravest concern was that the People's Army "represents a huge revolutionary force and . . . will play a decisive role in determining the economic and social life, the political system of a future Spain." The reason was that Prieto's "overall political conception . . . does not allow the development of the Spanish revolution to step beyond the limits of a classical bourgeois-democratic republic."[60]

By August Palmiro Togliatti, Dimitrov's chief lieutenant for Western Europe, had been in Spain for a month and was about to take over the reins as chief adviser. His long report to the Comintern on August 30 was only slightly more optimistic than Stepanov's. The Communists were making some progress with the Negrín government, but all the basic problems remained. The government still had not prepared a plan for nationalization of industry, a basic Communist goal, and now, after a year of war, "part of the population is already beginning to feel tired." A "bloc" of the extreme left, made up of anarchists and caballeristas, largely controlled the economy and continued to insist that Communist policy was "counterrevolutionary." "It is not enough to say that Negrín has a weak character," which was true enough, but basically the government remained severely divided and therefore still could not act effectively.[61]

Togliatti reported ingenuously that the PCE "is popular and beloved by the people," but the overthrow of Largo Caballero and the rise of Negrín "undoubtedly turned the heads of some comrades" and gave them delusions of grandeur. They attributed it all to Communist strength, forgetting the crucial role of the prietistas. Thus they have been making the mistake of thinking that "the party could already raise the question of its *hegemony*, openly struggling for hegemony in the government and in the nation as a whole." When new problems had arisen with the Negrín government, their solution was to force another crisis that would "create a government with the dominant portions for the Communists." The PSUC had recently been more culpable than the PCE in this regard. "In Catalonia this confusion has led the comrades to make the central task 'struggling for the destruction of all capitalist elements' . . . , arriving, of course, at the idea that such a task can be accomplished only by a purely proletarian and Communist government. I will send you one of the copies of the pamphlet [an open letter to the UGT] in which this theory is propounded." Such foolish ambitions had to be curtailed, for the time had not yet come for the open hegemony of the party.[62]

The PSUC leaders had been particularly arrogant in their dealings with the CNT. "Trade union work . . . is the weakest part of the party's work." That weakness was all the more serious because the unions held such great economic power in the Republican zone. The anarchists complained that the Communist goal of nationalization meant the "expropriation" of the unions. Togliatti therefore put the question to the Comintern bosses: "Is it possible to find a slogan that is an intermediate organizational form that would not immediately remove the trade unions from running industry, but would allow the government's organs to enter into this leadership, which might prepare for nationalization?"[63]

Another report by Pedro Checa of the politburo gave the party leadership's own estimates of their strength. The PCE had nearly tripled its membership in a little more than a year of civil war, reaching 328,978 members (of whom 116,372 were categorized as workers, 91,210 as farmworkers, and 91,463 as peasants; about 30,000 were women), "of whom 167,000 are at the front." The JSU had 350,000 members and the UGT approximately two million (including 758,000 farmworkers), of whom about 480,000 were in Catalonia. It was judged that the UGT was about 55 percent Communist in sympathy (though both this figure and the national total for the UGT were probably exaggerations). But Socialists abroad and the extreme left and other opposition elements in the Republican zone claimed "that the party wants to seize all power for itself in order to set up a dictatorship and that the Soviet government intends to make Spain an appendage of the USSR." Fortunately, "the party . . . now has hegemony in the army, and this hegemony is developing and becoming more and more firmly established each day both in the front and rear units." The chief traitor among the party leaders, the "Trotskyist" Astigarrabía, secretary of the party's Basque section, had been removed.[64]

Nonetheless, Togliatti reported, the party's central committee had become "confused," its leaders "tired, overworked, sick." Stress had taken a great toll, and the party had not been well advised. Codovilla must be restrained and kept from interfering too much, and the party needed more Comintern instructors. Togliatti later sent on remarks Codovilla had made in a meeting of July 30 in which the Comintern adviser clearly exceeded the Comintern's own strategy, since he had called for the intensification of the class struggle, the clear-cut hegemony of the PCE, and requiring the government to "cast off the bourgeois ballast."[65] Codovilla was finally recalled in September 1937 and the much shrewder Togliatti remained as senior adviser to the end of the war.

Stalin's Demand for New Elections

Despite certain improvements under the Negrín government, the People's Army was undergoing defeat after defeat as Franco was in the process of overrunning the entire northern Republican zone. Therefore the party's central committee developed a series of questions about how to proceed in key problem areas, which Dimitrov passed on to Stalin on September 8. In response, the ECCI Secretariat held discussions in Moscow in mid-September in consultation with Stalin and with some of the PCE leaders. Stalin personally insisted that new elections were needed. and these instructions were dispatched to the PCE on September 20.[66]

The first priority was new elections for a new parliament, the present one having become "unrepresentative." If what was left of the Republican rump parliament (after some of its members had been executed and others had fled in terror) refused to authorize new elections, then the president of the Republic should do so.[67] The elections should take place Soviet-style, with a single Popular Front list, though nominal terms of "universal, equal, direct, and secret suffrage" should officially prevail. If a general Popular Front list could not be agreed upon, then a single unified list of the PCE, PSOE, and JSU was absolutely indispensable. There should be similar unified-list elections for provincial assemblies and municipal councils. Other priorities were a new minister of the interior who was either a reliable Communist or a pro-Communist Socialist, creation of a special ministry of armament to be led by the same kind of person, naming of a single reliable commander in chief for the entire army, a major purge of the rear guard, development of trade union unity with the CNT, and a program of nationalization of "all the large industrial and commercial enterprises," together with all banks, under a single unified national economic plan. "The entire war industry should be not only nationalized but militarized as well," and its workers "should be considered conscripted." The PCE was instructed not to incur any unnecessary friction by trying to force the unification of the two parties, though it must achieve the "united action" of the two parties in all the key policy areas. The central committee of the PCE "should establish closer cooperation" with the PSUC to instruct it in developing united action with the CNT, and to help it overcome "its false assumption that Catalonia has already passed through the period of bourgeois-democratic revolution and has entered the phase of proletarian revolution." The Spanish Republic must remain within the framework of the "democratic republic of a new type."[68]

Only three weeks earlier, Togliatti had concluded, "I am not thinking about the possibility of elections . . . , since . . . elections would end with weapon fire."[69] The PCE politburo responded quite negatively, arguing that new elections would merely sharpen political conflicts in the Republican zone. Hernández observed that other parties would not join such an electoral bloc for fear of being dominated by the Communists and that elections would lack legitimacy anyway because only half the country could participate, while Ibárruri warned of the "danger that the Socialists would join the anarchists against us," as would indeed eventually happen during the final phase of the war.[70] This was only the most notable of several occasions in which PCE leaders had difficulty swallowing sharp new Comintern directives, the major preceding controversy having been resistance to liquidating the POUM. Nonetheless, the party was always ultimately directed from Moscow, and politburo members had no alternative but to submit once more, transmitting this proposal to the government.

It was taken up at a cabinet meeting on September 30. Prieto responded firmly that valid elections could not be conducted in the middle of a civil war, and Negrín agreed; Azaña was apparently of the same opinion. Communist leaders tried to convince Negrín privately on the following day, and he agreed to think about it. In the PSOE-PCE National Liaison Committee, one Socialist opined that such a proposal "could be made only by agents of the Gestapo," and that it would be a mistake to dissolve the present rump Cortes because it had a national electoral legitimacy while any new one would represent only part of Spain.[71] Thus Stalin's new idea quietly fizzled.

The Military Situation Deteriorates

The first months of the new government coincided with serious new defeats for the Republican army. Between April and October Franco's major forces concentrated primarily on the conquest of the northern Republican zone, which they fully completed. The Republicans were unable to achieve any concentration of resources. Each of the three main segments of the northern zone went down to defeat seriatim, with only limited assistance from other sectors. Though Franco's forces advanced slowly in the mountainous terrain, their commander had adopted a sound strategy, tactically assisted for the first time by effective air-to-ground support from the German, Italian, and Spanish Nationalist air forces, marking an important innovation in modern warfare. The Soviet and Communist commanders discouraged very much assistance to the north, preferring to concentrate new Soviet arms and the best Republican units, which heretofore had been decisive, in the central zone.[72] Soviet advisers did, however, participate in trying to maintain the defense of the northern zone, while there is no indication of any great disagreement concerning priorities within the Republican government.[73] The Soviet evaluation of the leadership and administration of the northern zone was not high, though the advisers could not ignore its importance, for its complete loss by October, together with other concurrent developments, began to shift the balance of power clearly in the direction of Franco. In the northern zone the Ejército Popular lost its entire northern army; more than 100,000 men were taken prisoner. The northern provinces had provided the highest rate of volunteers and some of the best soldiers for the Republican forces, and their loss would never be made good. It has been estimated that while as of August 1937 the correlation of total troop strength and matériel stood at 10:9 in favor of the Republicans, by the end of October it had declined to a ratio of 86:100.[74]

The Republican command attempted a series of four offensives in the center and northeast during these months to relieve the pressure and try to take Franco's main assault forces from the rear, but all failed. Indeed, Largo Caballero's planned assault in Extremadura might have been strategically more effective. These offensives revealed the continuing weaknesses of the People's Army, which would never be overcome—lack of operational cohesion, limited capacity for combined arms, severe deficiencies at middle and junior officer ranks, and lack of initiative. The larger number of German officers who assisted in training officers for Franco's army proved generally more useful than the very small number of Soviet officers assisting in the training of the People's Army, which was rarely effective on the offensive and fought cohesively only on the defensive.[75]

A particular Soviet concern was the decline in numbers, morale, and efficiency of the International Brigades. They had been repeatedly employed in the heaviest fighting, often as shock troops, and their losses had been proportionately heavier than in any other part of the Republican forces. Morale had inevitably declined. On the first night of the Brunete offensive in July an entire company on the verge of desertion had to be disarmed; eighteen of its members were shot, including one lieutenant.[76] Discipline had always been more strict in the International Brigades than in regular Republican units, and the execution of both officers and men for failures and infractions was not uncommon. By mid-1937 the flow of new volunteers was greatly reduced, and to maintain their troop strength the brigades had to recruit more and more Spaniards. Some of the brigades were now international in name only, and, as their morale and quality declined, Soviet advisers recognized that the best of the regular Spanish Brigadas Mixtas were now militarily superior to the internationals.[77] Problems also arose with regard to ethnic rivalries, disdainful attitudes toward Spaniards, and issues of training, administration, and weaponry.[78] To try to overcome some of these problems, the International Brigades, heretofore commanded by the Soviets as separate units, were finally incorporated into the regular structure of the Ejército Popular in September 1937.

Developments at sea during those months were equally favorable to Franco. Soviet naval forces were weak, though Stalin hoped to overcome this problem with the massively ambitious plan for a "bolshoi flot"—a great fleet of high-seas warships. For the time being, however, Soviet naval policy was very cautious. When on May 29 Soviet bomber crews flying with the Republican air force bombed the German pocket battleship *Deutschland* by mistake, Voroshilov immediately dispatched an order from "the boss" that great care should be taken not to repeat the mistake.[79] Meanwhile, an enraged Hitler thought momentarily of declaring war on the Republic but then decided to order German warships to bomb the port of Almería in reprisal. While considering the Republican response, Prieto reflected once more on the odds against a clear-cut Republican military victory in the Civil War, and proposed a retaliatory attack on the German fleet that might trigger a German declaration of war and a complete change in the international equation, with Germany's enemies coming to the Republic's aid. His fellow ministers, however, were not so audacious, and from the Soviet point of view, in which war with Germany was to be avoided, the Communist ministers could not support such an action.[80]

Much more important developments took place in the Mediterranean during the late summer of 1937, when Franco launched an offensive against Republican shipping in the western Mediterranean with the covert but active participation of the Italian submarine fleet.[81] Stalin had always proceeded with caution, and after three Soviet ships had been sunk and ninety-six others seized, albeit in the vast majority of cases temporarily, he had stopped using Soviet ships on the direct Mediterranean route by the early months of 1937. This ruthless new campaign, waged in defiance of international law, had the effect of making Stalin draw back further. By the first of September two Soviet merchant ships had been sunk, and indeed after two Republican ships arrived with Soviet arms on August 10, Stalin became extremely reluctant to risk not merely Soviet ships but even Soviet arms on Spanish ships on the direct Mediterranean route, and he abandoned it altogether by October, even though the vigorous new naval patrol system imposed by Britain and France had eliminated the Italian submarine attacks. From that time nearly all Soviet arms shipments would normally be carried by the vessels of France Navigation, the company set up by the French Communist Party with Republican funds, and would rely exclusively on the northern route to French ports, whence they would have to depend on sometimes uncertain French facilities for transshipment, reducing further the already diminished flow of supplies. Equally troublesome was the fact that with the liquidation of the northern Republican zone, after October Franco was able for the first time to concentrate most of his naval strength in the western Mediterranean, basing his ships at Mallorca. This development highlighted another failure of the Republicans' strategy: they had failed to make a major effort to occupy the island earlier, when it had been weak and isolated. Now Franco could harass nearly all Republican shipping, while the Republican fleet was kept perpetually on the defensive.

Changing Soviet Priorities

The second major new influence on Soviet policy in the summer of 1937 was Japan's invasion of China, which began on July 25. Soviet authorities were well aware that the Japanese military command at that time considered the Soviet Union Japan's number one enemy, and Stalin had to face the possibility that an easy triumph in China might allow Japan to turn against the Soviet Union next. Ignoring the civil war that until recently had been waged in China between Communists and their opponents, Stalin soon moved to major military support of the Chinese Nationalist regime against Japan. In September the Operation X administration, which had supervised arms shipments to Spain, was taken over directly by the General Staff of the Red Army, since the army would be in charge of the new shipments to China.[82] By 1938 Stalin was sending almost as many arms to China as he had sent to the Spanish Republic late in 1936. The effect was to guarantee that the lower rate of supply to the Republic would be unlikely to increase in the future. By the fall of 1937 the Republic no longer held the same priority for Stalin as it had a year earlier, but neither did he intend to abandon it. In September 1937 the problem of increasing the political strength of the PCE in Spain still drew his personal attention, but the Republic would have to organize itself and defend itself more effectively, even with diminished resources. Thus official Soviet sources recognize fifty-two shiploads of arms to Spain between September 1936 and September 1937 but only thirteen during 1938 and only three more in January 1939.[83]

Whereas Stalin showed more interest in the Spanish war than Hitler did in the autumn of 1936, those policies diverged somewhat less by the autumn of 1937. Unlike Hitler, Stalin maintained a powerful political presence in the peninsula but he was not willing to make another major new commitment to Republican victory, though he did help to maintain Republican resistance while awaiting broader international developments.[84] For Hitler Spain was rather more secondary, yet there were no logistical impediments to his continued military intervention. He was about to start expansion in Central Europe, and on November 5 he told his military advisers that "a 100 percent victory for Franco" was not desirable "from the German point of view." Germany's "interest lay rather in a continuance of the war and the keeping up of the tension in the Mediterranean" to distract international concern from Central Europe.[85] Stalin, conversely, was always careful to leave an opening for Hitler. On Christmas Day, 1937, Litvinov told the French correspondent of Le Temps in Moscow that a rapprochement between Germany and the Soviet Union was still perfectly possible. Of the three major dictators, only Mussolini, who proportionately invested much more militarily and economically in a country near his own, was totally committed to a complete and rapid Nationalist victory. He agonized endlessly over the slowness of Franco's advance.

By October Soviet advisers reported an increase in anticommunist and anti-Soviet sentiments in the Republican zone. All manner of rumors were afloat, ranging from the idea that it was the Soviets who were keeping the war going for their own purposes (which was not necessarily incorrect) to the notion that the diminished flow of supplies indicated that the Soviets would simply pull out and leave the Republicans at the mercy of Franco. Soviet reports made clear the need of the Republican forces for arms and also for further Soviet air crews, though it was judged that Republican tank personnel were now adequate. More than a year into their labors one Soviet adviser judged Russian military personnel "confused" about the politics and geostrategy of the situation in which they found themselves, and in a number of cases convinced that the main purpose of it all was simply to try out new Soviet weaponry.[86]

The Comintern slackened relatively little in support of the Republic, launching a renewed international aid campaign in October 1937, which continued through the greater part of the following year.[87] What it could no longer do was to mobilize new military volunteers, as it had done between September 1936 and the spring of 1937.

Commercial, Cultural, and Financial Relations

Commercial trade between the Soviet Union and Republican Spain remained at the somewhat higher level that the war had produced, though it too declined from the last months of 1937. In 1936 Soviet commercial exports reached $6 million, which, though not a large sum, represented a distinct increase over that of the preceding year, since it was concentrated in the second half of the year and in only half of Spain. Exports reached $18.5 million in 1937 before dropping to $10.5 million in 1938. Spanish exports to the Soviet Union had amounted to approximately $0.5 million in 1936, in itself a significant increase over the preceding year and concentrated in the second half, totaling $4.5 million in 1937 and rising to $5.3 million in 1938.[88] These were substantial amounts compared with prewar trade but in themselves not very impressive.

Cultural relations between the Soviet Union and the Republic had increased considerably since the last months of 1936. Much propaganda material had been sent to Spain well before the war began, and from November 1936 shipments of Soviet books, pamphlets, and journals, as well as of posters, recorded music, and films, were substantial. Soviet films were especially popular, but Soviet propaganda and cultural facilities were at first not prepared to deal with a large volume of activity in Spanish and some of the early material was in other Western languages. There was extensive contact with the numerous Communist front and pro-Soviet social and cultural organizations that flourished in the Republican zone, but this was not a one-way street, for a sizable volume of Spanish cultural products was also dispatched to the Soviet Union, including a variety of performers, agitprop groups, and several athletic teams (one Basque football team was especially triumphant in Russian cities). Though this activity began to decline late in 1937, it roused a favorable response in at least part of the Soviet public, and interest in things Spanish increased. By 1937 the Spanish language was being taught more widely than before, and new Russian translations of major works of contemporary Spanish literature had been undertaken.[89] Major cultural exhibitions were held in both countries. There was even a large exhibit on "revolution in Spain" at the official Moscow Revolutionary Museum. It ran for months, for the extent of the revolution was never disguised to Soviet citizens in the way it was in propaganda abroad. The Soviet Union also took in Spanish refugee children. Though most of the 31,000 to 34,000 Spanish children sent abroad went to Western Europe or Mexico, between the spring of 1937 and the summer of 1938 approximately 4,000 were received in the Soviet Union; most of them remained for many years, some forever.[90]

The ultimate concern remained weaponry and military assistance. During 1937 the frequency of Republican requests for new arms shipments declined somewhat. The first part of that year saw the Ejército Popular at probably the highest level of weaponry it attained during the war, but the trickle of variegated weaponry coming in from Western sources could not possibly make up for the decline in Soviet shipments during the last five months of 1937. Soviet shipments became increasingly few and far between, though they did not disappear, and Soviet agents remained active in purchasing matériel in the West.[91]

The Republican government continued to transfer portions of the gold on deposit in the Soviet Union to pay for shipments and purchases. A total of fifteen such orders were given during 1937. Approximately $265 million was assigned to Soviet, Comintern, and Spanish accounts in Paris, while more than $131 million of gold was used to pay for the direct Soviet arms shipments. Use of the gold became more important than ever, for the only aspect of the Republican economy that was functioning reasonably well was farm production. In the face of continuing revolution and military defeat, the other kinds of credit and payment resources that the Republican government could mobilize were extremely limited. Two more orders to sell gold were dispatched to Moscow during the first five weeks of 1938.[92]

In February 1938 Ambassador Pascua had a series of meetings with high-level Soviet officials, including Stalin and Molotov. He was informed that the nearly $430 million worth of gold that had already been sold to the Soviet government was inadequate to cover all Republican expenses, which were now at least $15 million in arrears. At this rate of spending (or accounting), the gold would obviously soon run out, and Pascua had been authorized to request terms of credit from the Soviet government. Stalin agreed to a credit of $70 million at 3 percent interest, half of which was to be guaranteed from the remaining gold deposit, the latter 50 percent to revert to the Soviet government within two years if otherwise unpaid. With one additional payment, all of the

510 tons of Spanish gold originally shipped to the Soviet Union would be liquidated through Soviet accounts by April 1938. This arrangement did expedite
the last major arms shipments during the spring and summer of 1938, absolutely necessary to restore the Ejército Popular after the defeats of the first four
months of the year, but it required future assistance to rely on Soviet credit.
Stalin would extend a second line of credit of $60 million in August 1938.[93]

Conflict between Prieto and the Communists

Prieto was increasingly frustrated by his inability to enforce the decree that
had attempted to end the politicization of the armed forces, while the Communists aimed at the very opposite.[94] Ibárruri later wrote that Prieto's concern
was due to the fact that he knew the People's Army "would play a decisive and
determining role in the future political regime of Spain," and she was doubtless correct.[95]

Prieto had no illusions about either the need for Soviet aid or the importance of Communist military power, or about the appropriateness of many of
the Communist demands for more effective military mobilization. Thus he
accepted the suggestion, perhaps originally made by Orlov, that the Republican military needed a superior intelligence service, and created a new Servicio
de Inteligencia Militar (SIM; Military Intelligence Service) within the Ministry
of National Defense. Orlov has written that he tried to convince Prieto that
such an important service should be organized by an experienced veteran such
as the NKVD chief himself, but that the Republican minister replied that "having the intelligence apparatus in your hands, one day you will come and arrest
me and the other members of our government and install our Spanish Communists in power." Orlov allegedly countered that Prieto could control all appointments in the SIM, but Prieto insisted on appointing his own director. He nonetheless made a major concession to the Communists by appointing the very
able young Communist Gustavo Durán (a pianist and composer before the
war) to organize the important Madrid section, with a prietista Socialist as the
number two chief there.[96] This was an important concession, according to
Prieto, because Durán is said to have quickly appointed several hundred
Communist agents and only three or four Socialists. Prieto finally summarily
dismissed Durán.[97] Orlov admits that he personally demanded that Durán be
reinstated, though without success. Jesús Hernández would later write that
Orlov then toyed with the idea of having Prieto murdered, since he was the
main obstacle to full Communist predominance in the armed forces.[98]

Communist Labor and Economic Policy

As this struggle within the Republican military command continued, the PCE worked to complete the final political destruction of Largo Caballero and expand Communist influence into the two great syndical organizations, where it was the weakest. The former prime minister had regained the post of secretary general of the UGT and on July 30 had established a provisional alliance with the CNT—particularly annoying Togliatti, who reported to Moscow that the Communists ought to have made such a move themselves.[99] Since his ouster from the government, Largo Caballero had turned the Communists' standard argument regarding the international context of war and revolution against them, loudly opining that the extent of Communist influence in the government guaranteed that Britain and France would never change their policies toward the Republic. He insisted that the Communists sought power only for themselves and would ruin Spain, leading *Frente rojo* to complain on July 10 that the executive committee of the UGT was made up of "enemies of the people" (*vragy naroda*—the standard political denunciation used during the Great Terror in the Soviet Union). The CNT press for its part complained bitterly that the constant Communist denunciation of the shortcomings of the other leftist forces made it appear that "in Loyalist Spain there is only garbage and scum."[100]

In his report of September 15, Togliatti acknowledged that the Communists had little influence at the workplace in the Republican zone and that their "ties with the working masses in the factories are weak." He also acknowledged that PCE propaganda was often heavy-handed and that it was counterproductive to continue to call the caballeristas "counterrevolutionaries" (just as the caballeristas called the Communists).[101] The PCE, however, already had the support of a minority of the members of the UGT executive committee and launched a campaign in September to take over, or at least strongly influence, the Socialist syndical organization. It succeeded in forming a general anti-Caballero front, which ousted the old leader from the secretary generalship on October 1, replaced him with Ramón González Peña, and gained other seats on the executive committee for cooperative leaders. When the rump Cortes opened for another session on October 1, Largo Caballero was removed from his two remaining parliamentary positions, and after he denounced the government at a public meeting in Madrid on the 17th, he was banned from further public appearances. Largo's subsequent appeal to the permanent committee of the Cortes was rejected by a vote of 16 to 1, and the onetime "Spanish Lenin" was silenced for the rest of the war. Though the caballeristas had retained control of the party apparatus in Madrid and Valencia, the new leadership of the UGT was able to use the Carabineros to seize all their publications, leaving them voiceless. The struggle against Largo Caballero within Socialist institutions rested on an informal alliance between prietistas and those pro-Communists who were now becoming known as negrinistas, but it was a highly unstable relationship.[102]

The Communists having now reached a new height of influence in the UGT, good relations were finally restored between the Communist-dominated Catalan UGT and the national UGT, and the Communists next sought to improve their relations with the CNT. The new UGT executive commission began negotiations with the CNT, the importance of which was emphasized by Togliatti in his reports to Moscow of November 15 and January 28. The chief Comintern adviser observed that "if we do not carry out a unitary policy with the CNT, the latter, on the basis of its new positions, will grow stronger, because its cadres are more active than those of the UGT," and they had the advantage of not being in the government, which made it easier for them to gain support by criticizing official policy.[103] It was more difficult to penetrate and influence the anarchosyndicalist leadership than that of the UGT, however, and the unity of action pact would not be achieved until the Republicans next faced a maximal military crisis in March 1938.

The Communists had generally been stymied in their efforts to obtain greater centralization and control of Republican industry and to challenge worker control and collectivization. The PCE continued to issue periodic calls for the nationalization of major industry, particularly war industry, and for the development of a unified general economic plan, but could not gain very much support. This was one of the principal Soviet frustrations in Spain, and was even taken up directly by Stalin during his interviews with Ambassador Pascua in Moscow, in which the Soviet dictator insisted that Republican industry must become better organized and more productive. Military production had been expanded in the factories of Catalonia and the Levant, and the Soviet Union had facilitated plans and provided engineers to develop the manufacture of a certain amount of late-model matériel. Soviet sources declare that altogether Republican factories using Soviet plans or assisted by Soviet engineers manufactured or repaired 320 airplanes and produced 337 armored vehicles.[104]

In this regard the PSUC and the Catalan UGT played an important role in the Catalan industrial heartland. The public discourse of the PSUC, which had to compete daily with the FAI-CNT and until June 1937 with the POUM, was generally to the left of the PCE's, sometimes to the annoyance of the Comintern advisers. Though the PSUC's actual role was sometimes to defend the

Catalan lower middle classes, its public face was usually more revolutionary than that of the PCE, and it advertised itself as the "sole Bolshevik revolutionary party of Catalonia."[105] The PSUC leader Estanislau Ruiz i Ponsetí, undersecretary of the Council of Economics in the Catalan Generalitat in 1937, declared in a major speech in September that all the worker left should be proud of the revolutionary accomplishments of the Catalan wartime economy. He declared that it had followed the path of the fathers of proletarian revolution, the Soviets, more rapidly than the Bolsheviks had done themselves, moving from primitive "war communism" to a situation analogous to the Leninist New Economic Policy of 1921 in less than a year. What had taken nearly four years in the wartime Soviet Union had required only a fraction of that time in Catalonia and in some other parts of the Republican zone. Though the industrial collectives were too entrenched to attack directly, Ruiz i Ponsetí denounced independent CNT initiatives, such as the formation of *agrupamientos industriales*, which had allowed collectivized concerns to squeeze out private competitors on their own. He praised instead governmental action under the Generalitat which had carried out "municipalization" of housing and public services on the local level, while avoiding collectivization.

When we want to establish the initial parallel between the transformation carried out in the Union of Soviet Socialist Republics and the transformation carried out in our land, we can say that the beginning of the transformation was about the same; the first steps were quite similar. There the evolution has been long and painful and has presented great difficulties at certain times. In our country we have tried to carry out the same transformation in the most rapid way possible. It would be senseless not to try to profit by the experience of others. . . . And so since our Russian comrades, after long years of war communism followed by misery and hunger, finally arrived at the adoption of the N.E.P., . . . here we have tried to avoid that painful experience . . . and leap in a single jump . . . from the primitive war communism that we experienced during the first months to our own period of the New Economic Policy, to the period of the existence . . . in good comradeship of socialized property side by side with private property.

It is clear that private property will be eliminated, and among us will be eliminated rapidly, by collectivized property. But it is also clear that no country in the world can afford the adjustment required by immediate and total collectivization. That is such a complex step that no one would recommend that total immediate collectivization be attempted.

We are already under the New Economic Policy, trying to make the principle of private property compatible with collective property. And this is the strongest, most sure and humane formula—and also the most efficient—to conquer the principle of private property rapidly, and to conquer it with precisely its own weapons.[106]

In other words, the sole Bolshevik revolutionary party of Catalonia was proceeding toward socialism both more firmly and more rapidly than the revolutionary extreme left precisely because, among other things, it refused to collectivize all property immediately. This was not the sort of news the official Republican information service transmitted outside of Spain. The next year the PSUC would lead the campaign in Catalonia to move toward nationalization of industry, and especially toward full militarization.

The Crisis of the First Negrín Government

In December the Republican forces launched a preemptive campaign to abort Franco's next major offensive, with the objective of pinching off the Teruel salient, which jutted into the Republican lines in Aragon. In their first successful offensive, the Republicans seized the city of Teruel. It was the only occasion during the Civil War when the Nationalists lost a provincial capital. Franco scrapped his own offensive and concentrated his forces to retake Teruel, but did not manage a full breakthrough until February 1938.

The four months between October 1937 and February 1938 thus constituted the last potentially hopeful phase of the Republic, a brief period in which it suffered no major defeat and scored one temporary victory. The PCE remained under orders to try to advance Stalin's plan for new general elections, and despite the rebuff from the cabinet at the end of September, it gave this item priority on the agenda of the central committee meeting at Valencia held from November 13 to 16. Nonetheless, the other parties continued to stonewall the proposal and the PCE had to give it up.

A new report by Togliatti painted a grim picture. War weariness was spreading, and more than ever people were saying in the ration queues that the Communists were merely prolonging the war, or that their departure from the government would bring aid from Britain and France. Despite recent political successes, the caballeristas and especially the anarchists remained a problem. Prieto, too, continued to be an obstacle: "He wants to defeat Franco, but at the same time he wants to subdue the Communists in the army."[107]

With the situation stalemated, Stalin held a consultation with Molotov, Dimitrov, and Manuilsky in Moscow on February 17 and decided against continued Communist participation in the government. According to Dimitrov, the Soviet dictator declared:

> The Spanish Communists must leave the government. They have two second-rate positions in it. If they leave, this will help the disintegration of Franco's front, and to some extent it will help the international position of the Spanish Republic. Quitting must not be demonstrative, not as a consequence of unhappiness with the government, but in order to ease the government's tasks. [They should say that] since the anarchosyndicalists are not in it, the Communists consider it inappropriate to be in the cabinet. Support the government but don't enter it—such must be our position at this given stage.[108]

This message was transmitted through a small Spanish Communist delegation that was about to return from Moscow. Before it had time to reach Barcelona, Dimitrov received Togliatti's report saying that at Dimitrov's earlier request the question of continued government participation had been thoroughly discussed with the PCE leaders. They strongly believed that withdrawal from the government would be viewed as a "capitulation" that would gravely weaken the political situation and that of the army. It would mean the collapse of Negrín's leadership and a dominant position for Prieto.[109] The politburo argued that "the departure of its ministers from the government would neither be understood by the people nor strengthen the Republic, especially following the loss of Teruel and the proliferation of capitulationist tendencies."[110] Nonetheless, after receiving Stalin's instructions, the Spanish leaders had no alternative but eventually to accept them.[111]

Franco recaptured Teruel on February 22, and this defeat marked the beginning of the new political crisis, now aimed at the elimination of Prieto and a yet more centralized and determined resistance, which might defend the Republic until there was a change in the international situation or possibly a broader war.[112] Hernández launched the campaign with a virulent article against Prieto in La Vanguardia on February 24, which was followed with a major speech by Ibárruri three days later. Afterward, Togliatti severely criticized Ibárruri for failing to follow the party line, being too leftist in declaring the constitution subordinate to worker demands, and attacking the petite bourgeoisie.[113]

The month of March was full of dramatic developments, primarily negative for the Republic. On March 9 Franco launched his new offensive in Aragon, which threatened to cut the Republican zone in two. Three days later Hitler occupied Austria without opposition from the Austrians or anyone else. The *Anschluss* in turn precipitated a political crisis in France, where the government of Camille Chautemps had secretly opened the border directly for passage of arms to the Republic between November 1937 and January 1938. The German expansion was so threatening to Paris that Maurice Thorez, leader of the PCF, inquired of his Moscow masters whether the French Communists ought to enter a new government of national unity. The Comintern said no, that such a step should be taken only in the case of a direct war of fascist aggression. Blum returned to power briefly, and the Spanish frontier was officially opened for three months, March 12 to June 13, facilitating the passage of military equipment.

On March 16 the Communists approached Mariano Rodríguez Vázquez, secretary of the CNT national committee, about the need for unity and continued determined resistance. Agreement was reached among representatives of the PCE, PSOE, UGT, FAI, and CNT to reject a new French mediation plan, to continue the war to the bitter end, and to eliminate *elementos vacilantes* from the government. That afternoon the PSUC and PCE mobilized a large demonstration featuring the participation of Ibárruri and crying "Down with the government of traitors!" outside the windows of the Pedralbes palace, Azaña's residence on the Diagonal in Barcelona, where a cabinet meeting was under way. The demonstration broke up only after Negrín addressed the crowd and promised that the war would continue. It was clearly directed against Prieto, who protested in a cabinet meeting the next day against such attempts to pressure the government. Negrín, however, defended the crowd, and Azaña, as usual, did nothing. On the following day, March 18, under the pressure of Franco's successful new offensive, the CNT and UGT finally signed a unity of action pact.

That day Togliatti reported to Moscow that with the military situation deteriorating more rapidly than ever, President Azaña and the left Republicans wanted to find a way out of the war. To maintain resistance it might be necessary to form a new government of the two syndical organizations and the Communists. On the 20th word arrived that Stalin had withdrawn his directive to leave the government; the Communists could retain at least one ministry in the next reorganization.[114]

Prieto had already told his fellow cabinet ministers that he feared the war had been lost, and after he reiterated his pessimism at a meeting on March 29, Negrín concluded that he could no longer remain as defense minister. Within two days or so the prime minister called together several top Socialist leaders and made it clear that in order to maintain effective resistance it would be necessary to replace Prieto and also the foreign minister, José Giral, who had made a habit of telling everyone he met that the war was lost. President Azaña personally wished to get rid of Negrín rather than Prieto, but the fragmentation of the Socialists was reflected in the other leftist parties as well. Only Negrín and the Communists showed strength and resolution, in the face of which the left Republicans and other Socialist leaders showed little resistance.[115]

The spreading of a rumor that Prieto was resigning alarmed some of the top leaders of the CNT, who considered him their most reliable representative in the government. Horacio Prieto, Segundo Blanco, and Galo Díez went to reason with him, and are said to have told him that the CNT would join forces with him to overthrow the power of the PCE by force.[116] Prieto thanked them for their support but replied that any new initiative would come too late to affect the outcome of the war. A special national plenum of CNT leaders then took place, possibly on March 31, at which Horacio Prieto declared that the military situation was becoming so hopeless that the CNT should join with the Socialists and left Republicans in a major effort to achieve a compromise peace, and thus, in his words, "stop unconsciously playing the game of the Russians, who want to continue a war that is ruining Spain and bleeding the libertarian movement for a cause that only appears to be ours. Thus we would save many lives, spare our people great suffering, and enable ourselves to rebuild our movement with less difficulty than if we continued resisting out of vanity."[117] These words provoked a tumult, with most CNT representatives disagreeing. Nonetheless, the Communists still had no confidence in the support of Mariano Rodríguez Vázquez because of his tendency to vacillate and because he took the position that the only change needed in the present government was to include representatives of the UGT and CNT.[118]

Negrín and the Communists had their way. The second Negrín government was formed on April 3 without either Prieto or Giral. Only one Communist remained, Uribe in Agriculture, but Segundo Blanco entered as a representative of the CNT. The Soviets, as usual, were very concerned to maintain as many left Republicans as possible for window dressing, and so the final composition was three Socialists (including the prime minister), five left Republicans (including one Catalanist), and one representative each of the PCE, UGT, CNT, and the PNV (Partido Nacionalista Vasco; Basque Nationalist Party).

The formation of the second Negrín government marked the apex of Soviet and Communist influence. Negrín himself took over the Defense Ministry (with Zugazagoitia a figurehead secretary general of the ministry), assuring maximal cooperation.[119] Del Vayo returned as foreign minister, with the Communist Manuel Arcas as his undersecretary. The leading fellow traveler in Izquierda Republicana, Bibiano Ossorio Tafall, became *comisario general de guerra*, while the outgoing Communist minister Hernández was named head military commissar for the central and southern zones. The most trusted Communist in the Republican high command, Colonel Antonio Cordón—whom Prieto had dismissed—became undersecretary of the army and the Communist officer Carlos Núñez Maza become undersecretary of the air force, an absolute Communist fiefdom. The SIM was placed under the Socialist Santiago Garcés, who had already been recruited as an NKVD agent.[120] Major Eleuterio Díaz Tendero, earlier removed by Largo Caballero, was restored to direction of the office of personnel in the Ministry of Defense. Thus Communists gained control of even more of the command structure of the armed forces. The Ministry of the Interior remained under a Socialist, but the Communists retained most of the key positions within it, and the Communist Eduardo Cuevas de la Peña was made director general of security. A member of the PSUC, Marcelino Fernández, replaced a prietista as director general of Carabineros. Togliatti's report of April 22 expressed his satisfaction with the outcome with regard to personnel and the government's strength and unity, though he recognized that the Socialists, anarchosyndicalists, and left Republicans still challenged some of Negrín's policies and accused him of being an "agent of the Communists."[121] But the Communists had become the war party par excellence, something the Comintern had hitherto sought to avoid, and now were more identified than ever with the military resistance. Moreover, this development came in the worst possible circumstances: during the first half of April the Republican front in Aragon collapsed, much of it disintegrating in a panicked rout on a scale the People's Army had never experienced before. On April 15 Franco's forces arrived at the Mediterranean; the Republican zone had been cut in two.

Negrín and Communism

Negrín had now become indispensable, not merely to the Communists in a way that he had not been in May 1937 but also to the resistance strategy of the Republic. War weariness was a serious problem, as were growing shortages, which by the latter part of the year would impose major strains on the civilian population in much of the Republican zone. There was also growing alienation even among the workers who were supposed to have benefited from worker control, collectivization, or state intervention.[122] At that point it was inconceivable that any other leader could have maintained equivalent unity and determination.

Similarly, from this point on the perception that Negrín was hand in glove with the Communists and was implementing a Soviet rather than a truly Spanish policy became increasingly common in the Republican zone, though it would not reach massive proportions until the end of the year. It is clear from the evaluations of Negrín in Comintern reports that the Communists were grateful for his extremely broad cooperation with them, which made it possible to implement many Communist designs more effectively than ever. They did not consider him either an agent or a crypto-Communist, but rather a pro-Soviet Socialist who maintained a political identity of his own. In his final summing up of the struggle, written on May 21, 1939, Togliatti concluded that the second Negrín government "was without doubt the one that most closely collaborated with the leadership of the Communist Party, and accepted and put into practice the Party's proposals more fully and rapidly than any other."[123] At the same time, he did not give them everything they wanted and refused to do certain things they desired. As one of his most severe scholarly critics, Burnett Bolloten, has written, Negrín was not in every way "totally amenable to the PCE," which "could not afford to alienate him by attempting to impose all of its proposals."[124] Though he gave the Communists just about everything they asked for in military assignments and policy, he refused to give them certain key economic positions they thought they must have to maximize military production. He also left many friends and Socialist Party colleagues in positions that the Communists did not think they should retain. Thus in his report Togliatti criticized Negrín for tolerating "the presence of a series of undesirable elements, disloyal to the cause of the Republic, and on occasion thieves, speculators, and saboteurs." In addition, he criticized Negrín for refusing to seize the leadership of his own party and bring it to submission. To a certain degree Negrín respected the autonomy of his old party, though not the policies of its leaders, and a stronger role within the PSOE would have been difficult for someone like him, who had joined the party relatively recently and had no major personal constituency within it. Though a group of negrinistas did develop in 1937–38 as a result of his government leadership, he had no genuine base within the party. Indeed, Negrín was not even political or a politician in the normal sense so much as an administrator and an authoritarian leader. To Togliatti he seemed torn between keeping faith with the Communists on the one hand and avoiding total alienation from his old Socialist comrades on the other. But without control of his own party, he had to make "continual concessions . . . to those he knew were his enemies." Moreover, Togliatti judged that the main reason Negrín continued to permit what from the Communist viewpoint was too much freedom of the press and of speech was fear of the censure of his Socialist Party colleagues.[125]

The Communists naturally soon became aware of his extraordinary personal vices and indulgences and sought to exploit them. In a Comintern report of November 25, 1937, Togliatti described Negrín as "a man without scruples," though it is not clear whether this remark, coming from a top Communist, was intended as criticism or compliment. The left Socialist Justo Martínez Amutio has written that the Soviets early discovered his penchant for bulimic *comilonas* (blowouts) that were "real binges" and made use of them. Togliatti also criticized "his work style, that of an undisciplined intellectual, blustering, disorganized, and disorganizing, and his personal life, that of a bohemian not without some sign of corruption (women)." Though in earlier years a meticulous scientist, in politics and public administration he seems almost to have been the reverse—a disorganized administrator who kept irregular hours. As Bolloten says, there can be little doubt that he dissipated much of his energy on personal indulgences that undermined his capacity for work.[126] Whereas Prieto was clearly cyclothymic, Negrín seems to have been something approaching a unipolar manic in psychiatric terms, and part of the time he was completely unable to discipline his mania and apply it effectively to his work.

An ultimate question is: What were Negrín's personal goals and ideals? Since he wrote almost nothing, this question is all the harder to answer. Martínez Amutio observed that Negrín "was not by conviction a Communist, nor even a Socialist militant of firmly held conscience and ideals. He scorned the trade union base, with which he had no contact,"[127] and that judgment seems to be correct as far as it goes. As Togliatti put it, "He has no ties to the masses. In the P[artido] S[ocialista] he was a rightist."[128] Bolloten recognizes that "it would be a mistake to argue that he had no apprehension or qualms of conscience about the role he was playing."[129] The key Communist military officer Antonio Cordón wrote in his memoirs that Negrín in fact seemed to be worried about being considered too pro-Communist.[130] That fear, Bolloten concludes, may explain why, despite his strong leadership of the resistance, he sometimes seemed uncertain with regard to individual policies. Hugh Thomas, who has a fairly high opinion of Negrín, has written that "it would be foolish to suppose that so independent-minded an intellectual, with so bad a temper, could be subservient to anyone," but Juan Simeón Vidarte recalls that Negrín admitted to him that this was indeed the case, saying at one point in 1938: "Don't you think that this odious servility is weighing on me, as it would on anyone? But there is no other way . . . unless to surrender unconditionally."[131]

However amoral part of his personal life may have been, Negrín undoubtedly had a political goal and certain ideals, though they had little to do with the working class, equality, or any specific elaborate ideology, such as any concrete form of Marxism. Helen Graham, one of his most ardent champions, holds that Negrín's goal was to maintain Spanish independence and to build a strong, progressive modern state.[132] This is no doubt true as far as it goes, but it is inadequate.

By his own standards, Negrín—unlike much of the left—was not merely a Spanish patriot but even a bit of a Spanish nationalist. Again, unlike much of the left, he did not reject his country's history, but accepted it and, to a degree, endorsed it.[133] Like nearly all the left, he was a strong sectarian, convinced that rightist rule would be the ruin of his country. He simply could not conceive that Spain might ever become a prosperous modern country under Franco, though in fact it did. If Negrín was not an intense left revolutionary, neither was he any kind of democrat. He believed that the salvation of Spain lay in a strong authoritarian leftist state, with a left-statist economic policy based on extensive nationalization but not on extreme revolutionary collectivization, and this conviction happened to coincide up to a point with Communist policy. He did not, however, seek a Communist regime in Spain, and probably hoped desperately to avoid it in some undetermined fashion, but recognized that for the time being—and possibly for some time into the future—Spain would be dependent on the Soviet Union. His political ideals overlapped with those of the Communists to the extent that he too sought a "democratic republic of a new type"—that is, an authoritarian leftist regime—but from his point of view not one that was merely dominated by the Communists. He apparently believed the left's propaganda—that Hitler and Mussolini had taken control of the Franco regime—more than most other leftist leaders did, though this credulity is surprising in someone of his level of education and intelligence. In a moment of candor just before the final collapse in Catalonia he said to his old Socialist colleague Zugazagoitia that the Republican political situation was terrible, the leftist parties were no better than the rightist ones, but nonetheless the Republic was the only way to save Spain as a country: "I have to resist letting Spain disappear."[134] There is no denying his growing fanaticism on this score. Conversely, after World War II, when he saw that such was not the case, he broke with the Communists with several articles in the *New York Times* urging the inclusion of Spain in the new Marshall Plan, simply because he realized how important that program might be to the future development of the country.

The Second Negrín Government

The domestic policies followed under the second Negrín government accorded with the general rule that the greater the degree of Communist influence, the more moderate the immediate domestic policy line. During the winter and spring of 1938 Stepanov, who had been to Moscow in February, kept repeating to the PCE politburo that the present line was the correct one, that despite the reduction in military supplies in the latter part of 1937 the Soviet Union was maintaining its same Spanish policy. He reemphasized that the left was fighting for the "democratic republic," which guaranteed "free political activities" (though not, of course, to rightists), and that Soviet policy, together with stout resistance by the Republic, would eventually force Britain and France to intervene.[135]

The crisis of March 1938 encouraged some Communist leaders to think that Comintern policy had become too timid and that the only solution was for the PCE to take over the Republican government. Thus *Mundo obrero* opined on March 23 that "it cannot be said, as in one newspaper, that the only solution to the war is that Spain be neither fascist nor communist, because France wants it that way. The Spanish people will win against the opposition of capitalism." Such a formulation leaned toward heterodoxy, and Díaz corrected the party line in *Frente rojo* one week later: "The affirmation that 'the only solution to our war is that Spain be neither fascist nor communist' is fully correct. . . . Our party has never thought that the solution to our war could be the installation of a Communist regime. . . . A Communist regime would not be accepted by all Spaniards." It was vital not to "forget the international character of our struggle"; "all the democratic states" should support one another. Togliatti reported on April 21–22 that "the tendency against which I have had to take a position on various occasions has been to think that all problems could be solved as soon as the Party took all the levers of power in its own hands. Some vacillation, even in Pepe [Díaz], in the form of an orientation toward a purely worker government." The ECCI categorically ratified Togliatti's position: there must be no thought of seizing power directly, but only of reinforcing the Popular Front.[136]

The new government definitively tilted the balance of power in Catalonia toward the PSUC. In April a number of worker collectives began to break up. All remaining worker committees were dissolved, replaced by a government *interceptor* in every enterprise of a certain size. Title in many cases was restored to the previous owners, though in fact only a few returned to take over. Ruiz i

Ponsetí became councilor of economics and began a new policy of nationalization of several key industries. Much publicity was given to the return of collectivized enterprises to foreign owners, though in fact very few reverted directly at that time. Worker morale and productivity declined further, though not for political reasons alone.[137]

Another change that followed somewhat later was the beginning of the return of public religious services, proscribed in practice in the Republican zone since the first days of the war. On June 25 Negrín restored services in the military, and a public religious procession was seen in Barcelona for the first time in more than two years during the funeral for a Basque captain on October 17. On December 8 Negrín created a General Commissariat of Religion in his personal offices, with jurisdiction over all religious regulations, nominally guaranteeing religious freedom. There is no indication that anticlericalism had been very important to Negrín personally, and the slow change in religious policy, like the reversal of collectivization, was calculated to win support among the middle classes and appear attractive to the Western democracies. It was too little, too late, and there is no indication that it had the slightest effect among either constituency.

The most important public relations gesture of the new government was the release of Negrín's "Thirteen Points" on April 30, specifying the Republic's war aims. They were intended to appeal to moderate opinion and, once more, to the democracies. It was apparently first suggested by the British Communist film producer Ivor Montagu, who told Del Vayo that the Republic needed a program for international consumption rather like Wilson's Fourteen Points. When the new cenetista minister Segundo Blanco requested that each of the government parties have a chance to approve it first, Negrín refused, allegedly saying: "It is not a matter of following every single detail of the declaration, since rather than being something that can be applied completely, instead it has the form of a declaration primarily useful for external consumption."[138]

In the Thirteen Points, Negrín declared that his "Government of National Union" stood for "the absolute independence and total integrity of Spain," "a Spain totally free of outside interference, whatever its character and origin." The second point stipulated the "liberation of our territory from all the foreign military forces that have invaded it," as well as of "those elements that have come to Spain since July 1936, and with the pretext of technical collaboration intervene in or try to dominate Spanish economic and legal affairs to their own advantage." As Elorza and Bizcarrondo comment, this sounded as though it might be referring to the Soviet Union, and indeed, as Bolloten notes, two weeks later, on May 14, *Mundo obrero* had to publish a clarification that it referred to the activities of Germany and Italy in the Nationalist zone.[139] The points went on to call for a people's republic based on "principles of pure democracy," with "universal suffrage." Its "legal and social structure" would be determined by a national plebiscite as soon as the fighting ended. The points promised "regional liberties," full civil rights, agrarian reform, advanced social legislation, and an army free of domination by any "party or tendency." This was a propaganda gesture designed for foreign consumption, obviously not a description of how the present *república popular* actually functioned, and although Negrín developed great enthusiasm for this ploy, abroad it preached only to the converted.

Negrín and Del Vayo maintained a policy—the chief slogan now was "Resistir Es Vencer" (To Resist Is to Win)—of prolonging the war until there was a change in the international situation, possibly even a bigger war that could rescue the Republic. This was the hope that Stepanov brought from Moscow. Despite their obedience, some of the PCE leaders had difficulty entertaining that hope. Ibárruri was a devout apostle of the resistance policy, but she told a plenum of the PCE central committee meeting in Madrid from May 23 to 25 that they should not wait to be saved by a great European war, for that might quickly have the effect of crushing what was left of the Republic.[140] For his part, Azaña thought such a strategy immoral. The Spanish war was bad enough without trying to turn it into an even greater drama of destruction.[141] He preferred another effort to make peace directly, but could find no opportunity.

The same issue of *Mundo obrero* that felt the need to explain that Point 1 was a propaganda device against Germany and Italy also returned to the theme of party unification, the formation of the "Partido Unico del Proletariado" (Sole Party of the Proletariat), a sort of PSUC for all the Republic, though it failed to add the PSUC's favorite self-description as *partido único bolchevique revolucionario*. In fact, this goal was becoming less and less realistic, as the various sectors of the Socialists grew increasingly resistant. The most sympathetic might have been the government-based group known as *negrinistas*, but since the autumn of 1937 the prime minister had also set himself against unification, in part because of the clear opposition in the PSOE and UGT, in part using the Communists' old arguments against them. Such a "partido único," he concluded, sounded too much like the official "partido único," FET de las JONS (Falange Española Tradicionalista and of the JONS), that Franco had created for his regime in April 1937.[142] It would receive a very bad press in the Western democracies.

One effect of the decisive strengthening of Negrín and the PCE, combined with the ouster of Prieto, was to inch toward a rapprochement between prietistas and caballeristas. As the two main sectors of the party began to restore some degree of amity among themselves, the likelihood that the Communists could simply pressure the party into unification dwindled. Gero had already reported to Moscow on May 7 that "the relations between our party and the PSOE are in general fairly tense in the majority of provinces and even more in the army. The liaison committees function very little, while in the Popular Front in the provinces (Madrid, Ciudad Real, Valencia, etc.) the party's role is quite reduced, with the frequent result that the party ends up isolated."[143] By June 19 Togliatti was reporting to Moscow what he termed a new intrigue against Negrín, to the effect that González Peña, who had cooperated with Negrín against Largo Caballero the autumn before, was now promoting the election of a new party electoral commission to be led by Julián Besteiro, the strongly anticommunist Marxist moderate who had opposed all revolutionism and had sought a peaceful solution to the war from the very beginning. He had served as Azaña's emissary in seeking British mediation in the spring of 1937 and Togliatti noted that he had declared recently "that the policy of the Popular Front had caused the war in Spain" (probably a more or less historically accurate judgment). The new initiative supposedly would combine most of the Socialists with left Republicans and Catalanists in asking Azaña to appoint a new prime minister who would seek to make peace. Togliatti called the left Republicans "the driving force" behind this plan, but warned that a situation was developing in which the Communists could—somewhat paradoxically—count on the CNT only for a policy of continued resistance. He observed that the situation was degenerating to the point where it might be necessary to declare martial law. Discussion of this possibility in the central committee had revealed "vacillations." Togliatti concluded that such a measure should not be opposed, but that "certain guarantees regarding the freedom of agitation" should be obtained. The second Negrín government was clearly the most authoritarian that the Republic had seen. It relied not on political development or the formation of consensus but on increasingly arbitrary administration, military expansion, propaganda, and Soviet support. Initially, its success in military administration was noteworthy, in some ways the most impressive of the entire war. Togliatti recognized that the changes Negrín introduced in military administration were essentially those the Soviets wanted, though he criticized the prime minister for moving very slowly with regard to the navy.[144] The administration of the People's Army was now directed by the Communist colonel Antonio Cordón, who has written that the new defense minister gave him "the task of resolving the largest possible number of matters related to the army," "with the exception of those that had to be carried out by formal decree and bear his signature, or others that had such political importance that I thought they required consultation."[145]

The Soviet advisers and the Communists already controlled the air force and the small armored units. Hernández calculated that by the spring of 1938 Communists had 70 percent of the command positions in the army, which would probably be correct for the army administration but would be a slight exaggeration for the army field corps.[146] All four corps of the newly forming Ejército del Ebro had Communist commanders, and the official Communist history recognizes that of the seventeen corps in the center and south, eight had Communist commanders, and there were Communist chief commissars in five of the other nine.[147] CNT leaders claimed that by September 1938 CNT officers commanded only nine of the seventy Republican divisions. The same report claimed that of 7,000 promotions under the new administration between May and September, approximately 5,500 went to PCE members.[148] Another anarchist source has claimed that during May 1938 alone some 1,280 commissioned or noncommissioned officer appointments went to members of the PSUC's 27th or Carlos Marx division alone.[149]

Also important was the Communists' influence in the SIM through the onetime prietista and still nominal Socialist Santiago Garcés Arroyo, one of the assassins of Calvo Sotelo in July 1936. Prieto had been unable to find a reliable chief for the military information service, one of his appointees having fled to Cuba with a suitcase full of jewels. Negrín made Garcés, a twenty-two-year-old captain of Carabineros, assistant director in April and then full head the following month, and Garcés allowed Orlov indirectly to control much of the SIM.[150] Its arrests, tortures, and killings became a political problem, drawing protests from Irujo, the former justice minister (now minister without portfolio), and from the leaders of the Esquerra, its excesses being more visible in Barcelona than elsewhere.

Yet even though Orlov was able to use much of the SIM as a branch of the NKVD, it is doubtful that it ever functioned exactly as he wished, for the control system was indirect, and was distinctly less effective in the Madrid district. Moreover, Orlov was frustrated by the chaos, multiplicity, and irregularity that still remained in Republican security operations. In one of his last reports from Spain early in July he complained that "Spain is unprecedented in Europe in its arbitrary rule of law," certainly an interesting observation from a top-ranking NKVD officer. "Any Special Department officer of the Spanish Republican Security Service has the right to arrest anyone without special permission, even the military staff." He claimed that "false cases are being trumped up"—something that he surely knew about—and that even a number of loyal Communists had been arrested and killed.[151]

The Disappearance of Aleksandr Orlov

In the middle of July, however, Orlov disappeared and for at least a month the NKVD had no idea what had happened to him. He had done effective work for Stalin in Spain and at one point it was even being rumored in Moscow that Orlov might become the next head of foreign intelligence for the NKVD, though that was before the arrest and execution of his cousin Zinovy Katsnelson.[152] What had happened was that on July 7 Orlov received a cryptogram telling him to go to Paris. There he would be taken by an embassy car to a Soviet ship in Antwerp harbor, where he was to report to someone "known to him." Not surprisingly, Orlov expected the worst. During the past two years nearly a million people had been executed in the Soviet Union. The best calculation is that 3,000 NKVD agents had been liquidated during 1937 alone, though an effort was made not to disrupt activities abroad. Orlov's superior, Avram Slutsky, had been poisoned in his office in Moscow. Rosenberg, Antonov-Ovseenko, Stashevsky, Berzin, Gorev, and Shtern had all been recalled and eventually liquidated. Orlov therefore immediately concluded that what was awaiting him was a rendezvous with a prison ship to take him to his execution.[153]

After receiving the cryptogram, Orlov wired his acceptance and almost immediately disappeared. He would later claim that he had already thought of defecting earlier and had placed his wife and daughter in a safer residence in France. Picking them up, he fled directly to Canada and later was able to enter the United States, where the Orlovs lived incognito for years. In August 1938 he wrote a letter to Yezhov saying that he was not defecting to the enemy but simply fleeing to save his life. He promised to reveal no secrets, pointedly mentioning the code names of the British spies Donald Maclean and Kim Philby, so long as no harm came to himself or his family. He warned that he had extensive, potentially very damaging documentation concerning Soviet intelligence deposited in a safe deposit box that was to be opened and publicized by his relatives living abroad in the event that any harm befell him or his family. The NKVD found $60,000 missing from the *rezidentura* safe in Barcelona. After receiving the letter, Yezhov gave orders that Orlov was not to be pursued.

Orlov did not surface publicly in the United States for thirteen years, until after the Korean War had begun. Though he testified before Congress, published more than a little, and was extensively debriefed by the FBI, he never revealed any significant secret information. About his experience in Spain he told many lies, and in his later years he worked as consultant on Soviet law at the University of Michigan Law School. Only years after his death, and after the collapse of the Soviet Union, was his NKVD file opened and his full story revealed.[154]

Orlov was replaced as *rezident* in Spain by his able lieutenant Leonid Eitingon ("Kotov"), who at this time developed the contacts he would use to employ a Catalan Communist to assassinate Trotsky in Mexico two years later. In September the Soviet chargé Marchenko reported to Moscow that Negrín had ordered that Eitingon, as NKVD chief, no longer deal directly with the Ministry of the Interior and the SIM, as in the past, but work indirectly through Negrín, who "is creating a special secret apparatus attached to himself." Marchenko commented that this order revealed the political pressure on Negrín from the other parties, the prime minister being "always extremely delicate with regard to our people."[155]

Temporary Recovery of the People's Army

The Soviet advisers were by this point gravely concerned about the strength and leadership of the People's Army. Togliatti reported on June 15 that the present Communist commanders alone were not enough, telegraphing Dimitrov:

> I beg you urgently to raise with the appropriate organs the question of providing more extensive and effective assistance to Republican Spain. This assistance is essential to increase the combat capacity of the army and, in particular, to strengthen and improve the command. We think that is the key to the whole situation. As a result of the army's reorganization, the Communist command staff plays a vital role at almost every front, but it is inept at commanding military units. Sometimes the disarray is even greater than it was previously, despite the fact that the situation with arms has improved. Negrín himself now has more opportunities to influence the course of operations planned by the general staff. Negrín insists that we help him more with people who know military science.[156]

Some of the points made in this report were further developed in a lengthy undated analysis by the best of the Soviet commanders in the People's Army, the Polish Red Army officer Karol Sverchevsky. Though he generally gave Soviet advisers good marks, he also noted that they had committed "many disappointing operational blunders," and he attributed to them at least part of the failure of all previous Republican offensives to maintain momentum. He accused the PCE stalwart Líster of "open sabotage" during the first Zaragoza offensive the preceding summer in refusing to subordinate himself to Juan Modesto, the other top PCE commander from the Frunze Institute. Sverchevsky characterized the second Republican Zaragoza offensive as so ill conceived as to be "criminal," and he judged that both Soviet advisers and Republican commanders had performed badly at Teruel, an offensive that had not been worth the effort. He thought that much of the planning was unrealistic and that "a large percentage" of Soviet advisers overestimated their own abilities. One Soviet tank officer held the fixed idea that the only purpose of being in Spain was to develop a "training ground" for the Red Army. But some of the Soviet advisers he ranked highly—Dmitry Pavlov, Yakov Smushkevich, Manfred Shtern, Rodion Malinovsky—and in general he believed the quality of the People's Army had improved.[157]

Togliatti's report of June 15 was passed on to Stalin, who had indeed been providing somewhat more matériel during the ninety days between March and June when the French border had been officially open. The great deficit that had existed in March was now at least partially made good, though the Soviets were naturally not above diverting matériel bought with Spanish money to their own uses. The Soviets reported that President Franklin D. Roosevelt was employing a subterfuge to permit arms for Spain to be sent to France, avoiding the appearance of violating the American Neutrality Act.[158]

The Republican forces then benefited from an extraordinary piece of strategic good luck. At the time of the great Nationalist breakthrough in April, Catalonia stood virtually undefended and Franco might readily have occupied it, virtually ending the war. Instead, Franco turned south toward Valencia, where he had to fight his way slowly across mountains and down a narrow coastal stretch. When the Nationalist offensive resumed, it made only slow progress. Franco's strategy sacrificed the greatest advantage the Nationalist Army possessed—its ability to maneuver in open country—and instead played to the Republicans' strength in good defensive terrain. Franco was presumably motivated by three factors, two of them of strategic concern and the third virtually irrelevant. To his subordinates he used the argument that the citrus exports of the Levant region would be very important to the balance of payments of Nationalist Spain—an argument that baffled them—but at that point, soon after the German *Anschluss* with Austria, he was probably at least as much concerned by a potentially hostile French reaction if he suddenly occupied the entire Pyrenees border. Franco was perfectly aware that a major part of Soviet and Republican strategy was still to encourage intervention by the Western democracies. This concern was apparently also stimulated by Hitler, who told one of his lieutenants that a slow-paced continuation of the Spanish war would continue to distract both France and Italy, discouraging Mussolini from creating complications elsewhere while also making it easier for Germany to extract resources from the Spanish Nationalist economy.[159]

All told, this gave Negrín and the commanders of the People's Army a three-month breathing space to build a significant army in Catalonia for the first time. A considerable number of the best Communist-led units had been shifted toward the northeast during the second half of 1937, and after the collapse of the following spring some of them ended up in Catalonia. Many of the most trusted Communist commanders were given posts in the brigades of the newly created Ejército del Ebro, which also received the best weaponry of the new Soviet shipments of 1938. A total of nearly 200,000 new troops were drafted, and Stalin sent at least 152 planes, most arriving between early June and early August.[160] These, together with the planes being produced in Catalonia and the Levant, made possible the reconstitution of the Republican air force, at least as far as its fighter squadrons were concerned.

After the collapse of March and April, the achievement of slowing Franco's advance to a crawl in the Levant amounted to a defensive victory for the Republicans. It also provided time to prepare for a counteroffensive from Catalonia. The Republican general staff followed a strategy something like that of the Confederacy in the American civil war, seizing the initiative through new offensives whenever possible. Since these offensives always failed, it may be asked whether a more purely defensive strategy might have been more effective. But the Republican command believed that it must seize the initiative, and the last major offensive was the assault southwestward across the Ebro River on July 25. Like all the other Republican offensives, it was designed to break through a quiet front and catch Franco's main forces from the rear.

Once more Franco was taken by surprise, demonstrating that despite the existence of a Nationalist fifth column in the Republican zone, he was not so well informed about the enemy's intentions as were the Republicans by Orlov's intelligence network. The resulting battle of the Ebro became the longest and most intense of the Civil War and followed the scenario of nearly all the other Republican offensives. The Ejército Popular achieved a tactical breakthrough but was unable to sustain it very long and then lost the strategic initiative, though it occupied and defended a sizable bulge of hilly terrain southwest of the river. Franco canceled his own offensive and devoted all his prime forces exclusively to a counteroffensive to regain the lost territory. The Republicans held their newly gained ground tenaciously, so that Franco's forces could proceed only very slowly, assisted by major air-to-ground support. With Republican air strength partially restored, the aerial warfare over the Ebro during late July, August, and September was probably the most intense in history to that date, until the Republican forces were ground down again through attrition. Republican air strength would have been more effective had it not been for deficiencies in the Republican/Soviet command system. General Vicente Rojo, the able Republican chief of staff, could not coordinate the use of air power completely, since it remained under autonomous Communist/Soviet command.

The Political Crisis of August 1938

During the early phases of the battle, when the situation still seemed somewhat favorable for the People's Army, the second governmental crisis of the year erupted in Barcelona. Negrín presented three new decrees on August 11. One militarized all Catalan war industry, placing it under central control and finally realizing one of the Communists' most cherished goals. The second militarized the special tribunals introduced the preceding year, while the third established a special new tribunal to combat contraband and the flight of capital. Sixty-four new death sentences were also approved. The first two proposals drew strong criticism from the Basque and Catalan ministers. After the decree on Catalan war industry was approved by the council of ministers, the head of its Catalan equivalent, Josep Tarradellas, implored Azaña not to sign such an infringement of Catalan autonomy, but to no avail. Irujo, who had soon returned to the government as minister without portfolio after his resignation, was scathing with regard to the death sentences and the militarization of the special tribunals. At the cabinet meeting on the previous day he had denounced the tortures and killings in the Sovietized checas of the SIM, saying that "with this regime of fascist cruelty we will have to lose the war," and then characterized the new measures as fascist, though of course he might as easily have said Soviet.[161] Negrín left the meeting to inform Garcés that the SIM must put an end to torture, but after the new decrees the Esquerra minister, Jaime Ayguadé, and Irujo resigned, the latter for good.

It was not difficult for Negrín to reorganize his cabinet because none of the other parties had supported the ministers from the two nominally autonomous regions. The division and passivity of the Republican parties continued, Azaña critical as ever but as impotent as ever. The outgoing ministers were then replaced by a more compliant Basque nationalist from the left-liberal Acción Nacionalista Vasca (Basque Nationalist Action, or ANV) and by a Catalan UGT leader who would soon join the PSUC. In the midst of the crisis, Undersecretary of the Army Antonio Cordón announced discovery of an alleged plot to overthrow the government by having troops assassinate officers throughout the army. This Moscow-style confabulation was then reinforced by the entry of Communist tank units from the XVIII Corps into Barcelona. By August 16 Negrín had completed formation of his new government, composed of three negrinista Socialists, one prietista Socialist, two Communists (one PCE, one PSUC), one negrinista CNT minister, four left Republicans (two of them negrinistas), and one negrinista Basque nationalist of the ANV. Negrín now had a cabinet more fully in accord with his policies than any he had led before, but its success would depend on military and international developments of the next few months.

A Soviet Exit Strategy in Spain?
New dangers encouraged even greater caution in Soviet policy, for on July 19 the Japanese army attacked Soviet positions near Lake Khasan, inside the Mongolian border, in some force. Soviet firepower and tenacity were sufficient to repel the Japanese in an intermittent battle that lasted more than three weeks, but the intensification of the threat facing the Soviet Union in the Far East called for a more careful policy in southwestern Europe. Concern was intensified during late August and much of September by the mounting crisis over the Czech Sudetenland, which seemed to threaten war between Germany and the Western democracies. These new developments in the Far East and in Central Europe encouraged increasing flexibility in Soviet policy in Spain; Stalin momentarily calculated that a show of moderation in the Civil War might now attract the support from the Western democracies that he had so long desired.

A possible change in the Soviet Union's Spanish policy was apparently first signaled by Ilya Ehrenburg in *Izvestia* on June 17, which for the first time mentioned the declining morale of the Republican troops and citizenry, and even referred to the (otherwise archfascist) Falangists as Spanish "patriots" on the other side of the trenches. The German ambassador in Moscow, Count Friedrich Werner von der Schulenburg, reported that Ehrenburg "intimates that their attitude could become significant for the further political development of Spain. . . . The Soviet press during recent weeks repeatedly carried reports about insubordination on the part of Falangists and explained these rebellions against Franco above all by the increasing hatred for foreigners. From these press statements one gets the impression the Soviets believe an understanding between the Falangists and parts of the Red Spanish side is possible."[162]

At approximately the same time Litvinov informed Jean Payart, the French chargé d'affaires in Moscow (who had recently come from a tour of duty in Valencia), that the Soviet Union was prepared to withdraw from Spain on the basis of the formula "Spain for the Spanish," provided that other powers did the same and a reasonable compromise could be reached between the two Spanish governments. On June 23 the Soviet foreign minister gave a speech stressing that it was the vital interests of Britain and France—not those of the Soviet Union—that were being threatened in Spain by Italy and Germany. Schulenburg observed that the Soviet government was trying to give the impression that it had "no power interests . . . at stake" in Spain, but was apparently preparing the Soviet people for the failure of the Republic and its own "disentanglement."[163]

In an unusual gesture toward Germany, Litvinov also referred publicly to the injustices of the Versailles Treaty and its amputation of German territory. Subsequently there seems to have been a verbal agreement between the Soviet foreign minister and Ambassador von der Schulenburg that the press in the two powers would cease personal attacks on each other's chief of state.[164]

On July 5 Schulenburg reported further that Robert Coulondre, the French ambassador, informed him that in a recent conversation Litvinov had observed that Stalin had intervened in the Spanish war "only upon the urging of the foreign Communist parties, especially the French Communists," and "chiefly for fear of a defection by foreign Communists." The Politburo had agreed, "guided more by considerations of ideology and sentiment," but the attitude of Litvinov had always been more circumspect. The Soviet foreign minister now "considered it best to withdraw from the Spanish venture without overly great losses. Under certain conditions, above all under the condition 'L'Espagne pour les espagnols,' Litvinov apparently was ready to accept an agreement between the two Spanish participants. M. Coulondre seemed to be of the opinion that Litvinov would have further success in gaining acceptance in the Politburo for his reasonable views."[165]

Togliatti was then recalled to Moscow, where between August 16 and 20 what was apparently the last major high-level Comintern debate on Spain was held as Togliatti, Marty, Codovilla, and Uribe met with the top Moscow leaders.[166] It was decided that for the time being "war without quarter" must be continued, though the present circumstances in which the PCE was identified in the Republican zone as the "war party" should be overcome. The latest changes in the international situation might make it possible to bring pressure to end German and Italian assistance to Franco, but conciliatory gestures might be both necessary and helpful.[167] The International Brigades, for example, had clearly outlived their usefulness, and had declined further during 1938. There were scarcely any new volunteers and morale had never altogether recovered. There had been cases of mutiny and a fair number of desertions.[168] The remaining military utility of the volunteers was scarcely equal to what the Soviets perceived as the political liability of their continued presence. The initiative in seeking their withdrawal came from Negrín, though he lacked the authority to do so on his own, since the brigades were still indirectly a Comintern force. The leaders in Moscow concluded on August 27 that the remaining foreign volunteers should be withdrawn. Two days later Dimitrov sent a recommendation to that effect to Stalin and Voroshilov.[169]

The same considerations also prompted—presumably on Stalin's instructions—the only sign of an exit strategy that the Comintern bosses ever signaled. Thus the Comintern leadership's resolution on Spain adopted September 3 espoused the usual demand for unswerving resistance but also sought to take advantage of the rapidly changing international situation, which very soon might limit the freedom of action of Germany and Italy. For the one and only time during the war the Comintern leadership proposed the possibility of "a loyal agreement between Spanish patriots made possible on the condition that foreign occupation troops be expelled from Spain." As Elorza and Bizcarrondo observe, this agreement would not necessarily impose or even save the new type of democratic republic, because it would presumably result in some sort of compromise peace, but it might extricate the Soviet Union from the war on terms attractive to France and Britain, and could also be presented as a Soviet and Communist success insofar as it saved Spain from any foreign domination, which had always been one of the main propaganda themes, so that a victory might be claimed for Soviet policy in terms of the country's freedom and independence.[170] The Soviet leadership was apparently at least momentarily willing to make concessions, so long as they did not redound to the advantage of Germany.

Officially, the Comintern still stood resolutely by the Republic. A resolution of the ECCI on August 28 urged all member parties to undertake new drives to send food and other supplies to Spain, and to try to encourage credits and loans from their governments.[171] In addition, Dimitrov and Manuilsky took up with Stalin and Molotov the possibility of alleviating the drastic food shortage in the Republican zone by starting yet another campaign among the Soviet trade unions, and asked whether the Republican government could buy still more supplies from the Soviet Union on credit. Stalin was at this point in no mood to increase his investment after having just agreed to new military credits for the Republic only two weeks before. The answer to both queries from the Comintern leaders was no.[172]

Shortly afterward Litvinov appeared before the League of Nations to propose the withdrawal of all foreign combatants from both sides and in the same forum on September 21 Negrín announced the unilateral withdrawal of the foreign volunteers of the International Brigades. Most of these maneuvers took place the following month, and after the end of October only a few hundred remained in the Republican zone. During September and October part of the remaining Soviet personnel were also recalled to the Soviet Union.

The crucial events of the final week of September, resulting in the Anglo-French capitulation at Munich, guaranteed that these last Soviet steps would have no political payoff whatsoever. After suspending deliveries to Franco for several weeks during the crisis, Hitler signed a new deal with him in October that pleased both dictators and guaranteed that the Nationalist forces would now be stronger than ever. Conversely, the Soviet Union was more isolated than ever before, its Spanish and Western European policy increasingly in shambles.

Franco's counteroffensive toward the Ebro was slow, unimaginative, and direct, fueled by superior firepower both on land and in the air. He committed his units piecemeal to what became the war's only long battle of attrition. Franco won slowly, as always, but was in little danger of losing. The Ejército del Ebro, the strongest section of the Republican forces, was slowly ground to pieces. The last Republican units finally retreated to the north side of the river in mid-November. Once more the Ejército Popular had been gravely weakened, indeed reduced to its lowest point in the war. When the ages of a group of 11,831 prisoners taken by one of Franco's army corps were checked, it was found that only 47 percent of them came from the age groups drafted for the Nationalist forces: 10 percent were younger and 43 percent were older men.[173] The People's Army was beginning to scrape the bottom of the barrel. Arguably, the end was in sight.

CHAPTER ELEVEN

Defeat

1938–1939

URIBE PRESENTED the Comintern's new line on the goal of the war—an understanding among Spaniards to end "the foreign invasion"— to the PCE central committee on September 29–30. The timing was fateful, for it coincided with the Munich agreement, which would demonstrate that the new line had no chance for success whatsoever. Some days later a telegram from Moscow informed Togliatti and Díaz that the Sudetenland settlement was a great blow and that the only means of assisting the Republic now lay in international worker mobilization, in itself a desperate sort of hope.[1]

The Soviet military presence was dwindling. At one time it may have numbered close to a thousand men, but by October 23 the total was approximately 250, and by January 4, 1939, it had dropped to 218.[2] This was a considerable reduction, but far from a liquidation. There is no indication that after the Comintern's new "September strategy" had become a nonstarter, Stalin either had or sought any exit strategy whatsoever. Soviet participation and exposure would be reduced but not ended; from the Soviet point of view, it was important not to give up. The combination of a strong common bastion and continued resistance in southwestern Europe might still have political or strategic utility. Dimitrov had announced publicly on several occasions that the chief responsibility of the Comintern's member parties was to contribute to the defense of the Soviet Union. The PCE was to see to it that the Republic continued to fight.

The Soviet advisers were well aware that all the other leftist parties were beginning to waver. Though the CNT remained committed to resistance, the peninsular committee of the FAI had first begun to discuss the possibility of an armistice in the summer of 1938. A long national committee meeting held by the CNT in Barcelona from October 16 to 30 produced great conflict. When Horacio Prieto joined Secretary General Vázquez in supporting Negrín, he was accused of holding "a concrete position of frank reformism, bordering on Marxism."[3] Vázquez, as usual, remained the staunchest proponent of collaboration and had accepted Negrín's thesis of trying to hold out until a general European war broke out, but the final resolution only approved a qualified "circumstantial political collaboration."[4] The leaders of the FAI were even more disillusioned than those of the CNT and sent a delegation to Azaña asking him to get rid of "the dictator." Azaña had indeed sought an alternative during the April crisis, but in August Negrín had simply ignored him and reorganized the government on his own initiative, leading Azaña to accuse him of a coup d'état. The *faístas* found Azaña "now completely intimidated."[5]

Negrín and Togliatti were, if anything, even more worried about the attitude of the Socialists. For some time many of the caballerista leaders had taken the position that they were living under little more than a Soviet dictatorship and that in the long run they would have to emigrate no matter who won. Araquistain wrote to his daughter, "For some time I have been saying that whether we win or lose, we independent Socialists will have to emigrate, because in the first case the Communists would shoot us and in the second case Franco."[6] When the political committee of the PSOE met on November 15, the growing strength of Julián Besteiro became apparent, as did the rapprochement between prietistas and caballeristas. The Communists later quoted Besteiro as saying at this time, "If the war were won, Spain would be Communist. All the rest of the democratic world would be against us and we could count on Russia alone. . . . And if we are defeated, the future will be terrible."[7] According to Ibárruri, the only person on the liaison committee still maintaining contact with PCE representatives was the Socialist Party secretary, Ramón Lamoneda, and he told Togliatti on November 21 that fusion was impossible, given the divisions and attitudes in the party.[8] The bitterness against the Communists in the PSOE was now enormous.

Ordinary members of the JSU had not learned until 1937 that the leaders of their unified organization created in the early spring of 1936 were in fact Communists. Anticommunist opposition in the JSU had begun to grow during the second half of 1937, and during 1938 rival leadership began to appear in a number of cities. Dissidence was strong in Madrid, and Carrillo's decision to move the national committee of the JSU back to Madrid to control it was ineffective. The opposition Committee of Young Socialists held their own conference in Madrid during November 1938, though they did not create a completely separate organization.

Even within the PSUC there was growing resentment about Soviet and negrinista domination. The PSUC in some ways followed a more revolutionary line than did the PCE, but much of its original membership was composed of ultra-left-wing Catalanists who resented external domination. Many of these people would leave the party altogether after the war ended.[9]

President Azaña made one final gesture of independence, summoning Besteiro to confer in Barcelona about another initiative to encourage British and French mediation, as Besteiro had sought to do in London the previous year. Besteiro informed him that it was now too late; neither the domestic nor the international situation would sustain such an endeavor.

The PCE was unable to maintain its position in some local political structures. In the Republican sector of Granada province, for example, it had earlier established a kind of hegemony in the Provincial Committee of the Antifascist Popular Front, but it began to collapse in the summer of 1938, and by the end of the year anticommunist sentiment was pervasive in the Republican zone.[10] The party's position in Popular Front groups (where they still existed) and in public opinion had weakened critically. The Communist position now depended more than ever on state power and the military, though the strongest Communist-led sector of the military, the Ejército del Ebro (which was also politically the most heavily Communist-officered Republican army), had been shattered by the battle it had waged for more than three and a half months.

On November 19 Erno Gero dispatched a long report to Dimitrov from Barcelona, which tried to put the best possible gloss on a bad situation. He admitted that the Republic would soon face its "most serious test" of the war, but in a Mussolini-like exaggeration, he declared that "the army currently has reached 1,200,000 men; that is, the Republican Army now significantly outnumbers the fascist army." Similarly gigantic figures were reported for PCE membership, which was allegedly benefiting from "a new inflow of the masses" and "currently numbers about 830,000 members," to which should be added 75,000 affiliates of the PSUC. This was a blatant example of the wishful thinking by that time rampant in the Communist enterprise. The only one of these statistics that may have been accurate is that for the PSUC, which Gero reported as gaining nearly a thousand members a month in Barcelona. The wildly inflated figure for the army could refer accurately only to the total number of soldiers to have passed through Republican ranks in the course of the war.

The real strength of the People's Army was around 800,000 men, often indiffer-
ently equipped. Franco's forces were now larger numerically and better armed.
Gero admitted that there had been "an increase in desertion lately" and that
"the adversary has a significant advantage in military matériel, especially in
aircraft (the proportion is 1 to 5) and also in artillery," while "the Republican
navy roughly equals the fascist navy in matériel" but "is inactive."[11]

Military stocks had dwindled dangerously during the battle of the Ebro
and no new Soviet supplies had arrived since August. Even before the battle
ended, Negrín decided that he must make a special effort to reopen the Soviet
pipeline. On November 11 he entrusted a personal letter to Stalin to the care
of the nominal Republican Air Force commander, Colonel Ignacio Hidalgo
de Cisneros (who, as explained earlier, maintained a checa in the basement of
his home in Alcalá de Henares). In this eighteen-page document, Negrín made
a major effort to explain political and military developments in terms satisfactory to the Soviets, including a pledge of the closest cooperation in the future
between the Soviet Union and a victorious Republic. Negrín insisted that "in
internal affairs we have achieved a degree of unity that is not perfect but, considering the period of anarchy we went through, is nonetheless satisfactory." He
explained: "It is possible that on occasion what has been interpreted as a weakness was no more than the realization that the strength to carry out a given
task did not yet exist. It is the responsibility of a statesman, especially when
he does not have a strong homogeneous party behind him, not to waste strength
in premature efforts. I believe that in the application of this norm I have proceeded correctly." Negrín clearly implied that he recognized that the semipluralism that existed in the Republican zone was inadequate from the Soviet point
of view—something that Soviets and Communists had no doubt impressed
upon him many times—and that he would endeavor to impose tighter control
when it became possible to do so. He admitted that a strong political campaign
was currently being waged against the PCE, but he assured Stalin that the
Communists were "my best and most loyal collaborators." Though "today we
cannot respond adequately because it would produce new conflict," he assured
Stalin that the PCE's position would be vindicated. He pledged to Stalin that
a major shipment of arms would carry a revitalized People's Army to victory
and that a victorious Republic would remain a firm political and military collabo-
rator of the Soviet Union in Western Europe:

> I do not want to close without assuring you that the recovery and
> reconstruction of Spain can be carried out with our own means in

a very few years. This is not the time to explain my recovery plans
to you, but please believe me when I say that with the potential
wealth of Spain, and with a united country and a government
directed by vigorous hands, such a task will be easy.

In the end we will find ourselves stronger than ever. With
many traditional obstacles removed, with people of energy and
authority forged by war, with a strong army and the industrial possibilities of our shipyards, we can not merely build a new merchant
and war fleet of some importance but also provide shipping to
other countries.

For many Spaniards it will always be an honor to think that if
at a later time there is in this western extremity of Europe a potent
military and naval force that can collaborate in common goals of
human progress with the USSR, this will be due in large part to
the encouragement, collaboration, and assistance that our Soviet
friends have disinterestedly lent us.[12]

Negrín may have included the extravagant claims for a future Republican navy
because he had learned of Stalin's search for foreign assistance in developing
his planned "bolshoi flot," a project still beyond the Soviet Union's economic
and technological grasp.

Hidalgo departed for Moscow, where he arrived before the end of the
month. Negrín requested a large shipment of arms, asking for 250 warplanes,
250 tanks, 650 pieces of artillery, and 4,000 machine guns, among other
things. It is doubtful that Stalin was much impressed by Negrín's boast about
the Republic's future military and naval strength, but the Soviet dictator did
assent after little delay, agreeing to satisfy at least a significant portion of the
request.[13] The preceding August the Soviet government had informed Republican representatives that only 1.5 ton of gold was left, and at that time extended
a credit of $60 million. In December a new line of credit was extended for
$103 million, the third Soviet loan of the year.

This final shipment of arms, prepared in the Soviet Union during December 1938, later became controversial in Civil War historiography when the
"abandonment thesis" was broached—the conclusion that Stalin had in fact
decided to abandon the Republic all the while that his representatives were inciting Republicans to fight to the last Spaniard. According to this thesis, the
arms shipment amounted to little more than a propaganda gesture and was
probably not even sent. Both Soviet and Spanish data, however, directly contra-

dict the abandonment thesis. Soviet records indicate that shipment was prepared for 15 torpedo boats, 134 warplanes, 40 tanks, 359 pieces of artillery, 3,000 machine guns, 40,000 rifles, and a sizable quantity of ammunition, at least some of which began to arrive in Catalonia in January before Republican defenses there collapsed.[14] It does seem, however, that nearly all of it arrived too late to be of much use in the defense of Catalonia. Since half of the $70 million credit conceded in April had been backed by gold, total Soviet loans granted during 1938 amounted to $198 million. However, much of the last $103 million was not used, for arms to that full value were never shipped. Later, when the use of the gold became an international issue after the death of Negrín in 1956 and transfer of the receipts to the Spanish government, the Soviet state would announce in *Pravda* on April 5, 1957, that all the gold had been used up, and that the Republic still owed at least $50 million—though there is evidence that before his death Negrín had rejected the Soviet accounting.[15]

After his request arrived in Moscow, Negrín also attempted to take decisive action to strengthen his domestic political position. While earlier he had opposed the idea of forming the unified "partido único del proletariado," in part because it sounded too fascistic, in the present dire situation Negrín concluded that a state party was needed to build government strength and generate necessary political unity. In December he began to sound out the leaders of the PCE about creating a new united Frente Nacional. Togliatti's notes indicate that the proposal would "preserve the parties" and that it would have to be carefully prepared, because "it cannot be done overnight." Togliatti was not sure to what extent it would simply rest on a "military dictatorship," since "parliament will not count" and there would have to be some kind of plebiscite. The proposal was apparently not to do away with the existing parties, since any such effort would mean the end of the Republic, but to create a greater new political superstructure with double membership. Togliatti wired Moscow that the Frente Nacional would function "outside of" the political parties, that it would not be seen as directed against any of them and particularly must not be seen as an initiative of the PCE. There might be either individual or collective membership for members of other parties or for the parties themselves. Stepanov later recalled that the idea was that "the Communist Party would be the real leader, but that such leadership would be exercised discreetly," while Togliatti indicated that the PCE "would provide the cadres to organize it," and Negrín also said that if the Communists did not agree to such a front, he would drop the idea. Negrín might even have been aware of Togliatti's speculation more than a year earlier about the possible utility of asking Azaña to "call for the creation of a mass patriotic organization," and the Comintern adviser reported that one of the prime minister's goals was to build a stronger political organization that would not be overtly Communist and would look better abroad.[16] In his unpublished memoirs, Uribe later wrote that Negrín "argued that in such a conglomeration or movement, with our strength and experience in political work we would be able to impose our line. For the formation of this Partido único administrative means were not excluded, because once this Partido único of the government, that is of Negrín, was formed, all other parties in the Republican zone would be prohibited."[17] That would not be the case in the initial phase, but would be the ultimate logic and outcome of the maneuver. This was the direction in which Franco had begun to move a full two years earlier.

Some days later, Negrín explained his thinking further to the Soviet chargé, Marchenko, who reported that Negrín had come up with his proposal because under present conditions the unification of the Socialist and Communist parties was simply impossible. According to Marchenko, who presumably was reflecting Negrín's thinking at this point, "the most that might be expected is that the Socialist party will be absorbed by the Communist party at the end of the war," even though the present Socialist leaders would never acknowledge the possibility and would try to maintain their own party. "But what kind of party is the government depending on? To depend on the Communist Party is unfavorable from the international standpoint. The existing Republican parties have no future. . . . What is needed, therefore, is an organization that would unify all that is best in all of the parties. . . . It seems to him [Negrín] that it ought to be based on individual membership, and he conceives of the membership in a threefold way: simple members, active members, and leading cadres, who ought to bear the title of full members. He permits a double membership, that is, members of the National Front may remain in existing parties, the activity of which will not be limited. . . . The leadership of the new party's organizational and propaganda work must be handed over to the Communists."[18] The whole concept seems somewhat similar to that of the Imperial Rule Assistance Association, set up the following year in Japan.

Marchenko added that "Negrín emphasized that he was not insisting on this idea if someone will indicate another way out of the situation." "There is no returning to the old parliamentarianism; it will be impossible to allow the 'free play' of parties as it existed earlier, for in this case the Right might once again force its way into power. This means that either a unified political organization or a military dictatorship is necessary. He does not see any other way." Here Negrín was simply being more honest than most of the left, many of whom had abandoned democracy as soon as they lost the elections of November 1933. Marchenko explained that his own response had been noncommittal. He was concerned that if the Republic should win a military success, Negrín would use the opportunity to "begin the formation of 'his' united-Spanish political party, ... even without the Communists (and that means against them) if they refuse," though he concluded that this matter was for the moment "not very pressing."

He also reported that Negrín expressed disdain for the counterrevolutionary policy of the Catalan Generalitat and said he could not explain why the PSUC ministers were so "reverential" toward Companys. The prime minister declared that "the Esquerra is striving to return to the situation that existed before 18 July. Such a return will not happen. The bourgeoisie will not recover their positions. All of the principal branches of Spain's economy will be nationalized. And Spain will be disposed least of all to restoring the privileges of the Catalan bourgeoisie."[19] Altogether, this Soviet document probably describes better than any other the gist of Negrín's political and economic thinking during the final phase of the Civil War.

That same day, December 10, however, the Comintern replied that Negrín's proposal was flatly unacceptable "because it contains a tendency toward personal dictatorship."[20] In Negrín's often simplistic political thinking, such a front might be seen as attractive, but the more sophisticated Comintern knew better. Equally important was the consideration that such a front would technically supersede the PCE itself, and in any case, it is doubtful that the Comintern leaders trusted Negrín that much. This Republican unity party would have been a device rather like the socialist unity parties that the Soviets created in the Eastern European people's democracies after 1945, but in the Spanish case they would at first not be in control and the military and international contexts were totally different.

Less than two weeks later (December 23), Franco opened his offensive against Catalonia. The international situation had changed decisively. France was not to be feared and Hitler was happy to see the Spanish struggle concluded as soon as possible. The People's Army still had 300,000 troops under arms in Catalonia, about the same number that Franco used in his offensive, but Franco's were much better organized, commanded, and equipped. Many of the new Soviet aircraft had been lost, and in Catalonia the Republican forces were down to 80 aircraft, 200 tanks and armored cars, and 360 pieces of artillery, much of this matériel of uncertain quality. Franco employed 500 warplanes and a much superior volume of artillery.[21] The small quantity of new Soviet matériel that arrived before the collapse was inadequate to right the balance. Though Franco's advance was, as usual, somewhat slow, it was steady and achieved multiple breakthroughs, preventing the Republican command from concentrating its defense. As the battle front neared Barcelona, the cry that "the Llobregat will be the Manzanares of Cataluña"—in other words, that Barcelona would resist like Madrid in 1936—proved hollow. There was now little appetite for diehard resistance in Barcelona, which fell on January 26. The remainder of Catalonia was occupied by February 10, as a mass exodus of refugees poured into France, most of them to return to Spain within a year.

This also marked the beginning of the end for the Republican government. Azaña and many of the other political and military leaders, including the chief of staff, Vicente Rojo, refused to return to the shrunken Republican zone, which now amounted roughly to the southeastern quarter of Spain, including Madrid. For them the war was lost, and they contended that the rest of the Republican government and command should simply face reality. With part of the government defecting, a serious problem of legitimacy would arise if the war effort were to continue.

Soviet policy, however, did not change. Stalin had no exit strategy for the Soviet effort in Spain, but gave orders for continued all-out resistance, on the grounds that complete resistance to fascism in Spain sustained a diversion that might limit the advance of fascism elsewhere. Togliatti telegraphed in reply on January 29 that such a policy would require the ultimate in mobilization and the harshest repression of dissent.[22] What the Soviet government would not contribute to such a policy of resistance was the remainder of the matériel in the last arms shipment—much of it still in transit across France—for fear that it would fall into Franco's hands, as was indeed the case with the new matériel that had already entered Catalonia. By February 16, 1939, further movement of this matériel was canceled, the main concern now being to recover arms currently in France awaiting transshipment.[23] Getting supplies through to the remaining Republican zone required double transshipment—by rail across France, then by boat from a port in southern France across the Mediterranean, in which Franco's forces were becoming increasingly dominant. Transport was too hazardous and further resistance somewhat uncertain. Only in this sense did the Soviet government "abandon" the Republic, but within three weeks Stalin was willing to consider a new shipment of matériel, if means could be found for its delivery. The Soviet government also donated 5 million francs for the relief of Republican refugees in France.[24]

The Soviet watchword was continued resistance to the end. All Soviet efforts toward rapprochement with Nazi Germany had thus far failed, and Stalin could not find any alternative to his basic Spanish strategy, though he was no longer willing to invest very much in it. Comintern agencies therefore continued their agitation for aid to the Republic.[25] If no further arms were being sent, at least for the time being, Stalin was still willing to send a few more Soviet military personnel. Though most of the latter had been withdrawn, their depleted ranks were slightly replenished by the last contingent to arrive, on February 7. This final group of twenty-five consisted of seven military advisers and instructors, twelve artillery specialists, two naval men, and four unidentified persons. In exchange, however, a larger group left Spain for the Soviet Union on the 27th, including the two remaining chief advisers, K. M. Kachanov and D. E. Kolesnikov.[26]

Togliatti later wrote that after the fall of Catalonia the general impression in the Republican zone was that further resistance was impossible, and that this was the opinion of nearly all the career officers in the People's Army, both Communist and noncommunist.[27] The Soviet line nonetheless permitted no wavering. Later Soviet publications greatly exaggerated the remaining strength of the Republican forces in the southeast in order to make it appear that the Communist position of continued resistance was reasonable. Colonel Segismundo Casado, commander of the Madrid district who led the overthrow of the Communists, wrote afterward that there were only about 400,000 troops remaining and 100 airplanes, whereas Soviet sources give figures of 700,000 or more, undoubtedly inflated.[28]

Martial law was finally decreed in the Republican zone on January 23, just before the fall of Barcelona, but only the Communist leaders seemed willing to follow the logic of extreme measures that martial law implied. Elorza and Bizcarrondo point out that the PCE chieftains still retained much of the ultraleft attitude of the old prewar revolutionary Bloque Popular, as distinct from the semipluralism of the Frente Popular. On February 2, scarcely a week before the final evacuation of Catalonia, the party bosses launched a PCE manifesto headed "The Communist Party reaffirms its faith and confidence in victory," in which they demanded a line of absolute intransigence. The manifesto strongly denounced the "treason of the capitulationists," specifically condemning "the shameful flight" of Largo Caballero to France immediately after the fall of Barcelona. The virulence and unilateralism of this manifesto quickly elicited strong criticism from all the other parties, no longer so cowed by the Communists as in the past.

With the collapse of Catalonia imminent, Stepanov, the number two

Comintern adviser, and Ibárruri were sent to Madrid on January 27 to shore up the situation there. Stepanov evidently began to share the thinking of the PCE leaders in Madrid, who spoke among themselves of the need for a new hard-line government, in good measure based on themselves. By the beginning of February, Stepanov began to talk of "a democratic revolutionary dictatorship, built largely on the PCE, which would crack down on defeatists. In such a scheme, the Negrín government would be replaced by a 'Special Defense Council of Labor and Social Security,' charged with administering the war and composed of two ministers, two or three politicians, and a pair of 'reliable and energetic' military men."[29] A provincial conference of the PCE in Madrid from February 9 to 11 took a similarly hard line; its climax was a violent speech by Ibárruri threatening condign punishment of "traitors." In addition, the Madrid leaders decided to reprint the party manifesto of February 2, distributing and posting it throughout Madrid, provoking a strong anticommunist reaction. The other parties were now beginning to lose their fear of the Communists and would no longer accept their constant demands, threats, and denunciations. The PCE was formally censured by the Popular Front committee of Madrid and even expelled from the committees in several provinces. Stepanov later reported to the Comintern that the party leadership had been out of touch with public opinion in the main Republican zone when it drafted the February manifesto in Figueras, and that he had recommended that it not be distributed widely in Madrid, but had managed to delay the distribution for only one day. The reaction revealed the party's growing isolation.[30]

Negrín, though profoundly depressed by the loss of Catalonia, returned from France to the Republic on February 11, as did Togliatti, the top PCE leaders, and the top Communist military commanders formerly in Catalonia. Purges of Communist officers who were not measuring up in September and January resulted in loss of command and expulsion from the party, but the officers who returned from France with Negrín were all Communists, in fact the core of the Communist military elite. When he learned of the new notion of the Madrid Communists, however, he is said to have told Uribe on the 16th that he had heard that the Communists were now declaring that they could obey or not obey the government as they pleased and angrily declared, "I am going to have the Communists shot." The situation was temporarily calmed when Togliatti returned to Madrid later that day, but Togliatti was concerned about the diminished strength and increasing isolation of the Communists in the central zone. On the 17th he telegraphed Moscow that the PCE was "isolated and attacked by everybody."[31]

Togliatti was displeased with the extremism of the Madrid leaders, the tone of their recent conference, Ibárruri's provocative speech, and the wide distribution of the last manifesto, nor was he impressed by Stepanov's response. Indeed, though Stepanov criticized the Figueras manifesto, he reported to Moscow that "I consider the line of the Madrid conference and Dolores's speech absolutely correct," because a strong appeal was necessary to overcome the "isolation" of the party.[32]

The Comintern advisers and PCE leaders were perplexed about how resistance was to be maintained if some sort of emergency dictatorship were not imposed, in view of the Republic's extreme weakness. On the 18th it was decided to send Stepanov to Moscow immediately for further instructions on this problem, and how to respond if either Negrín or other Republican forces decided to capitulate. In that case, would a Communist dictatorship have to be established to continue the war?[33]

Meanwhile, good relations were quickly restored between Negrín and the PCE, since each had so much need of the other. The party's politburo made a new attempt to improve its public relations with a manifesto prepared on February 23, with Togliatti's assistance, in somewhat more hopeful and conciliatory terms than its last broadside, which was published by *Mundo obrero* on the 26th. According to Togliatti, its final version was "personally corrected by Negrín," who now "conceded much more to the party than had been asked of him." The manifesto insisted that "it is a profound error to think that we have little or nothing to hope for from abroad, and that the democratic countries that have allowed Catalonia to be invaded by the Germans and Italians will not aid us now that we have lost such an important position. The international situation has never been more unstable than today." The fact that the aggressors had become yet bolder and more audacious would now begin to open the eyes of the democracies, while the great Soviet Union, "the powerful country that defends the cause of liberty, justice, and peace throughout the world," supported the Republic as firmly as ever. Likewise "the proletariat and the sincerely democratic forces" of all the Western countries that had provided great assistance in the past could provide decisive help in changing their governments' policies in the future, so that "what has not been obtained until now can be obtained in the future if we strengthen our resistance." Thus continued resistance "can change the situation, can permit new facts to develop, both in Spain and abroad, that . . . will open the possibility of victory to us." An end to the war was to be achieved through further resistance, so that a peace could be won that would maintain independence, freedom, and the absence of reprisals. The difference in this communication was that it spoke of "peace" and of how to "end the war," and that it emphasized "unity and antifascist brotherhood" "with all the parties, with all the leaders, with all the trade union, political and military organs." One day later, however, Togliatti once more asked Moscow whether the Spanish party should "take in its hands through forceful measures all the levers of power and direction of the war."[34] Despite the quick restoration of good ties with Negrín, the Communist leaders were beginning to question his will, for he had not overcome the deep depression that had gripped him since the loss of Catalonia. Moreover, Madrid was closely besieged on two sides by Franco, who might now overwhelm its defenses at any time. The government and the Communist leaders feared being caught in a trap, and on the 27th they abandoned the Republic's fourth capital in two and a half years, withdrawing far to the southeast. Symbolically, that same day Britain and France officially recognized the Franco regime as the government of Spain.

The Spanish Civil War generated more controversies than any other conflict of its dimensions during the entire twentieth century, and this most controversial of wars ended with yet another great political controversy. It also ended the way it began, with a political rebellion by a portion of the Republican army against the Republican government on the grounds that it was handing Spain over to communism—the final paradox of this most paradoxical of civil wars. Over the years, an entire literature has developed—primarily in Spanish—devoted to the thesis that the anticommunist revolt that brought the Republic and the war to an end was in fact the result of a cleverly designed Communist provocation, which was intended to shift the entire onus for surrendering to the anticommunists, and thus to enable the Communists (and the Soviet Union) to maintain untarnished the banner of antifascist resistance. In fact, the last book to present this thesis was published in 1998 by a ninety-year-old former Communist propaganda official who had become a vociferous anticommunist.[35] As Soviet documentation now available has made clear, however, there was in general no more to the end of the Spanish war than normally meets the eye.

The military commander of the central zone was a noncommunist professional officer, Colonel Segismundo Casado, who had participated in the early training and development of the People's Army, later commanded two corps in the Army of Andalusia, and had then been appointed by Negrín and Cordón commander of the central zone in May 1938. The conspiracy theorists have claimed that the very appointment of Casado was a clever Communist stratagem to set him up for his ultimate role, but this interpretation is unconvincingly complex and gives the Communists credit for clairvoyance. Though Casado early criticized the unequal distribution of Soviet arms among sectors of the People's Army—a criticism that cost him his first command—he had also afterward cooperated with the Soviet advisers and Communist commanders, even though he was known not to be a Communist. It is therefore more plausible that the People's Army simply was in desperate need of competent professional commanders who were loyal Republicans, and there were not nearly enough Communists in that category to go around. It was not surprising that *Mundo obrero* had initially hailed his appointment. By the first of February, Casado had become the military centerpiece of a loosely forming agreement among the noncommunist military and representatives of the other political parties in Madrid, led by the venerable Julián Besteiro, to make peace with Franco as soon as was feasible, without fighting another bloody battle. Aside from the very general desire for peace throughout most of the Republican zone, a driving idea behind the plot was the notion that professional noncommunist officers such as Casado and some of his colleagues would be much more likely than the communistoid Negrín regime to reach an honorable peace without reprisals, provided, of course, that the Negrín regime had first been removed from power. Togliatti would later claim that development of the conspiracy had been possible partly because of shoddy police and counterintelligence work in Madrid.[36] As has been pointed out, the SIM had not been as effective there as in Barcelona, whereas during the last months of the war the police chief in Madrid was Colonel Ricardo Burillo. Though a Communist, Burillo had been relieved of command of the Extremadura front in September 1938 and expelled from the party for deficiencies, but then received this new assignment from General José Miaja, who was always friendly to Communists but equally friendly to his fellow professional officers.

According to the conspiracy theorists, the detonator of the anticommunist revolt was supposed to be a very clever and provocatively conceived scheme to place in the hands of Communist officers all important commands not being held by Communists, announced officially in the *Diario oficial del Ministerio de Defensa Nacional* on March 3. This notion, however, involves considerable exaggeration, as will shortly be seen. Its main kernel of truth was that during the second half of February, while Casado was developing his contacts with Franco's agents, the few remaining Soviet professionals, the top Communist commanders, and the Comintern advisers were all insisting to Negrín that the Republican command needed to be tightened as much as possible, which in practice meant giving the Communists even more of the top commands.

Togliatti claimed that this was urgently brought to Negrín's attention on the 20th, but he at first failed to act, fearing to alienate further the other Popular Front parties.[37] On the 20th, the *Gaceta de la República* published a decree by Negrín promoting Casado to general, supposedly, according to the prime minister, to make it appropriate to appoint Casado to the post of chief of the General Staff in place of Vicente Rojo (who refused to return from France, judging the war to be over). That move would then make it possible to promote Lieutenant Colonel Emilio Bueno, Communist head of the Second Corps, to Casado's position as commander of the Army of the Center. Nonetheless, Negrín remained slow to move on the new appointments, but finally signed a large number of them late on March 2, and they appeared in the Ministry of Defense's *Diario oficial* on the following day.[38]

All copies of this issue of the *Diario* subsequently disappeared, or at least could not be found until the Spanish research assistants of Burnett Bolloten finally discovered a copy in the Archivo Histórico Nacional in Salamanca in 1985. These new assignments made major changes but not all of those later alleged by Casado or by the other conspiracy theorists. A number of Communist commanders were promoted and six received higher commands. Two other Republican commanders under political suspicion were demoted, but the new "provisional" head of the General Staff was the noncommunist general Manuel Matallana. The other appointments cited by the conspiracy theorists —Cordón as commander in chief of the armed forces and four top Communist officers given commands of the four distinct armies of the Center, the Levant, Extremadura, and Andalusia—simply were not made, though it is entirely possible that they were under contemplation.

On the following day, however, rather than completing plans for evacuation of the top Communists, as the conspiracy theorists would have it, Togliatti sent yet another telegram to Moscow nervously repeating his apparently unanswered query of five days earlier—in the likely event of a revolt against Negrín or the Communists, should the latter try to seize all power and impose a dictatorship of all-out resistance? He received an answer the following day, only hours before the Casado revolt broke out in Madrid. Rather than cunningly preparing to close down resistance, Stalin set conditions for yet another shipment of arms to the greatly shrunken Republic, provided that the government would pledge continued resistance and that reliable transshipment across France to the southern French ports could be reliably negotiated. The telegram also appears to have mentioned the possibility of forming not a Communist dictatorship, which the Comintern bosses doubtless realized was not likely to be successful and moreover would undercut the whole Soviet/Comintern political strategy, but simply a new Government of National Defense of all Popular Front parties willing to pledge continued resistance. Togliatti was also instructed not to undertake any new "missions or obligations" in that regard but to return to Moscow for further consultation.[39]

Clearly there was no cleverly planned Communist provocation. The Communists doubtless realized that Casado was no longer fully reliable and the failure to replace him earlier was due not to any diabolical Communist plan but simply to the torpor that Negrín had shown since the fall of Catalonia. Juan Modesto has claimed, in fact, that Negrín ordered Cordón to relieve Casado of command on the third, and Casado has claimed that an effort was made to lure him down to Negrín's new headquarters at Elda in Alicante province on the fifth. Further destitutions of noncommunists and key appointments of Communists may or may not have been made in the *Diario oficial* on the fourth. No copies of this publication have survived, but according to one version, that issue did not appear until the morning of the fifth and all copies were later destroyed by the anticommunist rebels.[40] It is unlikely that the controversy over the final appointments can ever be completely resolved, so that it cannot be known exactly how many new Communist commanders Negrín appointed down to March 5. The Communists have criticized Negrín for his depressive lethargy, and indeed he gave no sign of his customary mania. He dawdled for ten days about making the new appointments and then began to do so all at once in a politically provocative way.[41]

However all this may be, it is largely beside the point. The revolt against the Negrín government that Casado announced in Madrid by radio at midnight on March 5 was not something suddenly thrown together in response to new military appointments made scarcely forty-eight hours earlier. It had been in preparation for more than a month, and at most was slightly accelerated by the new appointments. As Bolloten and others have said, the revolt would have taken place no matter what, and Casado's pronouncement made no reference to any imminent Communist coup. A premature rebellion by pro-Nationalist Republicans and Falangist fifth columnists had broken out twenty-four hours earlier at the Cartagena naval base, but it found itself geographically isolated and was suppressed by loyal forces in less than forty-eight hours, though the remaining Republican fleet was under noncommunist command and departed the base en masse to seek internment in French Algeria. In Madrid, the immediate problem was that three of the four army corps in the area were under Communist leadership. Without instructions from the government or the party, they soon turned on the rebels, surrounding them for several days in the center of Madrid.[42]

The Communists would later claim that if Negrín had not been so slow in carrying out the new assignments, it would have been possible to avoid the revolt or suppress it easily once it began. This is possibly correct, though it would have made little difference in the long run. According to Líster, there was a feeling even among a good many of the Communists after they left Madrid on the 27th that the war was essentially lost. Manuel Tagüeña, who was ordered to move from Madrid to Elda on the fifth, only hours before the revolt began, has written that the attitude he found on arriving in the south confirmed his impression that the Communist leaders were not planning to take any new initiative for fear of being blamed for the final collapse of the Republic. That same day Jesús Hernández inquired of Togliatti and the other figures why the new Communist commanders had not yet taken over their posts and why the party had established such remote headquarters, 382 kilometers from Madrid.[43] The truth was that Togliatti and the party leaders were also uncertain of themselves and of how to respond in the current situation.

The response of Negrín and the Communists to the revolt was not to make a vigorous last stand, but briefly to play for time. It was clear that even if the Communist forces in the Madrid area were successful in repressing the revolt —technically they might have been strong enough to do so—this entire episode would so weaken the People's Army that further resistance would scarcely be possible. Moreover, since the fall of Catalonia the party had lost much of its prestige and its capacity for intimidation. In recent days even some military commanders who were members of the party had shown signs of unreliability. It was no longer clear how many nominally Communist units were still reliable.[44]

Therefore neither Negrín nor the Communists made much of an effort to destroy the rebellion militarily. The sixth of March was devoted to efforts at mediation and attempts to convince the fleet to return to Cartagena, but all these efforts failed. The last meeting of the Communist high command took place at Monóvar airfield near Alicante around ten P.M. The two most trusted Communist military commanders, Enrique Líster and Juan Modesto, both had earlier confirmed that effective military action against Casado was not possible. It was decided that they should use secondary leaders to negotiate with Casado to maintain the legal existence of the PCE, but in the early hours of the 7th two planeloads of Communist leaders left for France. Negrín followed in another plane some hours later. The last Soviet military advisers had to wait until the Soviet embassy in Paris dispatched a special plane to rescue them.[45]

Only Togliatti and a few leaders remained, now bound for Valencia. The Comintern adviser later explained that they could not give orders for all-out military action against Negrín, for that would mean the collapse of what was left of the People's Army. Besides, as he admitted, they were not sure how many of even the Communist commanders would obey.[46] In the search for scapegoats, the Communists at first sought to blame Negrín. Togliatti sent his first report to Moscow from Valencia on the tenth, ingenuously and dishonestly declaring that the prime minister's lack of resistance and flight had been "a tragic error," and that he even suspected the prime minister of being in complicity with Casado, warning that any future relations with Negrín must be examined very carefully.[47] This warning probably reflected an initial effort simply to deflect blame from himself and from the PCE. The negrinista/Communist alliance was later restored, and in subsequent years references to Negrín in PCE historiography were usually quite positive. Togliatti remained in the Valencia region until the 24th, trying to guarantee a more satisfactory position for the PCE under Casado's council, until he was flown out of the country to France.

Meanwhile, the final "battle of Madrid" was waged, not between the Nationalist Army and the People's Army but between the initially exiguous forces loyal to Casado and those of the Communist commanders in the central zone. The latter had received no specific orders from the Communist leadership and soon found themselves fighting not to restore the Negrín government but simply to impose a more satisfactory policy on Casado's council. The issue was finally decided by the intervention of the army corps in the Guadalajara region commanded by the cenetista Cipriano Mera, a loyal ally of Casado. A general truce was eventually patched up after nearly a week of fraternal strife, the last major casualties in the Civil War being those inflicted by this struggle between the Communist and anticommunist units of the People's Army. The Casado forces did require the execution on the 13th of three leaders of the Communist assault against them—the last executions in Madrid during the Civil War. In these final days the situation of the Communists in the Republican zone became highly confused. A number were arrested, though the majority remained at large and some devoted themselves to developing a clandestine organization.

The Casado junta could not achieve its main goal—a generous peace without reprisals. All that Franco would concede was the opportunity for Republican leaders to flee abroad. When he launched his *Ofensiva de la Victoria* on March 27, he met virtually no resistance.

As it turned out, Togliatti need not have worried. Though Stalin later roundly criticized the Spanish Communists simply for having lost the war,

Manuilsky allegedly told Togliatti that he and the Spanish Communists, as well as Negrín, had handled the situation very cleverly. They had maintained the policy of resolute resistance, but left Casado in place and then, when he rebelled, let Casado take the blame for capitulation. This was fortunate, since the war had already been lost. Hernández claims that he then objected that this was not what the Comintern and the Soviet government had been telling them down to March 5; "Manu" supposedly replied that the advisers had simply failed to explain the situation fully. In fact, the way the situation had been handled would help to guarantee the prestige and political future of Spanish communism.[48]

To the extent that this explanation was true, it was the result of serendipity. As seen earlier, Stalin had no exit strategy, and the Soviet advisers continued to insist on resistance to the last Spanish Republican. At the same time, the situation was becoming so desperate and the position of the Communists within the Republic so increasingly weak that Negrín could not bring himself to attempt a direct Communist takeover, nor did the Comintern dare recommend that he do so. The anticommunist revolt by Casado and his allies, though certainly not sought by the Communists, proved very useful in the long run, for it relieved them of any need to take responsibility for the final defeat.

An undetermined proportion of the membership of the PSUC and PCE (more the former than the latter) managed to flee abroad, mainly to France. It is said that about half petitioned for asylum in the USSR, but Stalin would admit only about 3,000 in 1939; another 2,000 moved to the western hemisphere. During February the Soviet Politburo had, at the request of Dimitrov and Manuilsky, agreed to let a small number of International Brigade volunteers who could not return to their own countries enter the Soviet Union, but limited that number to 300.[49]

Only a week after the final collapse of the Republic, Stalin, together with Dimitrov, Molotov, and Beria, received the top leaders of the Spanish Communist Party in the Kremlin. He praised the Spanish Republicans as "valiant and intrepid," but also called them "careless people," reproving them for not having resisted to the very end. Later, a postmortem was held in the Secretariat of the Comintern on July 28. The judgment of the Comintern bosses was harsh: they condemned all the attempted negotiations during the March crisis. Togliatti was strongly criticized for having been unclear and compromising. The PCE leaders were told that they should have organized total mobilization against Casado's council, and never should have fled (with the exception of Ibárruri). Top leaders such as Checa, Uribe, and Hernández were singled out for criticism. As Elorza and Bizcarrondo say, this discrediting of Togliatti's policy tended to rehabilitate the hard-line position taken by Stepanov, though it was notable that the Comintern leadership had failed to endorse a Communist takeover before March 5. Its conclusion was standard rhetoric of Stalinist *shturmovshchina:* the final resolution declared that any victory was possible for a Bolshevik party that acted with audacity. Thus the PCE had been "defeated by its own errors."[50] All this was the normal Stalinist critique of failure, and could not be called a serious analysis of the problems of the last months of the war.

CHAPTER TWELVE

Conclusion

THE TWENTIETH CENTURY was a great generator and destroyer of myths. By its end nearly all the major new political and ideological myths of the first half of the century had been discredited. Of them all, however, probably none has been more enduring than the myth of the Spanish Republic. The myth of fascism was rapidly destroyed, whereas myths connected with the varying forms of communism endured for years, with new forms emerging in the second half of the century. Nonetheless, by the end of the century they were dead or moribund. The myth of the Spanish Republic, by comparison, has retained its power to enlist the sympathy of later generations.

The classic definition propagated by the Comintern and by the propagandists of the Republic—"democracy versus fascism"—has retained some currency, despite the perfectly obvious fact that had democracy still obtained in Spain in July 1936, there could scarcely have been a great civil war. Democracy is incapable of provoking a ferocious civil war, but prerevolutionary violence, persistent major disorder, and refusal to enforce the law, if carried far enough, can do so. What Burnett Bolloten once called the "grand camouflage" of disguising the revolution into nonexistence failed to influence many politicians in the 1930s, but was effective in key milieux. Comparative studies of revolutions never include a discussion of the Spanish revolution, even though there is much to support the contention of Andreu Nin that the Spanish revolution was in many ways a more intense, spontaneous, and extensive worker revolution than that in Russia in 1917–18. The rise of fascism, the projection of the "third" or wartime republic as some sort of democracy, and the specter of World War II, which immediately followed, combined to overshadow the precise character of the Spanish war. The left lost the military struggle but more often than not won the propaganda war.

The basic cause of the civil war in Spain, though not the only cause, was the revolutionary process, whose roots lay in the late nineteenth century. The revolutionary process experienced its first genuine acceleration during 1917–23 and a major stimulus in 1931. It began to develop significant strength, however, only late in 1933 and in 1934, accelerating again during the prerevolutionary spring and early summer of 1936.

What would have occurred had it not been for the preemptive strike by part of the military on July 18? The country had undergone a kind of civic and constitutional collapse and was experiencing new economic distress, but it is often pointed out that the left was profoundly disunited and that most of the left had no specific coherent revolutionary plan. Both of these points are correct, though conversely there was not the slightest sign that any of the revolutionaries were abandoning their aspirations, which were killed only by the most ruthless counterrevolutionary action. Since the Popular Front had limited normal political and constitutional access to public life in Spain, the only other likely denouement would have been total breakdown and chaos, with unpredictable consequences. Arguably it would have been better to permit breakdown to occur, but in any polity there are limits to the degree of deterioration that can develop without provoking major counteraction.

It hardly need be said that the most desirable change would simply have been a new government based on a Republican realignment that could have brought political forces into balance through a firm return to constitutional norms. Something of that sort is what Azaña attempted on September 19, 1936, through appointment of the abortive Martínez Barrio government. The concept of that government was an all-Republican union that would include all the Republican parties of the center and left-center. Had this initiative been attempted even as much as a week earlier, it might have managed to avoid the conflagration. It involved rupture of the Popular Front, which was absolutely necessary to reequilibrate the Republic and avoid civil war.

Even so, the concept of the Martínez Barrio government was too narrow to have served as the basis of government for very long. A more enduring solution would have had to include either the right-center or more of the left-center, or ideally both. That would have involved splitting the Socialist Party into social democratic and revolutionary sectors, and in the case of the CEDA either reaching an agreement with Gil Robles or splitting the Catholic party into a minority Christian democratic sector and a broader corporative-authoritarian sector that could not have formed part of the government but might in certain circumstances have cooperated with it. Neither of these maneuvers would have been very easy to accomplish and may not have been realistic, but would simply have pointed in the direction of expanding a constitutionalist basis for a new coalition.

In politics, as in many other areas, timing is all-important. Until the fighting began, President Azaña simply sleepwalked his way toward civil war, permitting the situation to deteriorate until it was too late. Unlike caballeristas and POUMists, he and most left Republicans did not want civil war, but he also did not want to change the policies that were almost inevitably leading to civil war. When he finally responded to a fait accompli, the time for a compromise solution had passed.

The only two coherent revolutionary plans in Spain were those of the two extremist Marxist parties, the Leninist POUM and the Stalinist PCE. The plan of the POUM was to stimulate the left Republican government to complete its program as soon as possible, while organizing workers to replace it directly within a short period of time with a revolutionary worker government. This program was not important in itself, for the POUM was such a small movement that it could never have carried it out. The only significance of the plan lay in whatever stimulus the POUM's persistent agitation might give to other, more vaguely positioned revolutionary groups.

The other party with a coherent revolutionary plan was the PCE. Historians have tended to ignore this fact because of the supposedly "counterrevolutionary" or "moderate" character of Communist policy, a concept zealously propagated for many years, principally in fact by noncommunists. In consonance with this interpretation, Hugh Thomas titled the section of his classic history of the Civil War that dealt with the main phase of the conflict "The War of the Two Counterrevolutions." It has been observed that Communist policy and the role of the Soviet Union have been "the major mystery of the Civil War" and that it "has provoked more questions, mystification and bitter controversy than any other subject in the history of the Spanish Civil War."[1] As far as Communist policy and action have been concerned, that controversy has centered on the myth of counterrevolution, one of the most persistent of the many misperceptions that still cloud the historical understanding of the most mythified civil war of the twentieth century.

As has been explained earlier, the tactic of the Popular Front was outlined at the Comintern congress of August 1935. Historians and writers dealing with Popular Front strategy, however, have ignored the facts, customarily producing observations that it involved renouncing "revolution," espousing "moderation," and giving up the goal of socialism. The slightest direct acquaintance with the statements of that congress makes it clear that such tactics, to the extent that they obtained, were no more than temporary tactical adjustments. Georgy Dimitrov explained that that strategy remained unaltered. In the era of the growth of fascism, the Popular Front was simply a tactic to assist in defeating fascism and to find a more direct route to the "democratic republic of a new type" that would be the antechamber to socialism.

That type of democratic republic had nothing to do with liberal moderation, though it was conceived to maintain some of the outward forms of Western democracy as political camouflage. As Comintern and PCE leaders made abundantly clear, this kind of regime was intended to achieve a permanent leftist monopoly of political power while maintaining an appearance of pluralism. This monopoly would make it possible to eliminate all significant nonleftist political, social, and economic forces permanently and to begin irreversible social and economic changes, involving extensive confiscation of agrarian land and the nationalization of industry—a kind of Western NEP not under Bolshevik dictatorship but under Western leftist semipluralism. As in the Soviet Union under the NEP, most forms of small private property would still be tolerated.

Introduction of the "democratic republic" would proceed by stages, the first stage being primarily a semipluralist political stage, though accompanied by major social and economic reforms. Acquisition of predominant political power would make possible the permanent elimination of the rightist forces, at the same time that major social and economic changes began. In a country such as Spain, where the conservatives were already weaker, the Communist Party from the beginning publicly announced a two-track strategy, agitating for the planning and organizational predevelopment of the "worker-peasant government" that would succeed the initial Popular Front government as soon as the time came. By April 1936 the two-track strategy temporarily disappeared from view as the international situation became increasingly threatening and the danger began to develop that the more incendiary elements of the Spanish left might get out of control and try to precipitate a premature effort at revolution, or, failing at that attempt, nonetheless so grievously provoke the right as to drive it to armed revolt or civil war. All of this amounted to the only sort of realistic or even semirealistic concrete strategy for revolution to be found in Spain during the spring and early summer of 1936.

There were indeed fairly frequent calls for moderation from the PCE from April 1936 on. These were not in any way intended to preserve democracy or to effect counterrevolution. Their goal was simply to keep the revolutionary extreme left from getting totally out of control while the Popular Front program was being completed, preparatory to even more decisive changes. Stalin and the Comintern leaders knew much better than either the POUM or the anarchists and caballeristas that any direct attempt at some form of immediate revolutionary collectivism in Western Europe in 1936 was very likely to fail and that the goal must be approached more cautiously and indirectly.

The PCE's calls for moderation in incendiary ultraleftist and directly prerevolutionary activity were also accompanied by a series of concrete proposals for sweeping changes, nominally within the law, that Communist spokesmen made at the same time. As the final crisis was about to break, precipitated by the murder of José Calvo Sotelo, only the PCE had a concrete plan to take advantage of the situation to make decisive changes, presenting a new legislative proposal that would have simply dissolved all the rightist political groups and their public organs, turning the Second Republic into a strict political monopoly of the left. Thus the institutions of the "democratic republic" could be used to kill any political democracy. This was hardly a call for moderation. Those historians—and they remain fairly numerous—who still describe the PCE as a force for moderation have simply paid no attention to its own clearly announced policies.

Though the Communist Party was the only leftist group with a coherent revolutionary strategy, it was also the leftist group with the greatest practical concern to avoid civil war. Comintern strategists readily grasped that with the left holding a decisive political advantage as a result of the elections of February 1936, the right was likely to remain at a permanent political disadvantage so long as the left exploited the existing political situation in carefully calculated but not exaggerated and counterproductive ways. While the POUM and the caballeristas could say that they welcomed civil war as an inevitable concomitant of a true revolution (which in one sense was true enough), the Comintern bosses realized that a major armed insurrection by the right would alter the terms of conflict in ways that might not be to the advantage of the left. A situation had developed in which the right had been deprived of many normal means of political access and recourse, while a significant armed insurrection would introduce a completely new and dangerous equation in which the correlation of forces—even if they somewhat favored the left—could not possibly be as fully in their favor as was the correlation of forces on the strictly political level, so long as that level were not surpassed prematurely. Both Araquistain and Maurín argued that in a civil war the international situation would preclude any significant foreign intervention on behalf of the right, and that if necessary the Soviet Union would intervene on behalf of the left. Stalin and the Comintern strategists wished to avoid any danger of the former and did not wish to be placed in a situation in which they might be pressured to do the latter. In hindsight, the calculation of the Stalinists was altogether more objective and accurate than that of the extreme revolutionary left. As it turned out, Hitler and Mussolini agreed to undertake limited assistance of the counterrevolutionaries in little more than a week, while Stalin waited two months before beginning significant intervention on behalf of the left. This was not what the extreme revolutionary left had in mind. Major Soviet assistance, when it did arrive, was initially greater than that of the Axis powers, representing a significant escalation of foreign intervention and one that Stalin hoped would be decisive. It was too late for that, however; the Soviet intervention managed to block the victory of the right but its dimensions were not great enough to achieve the victory of the left. It was adequate only to guarantee a more prolonged civil war, and thus in the long run it proved to be counterproductive.

The "real goals" of Soviet policy have always been among the most controversial problems of the Spanish war. Rightists from the very beginning—and leftists by the latter part of the war—claimed that the goal was simply to create a Soviet-style regime in Spain. This interpretation is no doubt correct with regard to the very long-term Soviet strategic goal, but does not accurately describe short-term Soviet tactical goals in the war. In this regard, as Geoffrey Roberts has said, Soviet policy was less covert and complicated than it has sometimes been made out to be.[2]

The USSR had two basic goals in the Spanish war, the first geostrategic and the second dealing with internal Republican politics. The geostrategic goal was to frustrate the international growth of German power and influence—in Comintern jargon to "fight fascism"—and in the process to manage to convince Paris and London that it was both feasible and important to reverse their own policies toward Spain particularly and toward collective security more generally. The goal in domestic politics was to develop a more centralized and effective Republican war effort, advance broadly the power and influence of the Soviet Union and the PCE, and equally to channel and control what had quickly become an explosive revolutionary process. The channeling and controlling of the revolutionary process in turn were based on three related goals: to reduce the power of the revolutionary extreme left, to make possible a more disciplined and vigorous Republican war effort, and to camouflage the revolution from the view of the Western capitalist democracies.

To some of the more analytic scholars who have examined these problems, Soviet policy has seemed inevitably contradictory: How could a military intervention by the Soviet Union on the opposite side of Europe—in itself representing a major extension of Soviet strategic reach—designed to give victory to the only ongoing left collectivist revolution outside the Soviet Union, really be expected to encourage the capitalist democracies to join in on the same side? Strict logic is definitely against this proposition, yet there is abundant evidence that such indeed was Stalin's intent. To understand Soviet reasoning in this regard, one has first to remember that Leninist-Stalinist politicians had been accustomed to playing both ends against the middle for many years, sometimes with surprising success. A significant part of Soviet policy was always predicated on Lenin's metaphor of selling the capitalists enough rope to hang themselves with, and more than once the capitalists had shown willingness to collaborate in this endeavor. This was a matter not of strict empirical logic but of a psychology, style, and approach to politics. From Stalin's point of view there seemed to be a reasonable chance that a massive propaganda barrage about the "democratic republic," combined with some salutary political changes in Spain, might divert powerful Western interests sufficiently from the actual revolutionary content of the Republic to focus instead on the geostrategic implications of German influence, if not more broadly of "fascism," in southwestern Europe. From the perspective of Stalin's own arithmetic of power, there seemed to be reason enough for capitalists to be willing to give priority to addressing the danger inherent in the geostrategic situation, and doing so might lead them to consider the internal political content of what was otherwise a third-rate power to be an altogether secondary matter.

It was, of course, wishful thinking. Stalin miscalculated the extreme abhorrence of war that had set in within the two major Western European democracies, which would discourage military action except in the greatest of emergencies, something that Spain did not seem to present. Second, Stalin also underestimated at least in practical terms the extreme aversion to and distrust of the Soviet Union. Before the Second World War, the crimes of Lenin and Stalin had been infinitely greater than those of Hitler, and almost equally publicized. In peacetime this was a greater barrier than Stalin had been willing to acknowledge. Third, there were distinct limits to the efficacy of Comintern propaganda. During the first six months of the war, leftist atrocities had drawn rather greater publicity in France and England than had rightist atrocities, and significant portions even of the French Socialist and British Labour parties had set their faces against involvement with this sort of republic. And from there, moving right along the political spectrum, support dwindled accordingly.

The Communists were greatly irritated, indeed outraged, by all the political commentary and propaganda, coming primarily from other sectors of the Spanish left, that labeled them "counterrevolutionaries." The official PCE history, *Guerra y revolución en España, 1936–1939,* contains various sarcastic references to the anticommunist rhetoric of the extreme left, and comments ironically on what it considers the frivolously irrelevant efforts of "bourgeois historians" to debate what was truly revolutionary and what was counterrevolutionary during the struggle, because of course only an orthodox Communist party such as the PCE was truly in a position to make such definitions and distinctions in a fully authoritative way.[3]

During the Civil War, Comintern and Communist discourse functioned on three levels: the international Comintern propaganda level; the PCE discourse on the national Republican level; and Communist discourse on the regional and local levels. On the first level, camouflage was total; the idea of violent revolution was held to be no more than a malevolent projection of fascist propaganda. On the Republican national level, the Communist line was the Spanish application of the old Leninist formula "Odin shag nazad, dva shaga vperyod" (One step back, two steps forward). A temporary channeling and restriction of the revolution were necessary purely as tactical measures to win the war, which was the only way to achieve an effective revolution in the future. On the regional or local levels, however, particularly in Catalonia, heartland of the anarchist revolution, the local Communist party—in this case the PSUC —was portrayed as the only truly revolutionary party, partly because it was part of triumphant Bolshevism, the only successful and triumphant revolutionary movement in the world, partly because only it could apply a tactic of revolution that could render Catalonia as felicitous as the Soviet Union. Thus the PSUC could represent itself as the *partit únic bolxevic revolucionari de Catalunya,* the one truly and coherently revolutionary force in the region, all the while that it sought to shelter sectors of the petite bourgeoisie from anarchosyndicalism.

The specific formula of the FAI-CNT, "libertarian communism," was indeed categorically rejected. Decentralized collectivization was directly at odds with the statist/centralist model of Communist nationalization. In this sense the Communists sought to roll back as much of the anarchosyndicalist revolution as was compatible with maintaining a degree of unity behind the war effort, with the remainder to be destroyed once victory had been achieved. It was not surprising that after the summer of 1937 members of the FAI-CNT had increasingly to ask themselves just what it was they were still fighting for. As the struggle hardened into the military attrition of two competing authoritarianisms, this was a question that more and more Spaniards on both sides of the barricade had to ask themselves. The almost uninterrupted sequence of military victories and strong economy of Franco's regime provided a more reassuring answer for most of his followers than did Negrín's Republic for the other side. It is a testimony to their devotion to their ideals, however flawed those ideals may have been, that the great bulk of the left persevered in the Republic's struggle.

In the end, it was declared not to be worth the effort because, as *El Socialista* put it on March 12, the day the final internecine struggle in Madrid ended, Casado's new council had prevented what was left of the Republic from becoming "a colony of the Soviet regime." The theme was naturally especially cultivated by the publicists of the POUM. After the Soviet Union established the totalitarian "people's democracies" in Eastern Europe following World War II, Julián Gorkín, the number two leader of the party during the Civil War, devoted a brief book to the theme, *España, primer ensayo de democracia popular* (1961), while more recently the POUM veteran Wilebaldo Solano has written that "the first experiment in a *people's democracy* was carried out in our country." He specifies the tactics involved "infiltration of the state apparatus; conquest of key positions in the government, the army, the police, the secret services; a growing monopoly of information (press, radio, films); censorship or repression of any action that might endanger the policy established by the Kremlin."[4]

The NKVD *rezident* in the Netherlands during those years, Walter Krivitsky, wrote in 1939 that Stalin's goal was to "include Spain in the sphere of the Kremlin's influence" and build a regime "controlled by him," although not officially so. E. H. Carr, scarcely a historian hostile to the Soviet Union, concluded in his final, posthumous book that the Republic had eventually become "what its enemies called it, the puppet of Moscow."[5]

More recently, the senior Russian army officers and military historians Oleg Sarin and Lev Dvoretsky have come to similar conclusions:

Judging from numerous papers that we have examined, Stalin began to see the Spanish government as some kind of branch of the Soviet government obedient to dictates from Moscow. For example, late in 1937 when the Spanish situation was discussed at a Politburo meeting, a comprehensive directive to the Spaniards was approved. It covered among other things that it was necessary to remove all saboteurs and traitors from the army, to develop measures to mobilize industry for military production, and to clear rear areas of Fascist spies and agents. Other matters were included in the directive, such as governmental problems and laws regarding agriculture, industry, trade and transportation, and propaganda in territories occupied by the enemy. It is not just the listing of problems and points for attention that is important, but the language itself. The words chosen and the terms used were so bad that they resembled directives to a district Party committee or some ministry as opposed to friendly messages of advice.[6]

Spanish Communist commentators and Soviet historians have themselves advanced the "people's republic" interpretation. José Díaz, the PCE's secretary general, and many other party spokesmen during the course of the war were categorical and emphatic that the "Third Republic" had very little in common with a Western liberal democracy except for a certain cosmetic facade, being exclusively "a democratic and parliamentary republic of a new type with profound social content," as Díaz put it in his marathon address to the party's central committee on March 5, 1937.[7] Stalin's favorite Spanish Communist, Dolores Ibárruri, who rose to the top of the PCE hierarchy soon after the Civil War began, wrote years later in her orthodox Stalinist autobiography that in the Republican zone "the democratic bourgeois Republic was transformed into a People's Republic, the first in the history of contemporary democratic revolutions." She goes on to say that whereas in 1905 the Russian people had created the first soviets, in Spain during "the national revolutionary war" the Spanish people had created "a people's democracy, which after the Second World War has been in some countries one of the forms of peaceful transition to socialism."[8] In December 1947, while the new Eastern regimes were still in process of construction, the veteran PCE leader, publicist, and later vehement anticommunist Félix Montiel published an article titled "España fue una República popular y volverá a serla" (Spain was a People's Republic and will be so again) in the party's main theoretical monthly Nuestra bandera. Later, in the first volume of the official party history, which appeared in Moscow in 1966, the editors emphasized that the regime became "a new republic" with the establishment of the first Giral government on July 19, 1936, and that this produced "a rapid acceleration of the entire process of the Spanish democratic revolution," resulting in "a republic of a new type in which, together with usable sectors of the old state not contaminated with fascist and reactionary infection, new organisms created by the masses were integrated." This is also the interpretation presented by José Sandoval and Manuel Azcárate in 1963.[9]

The inventor and avatar of Spanish Eurocommunism, Santiago Carrillo, has on occasion been equally forthright. He declared before the Conference of Communist Parties held in Moscow in 1969 that "it must not be forgotten that Spain had been the first people's democracy in Europe," and even admitted as late as the Orwellian year 1984 that "if the Republic had triumphed, we would have provided the first example of a people's democracy, created not by the intervention of the Soviet army but by the struggle of the people, with a plurality of political forces."[10]

The official terminology of internal Comintern and later Soviet discourse, and also of Russian historiography after the disappearance of the Soviet Union, would continue to employ the concept of the "national revolutionary war" as initially defined by Dimitrov, Manuilsky, and Togliatti in September–October 1936. The term "people's republic," introduced in Mongolia in 1924, had largely disappeared from Soviet and Comintern usage by 1928 with the new doctrine of the Third Period of immediate European and world revolutionary upheaval. The concept, though not quite the original term, was reintroduced with the yet newer doctrine of the "democratic republic of a new type" in association with Popular Front strategy by the Comintern in 1935. At that point the old terminology of "people's republic" or "people's democracy" would have smacked too much of the Soviet conquest of Mongolia, so that it could not officially be reintroduced until Eastern Europe was safely under complete Soviet military control in 1945.

One of the first nominally scholarly Soviet accounts of the Spanish war, published in 1960, declared that the conflict "was the greatest armed confrontation of the international proletarian revolution with world imperialism in Europe between the two world wars," a forerunner of "the following war and revolution in Europe."[11] A short history of the Comintern published in 1969 concluded that "the course of events in Spain revealed a fact of paramount importance, namely, that the popular front, the new democracy, was a connecting link between the defensive antifascist struggle and the ultimate aim—the struggle for socialism. The significance of the Spanish experience for an understanding of the means of approach to the socialist stage of the revolution was fully grasped and appreciated by the Comintern."[12] The Red Army's official history of the Second World War is more explicit yet in its section on the Spanish conflict: "Because of its character and content the democratic revolution in Spain went far beyond the framework of typical bourgeois revolutions. This was a people's national antifascist revolution in which the role of the proletariat, acting in unity with the peasantry and the middle and petite bourgeoisie, united in the Popular Front, steadily increased. On ancient Iberian soil a democratic republic of a new type was born. Spain was the first country of western Europe in which was established the democratic dictatorship of a broad coalition of political forces—from Communists to Catholics, based on parliament."[13]

The veteran Stalinist NKVD official Pavel Sudoplatov put it somewhat differently: "Stalin in the Soviet Union and Trotsky in exile each hoped to be the savior and the sponsor of the Republicans and thereby the vanguard for the world Communist revolution. We sent our young inexperienced intelligence operatives as well as our experienced instructors. Spain proved to be a kindergarten for our future intelligence operations. Our subsequent intelligence initiatives all stemmed from contacts that we made and lessons that we learned in Spain. The Spanish Republicans lost, but Stalin's men and women won."[14]

Sarin and Dvoretsky see matters more starkly:

In this unnecessary war, many hundreds of young Soviet men suffered and died for no good purpose. Stalin and his team pursued an unrealistic goal: to turn Spain into a Communist country beholden to the Soviet Union as a first step to creating Communist governments in other countries of the western world. As with Germans and Italians, it gave Stalin a fine place to test Soviet equipment and procedures in a modern war. Soviet participation in this war was the first serious attempt to change the social system of another state by force after the Revolution of 1917. It failed dismally.[15]

The great majority of historians tend to agree concerning the predominant, virtually hegemonic position gained by the Communists in the army and in certain state institutions, but also regard the wartime Republic as a semipluralist system that did not completely succumb to Communist control. Their judgments in this regard, however, vary considerably. Burnett Bolloten devoted much of his life to compiling a great mass of primary and secondary data that would achieve what the Communists themselves would have called the "unmasking" of the extent of Communist power in the wartime Republic. David T. Cattell, author of the first published study on Communism and the Spanish war, concluded that "from the evidence it seems clear that the party was in a position to seize absolute power in the Loyalist government when and if it wanted to."[16]

Antonio Elorza and Marta Bizcarrondo, ending their careful study of Comintern policy, have written that "the process is well known . . . and . . . was clearly outlined in the Spain of 1937. Thus, without complete institutional similarity, it can be said that the policy of the Comintern in Spain pointed, without doubt, to the model of the people's democracy," though frustrated in the Spanish case by the military defeat of the Republic. Their conclusion is that nonetheless some remnants of a state of law survived as residue of the prewar Second Republic and succeeded to some extent in frustrating Stalin's full designs, and they point out that his plan for manipulated elections, which would have been a major step in developing a new system, was effectively rejected by the other parties.[17]

François Furet, in his magisterial analysis of Communism, says of the Spanish war:

> I do not consider it accurate to write, as Hugh Thomas does, that after the anarchist defeat of May 1937 and the formation of the Negrín government, "two counterrevolutions" faced each other: that of Franco and that led by the Spanish Communist Party, in the shadow of the new prime minister. This definition fits Franco, but not the other side. It is true that the Communists have suffocated a revolution in Barcelona, but only to substitute one of their own. They suffocated the popular revolution, annihilated the POUM, subjugated Catalan separatism, regimented anarchism, split the left and right of the Socialist Party—that is, Caballero and Prieto, respectively; obliged Azaña and Negrín to follow them. But with that the Spanish Republic has lost its spark. The authority that it could finally offer to defeat Franco was less republican than pretotalitarian.
>
> . . . What is being tested in Spain is the political technique of "people's democracy," as it would flourish in Central and Eastern Europe after 1945. There is even a theory that the democratic Spanish Republic . . . is, in reality, a republic "of a new type."[18]

Furet's conclusion is that Stalin's goals for Spain were potentially dual, either to use it as a bargaining chip if no more could be gained or to move toward a Soviet-style revolution such as occurred in Eastern Europe after 1945.

Ronald Radosh, Mary R. Habeck, and Grigory Sevostianov have written in their extensively annotated volume of new Soviet documents on the Spanish war that "as some historians have long suspected, the documents prove that advisers from Moscow were indeed attempting to 'Sovietize' Spain and turn it into what would have been one of the first 'People's Republics,' with a Stalinist-style economy, army, and political structure."[19]

There is no doubt that the "democratic republic of a new type" preached in the Popular Front era was essentially the same kind of transition regime to socialism constituted first by the People's Republic of Mongolia in 1924 and later by the people's democracies established by the Soviet Union in Eastern Europe after 1945. When the onetime Comintern boss Georgy Dimitrov returned to his native Bulgaria after the war to lead the new Bulgarian Communist regime, he defined the goal of the new states as "a people's republic and not a capitalist republic, . . . a people's republican government and not a bourgeois republican government," in language similar to that used by PCE spokesmen in Spain. More concretely, Dimitrov declared in March 1947 that "Spain was the first example of a people's democracy."[20] He understood this regime to constitute a system that was not the same as that of the Soviet Union in the 1930s and 1940s, but one that would retain a limited pluralism, though excluding all conservative and rightist forces, and still retain certain functions of private property that would be consistent with the initial development of a state collectivized economy. In 1948, however, shortly before his death, Dimitrov also made it clear that a "people's democracy" must carry out the basic functions of the dictatorship of the proletariat.[21]

Yet a detailed comparison quickly reveals that the wartime Spanish Third Republic, while very different from the Second Republic that had existed before the spring of 1936, was also not the precise sort of regime established by the Soviets in Eastern Europe. The differences remained fundamental: first of all, each of the Eastern satellites was thoroughly occupied and controlled by the Red Army. While the Communists gained a predominant position in the Spanish Ejército Popular, they did not totally control it in every way as the Soviets totally controlled all armed force in the Eastern countries. In the Eastern satellites—initially puppets more than satellites—new national people's armies were created, again absolutely controlled by the Communists. The same may be said of the police in the two cases.

Second, in the Eastern regimes the Soviets quickly formed unified Socialist-Communist parties and front organizations, which soon totally dominated all political activity. In Spain the PCE sought to unify the two parties from 1935, but its inability to carry out this plan became one of the greatest frustrations of Communist policy. In the Eastern countries, the Communists normally permitted one initial election that was partially free but also partially controlled.

After that all elections were totally controlled. The Spanish Popular Front certainly did not believe in democratic elections, as demonstrated by the fraudulent by-elections it held in Cuenca in May 1936, but after that it solved the problem by not holding elections. Stalin's proposal in the autumn of 1937 to hold carefully controlled elections in the violent and authoritarian atmosphere of Civil War Spain was clearly intended as a step toward the consolidation of the new type of regime, but all the other parties rejected it. Apparently even the PCE leaders did not favor the idea but merely supported it out of Comintern discipline.

Third, in the Eastern European regimes the state nationalized basic industries and in most cases carried out broad land confiscation, usually accompanied by state collectivization (though not always). Here the similarity would seem to be greatest, and indeed the Red Army's history of World War II boasts that in Spain the Communists carried out a broad program of nationalization.[22] In fact, this was not precisely the case, and in economic policy and structure there were considerable differences between the Eastern regimes and the Spanish case. In the Eastern satellites, sweeping economic changes were carried out by a monolithic, all-powerful totalitarian state. In the Third Spanish Republic the state at first almost disappeared, and after it began to be restored remained a semipluralist state in which there was much conflict over economic policy. The policy of state control and nationalization favored by the Communists could never be carried out completely. Initially, collectivization of agriculture meant the formation of autonomous collectives by revolutionary movements independent of the state—very different from the centralized statist policy favored by the Communists (though in one sense vaguely analogous to the way independent peasant groups and villages in Russia in 1917 seized those portions of farmland that were owned by the middle and upper classes). The Communist program of statist agrarian reform and centralized process could never entirely reverse the libertarian revolution in much of the Republican countryside. Similarly in Catalan industry the state established a system of direct and autonomous collectivization of larger factories, and the Communists were never able to convert it into a program of complete nationalization.[23]

The Soviet economic model for Spain, as for the initial phases of the people's democracies, was the New Economic Policy introduced by Lenin in the Soviet Union in 1921, which combined nationalization of what Lenin called the "commanding heights" of major industry with autonomous peasant agriculture and private property in ordinary small production and commerce. A Catalan NEP was announced by Estanislau Ruiz i Ponsetí while he was undersecretary of economics in the Catalan government in September 1937, but in fact such an economic program could not be fully carried out.

The revolutionary Spanish Republic of the Civil War was a unique kind of regime that has no exact historical counterpart. In a contradictory process, the wartime Spanish Republic combined autonomous libertarian collectivization with a restored centralized state, increasing state control, and a degree of nationalization. It involved an initial policy of increasing local and regional autonomy (July to October 1936) with progressive restriction of autonomy (from approximately December 1936 on). Politically it remained a semipluralist regime, in that each of the four main leftist sectors remained autonomous. Only the POUM could be suppressed by the Communists, and even there certain legal limits had to be observed. The Third Republic was not democratic—only the Second Republic was democratic—but it did remain semipluralist and restore a limited framework of law.

The Communists established a military and police predominance, and under Negrín a certain political predominance as well, but there were limits to this predominance, which was not the same sort of thing as a direct dictatorship. Though there were certain limits to its sovereignty vis-à-vis the Soviet/Comintern military and the NKVD, the Third Republic remained a sovereign state and was not a mere satellite of the Soviet Union, though such was undoubtedly Stalin's long-term goal. The Soviet dictator clearly did not seek at that time an overtly Communist regime in Spain, partly for reasons of international politics. Even had Soviet policy come to agree with those among the Spanish Communist leaders who wished to take power directly, it is not at all clear that they could have done so effectively. The strength of the Communists in the Republican military was to some degree predicated on the fact that they subordinated other factors to military discipline and to military victory over Franco. Had it come to a final showdown at any time before March 1939 between Communist and noncommunist sectors of the People's Army, it is not clear that all Communist units would necessarily have collaborated fully in trying to impose a Communist dictatorship on the noncommunist left. Even if they had, such an internecine struggle would at most have been no more than a pyrrhic victory, for the noncommunist units were sufficiently large that the cost of overcoming them would have fatally weakened the Communists in efforts to pursue the Civil War further.

There is a sense, of course, in which all the leftist groups sought some form of people's republic—that is, a purely leftist and hence nondemocratic regime—rather than a liberal democracy. Each differed, however, as to the kind of nondemocratic all-leftist regime it sought. The left Republicans sought only limited deviations from a capitalist democratic regime, the anarchists sought their distinct utopia, while the PSOE was divided. Prietistas sought only a rather more socially advanced version of the left Republican regime, while the caballeristas initially claimed to want a Leninist system, as did, in more clear-cut and extreme fashion, the POUM. Yet none of these other Spanish leftist versions of an all-left regime was the same as a Stalinist people's democracy, though the POUMist and caballerista versions—and also the later negrinista version—came closest to it. Negrín certainly went farthest in accommodating the new type of regime, and he did give evidence in the last months of the war that he sought to move Spain toward such a model, with a one-party state and nationalized industry. Yet even Negrín insisted that it be a sovereign Spanish state—despite his seemingly endless concessions to the Communists—and not a mere puppet of Moscow. Basically, the Spanish Third or revolutionary Republic was a unique case, with no exact parallel among twentieth-century revolutionary regimes. Any comparison with the Eastern European people's democracies can refer only to the very first pretotalitarian phase of those regimes.

Therefore the most that can be claimed would seem to come down to two factors: first, that the Spanish Third Republic was the nearest approximation to a people's republic in the history of Western Europe, though it was not merely incomplete but in some ways basically different from the Soviet model; second, that the struggle in Spain provided the Soviets with experience that they applied in Eastern Europe, where they were able to proceed more forth-rightly than in Spain.

A second basic question concerning Soviet policy is: To what extent did the Comintern's activity and the Soviet military intervention benefit the Soviet Union? This matter involves quite a different set of considerations. For example, Dimitrov had declared publicly on various occasions that the number one re-sponsibility of all Comintern parties was to contribute to the security of the Soviet Union, bulwark of the world proletarian revolution. Though the Soviet intervention was calculated to advance that goal, it cannot be argued that the Soviet and Comintern project in Spain contributed significantly to achieving this end, and in fact may have detracted from it. The Soviet Union was more isolated internationally in April 1939 than in July 1936. The great Comintern propaganda campaign that accompanied the war did serve to enhance the im-age of the Soviet Union as the mainstay against fascism, but the positive senti-ment that image generated in left-liberal circles could not in 1939 be translated into influence on the state policy of Western countries. On the other hand, one of Stalin's goals in September 1936 seems to have been to take concrete military action that would, among other things, check a German proxy war and thereby inhibit German strategy. Though that effort failed militarily and might even be considered therefore strategically counterproductive, the fact that the Soviet Union had been willing to act, to some degree with persistence, may have influenced Hitler to some extent in 1939. It may have been one factor in encouraging him to think that it was necessary to undertake rapprochement with the Soviet Union (however temporarily), to solidify the geostrategic position on the basis of which Germany could go to war. From Stalin's devious, amoral, and often completely erroneous point of view, the Soviet dictator could not have asked for more.

The Soviet effort was certainly economical, an unusual occurrence in the history of a regime characterized above all by its profligacy in wasting human and economic resources. The whole enterprise cost Stalin nothing financially. Indeed, given its dishonest bookkeeping, the Soviet regime may even have turned a profit, ending the war by confiscating nine Spanish Republican ships found in Soviet ports.[24] Moreover, it was a highly efficient undertaking in the relationship of means to ends. At virtually no cost, and never employing more than about 3,000 Soviet military and related personnel, with a loss of life of no more than about 200 (less than insignificant from a Stalinist point of view), the Soviet Union helped to prolong Republican resistance for two and a half years and enable the Communists to achieve a predominance that, though incomplete, was and would forever remain unparalleled in the history of any other Western European country. The fact that Hitler himself was perfectly pleased to see the Spanish war prolonged through 1937 and 1938 was something that Stalin probably did not understand.

The Soviet institution that most benefited from involvement in the Spanish war was the NKVD. The NKVD "used the war in Spain for deep penetration into the military and the political structures of the Republic. They created cells which they planned to expand significantly in order to increase secret operations in other European countries and the United States."[25] The loyal Soviet dropout Aleksandr Orlov and the arch-Stalinist Pavel Sudoplatov have both offered their own testimony in this regard. Never before had the NKVD enjoyed a major secure base all its own in a large Western country. Not merely did the NKVD develop a major network within the Republican zone, as well as a significant intelligence system inside the Nationalist zone, but it acquired experience, opportunities, new personnel from a variety of countries from the International Brigades, and purloined documentation to expand its operations significantly.

Espionage in the United States, in particular, was greatly enhanced. The International Brigades proved a major reservoir for the development of new agents and also for the development of Comintern activists in other countries. Former members of the brigades often rose to the top in the hierarchies of the new people's democracies after 1945, particularly in the military, security, and intelligence forces.

Much has been made of the role of military intervention in Spain in testing and evaluating new weaponry and tactics, especially in the case of the German Kondor Legion, which came to play so important a role in Franco's forces.[26] What has not generally been appreciated is that this sort of advantage accrued much more to the Soviet military command than to the Germans. Whereas the Germans were skeptical and carefully selective with the lessons they chose to draw from the Spanish conflict, the Soviet approach was much more extensive and also more credulous. Mary Habeck, the leading Western specialist in this area, writes that "Soviet officers . . . , unlike their German counterparts, believed that the conflict presented a valid picture of a future great war." The Soviet "command staff became convinced that the conflict was a reliable model of modern war and treated each new experience of combat as a valuable lesson for how the Soviet army should fight in the future." Soon after the Soviet military intervention began, "Defense Commissar Kliment Voroshilov issued orders detailing the specific tactics and technology that his men were to study." Copious and detailed reports were sent home by the Soviet military advisers, ultimately composing an entire section in the Red Army archives.[27] "Specialists returning home after combat in Spain were interrogated exhaustively on the effectiveness of the equipment being supplied and the methods of its employment."[28]

No other major European army devoted as much attention to the presumed lessons of the Spanish war as did the Red Army. The study of operations in Spain was massive. By November 23, 1937, the Ministry of Defense had prepared fifty-seven informational notebooks and had already published three books and thirteen pamphlets on the subject of the war in Spain. Within a few months three more books and four more pamphlets appeared, with extensive press runs of 6,000 to 10,000 copies. Altogether, Yury Rybalkin has counted a total of fifty-six military books and articles on military operations in Spain published in the Soviet Union between 1937 and 1941, not counting a long list of articles that appeared in the Soviet military journals *Krasnaya zvezda*, *Voennaya mysl*, *Morskoi sbornik*, *Voenno-istorichesky zhurnal*, *Voenny vestnik*, and others. In addition, unpublished studies were carried out at the Soviet military academies. Many lectures were presented and numerous discussion groups were formed.[29]

The massive and highly detailed Soviet examination of the Spanish war covered virtually every aspect of weaponry and operations. It ranged from the use of combined arms, tanks, aircraft, naval affairs, artillery, antitank guns, all manner of infantry weapons, and tactics to military administration, intelligence, communications, medical and sanitary affairs, topography, engineering, the functioning of military commissars, reconnaissance, and the study of German and Italian equipment.[30]

But the question has been raised as to whether the Red Army commanders learned accurate lessons, or whether in fact they managed to deceive themselves, and here the situation is complex. The aspect of Soviet planning that has generally drawn the attention of historians was the decision taken during those years to discard the offensive doctrines of massed armor and "deep operations" developed under Marshal Mikhail Tukhachevsky and his colleagues who perished in the Great Terror—exactly in the opposite direction from the structure and tactics of the German Wehrmacht, which contributed so decisively to its astounding conquest of France in 1940. As Habeck has pointed out, however, it is a mistake to conclude, as some have done, that this grievous error was due exclusively to the very limited achievements of Soviet armor in Spain. Such a flawed change in military policy stemmed as much or more from the decision to reject the policies of the commanders purged in 1937. The limited role of Soviet armor in Spain only encouraged this new orientation.[31] There had obviously been no deep offensive operations, and in November and December 1939 the Red Army tank corps were broken up, Soviet doctrines returning to the concept of "positional struggle" and the "continuous front," with the offense geared to "gnawing through" rather than quick penetrations. The only advantage of the new orientation was that it encouraged somewhat greater attention to defensive tactics, in which the Red Army was deficient.[32]

Soviet commanders obviously made a fundamental mistake in taking the Spanish conflict as a valid scenario for a future European war. The armies in Spain for the most part lacked the weapons, firepower, leadership, and training to provide many lessons applicable to major mid-twentieth-century campaigns. This is especially the case when Spain's topography is compared with that of Eastern Europe. Mountains often played a major role in the Spanish fighting but are absent in European Russia and most of Poland and eastern Germany.

The most egregious Soviet mistake in trying to learn from Spain lay in armor doctrine and organization, but it is a mistake to overlook improvements that the Red Army was able to make in many individual technical areas, ranging from military administration and engineering to specific weapons systems.

Though Soviet tanks were by far the best in Spain, they also revealed notable shortcomings, on the basis of which Soviet planners accelerated the development of the B-5 into the T-34 by 1941, which became ton for ton the best tank of World War II.[33] By 1937–38 Soviet aircraft were becoming obsolescent in comparison with the latest German models, and the need for replacements stimulated development of new models of faster and more efficient fighter planes and the very effective ground-attack aircraft that were being produced by 1942–43.[34] Improvements were also achieved in artillery and infantry weapons and in other kinds of technical equipment. The experience of the Spanish war was not uniquely decisive in any of these areas, and much Soviet equipment remained obsolescent in 1941 (partly the result of Stalin's obsession with military overproduction in the mid-1930s), but the highly intensive Spanish studies certainly played a role in the development of better Soviet weaponry and technical execution.

The Spanish war also had some effect on Soviet naval development, pointing up the extreme weakness of the Soviet navy. Stalin had apparently already made the basic decision to remedy this situation through the initial plan at the end of 1935 to create a bolshoi flot, and the disheartening naval experience of the Spanish conflict reinforced this orientation. Ivan Maisky, the Soviet ambassador in London and representative before the Non-Intervention Committee, on several occasions urged Soviet naval intervention in the Mediterranean during the winter of 1936–37, but was always opposed by the Soviet naval commander, Admiral Vasily A. Orlov, who held that the Soviet navy was simply too weak to undertake any such operations. Stalin accepted this position, but by July 1937 Admiral Orlov had been purged and Stalin redoubled efforts at major expansion of the Soviet navy. This program did not in general depend on information from Spain, but Soviet naval command in the Republican forces had been timid and inept and the entire experience underscored the weakness of the Soviet navy and its doctrinal deficiencies.[35]

Just as the revolutionary Spanish Republic was sui generis politically, the Civil War was unique militarily. It was typical neither of World War I nor of World War II, but rather represented a kind of transition war halfway between the two and exhibited certain characteristics of each. Most of the weaponry used was more typical of World War I, though occasionally the employment of armor and, much more frequently and importantly, of airpower was more characteristic of World War II. Neither the Nationalists nor the Republicans employed blitzkrieg tactics, for example, for the simple reason that the German doctrine at that moment was purely theoretical and had not been fully worked out even for the German army, much less for Franco's rudimentary forces. Though combined arms operations involving air-to-ground support became important for Franco's offensives during the last two years of the war, the two armies were inadequately developed to create other forms of combined-arms operations (for that matter, the same could be said of most armies in 1939). Much of the time, the defense enjoyed an almost World War I level of effectiveness. Though Franco was successful in most of his offensives, they developed and foreshadowed those of World War II only to a very limited degree.

If the Red Army sometimes drew inaccurate lessons from the war, it was not alone. For French analysts, the Spanish war tended to reconfirm the importance of the defensive and of antitank weapons.[36] For the Italian military, the success of their small units most of the time, together with the victory of Franco, merely reconfirmed their own otherwise generally inadequate priorities and policies. Moreover, Italy proportionately contributed much more in arms than did either Germany or the Soviet Union, and the effort somewhat reduced overall Italian stocks of arms (though probably not to the degree that has sometimes been alleged).

Once Soviet intervention had begun, the only European military command that drew the correct lessons, so to speak, was the German command, which concluded correctly that the Spanish conflict was a special kind of war from which it would be a mistake to draw any major new conclusions or lessons. The Germans did learn to perfect certain important new aerial techniques, especially air-to-ground support, which later became very important, but even the Germans did not altogether draw proper conclusions about the need to improve their basic antitank weapons, the slack in Spain having been sometimes taken up by the first use of the extraordinarily effective new 88-mm anti-aircraft gun, later one of the most famous weapons of World War II.

The only exit strategy that was ever developed for the Soviet involvement emerged obliquely during the summer of 1938 and then was quickly dashed at Munich. After that there was no indication of any other Soviet strategy for Spain other than to maintain assistance at a comparatively low level and stimulate Republican resistance to the last, while continuing the collective security policy. Nonetheless, signals concerning a possible reorientation of Soviet foreign policy could be seen during the final month of the Spanish conflict. On March 10, 1939, as Casado's forces fought with Communist units in Madrid, Stalin presented a major foreign policy speech to the Eighteenth Party Congress in Moscow. He declared that "a new imperialist war is already in its second year," dating the "second imperialist war" from the beginning of the German-Austrian

Anschluss a year earlier. He had no new policy to announce, but insisted that the rejection of collective security by the Western powers was due simply to a weakness of will. Stalin warned that the expectation of the Western powers that Germany would turn on the Soviet Union was probably mistaken, for Hitler had already given signs of turning his aggression against the West.[37] Though the speech presented no new alternative, it aroused speculations about a possible change in Soviet policy. One of Stalin's chief henchmen, General Lev Zakharovich Mekhlis, gave a more aggressive speech, declaring that the Soviet Union would use a second imperialist war to carry operations into enemy territory and multiply the number of soviet republics.[38] Given Hitler's lack of response to any gesture from the Soviet Union, however, in April Stalin made his last major effort to develop a collective security arrangement with Britain and France by attempting to encourage a sort of triple alliance against Germany, but this effort also failed.[39]

At the beginning of May, Maksim Litvinov, the foreign minister of collective security, was replaced by Vyacheslav Molotov. This appointment signaled further change, but Soviet policy remained in limbo, or transition, for nearly four months, until Hitler's own strategy changed, leading to the Nazi-Soviet Pact of August 1939. Antifascism as leitmotiv of Soviet policy suddenly disappeared for twenty-two months, as Stalin encouraged "new thinking," which included his personal speculation that German National Socialism might really be a form of "national populism" rather than fascism, and hence at least partially progressive.[40] Soviet policy now mirrored fascism as directly as possible as Stalin seized large chunks of territory in Eastern Europe. The American Communist volunteers who had formed the Veterans of the Abraham Lincoln Brigade Association and later liked to style themselves "premature antifascists," mocking the straight-faced charge of the Cold War congressional witch-hunters, in fact gave up antifascism altogether, marching in New York to oppose the United States' entry into the war, as they supported the policies of Stalin and Hitler.[41] When Stalin invaded Finland in December 1939, he immediately set up a Finnish puppet government under the Finnish Communist leader Otto Kuusinen at Terijoki, the first seaside village occupied by the Red Army inside Finland. It proclaimed for a hopefully puppet Finland a "democratic republic of a new type," using the Comintern language that had first been fully defined by Togliatti in October 1936 and then applied ad nauseam for two and a half years in Spain. There was no mention of "socialism" or "soviets," just as there had been none in Spain. In the Winter War of 1939–40, however, the ploy lasted less than two months. Finnish resistance was too tough, and Finnish quislings and Kerenskyites were in short supply. Finland was a fully democratic country; even members of the Communist Party fought loyally in the Finnish army against the Soviet Union.[42] The new formula would have to wait until 1945 for its effective application. In June 1941, with the German invasion, the Soviet Union could return to "antifascism" once more.

Antifascism in the broadest sense was what had held the alliance between the Communists and their unhappy allies together throughout the long and bitter Spanish war. Amid the mutual recriminations that followed for many years—and that have not entirely ceased even in the twenty-first century—antifascism remained the only thing they could still agree on, even though much of the noncommunist left would for many years charge the Communists with themselves following fascist practices. Nonetheless, they would agree that the purpose of their struggle had been to fight fascism, and that therefore the Spanish war had been the first round—or prelude or opening shot—of World War II. In the first contention, they were largely correct, even though the Spaniards against whom they fought were mostly not themselves fascists. Were they equally correct in the latter contention? Was the Spanish war so closely linked to the Second World War that it merely constituted the prelude or opening round? This was the thesis not merely of the Spanish left and the Soviet Union but of some scholarly studies, beginning with Patricia van der Esch's *Prelude to War: The International Repercussions of the Spanish Civil War* (1951).

In one obvious sense, the answer has to be no. The Spanish war was a clear-cut revolutionary/counterrevolutionary contest between left and right, with the fascist totalitarian powers supporting the right and the Soviet totalitarian power supporting the left. World War II, on the other hand, began only when a pan-totalitarian coalition was formed by the Nazi-Soviet Pact with the aim of allowing the Soviet Union to conquer a sizable swath of Eastern Europe while Germany was left free to conquer as much of the rest of the continent as it could. This was a complete reversal of the terms of the Spanish war, and would have meant in Spanish terms the equivalent of an embrace between Franco and La Pasionaria. It seems rather ridiculous to say that the Spanish conflict was the opening round of a pact between Franco and Ibárruri.

One might reverse the formula and conclude that the Spanish revolution and civil war constituted the last of the revolutionary crises stemming from World War I. Just as the military characteristics of the Spanish war resembled those of World War I as much as those of World War II, the Spanish situation had many more characteristics of a post–World War I crisis than of a domestic crisis of the era of World War II. Among those characteristics were (1) the complete domestic revolutionary breakdown of institutions, as distinct from the direct coups d'état and legalitarian impositions of authoritarianism typical of the World War II era; (2) the development of a full-scale revolutionary/counterrevolutionary civil war, common after World War I but elsewhere unheard of during the 1930s; (3) development of a typical post–World War I Red Army in the form of the People's Army; (4) an extreme exacerbation of nationalism, more typical of World War I than of World War II; (5) frequent use of World War I–style military matériel and concepts; and (6) the fact that it was not the product of any plan by any of the major powers, and thus more similar to post–World War I crises than to those of World War II. Similarly, the extreme revolutionary left both inside and outside of Spain hailed the Spanish revolution as the last and one of the greatest of the revolutionary upsurges of the post–World War I era.

It was the negotiation of the Hitler-Stalin Pact, rather than the Soviet intervention in Spain, that obeyed the classic Soviet doctrine of the "second imperialist war," as explained in Chapter 1. According to this doctrine, the Soviet Union should encourage war among the imperialist powers so long as it could avoid serious involvement, for war would have the effect of weakening the major capitalist states. The Soviet Union should strengthen itself as much as possible and then be prepared to enter the war at the decisive moment to determine its final outcome in order to open Europe to the advance of Communism. That was almost exactly the way it worked out in the long run, but Stalin had been severely frustrated between 1933 and 1939 by the fact that German aggression seemed to target the Soviet Union more than the West, and hence Moscow had turned to the collective security policy, which failed completely. The Nazi-Soviet Pact established exactly the terms that Soviet policy had earlier preferred, though this "pact with the devil" initially threw many of the Comintern parties into crisis.

The ECCI dutifully launched the slogan that the war between Germany and the Western democracies was an "imperialist war" in which Communists should not be involved. It would benefit them by hastening the day of revolution. Members of the PCE were less disturbed by the Hitler-Stalin Pact than were those in most other Communist parties, because the experience of the Spanish war left them with a great sense of bitterness against Britain and France, which they were now happy to leave to fight Germany alone. Dimitrov's diary for September 7 quotes Stalin as having said to him: "It wouldn't be bad if the position of the wealthier capitalist states (especially England) were undermined at Germany's hands. Hitler, not understanding and not wishing this himself, is weakening and undermining the capitalist system. . . . We can maneuver, support one side against the other so they can tear each other up all the better." As far as Poland was concerned, it was just another "fascist state," whose destruction by Germany was welcome. "The destruction of this state in the present circumstances would mean one less bourgeois fascist state! It wouldn't be bad if, as a result of the crushing of Poland, we extended the socialist system to new territories and populations."[43] Later in the month a Comintern circular went out explaining that "all efforts to kindle a world revolution have so far been unsuccessful. What are the natural prerequisites of a revolution? A prolonged war, as expounded in the writings of Marx, Engels, and Lenin. What, therefore, must the attitude of the USSR be to hasten a world revolution? To assist Germany in a sufficient degree so that she will begin a war and to take measures to insure that this war will drag on."[44]

Meanwhile, Franco, the victor of the Spanish war, never officially entered World War II. Some historians have therefore denied the Spanish war any significant effect on the broader issues of international affairs. Pierre Renouvin judged its consequences to be merely "modest," saying that "it would be an exaggeration to see in this war a 'prelude to a European war.'"[45] In his *Origins of the Second World War* (1961), A. J. P. Taylor judged that the Spanish conflict had no "significant effect" on the great powers. The author of *The Origins of the Second World War in Europe* (1986), P. M. H. Bell, concluded that the Spanish war was "much ado about nothing."

Stalin was of course too Machiavellian for his own good. By assisting Hitler in his war against France and Britain, he facilitated Germany's stunning victory over France, which then placed Hitler in a position the following year to launch a devastating one-front war that came very close to destroying the Soviet Union. No wonder that Stalin has often been quoted as having remarked depressively in the first days of the German invasion that everything the Communists had built was now in grave danger of being destroyed.

The Soviet Union was saved by Hitler's gratuitous and self-destructive act of joining in Japan's assault against the United States. By doing so he enabled the USSR eventually to achieve a victory in Eastern Europe that created a large new Soviet empire and made the Soviet Union a superpower. The war worked out almost as well for the USSR as Stalin had ever hoped, though it was the most destructive war in human history and victory cost the lives of nearly 30 million Soviet citizens.

In December 1941 an international "popular front" was created, primarily through the recklessness of Japan and Germany, which was politically much broader than the Popular Front in Spain, since it included very conservative major sectors of capitalist society in the United States, Great Britain, and other countries. Did not the Spanish war foreshadow this development? Not really, for the Spanish Republic represented essentially the forces of the revolutionary left, whereas the alliance of 1941–45 included the equivalent of many of the forces on Franco's side during the Spanish war.[46] Thus neither the European war of 1939–41 nor the truly world war of 1941–45 merely replicated the conflict of the Spanish war, though the war after 1941 obviously came closer.

Even though the Spanish war was no mere "prelude" to or "opening round" of World War II in Europe, it contributed significantly to the terms in which the European war developed. Without directly linking the Spanish war and World War II, historians often advance the argument that the Spanish war contributed greatly to the perceptions and psychology that precipitated the greater conflict. Thus it has not infrequently been contended that the behavior of Britain and France vis-à-vis the Spanish war stimulated the false perception by Hitler and Mussolini that the Western democracies lacked the will to fight, and therefore would not respond to much broader aggressions by the fascist powers. In this interpretation the Spanish war would therefore not be a unique "prelude" but would simply be the longest in a series of crises in which the fascist powers acted aggressively and the democracies passively: Ethiopia (1935), the Rhineland (1936), Austria (1938), the Sudetenland (1938).

Hitler's policy of using and prolonging the Spanish conflict as a grand international distraction to deflect attention from his own rearmament and expansion in Central Europe was generally successful. London and Paris often dedicated more attention to Spain than to Austria and Czechoslovakia, while the Spanish issue significantly divided France internally, as we have seen. Moreover, Spain was a very effective issue with which to bind Italy more closely to Germany and provided the original incentive for the Rome-Berlin Axis. In addition, the fascist intervention in Spain had the benefit of eliciting a Soviet counterintervention that Stalin would not expand sufficiently to permit Republican victory (for fear of the consequences), but had for Germany the benefit of intensifying the democracies' suspicion of and alienation from the revolutionary Soviet Union. The more Stalin intervened in Spain and the more aggressive the role of the Soviet Union in the Non-Intervention Committee, the wider the gap yawned. Soviet policy proved almost totally counterproductive, except for the gains made by the NKVD. In that particular game Hitler outsmarted Stalin, as he would do the second time in 1939–41 until he made the absurdly fatal mistake of trying to make war on both of the two largest powers in the world at the same time.[47]

The Soviet intervention was economic and efficient. In proportion to the means invested, it was surprisingly effective, even though the Soviets did not achieve success either in imposing all their policies on the Republican government or in stimulating a Republican victory. Stalin's cautiousness and refusal to make a more significant investment—such as those of Italy and Germany —made it impossible for his side to win in Spain, while the overall international consequences for the Soviet Union were counterproductive. For years the full extent of Soviet intervention was hidden even from the Soviet public, but by the 1960s it had become a cherished memory for personal memoirs and historical studies, presented as an idealistic struggle against fascism of which all Soviets could be proud. Compared with many other Soviet initiatives around the world, it was long cast as a saga that would always reveal the Soviet Union in a positive light. Soviet historians hid the full motives and activities of Soviet policy, as to some extent Russian historians still do today.

Notes

CHAPTER 1. SOVIET POLICY AND THE COMINTERN IN THE
EARLY YEARS

1. Cf. A. J. Mayer, *Dynamics of Counter-Revolution in Europe, 1870–1956* (New York, 1971).
2. V. Zubok and C. Pleshakov, *Inside the Kremlin's Cold War: From Stalin to Khrushchev* (Cambridge, Mass., 1996). On Russian and Soviet Messianism, see P. J. S. Duncan, *Russian Messianism: Third Rome, Revolution, Communism and After* (London, 2000).
3. General treatments of Soviet policy include M. Beloff, *The Foreign Policy of the Soviet Union*, 2 vols. (London, 1947–49); G. Kennan, *Russia and the West under Lenin and Stalin* (New York, 1961); R. Warth, *Soviet Russia in World Politics* (New York, 1963); R. Rosser, *An Introduction to Soviet Foreign Policy* (Englewood Cliffs, N.J., 1969); A. Ulam, *Expansion and Coexistence: The History of Soviet Foreign Policy, 1917–1967* (New York, 1968); and P. Zwick, *Soviet Foreign Relations: Process and Policy* (New York, 1990). T. T. Hammond, *Soviet Foreign Relations and World Communism: A Selected, Annotated Bibliography of 7,000 Books in 30 Languages* (Princeton, N.J., 1965), and R. H. Johnson, *A Guide to the Foreign Policy of the Soviet Union* (New York, 1991), provide further references.
4. Cf. P. Hopkirk, *Like Hidden Fire: The Plot to Bring Down the British Empire* (New York, 1994).
5. Quoted in E. R. Goodman, *The Soviet Design for a World State* (New York, 1960), 292–93; quoted in S. M. Walt, *Revolution and War* (Ithaca, N.Y., 1996), 159. Early Soviet diplomacy is treated in detail in two works by R. K. Debo, *Revolution and*

Survival: The Foreign Policy of Soviet Russia, 1917–18 (New York, 1979) and *Survival and Consolidation: The Foreign Policy of Soviet Russia, 1918–1921* (New York, 1992).

6. Quoted in Walt, *Revolution and War,* 165.
7. The literature on the Comintern is extensive. The most extensive single treatment of the first decade of its history, and one of the most pro-Soviet, will be found in E. H. Carr's ten-volume *History of Soviet Russia* (Harmondsworth, 1950–78), followed by his *Twilight of the Comintern, 1930–1935* (London, 1982) and the woefully incomplete, often inaccurate, posthumously published *The Comintern and the Spanish Civil War* (London, 1984). The account by K. McDermott and J. Agnew, *The Comintern: A History of International Communism from Lenin to Stalin* (Houndmills, Basingstoke, Hampshire, 1996), is succinct, reliable, and up to date, but very brief. T. Rees and A. Thorpe, eds., *International Communism and the Communist International, 1919–43* (Manchester, 1998), is another useful work. One of the best one-volume treatments is F. Claudín, *The Communist Movement: From Comintern to Cominform* (Harmondsworth, 1975), though the older works by F. Borkenau, *European Communism* (London, 1953) and *World Communism: A History of the Communist International* (repr. Ann Arbor, Mich., 1971), are still useful. For the initial phase, see J. W. Hulse, *The Forming of the Communist International* (Stanford, Calif., 1964), and A. Vatlin, *Komintern: Pervye desiat' lety* (Moscow, 1993). Shifts in doctrine and tactics in the later years are analyzed in K. E. McKenzie, *Comintern and World Revolution, 1928–1943: The Shaping of Doctrine* (New York, 1964).
8. A. Vatlin in Rees and Thorpe, *International Communism,* 118.
9. See T. C. Fiddick, *Russia's Retreat from Poland* (New York, 1990), 123–24.
10. Quoted in D. Volkogonov, *Lenin: Life and Legacy* (New York, 1995), 388.
11. The text of the Twenty-one Conditions may be found in J. Riddell, ed., *Workers of the World and Oppressed Peoples, Unite! Proceedings and Documents of the Second Congress, 1920,* 2 vols. (New York, 1991), 2:765–71.
12. Quoted in E. Nolte, *La guerra civil europea, 1917–1945: Nacionalsocialismo y comunismo* (Mexico City, 1994), 11.
13. At the Twelfth Communist Party Congress in 1923 Nikolai Bukharin stressed that the Nazi Party had "inherited Bolshevik political culture exactly as Italian Fascism had done." On June 20, 1923, Karl Radek gave a speech before the Comintern Executive Committee (ECCI) proposing a common front with the Nazis in Germany. That summer several Nazis addressed KPD meetings and vice versa, as the KPD took a strong stand for "national liberation" against the Treaty of Versailles and inveighed against "Jewish capitalists." Yet the two radicalisms proved mutually exclusive, and each went ahead with separate, equally unsuccessful efforts at insurrection. K. Radek, *Der Kampf der Kommunistische Internationale gegen Versaille und gegen die Offensive des Kapitals* (Hamburg, 1923); E. von Reventlow, *Volkisch-kommunistische Einigung?* (Leipzig, 1924); O.-E. Schuddekopf, *Linke leute von Rechts* (Stuttgart, 1960), 445–46; R. Abramovitch, *The Soviet Revolution* (New York, 1962), 259; and L. Luks, *Entstehung der kommu-*

nistischen Faschismustheorie (Stuttgart, 1985), as cited in M. Agursky, *The Third Rome: National Bolshevism in the USSR* (Boulder, Colo., 1987), 378.

14. The quotations, with minor amendment, are from Goodman, *Soviet Design*, 34–43.

15. As late as 1934 the Mongolian prime minister declared: "Our republic is a bourgeois democratic republic of a new type, gradually advancing on the road of noncapitalist development." Quoted in T. T. Hammond, "The Communist Takeover of Outer Mongolia: Model for Eastern Europe?" in *The Anatomy of Communist Takeovers*, ed. Hammond (New Haven, Conn., 1975), 107–44.

16. See ibid. and G. G. S. Murphy, *Soviet Mongolia: A Study of the Oldest Political Satellite* (Berkeley, Calif., 1966). In 1954 the Chinese Communist dictator Mao Zedong asked the post-Stalin government of the Soviet Union to "return" Outer Mongolia to China—though of course it was not Chinese, either—but the Soviets insisted on retaining control of their Mongolian puppet regime.

17. Quoted in McDermott and Agnew, *Comintern*, 51.

18. Ibid., 49, 98–99.

19. Both quotations are ibid., 52.

20. J. V. Stalin, *Sochineniia* (Moscow, 1946–55), 7:14, cited in Goodman, *Soviet Design*, 298.

CHAPTER 2. COMMUNISM AND REVOLUTION IN SPAIN

1. The best introduction to the history of organized labor in Spain in English is B. Martin, *The Agony of Modernization: Labor and Industrialization in Spain* (Ithaca, N.Y., 1990). In Spanish the three-volume work by M. Tuñón de Lara, *El movimiento obrero en la historia de España* (Barcelona, 1972), is somewhat one-sided and now dated.

The principal history of Spanish socialism is the five-volume *Historia del socialismo español* (Barcelona, 1989), ed. M. Tuñón de Lara, but see also the massive one-volume work by S. Juliá, *Los socialistas en la política española, 1879–1982* (Madrid, 1997). For the early years, V. M. Arbeloa, *Orígenes del PSOE (1873–1880)* (Madrid, 1972); A. Elorza and M. Ralle, *La formación del PSOE* (Barcelona, 1989); F. Mora, *Historia del socialismo obrero español* (Madrid, 1902); and J. J. Morato, *El Partido Socialista Obrero Español* (1918; Madrid, 1976). E. del Moral, ed., *Cien años de socialismo en España* (Madrid, 1977), presents the basic earlier bibliography. There are several brief general accounts, such as A. Padilla Bolívar, *El movimiento socialista español* (Barcelona, 1977).

2. The principal study of the origins of Spanish anarchism is J. Termes, *Anarquismo y socialismo en España: La Primera Internacional (1864–1881)* (Barcelona, 1972), but see also C. Lida, *Anarquismo y revolución en la España del siglo XIX* (Madrid, 1972). General accounts are R. W. Kern, *Red Years/Black Years: A Political History of Spanish Anarchism, 1911–1937* (Philadelphia, 1978); C. Lorenzo, *Les anarchistes espagnols et le pouvoir, 1868–1939* (Paris, 1969); M. Buenacasa, *El movimiento obrero español* (Barcelona, 1928); A. Padilla Bolívar, *El movimiento*

anarquista español (Barcelona, 1976); J. Maurice, *L'anarchisme espagnol* (Paris, 1973); and J. Gómez Casas, *Historia del anarcosindicalismo español* (Madrid, 1968) and *Historia de la F.A.I.* (Bilbao, 1977).

The leading works on early anarchist ideology are J. Alvarez Junco, *La ideología política del anarquismo español (1868–1910)* (Madrid, 1976), and G. R. Esenwein, *Anarchist Ideology and the Working-Class Movement in Spain, 1868–1898* (Berkeley, Calif., 1989). The most accurate treatment of anarchism in the south is probably J. Maurice, *El anarquismo andaluz* (Barcelona, 1990).

3. Though superseded in certain aspects, the basic book on the revolutionary left in Spain during the era of World War I is still G. Meaker, *The Revolutionary Left in Spain, 1914–1923* (Stanford, Calif., 1974). Principal studies of the origins and early years of the CNT are J. Romero Maura, *"La rosa de fuego"* (Barcelona, 1975); X. Cuadrat, *Socialismo y anarquismo en Cataluña (1899–1911)* (Madrid, 1976); and A. Bar, *La CNT en los años rojos* (Madrid, 1981). See also C. Forcadell, *Parlamentarismo y bolchevización: El movimiento obrero español, 1914–1918* (Barcelona, 1978).

On the problem of anarchist violence, see R. Núñez Florencio, *El terrorismo anarquista, 1888–1909* (Madrid, 1983); J. Romero Maura, "Terrorism in Barcelona and Its Impact on Spanish Politics, 1904–1909," *Past & Present* 41 (1968), 130–83; W. L. Bernecker, "Strategien der 'direkten Aktion' und der Gewaltanwendung im spanischen Anarchismus," in *Sozialprotest, Gewalt, Terror*, ed. W. Mommsen and G. Hirschfeld, 107–34 (Stuttgart, 1982); A. Balcells, "Violencia y terrorismo en la lucha de clases de Barcelona de 1913 a 1923," *Estudios de Historia Social* 3–4 (1987): 37–79; A. Pestaña, *Lo que yo aprendí en la vida* (Barcelona, 1934), reprinted in his *Trayectoria sindicalista* (Madrid, 1974), and his *Terrorismo en Barcelona*, ed. J. Tusell (Barcelona, 1979); León-Ignacio, *Los años del pistolerismo: Ensayo para una guerra civil* (Barcelona, 1981); A. del Rosal, *La violencia, enfermedad del anarquismo* (Barcelona, 1976); and C. Winston, *Workers and the Right in Spain, 1900–1930* (Princeton, N.J., 1985).

4. For the image of the Bolshevik revolution in Spain, see J. Avilés Farré, *La fe que vino de Rusia: La revolución bolchevique y los españoles (1917–1931)* (Madrid, 1999).

5. A. Barragán Mariana, *Conflictividad social y desarticulación política en la provincia de Córdoba, 1918–1920* (Córdoba, 1980); M. Tuñón de Lara, *Luchas obreras y campesinas en la Andalucía del siglo XX: Jaén (1917–1920), Sevilla (1930–1932)* (Madrid, 1978); and J. M. Macarro, *Conflictos sociales en la ciudad de Sevilla en los años 1918–1920* (Córdoba, 1984).

6. Quoted in Meaker, *Revolutionary Left in Spain*, 126, 143.

7. Ibid., 189.

8. Ibid., 247.

9. The son of a Russian Jewish immigrant, Phillips was originally named Charles Fischel, but years later, after abandoning communism, he changed it to Charles Shipman. Harvey Klehr has edited Shipman's memoir, *It Had to Be Revolution* (Ithaca, N.Y., 1993).

10. On these early years, see M. Izquierdo, *La Tercera Internacional en España, 1914–1923* (Madrid, 1995). The original official history of the PCE, directed by Dolores Ibárruri, is the *Historia del Partido Comunista de España* (Buenos Aires, 1961). Two critical one-volume accounts are J. Estruch Tobella, *Historia del PCE, 1920–1939* (Barcelona, 1978), and V. Alba, *The Communist Party in Spain* (New Brunswick, N.J., 1983). The most extensive treatment of the first years is P. Pagés, *Historia del Partido Comunista de España: Desde su fundación en abril de 1920 hasta el final de la dictadura de Primo de Rivera, enero de 1930* (Barcelona, 1978). E. Comín Colomer, *Historia del Partido Comunista de España*, 3 vols. (Madrid, 1965), remains the principal rightist account, based on access to police materials. J. Andrade, *Apuntes para la historia del PCE* (Barcelona, 1979), is part memoir, part historical essay by one of the early leaders. C. Llorens Castillo, *Historia del Partido Comunista de España: Desde los orígenes hasta el período de su conversión al reformismo (1956–1982)* (Valencia, 1982), is a brief patchwork. There are also several regional histories, such as F. Moreno Gómez, *La última utopía: Apuntes para la historia del PCE andaluz, 1920–1936* (Córdoba, 1995), and F. Erico, ed., *Comunistas en Asturias, 1920–1982* (Gijón, 1996). There is also a published guide to the party's archive: *Catálogo de los fondos del Archivo Histórico del Partido Comunista de España* (Madrid, 1997).

11. The most striking of several accounts published by the delegates was that of the CNT leader Angel Pestaña, *Setenta días en Rusia: Lo que yo vi* (Barcelona, 1924). Pestaña was a keen observer and, as an anarchosyndicalist, not disposed to be deceived by the new regime. He was appalled by the pervasive atmosphere of sadness, dreariness, and suffering under the revolutionary new order, and realized that urban workers in Spain enjoyed distinctly higher standards of living.

12. See V. Alba, *Andreu Nin, Joaquín Maurín* (Madrid, 1975); P. Pagés, *Andreu Nin: Su evolución política* (Madrid, 1975); and F. Bonamusa, *Andreu Nin y el movimiento comunista en España (1930–1937)* (Barcelona, 1977).

13. Y. Riottot, *Joaquín Maurín de l'anarcho-syndicalisme au communisme (1919–1936)* (Paris, 1997), 11. This is the most polished study, but also of interest are D. Bateman, *Joaquim Maurín, 1893–1973: Life and Death of a Spanish Revolutionary* (London, 1974); *Joaquim Maurín*, the fourth volume of V. Alba's *El marxisme a Catalunya* (Barcelona, 1975); A. Monreal, *El pensamiento político de Joaquín Maurín* (Barcelona, 1984); L. Rourera Farré, *Joaquín Maurín y su tiempo* (Barcelona, 1992); A. Bonsón Aventín, *Joaquín Maurín, el impulso moral de hacer política* (Lleida, 1995); A. Bonsón et al., *Joaquim Maurín* (Barcelona, 1998); and the lengthy dissertation by R. A. Tyree, "Toward the Second Revolution: The Political Thought of Joaquín Maurín, 1915–1936" (De Kalb, Ill., 1996).

14. Quoted in Meaker, *Revolutionary Left in Spain*, 425.

15. On Maurín's early initiatives, see Riottot, *Joaquín Maurín*, 20–59; and Meaker, *Revolutionary Left in Spain*, 385–403.

16. Meaker, *Revolutionary Left in Spain*, 449.

17. These and other texts have been republished by Albert Balcells with his own lengthy analytic introduction in *El arraigo del anarquismo en Cataluña: Textos de 1926–1934* (Barcelona, 1973).

18. The inadequacies of Spanish socialism are analyzed at length in P. Heywood, *Marxism and the Failure of Organized Socialism in Spain, 1879–1936* (Cambridge, Mass., 1990), 1–84.

19. On events during 1924–25, see Riottot, *Joaquín Maurín*, 64–90; A. Elorza and M. Bizcarrondo, *Queridos camaradas: La Internacional Comunista y España, 1919–1939* (Barcelona, 1999), 44–52; and A. Durgan, *B.O.C., 1930–1936: El Bloque Obrero y Campesino* (Barcelona, 1996), 29–35.

20. For a brief introduction, see E. Ucelay–Da Cal, *The Shadow of a Doubt: Fascist and Communist Alternatives in Catalan Separatism, 1919–1939* (Barcelona, 2002). With a rightist dictatorship controlling Spain, any temptation toward a semi-fascist "national socialism" was precluded, though some movement in that direction would later take place. Given the weakness of both socialism and communism in Catalonia, Estat Català would look intermittently toward a left alliance with the CNT. That would become a dead letter by 1932, however, and finally took shape only after the Civil War began. See Chapter 6.

21. J. Carner Ribalta, *De Balaguer a Nova York, passant per Moscou i Prats de Molló (Memóries)* (Paris, 1972), 2:305.

22. The most lucid account is X. Estévez, *De la Triple Alianza al Pacto de San Sebastián: Antecedentes de Galeuzca* (San Sebastián, 1991), 503–15. See also J. Carner Ribalta and R. Fabregat, *Macià: La seva actuació al'estranger*, 2 vols. (Barcelona, 1978).

23. Some of the Comintern reports and instructions for these early years have been published in Rossiiskaia Akademiia Nauk, *Komintern i grazhdanskaia voina v Ispanii* (Moscow, 2001), 22–31.

24. Quoted in Elorza and Bizcarrondo, *Queridos camaradas*, 59.

25. Ibid., 70.

26. Ibid., 74.

27. See ibid., 74–78; Riottot, *Joaquín Maurín*, 103–61; Durgan, *B.O.C.*, 35–49; and V. Alba, *El marxismo en España (1919–1939)*, Historia del B.O.C. y del P.O.U.M. (Mexico City, 1973), 9–64.

CHAPTER 3. COMMUNISM AND THE SECOND REPUBLIC

1. K. E. McKenzie, *Comintern and World Revolution, 1928–1943: The Shaping of Doctrine* (New York, 1964), 68–76.

2. Ibid., 71–72, 81–82.

3. Ibid., 72–73, 105.

4. Ibid, 73–77, 105.

5. Ibid., 78.

6. E. R. Goodman, *The Soviet Design for a World State* (New York, 1960), 292–93.

7. McKenzie, *Comintern and World Revolution*, 120–22.

8. Ibid., 95–191.

9. As Bruce Elleman says, "The 1929 Sino-Soviet conflict is perhaps China's least studied and understood war." He provides a useful summary in his *Modern Chinese Warfare, 1795–1989* (London, 2001), 178–93.

10. See K. G. P. Schuster, *Der Rote Frontkämpferbund, 1924–1929: Beitrage zur Geschichte und Organisationsstruktur eines politischen Kampfbundes* (Dusseldorf, 1975).

11. Quoted in K. McDermott and J. Agnew, *The Comintern: A History of International Communism from Lenin to Stalin* (Houndmills, Basingstoke, Hampshire, 1996), 101. A more recent account of the KPD under the Weimar Republic will be found in E. D. Weitz, *Creating German Communism* (Princeton, 1997).

12. McKenzie, *Comintern and World Revolution*, 130.

13. The fundamental account is D. R. Stone, *Hammer and Rifle: The Militarization of the Soviet Union, 1926–1933* (Lawrence, Kans., 2000).

14. See J. Haslam, *Soviet Foreign Policy, 1930–1933: The Impact of the Depression* (New York, 1983).

15. Ibid., 35.

16. P. Hopkirk, *Setting the East Ablaze: Lenin's Dream of an Empire in Asia* (New York, 1995), 226–37.

17. Haslam, *Soviet Foreign Policy*, 61.

18. Ibid., 64–65.

19. E. Rosenhaft, *Beating the Fascists? The German Communists and Political Violence, 1919–1933* (New York, 1983).

20. See C. Fischer, *The German Communists and the Rise of Fascism* (London, 1991). Historians have tried in various ways to make sense of the seemingly suicidal policy of the Comintern in Germany. In *Stalin in Power: The Revolution from Above, 1928–1941* (New York and London, 1992) and "The Emergence of Stalin's Foreign Policy," *Slavic Review* 36 (1977): 563–89, Robert C. Tucker argues that Stalin followed a Machiavellian policy of encouraging the Nazis to make trouble in Western Europe, hoping that such conflict would not involve the Soviet Union, which might then derive revolutionary advantages.

   T. Weingartner, *Stalin und der Aufstieg Hitlers: Die Deutschlandpolitik der Sowjetunion und der Kommunistischen Internationale, 1929–1934* (Berlin, 1970), takes an opposite approach. He argues that Soviet policy never consciously sought to abet the Nazis, and that Stalin never really anticipated any revolution in Germany at that time, but sought to maintain friendly relations with a Germany in which he expected the nationalist right, not the Nazis, to come out on top. See also K. Niclauss, *Die Sowjet Union und Hitlers Machtergreifung* (Bonn, 1966).

   In my view, both interpretations are inaccurate. Weingartner is correct that Soviet policy did not intentionally seek to bring the Nazis to power, but is wrong in concluding that it did not believe that a revolutionary destabilization of Germany could be carried out.

21. "The Revolution in Spain," Jan. 24, 1931, in L. Trotsky, *The Spanish Revolution* (New York, 1973), 67–88.

22. McKenzie, *Comintern and World Revolution*, 79–80.

23. McDermott and Agnew, *Comintern*, 106–7.

24. Cultural relations with the Soviet Union under the Republic are treated in D. L. Kowalsky, "The Soviet Union and the Spanish Republic: Diplomatic, Military, and Cultural Relations, 1936–1939" (Ph.D. diss., University of Wisconsin–Madison, 2001), 244–74.

25. See the dissertation by A. San Román Sevillano, "Los Amigos de la Unión Soviética (AUS): Propaganda política en España (1933–1938)" (University of Salamanca, 1994).

26. A. Elorza and M. Bizcarrondo, *Queridos camaradas: La Internacional Comunista y España, 1919–1939* (Barcelona, 1999), 146.

27. Ibid., 150.

28. D. Manuilsky, "La revolución española y la necesidad del viraje del Partido Comunista," ibid., 142, 153–54.

29. The Latin Section of the Comintern conducted an extensive review in Moscow on March 5, 1932. Rossiiskaia Akademiia Nauk, *Komintern i grazhdanskaia voina v Ispanii* (Moscow, 2001), 40–65. (Hereafter cited as RAN.)

30. Elorza and Bizcarrondo, *Queridos camaradas*, 155–60.

31. Ibid., 161–67. Years later Bullejos would publish his version of these events in *La Comintern en España: Recuerdos de mi vida* (Mexico City, 1972).

32. See M. V. Fernández Lucero, *José Díaz Ramos: Aproximación a la vida de un luchador obrero* (Seville, 1992). There is also, appropriately, a Soviet biography: M. T. Meshcheriakov, *Vsia zhizn'—Bor'ba: O Khose Diase* (Moscow, 1976).

33. Ibárruri's personal apologium is *El único camino* (Madrid, 1992). See also R. Cruz, *Pasionaria: Dolores Ibárruri, historia y símbolo* (Madrid, 1999); M. Vázquez Montalbán, *Pasionaria y los siete enanitos* (Barcelona, 1995); *Pasionaria: Memoria gráfica* (Madrid, 1985); C. F. Gallagher, *La Pasionaria* (Hanover, N.H., 1976); and P. Preston, "Pasionaria of Steel," in his *Comrades! Portraits from the Spanish Civil War* (London, 1999), 277–318.

34. Elorza and Bizcarrondo, *Queridos camaradas*, 444.

35. R. Cruz, *El Partido Comunista en la Segunda República* (Madrid, 1987), 160. Further top organizational changes in July 1933 are detailed in a report of the PCE Plenum of July 27. RAN, 85–86.

36. Elorza and Bizcarrondo, *Queridos camaradas*, 178, 180, 169–72; and see A. Elorza, "La 'Nation éclatée': Front Populaire et question nationale en Espagne," in *Antifascisme et nation: Les gauches européennes au temps du Front Populaire*, ed. S. Wolikow and A. Bleton-Ruget, 5–48 (Dijon, 1997). Potential revolutionary subversion of France might seem to contradict the official Soviet policy of nonaggression and positive diplomatic and commercial relations. Such a split-level policy—involving also revolutionary subversion in Indochina —constituted the standard circle that Soviet policy had been trying to square ever since 1921 and would continue to manipulate, mutatis mutandis, into the 1980s. In some instances, however, the Comintern seems to have issued

instructions to soft-pedal subversive activity so as not directly to undercut Soviet diplomacy.

37. For a thorough treatment of Soviet and Communist policy in the German crisis, see Weingartner, *Stalin und der Aufstieg Hitlers.*

38. McKenzie, *World Communism,* 135.

39. Elorza and Bizcarrondo, *Queridos camaradas,* 175–77.

40. Ibid., 181–82.

41. Cruz, *Partido Comunista,* 147.

42. Ibid., 170–73. There had been a few modest municipal electoral alliances in Córdoba province in 1931 and 1933.

43. McKenzie, *Comintern and World Revolution,* 125.

44. Quoted in Elorza and Bizcarrondo, *Queridos camaradas,* 186.

CHAPTER 4. FROM REVOLUTIONARY INSURRECTION TO POPULAR FRONT

1. A. C. Durgan, *B.O.C., 1930–1936: El Bloque Obrero y Campesino* (Barcelona, 1996), 49–71; V. Alba, *El marxismo en España (1919–1936),* Historia del B.O.C. y del P.O.U.M. (Mexico City, 1973), 65–93; and Y. Riottot, *Joaquín Maurín de l'anarcho-syndicalisme au communisme (1919–1936)* (Paris, 1997), 162–216.

2. Quoted in Durgan, *B.O.C.,* 89.

3. The ICE is treated in P. Pagés, *El movimiento trotskista en España, 1930–1935* (Barcelona, 1977); I. Iglesias, *León Trotski y España* (Madrid, 1977); and F. Bonamusa, *Andreu Nin y el movimiento comunista en España (1930–1937)* (Barcelona, 1937). Writings of Nin have been variously anthologized under the titles *Los problemas de la revolución española (1931–1937)* (Paris, 1971), *Por la unificación marxista* (Madrid, 1978), and *La revolución española* (Barcelona, 1978).

4. The secret report is dated June 14, 1932. Rossiiskaia Akademiia Nauk, *Komintern i grazhdanskaia voina v Ispanii* (Moscow, 2001), 65–82. (Hereafter cited as RAN.)

5. Quoted in Durgan, *B.O.C.,* 102.

6. Ibid., 102–17.

7. Ibid., 147–81.

8. *La Batalla,* Apr. 27, 1933, cited ibid., 192.

9. On the development of the Alianza Obrera, see ibid., 193–253, and Alba, *Marxismo en españa,* 1:135–57.

10. *El Socialista,* Sept. 24, 1933, quoted in P. Moa, *Los orígenes de la guerra civil española* (Madrid, 1999), 162.

11. *XIII Congreso del PSOE* (Madrid, 1932), 561–62. For further discussion of the confusions and contradictions in Socialist policy during this period, see P. Heywood, *Marxism and the Failure of Organized Socialism in Spain, 1879–1936* (Cambridge, Mass., 1990), 110–45.

12. A. Saborit, *Julián Besteiro* (Buenos Aires, 1967), 238–40.

13. Moa, *Orígenes de la guerra civil,* 178.

14. A. Balcells, *Crisis económica y agitación social en Cataluña de 1930 a 1936* (Barcelona, 1974), 29.

15. S. Juliá, *Historia del socialismo español (1931–1939)*, vol. 3 of *Historia del socialismo español*, ed. M. Tuñón de Lara (Barcelona, 1989), 79.

16. Quoted in Moa, *Orígenes de la guerra civil*, 220. This speech was not, however, published in *El Socialista*.

17. The text of the Socialist project may be found in Juliá, *Historia del socialismo*, 347–49, and in the official Communist history by D. Ibárruri et al., *Guerra y revolución en España* (Moscow, 1967), 1:52–57. Largo Caballero's version may be found in his memoir, *Mis recuerdos* (Mexico City, 1954), 134–35.

18. Quoted from the text of the instructions for the insurrection in *Largo Caballero: Escritos de la República*, ed. S. Juliá, in Moa, *Orígenes de la guerra civil*, 404–14, 271.

19. According to Moa, this work was last republished in the West in Paris in 1970.

20. See the remarks in Juliá, *Historia del socialismo*, 101–6. One of the best accounts of the planning is by a member of the committee, Juan Simeón Vidarte, *El Bienio Negro y la insurrección de Asturias* (Barcelona, 1978). See also A. del Rosal, *El movimiento revolucionario de octubre: 1934* (Madrid, 1983), and the documents in S. Juliá, ed., *Largo Caballero: Escritos de la República* (Madrid, 1985).

21. Juliá, *Historia del socialismo*, 115–16. See A. Shubert, *The Road to Revolution in Spain* (Urbana, Ill., 1987), and, more broadly, X. Paniagua, *La sociedad libertaria: Agrarismo e industrialización en el anarquismo español (1930–1939)* (Barcelona, 1982).

22. J. Avilés Farré, *La izquierda burguesa en la II República* (Madrid, 1985), 232–36, 243–44. This further leftward movement by the middle-class left may be compared with the "New Radical Movement" in the French Radical Party between 1926 and 1932. The differences were that the French Radicals were a much stronger, more broadly based group and in the long run were not won over by the new socioeconomic leftism. See M. Schlesinger, "The Development of the Radical Party in the Third Republic: The New Radical Movement, 1926–32," *Journal of Modern History* 46 (September 1974): 476–501.

23. This incident is treated in my *Fascism in Spain, 1923–1977* (Madison, Wis., 1999), 102–14.

24. Quoted in A. de Blas, *El socialismo radical en la II República* (Madrid, 1978), 118.

25. R. Cruz, *El Partido Comunista de España en la Segunda República* (Madrid, 1987), 184–86.

26. N. Greene, *Crisis and Decline: The French Socialist Party in the Popular Front Era* (Ithaca, N.Y., 1969), 4–39.

27. See R. Cruz, *El arte que inflama: La creación de una literatura bolchevique en España, 1931–1936* (Madrid, 1999), and A. Elorza and M. Bizcarrondo, *Queridos camaradas: La Internacional Comunista y España, 1919–1939* (Barcelona, 1999), 60–61, 193–206.

28. Cruz, *Partido Comunista de España*, 188–89.

29. Elorza and Bizcarrondo, *Queridos camaradas*, 215–20; Cruz, *Partido Comunista de España*, 193–94.

30. The best accounts of the strike are in E. E. Malefakis, *Agrarian Reform and Peasant Revolution in Spain* (New Haven, Conn., 1970), 317–42, and M. Tuñón de Lara, *Tres claves de la Segunda República* (Madrid, 1985), 130–53.

31. E. Ucelay–Da Cal and S. Tavera, "Una revolución dentro de otra: La lógica insurreccional en la política española, 1924–1934," in *Violencia y política en España*, ed. J. Aróstegui, special issue of *Ayer* 13 (1994): 115–46.

32. Alba, *Marxismo en España*, 1:164.

33. On the BOC in the revolt, see Durgan, *B.O.C.*, 283–305. For Catalonia as a whole, L. Aymamí i Baudina, *El 6 d'octubre tal com jo l'he vist* (Barcelona, 1935); E. de Angulo, *Diez horas de Estat Català* (Madrid, 1935); F. Gómez Hidalgo, *Cataluña-Companys* (Madrid, 1935); A. Estivill, *6 d'octubre: L'ensulsiada dels jacobins* (Barcelona, 1935); J. Miravitlles, *Crítica del 6 d'octubre* (Barcelona, 1935); S. Campos i Terre, *El 6 d'octubre a les comarques* (Barcelona, 1935); and more recently M. Cruells, *El 6 d'octubre a Catalunya* (Barcelona, 1970), and J. Tarín-Iglesias, *La rebelión de la Generalidad* (Barcelona, 1988).

34. J. D. Carrión Iñiguez, *La insurrección de 1934 en la provincia de Albacete* (Albacete, 1990), and J. P. Fusi, "Nacionalismo y revolución: Octubre de 1934 en el País Vasco," in G. Jackson et al., *Octubre 1934*, 177–96 (Madrid, 1985).

35. On the Asturian background, see Shubert, *Road to Revolution;* L. Paramio, "Revolución y conciencia preindustrial en octubre de 1934," in Jackson et al., *Octubre 1934*, 301–25; and A. Barrio Alonso, *Anarquismo y anarcosindicalismo en Asturias (1890–1936)* (Madrid, 1988).

36. On the role of the Communists in Asturias, see M. Grossi, *La insurrección de Asturias* (Madrid, 1978), 86–98, and J. Canel (pseud.), *Octubre rojo en Asturias* (Madrid, 1935), 153–54.

37. The fullest account, highly favorable to the revolutionaries, is P. I. Taibo II, *Asturias 1934* (Gijón, 1984), 2 vols. A. de Llano Roza de Ampudia, *Pequeños anales de quince días* (Oviedo, 1935), is one of the best of the contemporary narratives. See also Gen. E. López de Ochoa, *Campaña militar en Asturias de octubre de 1934* (Madrid, 1936); Reporteros reunidos, *Octubre rojo* (Madrid, 1934); I. Núñez, *La revolución de octubre de 1934* (Barcelona, 1935), 2 vols.; "Un testigo imparcial," *Revolución en Asturias* (Madrid, 1934); J. S. Valdivielso, *Farsa y tragedia de España en el 1934* (Oviedo, 1935); H. Iglesia Somoza, *Asedio y defensa de la cárcel de Oviedo* (Vitoria, 1935); J. C. Geijo, *Episodios de la revolución* (Santander, 1935); M. Martínez de Aguiar, *¿A dónde va el Estado español? Rebelión socialista y separatista de 1934* (Madrid, 1935); and V. Madera, *El Sindicato Católico de Moreda y la revolución de octubre* (Madrid, 1935).

Among the leading contemporary leftist accounts, in addition to those of Canel and Grossi (n. 36), are A. Ramos Oliveira, *La revolución española de octubre* (Madrid, 1935); M. D. Benavides, *La revolución fue así* (Barcelona, 1937); R. González Peña, *Un hombre en la revolución* (Madrid, 1935); M. Domingo, *La revolución de octubre* (Madrid, 1935); Ignotus (M. Villar), *El anarquismo en la insurrección de octubre* (Valencia, 1935); Solano Palacio, *La revolución de octubre*

(Barcelona, 1935); and J. Orbón, *Avilés en el movimiento revolucionario de Asturias* (Gijón, 1934).

Later detailed accounts include F. Aguado Sánchez, *La revolución de octubre de 1934* (Madrid, 1972); B. Díaz Nosty, *La comuna asturiana* (Madrid, 1974); J. A. Sánchez and G. Sauco, *La revolución de 1934 en Asturias* (Madrid, 1974); M. Bizcarrondo, *Octubre del 1934* (Madrid, 1977); E. Barco Teruel, *El golpe socialista (octubre 1934)* (Madrid, 1984); D. Ruiz, *Insurrección defensiva y revolución obrera: El octubre español de 1934* (Barcelona, 1988); R. de la Cierva, *La revolución de octubre: El PSOE contra la República* (Madrid, 1997); and A. Palomino, *1934: La guerra civil comenzó en Asturias* (Barcelona, 1998).

38. R. Ledesma Ramos, *¿Fascismo en España?* (Madrid, 1935), 38.

39. See the references in my *Spain's First Democracy* (Madison, Wis., 1993), 22–23.

40. J. S. Vidarte, *El Bienio Negro y la insurrección de Asturias* (Barcelona, 1978), 236, and S. Carrillo, *Memorias* (Barcelona, 1993), 16ff.

41. G. Brenan, *The Spanish Labyrinth: An Account of the Social and Political Background of the Civil War* (Cambridge, 1967); G. Jackson, *The Spanish Republic and the Civil War (1931–1939)* (Princeton, N.J., 1965).

42. Jackson, *Spanish Republic*, 166, estimates about forty murders by the left, including thirty-four clergy and seminarians and one conservative parliamentary deputy. There is an extensive literature on the persecution of the clergy. No systematic investigation of violence by the right was ever carried out. One of the fullest statements from the left was Ignotus (M. Villar), *La represión de octubre* (Barcelona, 1936).

43. Elorza and Bizcarrondo, *Queridos camaradas*, 221–22.

44. J. V. Stalin, *Sochineniia* (Moscow, 1955), 12:263; A. Eden, *Facing the Dictators* (Boston, 1962), 164. On the changes in Soviet policy, see J. Haslam, *The Soviet Union and the Struggle for Collective Security in Europe, 1933–1939* (London, 1984), 27–51, and J. Hochman, *The Soviet Union and the Failure of Collective Security, 1934–1938* (Ithaca, N.Y., 1984), 33–77.

45. On Dimitrov's policies and his relations with Stalin, see the Comintern documents in *Dimitrov and Stalin, 1934–1943: Documents from the Soviet Archives*, ed. A. Dallin and F. I. Firsov (New Haven, Conn., 2000).

46. J. Santore, "The Comintern's United Front Initiative of May 1934: French or Soviet Inspiration," *Canadian Journal of History* 16 (1981): 405–21.

47. K. McDermott and J. Agnew, *The Comintern: A History of International Communism from Lenin to Stalin* (Houndmills, Basingstoke, Hampshire, 1996), 126; Haslam, *Soviet Union*, 56.

48. D. P. Brower, *The New Jacobins: The French Communist Party and the Popular Front* (Ithaca, N.Y., 1968); J. Kergoat, *La France du Front Populaire* (Paris, 1986), 51–52; E. H. Carr, *The Twilight of the Comintern, 1930–1935* (London, 1982), 145.

49. The quotations here and in the following paragraphs are from McDermott and Agnew, *Comintern*, 130–32, 134, 155–59.

50. Cf. P. Spriano, *Stalin and the European Communists* (London, 1985), 30; McDermott and Agnew, *Comintern*, 133, 159.

51. Elorza and Bizcarrondo, *Queridos camaradas*, 250; McDermott and Agnew, *Comintern*, 132.

52. Elorza and Bizcarrondo, *Queridos camaradas*, 223–25.

53. Ibid., 225–26; Cruz, *Partido Comunista*, 229.

54. Elorza and Bizcarrondo, *Queridos camaradas*, 232.

55. As outlined in a report of the Romanskii Lendersekretariat of Feb. 8, 1935. RAN, 99–101.

56. See Elorza and Bizcarrondo, *Queridos camaradas*, 230–34.

57. Ibid., 236–44.

58. José Díaz, *Tres años de lucha* (Barcelona, 1978), 1:43.

59. Cruz, *Partido Comunista*, 214.

60. See J. C. Gibaja Velázquez, *Indalecio Prieto y el socialismo español* (Madrid, 1995), and E. Cornide Ferrant, *Indalecio Prieto: Socialista a fuerza de liberal* (La Coruña, 1995).

61. On the situation of the AOs in 1935, see Durgan, *B.O.C.*, 340–46.

62. Ibid., 346–49.

63. L. Trotsky, *The Spanish Revolution* (New York, 1973), 198–201. The best guide to these maneuvers is Durgan, *B.O.C.*, 350–59, but see also Riottot, *Joaquín Maurín*, 301–19, and Alba, *Marxismo en España*, 1:181–245.

64. Cruz, *Partido Comunista*, 228.

65. J. Díaz, *Nuestra bandera del Frente Popular* (Madrid-Barcelona, 1936), 31, 57; Cruz, *Partido Comunista*, 235–39, 245–46.

66. Elorza and Bizcarrondo, *Queridos camaradas*, 255.

67. The clearest discussion of these negotiations remains S. Juliá, *Orígenes del Frente Popular en España (1934–1936)* (Madrid, 1979), 70–149.

68. Cruz, *Partido Comunista*, 249–50.

69. Elorza and Bizcarrondo, *Queridos camaradas*, 263–64, 267.

70. Ibid., 261, 496–97.

71. J. Díaz, *Tres años de lucha* (Barcelona, 1978), 1:97–98.

72. Cruz, *Partido Comunista*, 254–55.

73. On the comparative background, see G.-R. Horn, *European Socialists Respond to Fascism: Ideology, Activism and Contingency in the 1930s* (New York, 1996); M. S. Alexander and H. Graham, eds., *The French and Spanish Popular Fronts: Comparative Perspectives* (Cambridge, Mass., 1989); and H. Graham and P. Preston, eds., *The Popular Front in Europe* (London, 1987). There is no general history of the Spanish Popular Front. On its French counterpart, see G. Lefranc, *Histoire du Front Populaire, 1934–1938* (Paris, 1965); J. Jackson, *The Popular Front in France: Defending Democracy, 1934–1938* (Cambridge, 1984); Kergoat, *La France du Front Populaire;* and K. G. Harr Jr., *The Genesis and Effect of the Popular Front in France* (Lanham, Md., 1987).

74. Riottot, *Joaquín Maurín*, 321–31; Durgan, *B.O.C.*, 402–10; Alba, *Marxismo en España*, 1:245–53; and Cruz, *Partido Comunista*, 267–68.

75. The principal study is J. Tusell et al., *Las elecciones del Frente Popular* (Madrid, 1971), 2 vols., but see also J. J. Linz and J. M. de Miguel, "Hacia un análisis

regional de las elecciones de 1936 en España," *Revista española de la opinión pública* 48 (April–June 1977): 27–67, who conclude that the Popular Front list alone drew 43 percent, the rightist list alone 30.4 percent, and a variety of right-center and center lists 21 percent, but that about three-quarters of the latter pertained to the right-center.

CHAPTER 5. COMMUNISM AND THE IMPLOSION OF THE REPUBLIC

1. D. Martínez Barrio, *Los orígenes del Frente Popular* (Buenos Aires, 1943), 61.
2. The first historian of the Republic, Josep Pla, referred repeatedly in his *Historia de la Segunda República española*, 4 vols. (Barcelona, 1940–41), to what he termed the "kerenskyismo ideológico" of Manuel Azaña.
3. For a description of this process, see my *Spain's First Democracy: The Second Republic, 1931–1936* (Madison,Wis., 1993), 281–384.
4. ECCI directive of Feb. 21, 1936, in Rossiiskaia Akademiia Nauk, *Komintern i grazhdanskaia voina v Ispanii* (Moscow, 2001), 104–7. Cf. the British Intelligence decrypt quoted by G. Roberts in C. Leitz and D. J. Dunthorn, *Spain in an International Context, 1936–1959* (New York, 1999), 102n42.
5. A. Elorza and M. Bizcarrondo, *Queridos camaradas: La Internacional Comunista y España, 1919–1939* (Barcelona, 1999), 257–70.
6. Ibid., 279.
7. *El Socialista*, Feb. 12, 1936.
8. Quoted in E. Comín Colomer, *Historia del Partido Comunista de España* (Madrid, 1967), 3:190; *Mundo obrero*, Mar. 2, 1936.
9. This was the front-page demand of *Mundo obrero* on Mar. 7.
10. *Claridad*, Feb. 11, 1936. On Araquistain, see M. Bizcarrondo, *Araquistain y la crisis socialista en la II República: Leviatán (1934–1936)* (Madrid, 1975), and the anthology edited by P. Preston, *Leviatán* (Madrid, 1976), as well as S. Juliá, *La izquierda del PSOE, 1935–1936* (Madrid, 1977), and A. de Blas Guerrero, *El socialismo radical en la II República* (Madrid, 1978).
11. In an article titled "Paralelo entre la revolución rusa y la española," *Leviatán*, Mar. 22, 1932, 32.
12. Elorza and Bizcarrondo, *Queridos camaradas*, 272–77. For the background of Carrillo and of the FJS, see R. Viñas, *La formación de las Juventudes Socialistas Unificadas (1934–1936)* (Madrid, 1978), and M. E. Yague, *Santiago Carrillo* (Madrid, 1978).
13. Fernando Claudín, *Santiago Carrillo (Crónica de un secretario general)* (Barcelona, 1983), 31–39.
14. This very lengthy document was widely publicized and appeared not only in *Mundo obrero* but also, at least in part, in other newspapers.
15. A critique of the "ultraleftism" of the caballeristas during these months is in D. Ibárruri et al., *Historia del Partido Comunista de España* (Paris, 1960), 114.
16. G. Mario de Coca, *Anti-Caballero: Crítica marxista de la bolchevización del Partido Socialista* (Madrid, 1936), 207, 211.
17. Elorza and Bizcarrondo, *Queridos camaradas*, 280.

18. Ibid., 282.

19. Comín Colomer, *Historia del Partido Comunista*, 3:242, 232; J. Díaz, *Tres años de lucha* (Barcelona, 1978), 165; Elorza and Bizcarrondo, *Queridos camaradas*, 282.

20. Quoted in Elorza and Bizcarrondo, *Queridos camaradas*, 282–83.

21. Díaz, *Tres años de lucha*, 165.

22. Quoted in B. Bolloten, *The Spanish Civil War* (Chapel Hill, N.C., 1991), 25.

23. G. Dimitrov, "The United Front of the Struggle for Peace," *Communist International* 13 (May 1936): 290–93.

24. Figures for the earlier dates are from R. Cruz, *El Partido Comunista de España en la Segunda República* (Madrid, 1987), 57, who calculates that by July 18 membership may have reached 83,867 (p. 60). Bolloten, *Spanish Civil War*, 83, cites an article by Manuel Delicado of the party's central committee that appeared in *La Correspondencia internacional*, July 23, 1939, and gave a figure of approximately 40,000 on the eve of the Civil War.

25. A. C. Durgan, *B.O.C., 1930–1936: El Bloque Obrero y Campesino* (Barcelona, 1996), 526, 411–16, 430–31; Y. Riottot, *Joaquín Maurín de l'anarcho-syndicalisme au communisme (1919–1936)* (Paris, 1997), 335–38.

26. Durgan, *B.O.C.*, 430–31.

27. Quoted ibid., 418.

28. J. L. Martín i Ramos, *Els orígens del PSUC* (Barcelona, 1977); L. V. Ponomariova, *La formación del Partit Socialist Unificat de Catalunya* (Barcelona, 1977); M. Caminal, *Joan Comorera: Catalanisme i socialisme (1913–1936)* (Barcelona, 1984); and R. Alcaraz i González, *La Unió Socialista de Catalunya* (Barcelona, 1987).

29. Durgan, *B.O.C.*, 428–29.

30. *Solidaridad obrera* (Barcelona), May 11 and 13, 1936; *El Congreso confederal de Zaragoza (mayo, 1936)* (Toulouse, 1955).

31. Riottot, *Joaquín Maurín*, 216–22; Durgan, *B.O.C.*, 432–44.

32. L. Trotsky, *The Spanish Revolution* (New York, 1972), 207–10, 215–24.

33. Durgan, *B.O.C.*, 435–36.

34. Ibid., 437–42.

35. Ibid., 444–76.

36. Ibid., 477–79.

37. Ibid., 480–84.

38. See the discussions in K. McDermott and J. Agnew, *The Comintern: A History of International Communism from Lenin to Stalin* (Houndmills, Basingstoke, Hampshire, 1996), 137, and N. Greene, *Crisis and Decline: The French Socialist Party in the Popular Front Era* (Ithaca, N.Y., 1969), 64.

39. See G. Lefranc, *Le Mouvement socialiste sous la Troisième République* (Paris, 1963) and *Histoire du Front Populaire* (Paris, 1965); J. Colton, *Léon Blum, Humanist in Politics* (New York, 1967); Colloque, *Léon Blum: Chef de gouvernement* (Paris, 1968); G. Ziebura, *Léon Blum: Theorie und Praxis einer sozialistischen Politik*, vol. 1 (Berlin, 1963); M. Perrot and A. Kriegel, *Le Socialisme français et le pouvoir* (Paris, 1966); and A. Prost, *La CGT à l'époque du Front Populaire* (Paris, 1964).

There is a good brief treatment in I. Wall, "French Socialism and the Popular Front," *Journal of Contemporary History* 5, no. 3 (1970): 5–20.

40. Elorza and Bizcarrondo, *Queridos camaradas*, 285. *Mundo obrero* had already boasted of the participation of party members in carrying out the arbitrary arrests that were a feature of Spanish life under the leftist government. On Apr. 20 it had quoted the civil governor of Oviedo, Fernando Bosque, as reporting: "I have appointed Popular Front delegates throughout Asturias, who have been carrying out antifascist sweeps [batidas] with very good results: they have jailed priests, doctors, municipal secretaries, anyone. They fulfill their tasks admirably. Some of the delegates are Communists, and even like Fermín López Irún, who was sentenced to death for his participation in the events of October. . . . The one in Taverga has jailed the local telegrapher and court secretary; the former is let out during the day to do his work and locked up at night. Among those in prison are two canons from Covadonga." This frank statement of what was going on in various parts of the country raised a scandal in Madrid, and the interior minister eventually dismissed Bosque.

41. M. V. Novikov, *SSSR, Komintern i grazhdanskaia voina v Ispanii, 1936–1939 gg.* (Yaroslavl, 1995), 2:76.

42. Elorza and Bizcarrondo, *Queridos camaradas*, 285–86.

43. Ibid., 287.

44. *Material de discusión para el Congreso Provincial del Partido Comunista que se celebrará en Madrid, durante los días 20, 21 y 22 de junio de 1936* (Madrid, 1936).

45. D. Ibárruri et al., *Guerra y revolución en España, 1936–1939* (Moscow, 1967), 1:66; J. Modesto, *Soy del Quinto Regimiento* (Barcelona, 1978), 63–67.

46. On the concept of constitutional dictatorship, see C. Rossiter, *Constitutional Dictatorship: Crisis Government in the Modern Democracies* (New Brunswick, N.J., 2002).

47. *Mundo obrero*, July 10, 1936.

48. The two principal studies of this affair are I. Gibson, *La noche en que mataron a Calvo Sotelo* (Barcelona, 1982), and L. Romero, *Cómo y por qué mataron a Calvo Sotelo* (Barcelona, 1982). The nature of the role of Ossorio Tafall was first explained to me by one of the two principal leaders of his Galician party, Emilio González López. Interviews in New York, May 1958.

49. Quoted in J. Tusell, "La recuperación de la democracia: El último Araquistain (1933–1959): Política y vida de un escritor socialista," his introduction to Araquistain's *Sobre la Guerra Civil y la emigración* (Madrid, 1983), 11–128.

50. Elorza and Bizcarrondo, *Queridos camaradas*, 291–92.

CHAPTER 6. COMMUNISM AND THE SPANISH REVOLUTION

1. There is no question that these materials had some effect in conservative circles both at home and abroad. See H. Southworth, *El mito de la cruzada de Franco* (Paris, 1963), 247–58; R. de la Cierva, *Historia de la Guerra Civil española* (Madrid, 1969), 1:709, 713–20; and *Los documentos de la primavera trágica* (Madrid, 1967), 428.

2. Quoted in J. Zugazagoitia, *Historia de la guerra en España* (Buenos Aires, 1940), 9.

3. C. Rama, *La crisis española del siglo XX* (Mexico City, 1960), 47.

4. There is a sizable literature on anarchosyndicalism during the Spanish war. The most systematic treatment is R. J. Alexander, *The Anarchists in the Spanish Civil War*, 2 vols. (London, 1999). The most detailed account in Spanish is the pro-cenetista publication by J. Peirats, *La CNT en la revolución española*, 3 vols., of which the most recent (fourth) printing came out in Cali, Colombia, in 1988. See also his *Los anarquistas en la crisis política española* (Buenos Aires, 1964). The older work by the French Trotskyists Pierre Broué and Emile Témime, *La révolution et la guerre d'Espagne* (Paris, 1961), also has extensive coverage of the CNT. The best longitudinal study is J. Casanova, *De la calle al frente: El anarcosindicalismo en España (1931–1939)* (Barcelona, 1997).

5. H. Prieto, *El anarquismo español en la lucha política* (Paris, 1946), 7. The quotation, technically correct, must be qualified by the fact that anarchist power became increasingly pluralistic, while that of the Bolsheviks soon became completely totalitarian.

6. Quoted in C. Serrano, *L'Enjeu espagnol: PCF et guerre d'Espagne* (Paris, 1987), 65.

7. On collectivization in Catalonia, see A. Pérez-Baró, *Treinta meses de colectivismo en Cataluña, 1936–1939* (Barcelona, 1974); A. Castells Durán, *Les collectivitzacions a Barcelona, 1936–1939* (Barcelona, 1993); J. M. Bricall, *Política económica de la Generalitat, 1936–1939* (Barcelona, 1970); and P. Pagès, *La Guerra Civil espanyola a Catalunya (1936–1939)* (Barcelona, 1997).

8. See the references in B. Bolloten, *The Spanish Civil War* (Chapel Hill, N.C., 1991), 225, 819.

9. For an approach to the revolutionary experience from the viewpoint of ordinary workers rather than of the revolutionary organizations, see M. Seidman, *Workers against Work: Labor in Paris and Barcelona during the Popular Fronts* (Berkeley, Calif., 1991), and his *Republic of Egos: A Social History of the Spanish Civil War* (Madison, Wis., 2002), on ordinary workers and soldiers during the war, as well as his articles "Work and Revolution: Workers' Control in Barcelona in the Spanish Civil War, 1936–38," *Journal of Contemporary History* 17 (July 1982): 409–33; "Towards a History of Workers' Resistance to Work: Paris and Barcelona during the French Popular Front and the Spanish Revolution (1936–1938)," *Journal of Contemporary History* 23 (April 1988): 193–219; "The Unorwellian Barcelona," *European History Quarterly*, March 1990, 163–80; and "Individualisms in Madrid during the Spanish Civil War," *Journal of Modern History*, March 1996, 63–82.

10. E. Malefakis, "La revolución social," in *La Guerra de España, 1936–1939*, ed. Malefakis, 319–54 (Madrid, 1996).

11. The most inclusive study of collectivization during the Spanish war is W. L. Bernecker, *Colectividades y revolución social: El anarquismo en la guerra civil española, 1936–1939* (Barcelona, 1982), which, as the title indicates, is devoted to the activity of the CNT, particularly in agrarian collectives. For a briefer and more general survey, see Bernecker's chapter "La revolución social" in *La Guerra Civil: Una*

nueva visión del conflicto que dividió España, ed. S. Payne and J. Tusell, 485–533 (Madrid, 1996). Another good brief study is L. Garrido González, F. Quilis Tauriz, N. Rodrigo González, and J. M. Santacréu Soler, "Las colectivizaciones en la Guerra Civil," in *Historia y memoria de la Guerra Civil,* ed. J. Aróstegui, 2:63–134 (Valladolid, 1988). These authors conclude that by 1937 39 percent of all the land in the Republican zone had been expropriated, though scarcely more than half of that figure was formally collectivized. The percentage of land that changed hands was considerably higher in Spain than in Russia during 1917–18.

Many monographs on collectivization in individual areas have appeared. A partial list of such studies includes A. Bosch Sánchez, *Ugetistas y libertarios (Guerra Civil y revolución en el País Valenciano, 1936–39)* (Valencia, 1988) and "The Spanish Republic and the Civil War: Rural Conflict and Collectivization," *Bulletin of Hispanic Studies* 75 (December 1988): 117–32; L. Garrido, *Las colectividades agrarias en Andalucía: Jaén, 1931–38* (Madrid, 1979); J. L. Gutiérrez, *Colectividades libertarias en Castilla la Nueva* (Madrid, 1978); N. Rodrigo González, *Las colectividades agrarias en Castilla–La Mancha* (Toledo, n.d.); F. Quilis Tauriz, *Revolución y guerra civil: Las colectividades obreras en la provincia de Alicante, 1936–1939* (Alicante, 1992); and A. Castells Durán, *Las transformaciones colectivistas en la industria y en los servicios de Barcelona (1936–1939)* (Madrid, 1992) and *El proceso estatizador en la experiencia colectivista catalana (1936–1939)* (Madrid, 1996). Useful accounts are also found in F. García, *Colectividades campesinas y obreras en la revolución española* (Madrid, 1977) and in the chapters by L. Garrido and J. Casanova in *Socialismo y guerra civil,* ed. S. Julià, 257–93 (Madrid, 1987). In addition, some of the numerous political monographs dealing individually with various cities and provinces sometimes contain brief accounts of the collectivization process in one locale.

12. According to the study by Garrido González et al., cited in n. 10.

13. C. Campoamor, *La Révolution espagnole vue par une républicaine* (Paris, 1937), 103.

14. The principal study is J. Paavolainen, *Poliittiset vakivaltaisundet Suomessa, 1918,* 2 vols. (Helsinki, 1967). In Spain there were more military fatalities than victims of the repression. This was not the case in Finland, where total fatalities amounted to 31,000. Military fatalities amounted to no more than 6,000–7,000, and the Red repression in Finland killed no more than 2,000–3,000 people. The White repression resulted in as many as 20,000 deaths, as many as 8,200 killed outright and another 11,800 dying in camps. See also A. F. Upton, *The Finnish Revolution, 1917–1918* (Minneapolis, Minn., 1980).

The first scholarly effort to tabulate the extent of the repression in both zones in Spain was R. Salas Larrazábal's *Pérdidas de la guerra* (Madrid, 1977). Though it correctly calculated the total number of deaths from all forms of violence in the Civil War—military and political—at approximately 300,000, the methodology employed to tabulate the repression province by province has been shown to be defective. Since that time a growing number of monographs have concentrated on the repression by one or both sides in individual districts or provinces. These studies vary greatly in methodology and quality, the most reliable being those by J. M. Solé Sabaté, *La repressió franquista a Catalunya, 1938–1953* (Barcelona, 1985) and (with J. Villarroya i Font) *La repressió a la reraguarda de Catalunya (1936–1939)*, 2 vols. (Barcelona, 1989–90). Broader syntheses have also appeared, such as the one edited by S. Juliá, *Víctimas de la Guerra Civil* (Madrid, 1999), which in large measure simply reverses the calculations of the total number of killings by left and right as earlier calculated by Salas Larrazábal, and the sober analyses by A. D. Martín Prieto, *Paz, piedad, perdón . . . y verdad* (Madrid, 1997) and *Salvar la memoria: Una reflexión sobre las víctimas de la Guerra Civil* (Madrid, 1999). Exact totals will never be known because reliable records do not exist. Whereas Salas Larrazábal calculated that there were twice as many executions by the left as by the right, the authors in the Juliá volume simply reverse that estimate. Martín Prieto has estimated a total of 60,000 killings by the left and 70,000 by the right. Those ratios are probably as accurate as they can be made, but the total number may be exaggerated. It should also be kept in mind that the Republicans carried out their executions within a steadily shrinking territory and a steadily narrowing demographic base. After the Civil War the Franco regime executed approximately 30,000 persons.

The Republican zone remained not at all "democratic," as the propaganda had it. It was at least semipluralistic and in general there was less planning and coherence in the Republican repression, even though nearly all executions were carried out by regular members of the leftist organizations. In almost every district of the Nationalist zone, conversely, the killings were under the overall control and direction of the military, even though they were sometimes carried out by individual Falangists and rightist bands on their own account.

The bulk of the killings took place during the first months; thereafter, blood lust partially sated, repression was more centrally organized and disciplined by both sides. Greater moderation and control began finally to be introduced in the Republican zone in December 1936 and in the Nationalist zone two months later.

15. E. Nolte, *La guerra civil europea, 1917–1945* (Mexico City, 1994), 239.

16. A. Elorza and M. Bizcarrondo, *Queridos camaradas: La Internacional Comunista y España, 1919–1939* (Barcelona, 1999), 294.

17. According to the British Intelligence decrypts quoted by G. Roberts in *Spain in an International Context, 1936–1959*, ed. C. Leitz and D. J. Dunthorn (New York, 1999), 100n11. The euphoria of these initial reports has to some extent been reflected in the secondary literature. Cf. A. Carabantes and E. Comirra, *Un mito llamado Pasionaria* (Barcelona, 1982), 119; M. Meshcheriakov, *Vsia zhizn'—Bor'ba (O Khose Diase)* (Moscow, 1971), 109–10; and J. Haslam, *The Soviet Union and the Struggle for Collective Security in Europe, 1933–1939* (London, 1984), 262.

18. R. Radosh, M. Habeck, and G. Sevostianov, eds., *Spain Betrayed: The Soviet Union in the Spanish Civil War* (New Haven, Conn., 2001), 10–11.

19. Ibid., 9, 11–13. The Russian text appears in Rossiiskaia Akademiia Nauk, *Komintern i grazhdanskaia voina v Ispanii* (Moscow, 2001), 110–13. (Hereafter cited as RAN.)

20. A. Dallin and F. I. Firsov, eds., *Dimitrov and Stalin, 1934–1943: Letters from the Kremlin Archives* (New Haven, Conn., 2000), 46. For the Russian text, see RAN, 113–14.
21. Radosh et al., *Spain Betrayed*, 14–15.
22. *Mundo obrero*, July 30, 1936.
23. D. Ibárruri et al., eds., *Guerra y revolución en España, 1936–39* (Moscow, 1966), 1:305–7.
24. Radosh et al., *Spain Betrayed*, 17–18.

CHAPTER 7. THE SOVIET DECISION TO INTERVENE MILITARILY

1. Cf. V. Peña Sánchez, *La cultura italiana del "ventennio fascista" y su repercusión en España* (Granada, 1995). See my *Fascism in Spain, 1923–1977* (Madison, Wis., 1999), 51–184, for details of this relationship.
2. Fernando Claudín has written: "The outbreak of the Spanish revolution—the only one that took place in Europe during the existence of the Communist International, apart from the ephemeral Hungarian soviet republic of 1919—caught the leaders of the 'world party' off guard": *La crisis del movimiento comunista* (Paris, 1970), 168. This may be true to a certain degree, but not entirely, for the Comintern leaders had for some time been seeking to manage affairs in Spain, which were developing so well from their point of view, so as to avoid any blowup—a possibility of which they were already painfully aware.
3. A. Amba, *I Was Stalin's Bodyguard* (London, 1952), 27–28, declares that on July 23 a small number of Soviet planes were shipped from Odessa, bound for Spain. This report seems unlikely. In *La révolution espagnole vue par une républicaine* (Paris, 1937), 174, the former Radical deputy Clara Campoamor wrote that "in August it was announced that a certain number of Russian planes had arrived in Madrid," but no confirmation has been found.
4. See the brief account in N. Greene, *Crisis and Decline: The French Socialist Party in the Popular Front Era* (Ithaca, N.Y., 1969), 78–81. The Soviet version may be found in R. Varfolomeeva, *Reaktsionnaia vneshniaia politika frantsuzskikh pravikh sotsialistov (1936–1939 gg.)* (Moscow, 1949). Soviet historians also detected somewhat similarly fell designs on the part of British Labour moderates, as in N. N. Nikolaev, *Vneshniaia politika pravykh leiboristov angliiskikh v period podgotovki i nachala Vtoroi Mirovoi Voiny, 1935–1940 gg.* (Moscow, 1953).
5. An account of French and British relations during these years will be found in M. Thomas, *Britain, France, and Appeasement: Anglo-French Relations in the Popular Front Era* (New York, 1996), 89–114. Earlier literature is extensive: J. Avilés Farré, *Pasión y farsa: Franceses y británicos ante la guerra civil española* (Madrid, 1994); W. L. Kleine-Ahlbrandt, *The Policy of Simmering: A Study of British Policy during the Spanish Civil War, 1936–1939* (The Hague, 1962); E. Moradiellos, *La perfidia de Albión: El gobierno británico y la guerra civil española* (Madrid, 1996) and several articles, such as "The Origins of British Non-Intervention in the Spanish Civil War: Anglo-Spanish Relations in Early 1936," *European History Quarterly* 21 (1991): 339–64; T. Buchanan, *Britain and the Spanish Civil War*

(Cambridge, 1997); D. W. Pike, *Les français et la guerre d'Espagne (1936–1939)* (Paris, 1975); C. Breen, *La droite française et la guerre d'Espagne (1936–1939)* (Geneva, 1973); L. Pala, *I cattolici francesi e la guerra di Spagna* (Urbino, 1974); M. D. Gallagher, "Léon Blum and the Spanish Civil War," *Journal of Contemporary History* 6, no. 3 (1971): 56–64; and D. Little, "Red Scare: Anti-Bolshevism and the Origins of British Non-Intervention in the Spanish Civil War," *Journal of Contemporary History* 23 (1988): 291–311.

6. See G. Howson, *Arms for Spain: The Untold Story of the Spanish Civil War* (London, 1998).

7. The initial effort by Madrid and Moscow to establish official relations in 1933 is described by D. L. Kowalsky, "The Soviet Union and the Spanish Republic: Diplomatic, Military, and Cultural Relations, 1936–1939" (Ph.D. diss., University of Wisconsin–Madison, 2001), 78–87.

8. R. Radosh et al., eds., *Spain Betrayed: The Soviet Union in the Spanish Civil War* (New Haven, Conn., 2001), 21.

9. See J. Hochman, *The Soviet Union and the Failure of Collective Security, 1934–1938* (Ithaca, N.Y., 1984), 95–124.

10. Scholarly investigation of the role of the Soviet Union in the Spanish war was begun by D. E. Allen, "The Soviet Union and the Spanish Civil War" (Ph.D. diss., Stanford University, 1952), who treats the Soviet press coverage on pp. 430–49. See also P. Broué, *Staline et la révolution: Le cas espagnol* (Paris, 1993), 71–73.

11. W. Krivitsky, *In Stalin's Secret Service* (New York, 2000), 76.

12. Krivitsky (ibid.) tended to agree with that conclusion, though his broader analysis of Soviet policy is more complex. This is also the thesis of "La guerra civil española vista por un disidente ruso," an interesting unpublished study by the émigré former dissident Mijail Yevslin. A book by two senior Russian army officers, Gen. Oleg Sarin and Col. Lev Dvoretsky, *Alien Wars: The Soviet Union's Aggressions against the World, 1919 to 1989* (Novato, Calif., 1996), also concludes that the goal was to make Spain "a Communist country." Ultimately, of course, that was the goal of Soviet policy toward the entire world. The question of timing and degree remains.

13. D. Boffa, *Istoriia Sovetskogo Soiuza*, 2 vols. (Moscow, 1994), 1:466, quoted in Sarin and Dvoretsky, *Alien Wars*, 3–4.

14. D. T. Cattell, *Soviet Diplomacy and the Spanish Civil War* (Berkeley, Calif., 1957); D. Puzzo, *Spain and the Great Powers* (New York, 1962); J. Haslam, *The Soviet Union and the Struggle for Collective Security in Europe, 1933–1939* (London, 1984); and D. Smyth, "'We Are with You': Solidarity and Self-Interest in Soviet Policy towards Republican Spain, 1936–1939," in *The Republic Besieged: Civil War in Spain, 1936–1939*, ed. P. Preston and A. L. McKenzie, 85–107 (Edinburgh, 1996).

15. For example, G. Roberts, "Soviet Foreign Policy and the Spanish Civil War, 1936–1939," in *Spain in an International Context, 1936–1959*, ed. C. Leitz and D. J. Dunthorn, 81–103 (New York, 1999), and the unusually shrewd senior

thesis of D. J. Hopkins, "The Soviet Eclipse: Ideology and the Evolution of the USSR's Domination of Republican Spain, 1936–37" (Harvard College, 2000).

16. S. Pons, "The Papers on Foreign and International Policy in the Russian Archives," *Cahiers du monde russe* 40 (1999): 237, cited in Hopkins, "Soviet Eclipse," 40; Haslam, *Soviet Union*, 122.

17. Krivitsky, *In Stalin's Secret Service*, 82.

18. The basic study remains R. Conquest, *The Great Terror: A Reassessment* (New York, 1990).

19. K. McDermott, "Stalinist Terror in the Comintern: New Perspectives," *Journal of Contemporary History* 30 (1995): 123; M. Alpert, *A New International History of the Spanish Civil War* (New York, 1994), 51.

20. Haslam, *Soviet Union*, 115;. G. Howson, *Arms for Spain: The Untold Story of the Spanish Civil War* (London, 1998), 123.

21. Loy Henderson to Cordell Hull, Aug. 4, 1936, in *Foreign Relations of the United States, 1936* (Washington, D.C., 1954), 2:461. Later the German ambassador, Count Friedrich Werner von der Schulenburg, reported that the Soviet government felt the need to "save face" and to "reassure the faithful disturbed by the purges," and to avoid "abandonment of the Spanish proletariat for opportunistic reasons." U.S. Department of State, *Documents on German Foreign Policy, 1918–1945* (Washington, D.C., 1949–83), ser. D, 3:108–9. Robert Coulondre, the French ambassador, agreed, concluding that Stalin was making concessions to Communist ultras and to the Comintern parties to maintain their support, according to Broué, *Staline et la révolution*, 138–42, 296.

As Krivitsky put it, "To a few veteran leaders of the Comintern, still inwardly devoted to the ideal of world revolution, the fighting in Spain brought new hope. These old revolutionaries really believed that the Spanish civil war might once more kindle the world." He adds that Stalin personally "was also moved . . . by the need for some answer to the foreign friends of the Soviet world who would be disaffected by the great purge and the shooting of his old Bolshevik colleagues. The Western world does not realize how tenuous at that time was Stalin's hold on power, and how essential it was to his survival as a dictator that he should be defended in these bloody acts by foreign Communists and eminent fellow travellers like Romain Rolland. It is not too much to say that their support was essential to him. And his failure to defend the Spanish Republic, combined with the shock of the great purge and the treason trials, might have cost him their support. (*In Stalin's Secret Service*, 79, 81.)

22. Iu. Rybalkin, *Operatsiia "Kh": Sovetskaia voennaia pomoshch respublikanskoi Ispanii (1936–1939)* (Moscow, 2001), 30; Haslam, *Soviet Union*, 225.

23. For example, R. Tucker, *Stalin in Power* (New York, 1990), 351; M. Malia, *Russia under Western Eyes* (Cambridge, Mass., 1999), 315–19; J. Hernández, *Yo fui un ministro de Stalin* (Madrid, 1974), 63; and M. V. Novikov, *SSSR, Komintern i grazhdanskaia voina v Ispanii, 1936–39 gg.* (Yaroslavl, 1995), 29. These citations are from Hopkins, "Soviet Eclipse," 42–46. Krivitsky also to some extent subscribed to this view.

24. François Furet writes that "from the Soviet viewpoint" the collective security policy "was as much a warning to Hitler as a commitment to the side of France. Stalin understood the game of the British Conservatives and of part of the French right all the more easily since he had the same intention they did, but in an inverse sense: he wanted to divert Hitler's storm toward the west. The Spanish Civil War gave him the opportunity to do so, because to the extent that it became internationalized, it would draw the attention of the fascist powers to the west, with a good chance of at least compromising France, where the left was in power. But it would be necessary for the war to continue, and therefore for the Republic to receive the means to fight. Should Franco win, it would at least have fixed the struggle between fascism and antifascism in a distant locale, without greater risk for the USSR. If he lost, it would leave a gravely weakened Spanish Republic that would be converted into a Soviet satellite that might be used on any opportune occasion. In either case, Spain would become a low-cost showplace for Soviet antifascist propaganda, at the same time that it sent a coded message to Hitler." (F. Furet, *El pasado de una ilusión* [Mexico City, 1995], 290–91.)

25. Quoted in Cattell, *Soviet Diplomacy*, 5.

26. The best brief study will be found in Kowalsky, "Soviet Union," 167–241. The statistics are drawn from V. A. Tolmachaev, "Sovietskii Soiuz i Ispaniia: Opyt i uroki internatsionalnoi pomoshchi (1936–1939 gg.)" (Ph.D. diss., Leningrad University, 1991), 68–69, in Kowalsky, 185. The principal Soviet publication in this area is Academy of Sciences of the USSR, *International Solidarity with the Spanish Republic, 1936–1939* (Moscow, 1975). In addition to Tolmachaev's, two other Soviet dissertations deal with this topic: A. A. Komshukov, "Natsional'no-revoliutsionnaia voina ispanskogo naroda, 1936–1939 gg., i sovetskaia obshchestvennost" (Kharkov University, 1979), and V. A. Talashova, "Sovietskii Komsomol—Aktivnei uchastnik dvizheniia solidarnosti s respublikanskoi ispaniei v period natsional'no-revoliutsionnoi voiny, 1936–1939 gg." (Vologda University, 1972), cited by Kowalsky. See also Novikov, *SSSR, Komintern*, 2:152–63, and Rybalkin, *Operatsiia "Kh,"* 23–25. The campaigns were first treated in English in Allen, "Soviet Union," 419–49.

27. J. Peirats, *La CNT en la revolución española* (Cali, 1988), 2:122–24.

28. The first study of the Non-Intervention Committee was P. van der Esch, *Prelude to War* (The Hague, 1951), followed by W. E. Watters, *An International Affair: Non-Intervention in the Spanish Civil War* (New York, 1971). See also W. Schieder, ed., *Der spanische Burgerkrieg in der internationalen Politik (1936–1939)* (Munich, 1976).

29. House Un-American Activities Committee, *Guide to Subversive Organizations and Publications*, doc. no. 398 (Washington, D.C., 1951), cited in C. Vidal, *Las Brigadas Internacionales* (Madrid, 1998), 50.

30. According to A. Elorza and M. Bizcarrondo, *Queridos camaradas: La Internacional Comunista y España, 1919–1939* (Barcelona, 1999), 307.

31. *Daily Worker* (New York), Aug. 5, 1936.

32. C. Serrano, *L'enjeu espagnol: PCF et guerre d'Espagne* (Paris, 1987), 20–22.

33. D. W. Pike, "Reaction in France to the Frente Popular (January to July 1936)," in *Spain in an International Context, 1936–1959,* ed. C. Leitz and D. J. Dunthorn, 19–40 (New York, 1999).

34. C. Breen, *La droite française et la guerre d'Espagne* (Geneva, 1973); D. W. Pike, *La crise espagnole de 1936 vue par la presse française* (Toulouse, 1966) and *Les français et la guerre d'Espagne, 1936–1939* (Paris, 1975); J. Martínez Parrilla, *Las fuerzas armadas francesas ante la Guerra Civil española (1936–1939)* (Madrid, 1987); J. Borrás Llop, *Francia ante la guerra civil española: Burguesía, interés nacional e interés de clase* (Madrid, 1981); J. Sagnes and S. Caucanas, eds., *Les français et la guerre d'Espagne* (Perpignan, 1990); and P. Jackson, "French Strategy and the Spanish Civil War," in Leitz and Dunthorn, *Spain in an International Context,* 55–80; J. Colton, *Léon Blum* (New York, 1966), 264.

35. Quoted in M. D. Gallagher, "Léon Blum and the Spanish Civil War," *Journal of Contemporary History* 6, no. 3 (1971): 63; *Le Populaire,* Oct. 15, 1945, quoted in Colton, *Léon Blum,* 64.

36. Quoted in Greene, *French Socialism in Crisis,* 135.

37. Quoted ibid., 115. See also I. M. Wall, "French Socialism and the Popular Front," *Journal of Contemporary History* 5, no. 3 (1970): 3–20.

38. Rybalkin, *Operatsiia "Kh,"* 37.

39. M. T. Meshcheriakov, "SSSR i grazhdanskaia voina v Ispanii," *Otechestvennaia istoriia* 3 (1997): 87, as well as the same author's *Ispanskaia Respublika i Komintern* (Moscow, 1981), which, despite its title, begins only with the war. The first commentator to make this point was Krivitsky, *In Stalin's Secret Service.* The Russian army historians Sarin and Dvoretsky agree: "Not a single document concerning the Spanish war escaped his attention. This enabled him to be knowledgeable on all developments and to react to them promptly" (*Alien Wars,* 3).

    Novikov is yet more explicit: "The war in Spain occupied an important, if not the principal, place (at least during 1936–1937) in Stalin's foreign policy plans and interests. He attentively followed the political, diplomatic, and military situation in the Iberian peninsula and its environs. Scarcely a single important document on the Spanish question escaped his attention. Receiving extensive information from the foreign ministry and from political and military intelligence, from the executive of the Comintern and its representatives in Spain, Stalin indubitably was involved in all Spanish developments and worked out his own approaches to the earlier or later problems of the civil war" (*SSSR, Komintern,* 7).

40. J. Costello and O. Tsarev, *Deadly Illusions* (New York, 1993), 254.

41. Ibid. Costello and Tsarev state that "on July 20, 1936, . . . the Politburo approved sending Orlov to Spain" (253). This is unlikely. It may either be a careless mistake or reflect the fact that Orlov was assigned to coordinate NKVD activities for Spain right after the fighting started. The dates are according to Orlov's response to the questionnaire I sent him, which he dated Apr. 1, 1968. The text has been published as "The NKVD in Spain: Questions by Stanley Payne, answers by

Alexander Orlov. With an introduction by Frank Schauff," *Forum für osteuro-paische Ideen- und Zeitgeschichte* 4 (2000): 229–50.

42. The Soviet pilot G. Prokofiev has testified that he and a fellow Soviet flyer arrived in central Spain via Toulouse and Alicante during the first days of September. They were met in Alcalá de Henares by Boris Sveshnikov, the new air attaché, and were immediately assigned to a mixed international squadron of Republican pilots, which already included several Soviets who had arrived shortly before. G. Prokofiev, "El cielo español en llamas," in *Bajo la bandera de la España republi-cana* (Moscow, n.d.), 366–73. See also A. García Lacalle, *Mitos y verdades* (Mexico City, 1973), 134–39, who dates the arrival of the first Soviet airmen as slightly later (early to mid-September). Curiously, it was approximately at this time, on Aug. 28, that Hitler rescinded the ban on German military personnel participat-ing in combat in Spain.

43. On Koltsov's role in Spain, see B. Bolloten, *The Spanish Civil War* (Chapel Hill, N.C., 1991), 308, and Haslam, *Soviet Union*, 198, 262–63. There is a volume of reminiscences by his brother, B. Efimov, *Mikhail Kol'tsov: Kakim on byl: Vospomi-naniia* (Moscow, 1975). Kol'tsov's memoirs, "Ispanskii dnevnik," first appeared in installments in *Novyi mir* in 1938 and were published in book form in Moscow only in 1956, after Stalin's death. They would later be translated into Spanish as *Diario de la guerra de España* (Paris, 1967).

44. Ehrenburg refers to his Spanish adventures in his memoir, *Lyudi, gody, zhizn*, vol. 9 of his *Sobranie sochinenii v deviati tomakh* (Moscow, 1967), 100. The Span-ish material has been translated as *Corresponsal en la guerra de España* (Madrid, 1979). Koltsov would later be executed by Stalin, but Ehrenburg played no politi-cal role in Spain and was further removed from the Soviet dictator, a circum-stance that may have saved his life.

45. On the two Soviet filmmakers, see Kowalsky, "Soviet Union," 313–16.

46. Broué, *Staline et la révolution*, 133–34.

47. Cited ibid., 136.

48. Reported from London in *La Humanitat* (Barcelona), Aug. 13, 1936, in Bolloten, *Spanish Civil War*, 115.

49. Elorza and Bizcarrondo, *Queridos camaradas*, 308.

50. A good example is F. Claudín, *La crisis del movimiento comunista* (Paris, 1970), 1:180–81 and passim. *Pace* Claudín, in their serious discussions and publica-tions the Communists never disguised the fact that there was an extensive non-communist collectivist revolution in the Republican zone, but held that this effort was centrifugal and destructive to the war effort—as indeed it was—and that it should be reduced and channeled through the controlled, partially but not totally revolutionary program of the people's republic. To pretend that that extensive program of industrial nationalization, agrarian expropriation, and partial collectivization was merely "counterrevolutionary" is idiotic.

51. According to M. Kol'tsov, "Ispanskii dnevnik," *Novyi mir*, April 1938, cited in Bolloten, *Spanish Civil War*, 121. As Bolloten notes, this report has been corrobo-rated by other sources, such as the memoirs of Jesús Hernández and Julio

Alvarez del Vayo, and by the official Communist *Guerra y revolución en España* (Moscow, 1966), 2:47. Later the Bulgarian Comintern adviser Boris Stefanov/ Stepanov (pseud. of Stoian Minev, known in Spain as Moreno), sometime comrade of Lenin and personal friend of Stalin, would claim that there was no choice in the matter because the ultrarevolutionaries at that point were strong enough otherwise to take over the government by force. "Las causas de la derrota de la República española," 19, cited in Bolloten, *Spanish Civil War*, 122.

52. Dimitrov to Díaz, Sept., 2, 1936, in *Dimitrov and Stalin, 1934–1943: Letters from the Kremlin Archives*, ed. A. Dallin and F. I. Firsov (New Haven, Conn., 2000), 49; Elorza and Bizcarrondo, *Queridos camaradas*, 309–10.

53. Dallin and Firsov, *Dimitrov and Stalin*, 49.

54. Cf. J. Zugazagoitia, *Historia de la guerra de España* (Buenos Aires, 1940), 135.

55. The basic study is A. Viñas, *El oro de Moscú* (Madrid, 1979), 21–101. See also A. del Rosal, *El oro del Banco de España y la historia de la Vita* (Madrid, 1976).

56. M. Litvinov, *Notes for a Journal* (London, 1955), 208.

57. Novikov, *SSSR, Komintern*, 9; Sarin and Dvoretsky, *Alien Wars*, 2.

58. Krivitsky later wrote that on Sept. 2 Soviet agents in Western Europe had been ordered to create a clandestine organization for purchasing and shipping arms to the Republic. *In Stalin's Secret Service*, 100.

59. The credits are detailed in Rybalkin, *Operatsiia "Kh,"* 28–30; the likelihood of reimbursement is the conclusion of Lt. Col. Rybalkin, in his articles in *Argumenty i fakty*, Apr. 4, 1996, and *El País*, Apr. 8, 1996.

60. Rybalkin, *Operatsiia "Kh,"* 37, admits that the reserve stock involved was not of the highest quality but claims that it constituted only a minor proportion of the infantry weapons sent.

61. On the initial plan, see Sarin and Dvoretsky, *Alien Wars*, 1–3; Novikov, *SSSR, Komintern*, 8–9; and M. T. Meshcheriakov, "Sovetskii Soiuz i antifashistskaia voina ispanskogo naroda (1936–1939 gg.)," *Istoriia SSSR*, January 1988, 85–93.

62. Elorza and Bizcarrondo, *Queridos camaradas*, 314–20, 323, 324; Serrano, *L'enjeu espagnol*, 47–63.

63. A. I. Sobolev et al., *Outline History of the Communist International* (Moscow, 1971), 416–17, 436; Elorza and Bizcarrondo, *Queridos camaradas*, 321.

64. *International Press Correspondance* 16, no. 48 (Oct. 24, 1936): 1292–95.

65. Haslam, *Soviet Union*, 115–20.

66. According to Rybalkin's research for the Catalan television production of "L'or de Moscú," cited in Howson, *Arms for Spain*, 126, 322.

67. This date is attested to in Meshcheriakov, "Sovetskii Soiuz i antifashistskaia voina"; Sarin and Dvoretsky, *Alien Wars;* and Rybalkin, *Operatsiia "Kh,"* as well as B. B. Gagin, *Vozdushnaia voina v Ispanii* (Voronezh, 1998), 12.

68. Quoted in Roberts, "Soviet Foreign Policy," 101.

69. Ibid., 84

70. On Oct. 11, 1936, the ECCI approved a new nine-point campaign on behalf of the Republic. It would include a new campaign within Spain itself, the swift convening of an international women's conference in Paris for aid to Spain,

agitation at the League of Nations, new pressure on trade unions and Socialist parties, a massive propaganda campaign (including a special "red book" on the crimes of Spanish fascism), a major effort to mobilize Western political parties and parliaments, an energetic attempt to mobilize a new international diplomatic campaign, and the sending of a Spanish Republican delegation to the western hemisphere. The entire campaign would focus on the democratic countries of Western Europe (Britain, France, Czechoslovakia, Holland, Belgium, Sweden, and Switzerland) and the United States and Argentina, but with special emphasis, as usual, on France. It was to be directed by a troika consisting of the French leader Maurice Thorez, Harry Pollit of Britain, and Willy Münzenberg, West European propaganda chief for the Comintern and undoubtedly the leading propagandist of the Spanish Civil War. Rossiiskaia Akademiia Nauk, *Komintern i grazhdanskaia voina v Ispanii* (Moscow, 2001), 145–48.

71. The lengthiest treatment will be found in H. Geiss, "Das 'Internationale Komitee für die Anwendung des Abkommens über die Nichteinmischung in Spanien' als Instrument sowjetischer Aussenpolitik, 1936–1938" (Ph.D. diss., University of Frankfurt am Main, 1977). See also Cattell, *Soviet Diplomacy;* Novikov, *SSSR, Komintern,* 12–41; and Allen, "Soviet Union," 121–230.

72. *Documents on British Foreign Policy, 1919–1939* (London, 1946), 2d ser., 17:496.

73. Quoted in J. Degras, ed., *Soviet Documents on Foreign Policy* (Oxford, 1953), 3:212.

74. Thus it provided the title for the widely diffused Soviet publication *Delo Ispanii ne chastnoe delo ispantsev* (Moscow, 1937). Other principal Soviet publications on the war include *Ispaniia v bor'be protiv fashizma: Sbornik statei i materialov* (Moscow, 1936); *Geroicheskaia Ispaniia: Sbornik* (Moscow, 1936); *SSSR i fashistskaia agressiia v Ispanii: Sbornik dokumentov* (Moscow, 1937); *Ispanskii narod pobedit* (Moscow, 1937); *Ispanskaia Kompartiia boretsia za pobedu: Sbornik materialov* (Moscow, 1938); *Kompartiia Frantsii v bor'be za Narodnii Front* (Moscow, 1938); *Govorit' Ispaniia: Sbornik* (Moscow, 1939); N. Gorozhankina, *Rabochii klass Ispanii v gody revoliutsii* (Moscow, 1936); M. Korolkov, *Ispaniia v ogne* (Moscow, 1936); E. Varga, *Ispaniia v revoliutsii* (Moscow, 1936) and *Portugaliia i fashistskaia interventsiia v Ispanii* (Moscow, 1938); E. A. Aksonov, *Portugaliia i ee rol v fashistskoi interventsii v Ispanii* (Moscow, 1937); I. Ehrenburg, *Ispaniia,* 2 vols. (Moscow, 1937); I. P. Trainin, *Baski v bor'be za svoiu natsionalnuiu nezavisimost'* (Moscow, 1937); G. Dimitrov, *Ko vtoroi godovshchine geroicheskoi bor'by ispanskogo naroda* (Moscow, 1938); G. Dashevskii, *Fashistskaia piataia colonna v Ispanii* (Moscow, 1938); and A. Volkov, *Za chto boretsia ispanskoe krestianstvo* (Moscow, 1938).

75. Viñas, *Oro de Moscú,* 102–45. See also the brief synopsis by Viñas, "Financing the Spanish Civil War," in P. Preston, ed., *Revolution and War in Spain, 1931–1939,* 266–83 (London, 1984).

76. A. Henshaw, *The Flight of the Mew Gull* (London, 1980), 101, quoted in Howson, *Arms for Spain,* 67. The best accounts of the chaotic Republican purchasing efforts in the West will be found in Howson and in F. Olaya Morales, *El oro de Negrín* (Madrid, 1998).

77. This is the conclusion of the Russian military historian Iurii Rybalkin, in his articles in *Argumenty i fakty,* Apr. 4, 1996, and *El País,* Apr. 8, 1996.
78. According to the testimony of the foreign minister and close Communist fellow traveler Julio Alvarez del Vayo, in his memoir *The Last Optimist* (New York, 1950), 291.
79. Krivitsky, *In Stalin's Secret Service,* 99–100; A. Orlov, "How Stalin Relieved Spain of $600,000,000," *Reader's Digest,* December 1966, 31–43.
80. According to the new Republican ambassador to Moscow, Marcelino Pascua, who would later present the originals in the Soviet capital, though they had presumably been transmitted by telegraph. Pascua, "Oro español en Moscú," *Cuadernos para el diálogo,* June–July 1970.
81. Rybalkin, *Operatsiia "Kh,"* 92–93.
82. Rybalkin in *Argumenty i fakty,* Apr. 4, 1996, and *El País,* Apr. 8, 1996, and the testimony in U.S. Senate, Subcommittee to Investigate the Administration of the Internal Security Act, *The Legacy of Alexander Orlov,* 93rd Cong., 1st sess. (Washington, D.C., 1973).
83. Orlov, "How Stalin Relieved Spain of $600,000,000."
84. The principal synthetic accounts of the gold shipment are in Viñas, *Oro de Moscú,* 146–93, 246–63, and Bolloten, *Spanish Civil War,* 140–58. Howson, *Arms for Spain,* 133, notes that one of the four Soviet ships employed, the *KIM,* was soon shifted to the Far East to transport gulag prisoners to Magadan. In the winter of 1937 a cargo of 3,000 prisoners rebelled, and the guards flooded the ship's hold in subfreezing weather. The prisoners arrived in Magadan as a block of ice.

    The former NKVD officer Pavel Sudoplatov has claimed that the third secretary of the Soviet embassy in Paris soon cabled Moscow that he suspected that part of the gold shipment had been embezzled, either by Spanish Communists or by other Republicans. His suspicion led to a further check by the NKVD's chief accountant, who found everything in order. P. and A. Sudoplatov, with J. L. and L. P. Schecter, *Special Tasks: The Memoirs of an Unwanted Witness, a Soviet Spymaster* (Boston, 1995), 42–43.
85. U.S. Congress, Senate, *Scope of Soviet Activity,* 3431, 3433–34, in Bolloten, *Spanish Civil War,* 798.
86. F. Largo Caballero, *Mis recuerdos* (Mexico City, 1954), 203–4.
87. According to the Soviet naval attaché Capt. Nikolai Kuznetsov (who became the chief adviser to the Republican navy), in *Pod znamenem ispanskoi respubliki, 1936–1939: Vospominaniia sovetskikh dobrovoltsev-uchastnikov* (Moscow, 1965), 241–44. Kuznetsov was in charge of arranging protection for the convoy as it traveled across the Mediterranean. His testimony in this regard is convincing, so that the allegation of the Republican ambassador Pascua (in "Oro español en Moscú") that the Soviet vessels departed at night and traveled without escort in an effort to avoid suspicion may be dismissed, as Bolloten has pointed out in *Spanish Civil War.* Kuznetsov's account largely coincides with that of Orlov both

in his testimony before the U.S. Senate and in "How Stalin Relieved Spain of $600,000,000."

88. I. Prieto, *Convulsiones de España* (Mexico City, 1967), 2:125–33; Pascua, "Oro español en Moscú." Orlov, conversely, has claimed that Azaña was apprised of the shipment. Costello and Tsarev, *Deadly Illusions*, 259.

89. A. Viñas, *El oro español en la guerra civil* (Madrid, 1976), 187. This judgment was removed from the revised edition.

90. This operation is fully studied in D. Grisoni and G. Hertzog, *Les brigades de la mer* (Paris, 1979). See also Serrano, *L'enjeu espagnol*, 89–107.

CHAPTER 8. SOVIET MILITARY PARTICIPATION

1. Though thin, the chief study is Lt. Col. Iurii Rybalkin, *Operatsiia "Kh": Sovetskaia voennaia pomoshch respublikanskoi Ispanii (1936–1939)* (Moscow, 2000). Rybalkin has also provided a brief summary in his article "La ayuda militar soviética a la España republicana: Cifras y hechos," *Ejército*, January 1992. There is an excellent account of the Soviet military intervention in English in D. L. Kowalsky, "The Soviet Union and the Spanish Republic, 1936–1939: Diplomatic, Military, and Cultural Relations" (Ph.D. diss., University of Wisconsin–Madison, 2001), 325–517. The early study by R. L. Plumb, "Soviet Participation in the Spanish Civil War" (Ph.D. diss., Georgetown University, 1956), was a good account for its time, and was generally accurate, but unavoidably lacked Soviet documentation.

2. The principal comprehensive study of Soviet casualties, Col.-Gen. G. F. Krivosheev, ed., *Soviet Casualties and Combat Losses in the Twentieth Century* (London, 1997), 46, lists only 115 officers and 43 NCOs, but other Soviet accounts give the higher figure.

3. On the logistics of Operation X, see Kowalsky, "Soviet Union," 333–49.

4. G. Howson, *Arms for Spain: The Untold Story of the Spanish Civil War* (London, 1998), 142. Howson gives a detailed listing of all the arms shipments for which records can currently be located in the Russian archives on pp. 278–301.

5. C. Vidal, *La guerra de Franco: Historia militar de la guerra civil española* (Barcelona, 1996), 536.

6. G. Soria, *Voina i revoliutsiia v Ispanii, 1936–1939 gg.* (Moscow, 1987), 1:273, cited in M. V. Novikov, *SSSR, Komintern i grazhdanskaia voina v Ispanii, 1936–1939 gg.* (Yaroslavl, 1995), 52.

7. For figures on Nationalist war supplies, see my *Franco Regime, 1936–1975* (Madison, Wis., 1987), 158.

8. See E. Abellán Agius, *Los cazas soviéticos en la guerra aérea de España, 1936/1939* (Madrid, 1999), 14–18.

9. J. Salas Larrazábal, *Intervención extranjera en la guerra de España* (Madrid, 1974), 424–29.

10. These conclusions are generally accepted, but see Abellán Agius, *Cazas soviéticos*; J. A. Guerrero, *Polikarpov I-16 "Mosca"* (Madrid, 1978); L. Moya Pimental, "Polikarpov I-16 Rata/Mosca," *Revista española de historia militar* 1 (January–February 2000): 42–43; and Howson, *Arms for Spain*, 136–38.

11. See Howson, *Arms for Spain*, 138–43, 105–13.

12. A. Orlov, *Handbook of Intelligence and Guerrilla Warfare* (Ann Arbor, Mich., 1963), 20–21.

13. Howson, *Arms for Spain*, 150–51.

14. Ibid., 151–52. Some of these special charges are also mentioned in Rybalkin, *Operatsiia "Kh,"* 99.

15. Ibid., 146–52.

16. R. González Echegaray, "Las pérdidas soviéticas en la guerra de España," *Revista de historia naval* 7 (1984): 25–42, and W. Frank, "Politico-Military Deception at Sea in the Spanish Civil War," *Intelligence and Naval Security* 5 (July 1990): 84–122. M. T. Meshcheriakov reported that, according to Soviet sources, no individual boatload of Soviet arms was ever sunk. During the course of the war, a total of sixty-six arms shipments (code-named *igreky*, or Y's) were dispatched. Of these, sixty-four got through. The other two shipments were not sunk, but had to turn back. Meshcheriakov, "Sovetskii Soiuz i antifashistskaia voina ispanskogo naroda (1936–1939 gg.)," *Istoriia SSSR* 1 (1988): 30.

17. Kuznetsov later claimed that the chief priority had to be the defense of Republican shipping. See his memoir, *Na dalekom merediane* (Moscow, 1966), and his piece in *Bajo la bandera de la España republicana* (Moscow, 1967), 170–208.

18. According to the former high-ranking Soviet intelligence officer Pavel Sudoplatov, in his frequently misleading memoir: P. and A. Sudoplatov, with J. L. and L. P. Schecter, *Special Tasks: The Memoirs of an Unwanted Witness, a Soviet Spymaster* (Boston, 1995), 24–25. He claims that they succeeded in sinking at least one Polish vessel bound for Nationalist Spain.

19. Quoted in J. Costello and O. Tsarev, *Deadly Illusions* (New York, 1993), 255.

20. For a guide to this literature, see the summary by the leading Russian historiographer of the Spanish conflict, M. V. Novikov, *Sovetskie i zarubezhnye istoriki i memuaristy o natsional'no-revoliutsionnoi voine ispanskogo naroda: 1936–1939 gg.* (Yaroslavl, 1992). Some of these works are also treated in English in chap. 1 of Kowalsky, "Soviet Union."

21. A more objective evaluation of the role and relationships of the Soviet advisers is found in Kowalsky, "Soviet Union," 388–464.

22. Ambassador Pascua to Madrid, Oct. 22, 1936, ibid., 394, which also cites other Soviet sources in this regard. As Kowalsky says (p. 395), "there is no evidence that any Russian who volunteered in this fashion to fight in Spain was ever sent."

23. A. Grechko, ed., *Istoriia Vtoroi Mirovoi Voiny* (Moscow, 1974), 2:55, and *Sovetskaia Voennaia Entsiklopediia* (Moscow, 1978), 5:550, the latter cited in Bolloten, *Spanish Civil War*, 799. Novikov, however, raises the total to 4,000 in *SSSR, Komintern i grazhdanskaia voina v Ispanii, 1936–39 gg.* (Yaroslavl, 1995), 2:68. The leading study from the Nationalist side is J. L. Alcofar Nassaes, *Los mexicanos: Los asesores soviéticos en la guerra civil española* (Madrid, 1971), which lists 300 Soviet advisers and other military personnel by name, though with some inaccuracies.

24. W. Krivitsky, *In Stalin's Secret Service* (New York, 2000), 77.
25. Louis Fischer (an important American correspondent who served as a sort of Soviet agent or source of information in the Republican zone) to R. L. Plumb, Nov. 5, 1954, in Plumb, "Soviet Participation," 304.
26. According to Mikhail Koltsov in *Novyi mir*, April 1938, 41–42, quoted in Bolloten, *Spanish Civil War*, 253.
27. The Buró de Milicias created by the Giral government eventually recognized the recruitment of 146,936 militiamen. Comandancia General de Milicias, *Un esfuerzo en 1936* (Madrid, 1937).
28. The only book-length account is E. Comín Colomer, *El comisariado político en la guerra española, 1936–1939* (Madrid, 1973). Predictably, the PCE was the first Republican group to urge the establishment of political commissars (e.g., Antonio Mije in *Mundo obrero*, Sept. 9, 1936). The look of the People's Army uniforms and other insignia is presented in C. Flores Pazos, *Uniformes y pertrechos: Ejército Popular republicano, 1936–1939* (Madrid, 1997). There are two general histories of the Republican army: R. Salas Larrazábal, *Historia del Ejército Popular de la República*, 4 vols. (Madrid, 1973), and M. Alpert, *El ejército republicano en la guerra civil* (Barcelona, 1977).
29. C. Engel, *Historia de las Brigadas Mixtas del Ejército Popular de la República, 1936–1939* (Madrid, 1999). Though various Soviet sources give the credit to the Soviet advisers, Col. J. Martín Blázquez is probably more nearly correct when he describes it as the joint creation of Spanish Republican officers and the Soviet advisers: *I Helped to Build an Army* (London, 1939), 294–95. As originally described in *La Gaceta de Madrid* on Oct. 9, the Mixed Brigade was to be a miniature division combining units of all sorts, with artillery, engineers, and even its own trucks in addition to infantry. The argument was that such units would be easier to organize and command in a new army being created from scratch.
30. "No one can doubt that the axis of our army is today our heroic people's militia. . . . No one could possibly think that in the present circumstances of struggle anything could be created in opposition to our glorious people's militia. What is really needed is simply to complement and reinforce the people's army in order to achieve greater efficiency and end the war as soon as possible." *Mundo obrero*, Aug. 21, 1936.
31. E. Líster, *Nuestra guerra* (Paris, 1966); J. Modesto, *Soy del Quinto Regimiento: Notas de la guerra de España* (Paris, 1974). Líster declared that he had received fourteen months of training in the Frunze Academy.
32. According to the very long report that Shtern prepared on Dec. 14, 1937, after his return to the Soviet Union. R. Radosh et al., eds., *Spain Betrayed: The Soviet Union in the Spanish Civil War* (New Haven, Conn., 2001), 295–368.
33. This is the conclusion of J. A. Blanco Rodríguez, *El Quinto Regimiento en la política militar del P.C.E. en la guerra civil* (Madrid, 1993). The Soviet writer A. Samarin, who wrote the principal Soviet account of the struggle for Madrid, *Bor'ba za Madrid* (Moscow, 1940), 25–28, estimated that about half the recruits of the Quinto Regimiento were (often newly professed) Communists,

approximately 25 percent were Socialists, some 15 percent left Republicans, and the rest without political affiliation.

34. Radosh et al., *Spain Betrayed*, 298.

35. Samarin, *Bor'ba za Madrid*, 21–23.

36. M. T. Meshcheriakov, "Narodnaia Armiia Ispanskoi Respubliki," *Voprosy istrorii* 11 (1979): 37–59.

37. For a thorough critique of this dubious propaganda maneuver, see R. de la Cierva, *Brigadas Internacionales: La verdadera historia* (Madrid, 1997), 15–40. The literature on the International Brigades is enormous. The best single history is C. Vidal, *Las Brigadas Internacionales* (Madrid, 1998). Other worthwhile accounts include V. Brome, *The International Brigades* (New York, 1966); V. B. Johnstone, *Legions of Babel: The International Brigades in the Spanish Civil War* (University Park, Pa., 1967), at the time of publication the best history available; J. Delperrie de Bayac, *Les Brigades Internationales* (Paris, 1968); A. Castells, *Las Brigadas Internacionales en la guerra de España* (Barcelona, 1974), the most thorough to that date; R. D. Richardson, *Comintern Army: The International Brigades and the Spanish Civil War* (Lexington, Ky., 1982); and M. Jackson, *Fallen Sparrows: The International Brigades in the Spanish Civil War* (Philadelphia, 1994). Of the several right-wing Spanish accounts, the best is Cierva, *Brigadas Internacionales*. The principal Soviet study is M. T. Meshcheriakov, "Sud'ba Interbrigad v Ispanii po novym dokumentam," *Novaia i noveishaia istoriia* 5 (1993): 18–41. There are numerous memoirs, primarily by Communists.

38. In "Sud'ba Interbrigad," Meshcheriakov concludes that the "immense majority" of volunteers were Communists, while Vidal, *Brigadas Internacionales*, 66, judges that they accounted for 85 percent of the total. During the war, Comintern leaders boasted in their reports that no more than 5 percent were "social democrats." Rossiiskaia Akademiia Nauk, *Komintern i grazhdanskaia voina v Ispanii* (Moscow, 2001), 199–207, 253–76.

39. W. Herrick, *Jumping the Line* (Madison, 1998), 16. Herrick has testified that the American volunteers were told to say "that we were antifascists, not to say we were Communists when asked the question in Spain." Herrick to B. Bolloten, Feb. 7, 1986, in Bolloten, *Spanish Civil War*, 289. See also the memoir by S. Voros, *American Commissar* (Philadelphia, 1961). In a paper delivered at Siena College, June 6, 1986, Herrick declared: "The irony is that though nearly all of my comrades in the International Brigades were Leninists and Stalinists, believers in the great proletarian revolution, only a few . . . recognized that what had taken place in Catalonia and Aragon led by the ridiculed Anarchists and abetted by the hated POUMists was that very proletarian revolution, the thought of which permeated every moment of our lives. It would seem that our greatest loyalty was to the Communist Party and Joseph Stalin and not to our ideals." Quoted in Bolloten, *Spanish Civil War*, 832.

40. On the repression in the International Brigades, see, inter alia, H. Romerstein, *Heroic Victims: Stalin's Foreign Legion in the Spanish Civil War* (Washington, D.C., 1993), and H. Klehr, J. E. Haynes, and F. Firsov, *The Secret World of American*

Communism (New Haven, Conn., 1997), 151–87. André Marty, the superintendent of the International Brigades, has been widely quoted as stating at a Communist meeting in France that it had been necessary to carry out "only 500" disciplinary executions. There is no clear evidence, however, that such an admission was ever made. See C. Serrano, *L'enjeu espagnol: PCF et guerre d'Espagne* (Paris, 1987), 127–28.

41. As Krivitsky put it, "Genuine American passports were highly prized at OGPU headquarters in Moscow." *In Stalin's Secret Service*, 95. Cf. C. Haldane, *Truth Will Out* (New York, 1950), 117. One subsequent State Department report gave a list of 580 American volunteers who complained that their passports had never been returned. *Scope of Soviet Activities*, 1221, cited in Vidal, *Brigadas Internacionales*, 274.

42. K. L. Maidanik, *Ispanskii proletariat v natsional'no-revoliutsionnoi voine* (Moscow, 1960), 172–73; Academy of Sciences of the USSR, *International Solidarity with the Spanish Republic, 1936–1939* (Moscow, 1974), 370; Meshcheriakov, "Sud'ba Interbrigad," 22. The figure of 51,000 is generally confirmed by a Soviet report to Marshal Voroshilov of July 26, 1938, in Radosh et al., *Spain Betrayed*, 464–68, and of Nov. 27, 1938, in A. Elorza and M. Bizcarrondo, *Queridos camaradas: La Internacional Comunista y España, 1919–1939* (Barcelona, 1999), 462.

43. Meshcheriakov, "Sud'ba Interbrigad," 20.

44. C. Geiser, *Prisoners of the Good Fight: The Spanish Civil War, 1936–1938* (New York, 1994), studies the fate of Brigade prisoners. Of 287 known to have been captured, 173 were executed. However, one batch of 87 captured in 1938 were saved by Italian officers who sought to exchange them for Italian soldiers captured by the Republicans.

45. Kowalsky, "Soviet Union," 474–77; Rybalkin, *Operatsiia "Kh,"* 68. Even so, the differential casualty rate for Republican and Nationalist flyers in Novikov, *SSSR, Komintern*, 65, seems excessive.

46. Kowalsky, "Soviet Union," 481; I. M. Zhoga and I. I. Kuznetsov, "Geroi boev s fashistkami v Ispanii," *Istoriia SSSR* 4 (1970): 76. More broadly, on aircraft and airmen in the Spanish conflict, see G. Howson, *Aircraft of the Spanish Civil War, 1936–1939* (London, 1990), and P. Laureau, *L'aviation républicaine espagnole* (Paris, 1978); and from the Nationalist viewpoint, J. Salas Larrazábal, *La guerra de España desde el aire* (Madrid, 1969), and *Guerra aérea, 1936/39*, 2 vols. (Madrid, 1998).

47. The commander was Red Army Capt. Pol (or Pavel) Arman (or Armand), son of Lenin's lover Inessa Armand. He would be killed in action on the Soviet northern front in 1943, not far from the position of the Spanish Blue Division.

48. See R. Simpkin, *Deep Battle: The Brainchild of Marshal Tukhachevskii* (London, 1987).

49. Kowalsky, "Soviet Union," 431.

50. Krivoshein later wrote a brief memoir, "Tanquistas voluntarios soviéticos en la defensa de Madrid," in *Bajo la bandera de la España republicana*, 315–28 (Moscow, 1971). Pavlov would be executed by Stalin in 1941, after the disasters of the initial

phase of the German invasion. On Soviet armor and armored personnel in Spain, see the summary in Kowalsky, "Soviet Union," 482–96; S. J. Zaloga, "Soviet Tank Operations in the Spanish Civil War," *Journal of Slavic Military Studies* 12, no. 3 (1999): 134–62; J. L. S. Daley, "The Theory and Practice of Armored Warfare in Spain, October 1936–February 1937" and "Soviet and German Advisors Put to the Test: Tanks in the Siege of Madrid," *Armor*, May–June 1999, 30–43; and Col. A. J. Candil, "Soviet Armor in Spain: Aid Mission to Republicans Tested Doctrine and Equipment," *Armor*, March–April 1999, 31–38.

51. O. Sarin and L. Dvoretsky, *Alien Wars: The Soviet Union's Aggressions against the World, 1919 to 1989* (Novato, Calif., 1996), 14. This observation is confirmed by Rybalkin, *Operatsiia "Kh,"* 73–75.

52. For brief general accounts of the Republican naval war, see M. Alpert, *La guerra civil española en el mar* (Madrid, 1987), and J. Cervera Pery, *La guerra naval española (1936–39)* (Madrid, 1988).

53. M. Alpert, *El ejército republicano en la guerra civil* (Barcelona, 1977), 295.

54. B. Whealey, *Guerrillas in the Spanish Civil War* (Detroit, 1969), 3, 7.

55. See Kowalsky, "Soviet Union," 419–24; on the situation in Catalonia (the main center of Republican war industry), E. Ucelay da Cal, "Cataluña durante la guerra," in *La guerra de España (1936–1939),* ed. E. Malefakis, 321–54 (Madrid, 1996).

56. Cf. Rybalkin, *Operatsiia "Kh,"* 47–48, 55–57.

57. According to Novikov, *SSSR, Komintern,* 2:57. Rybalkin, *Operatsiia "Kh,"* 58, corroborates this approximate figure.

58. Alpert, *Ejército republicano,* 258. Bitterly anticommunist by the end of the war, Col. Segismundo Casado wrote immediately afterward: "I can state clearly that during the whole war neither the Air Force nor the Tank Corps was controlled by the Minister of National Defense, nor in consequence by the Central General Staff. The Minister and his staff were not even aware of the quantity and types of their machines and only knew the situation of those which were used in actual operations. In the same way the Minister and his Staff were not aware of the situation, and even of the existence, of a great number of unknown 'flying fields' (aerodromes) maintained in secret by the 'friendly advisers' and certain of the aviation chiefs who were entirely in their confidence." (Casado, *The Last Days of Madrid* [London, 1939], 54.)

59. Novikov, *SSSR, Komintern,* 2:60, 125.

60. Quoted in Kowalsky, "Soviet Union," 437.

61. On these problems and the shortcomings of many of the Soviet advisers, see ibid., 431–46.

62. J. Tusell, "¡Menos mal que los rojos son peores!" *Aventura de la historia* 2 (February 2000): 22–36.

CHAPTER 9. THE POLICY STRUGGLE UNDER THE LARGO CABALLERO
GOVERNMENT

1. *Política* (Madrid), Sept. 5, 1936.
2. According to the report later given by one of them to *Manchester Guardian*, Nov. 25, 1936; B. Bolloten, *The Spanish Civil War* (Chapel Hill, N.C., 1991), 160, 799.
3. Santos Juliá emphasizes this dual perception in "La guerra de Manuel Azaña: Defensa en el interior para no perder en el exterior" (unpublished paper presented at the Conference on Contemporary Spanish History at Tufts University, October 2001).
4. C. Sánchez Albornoz, *Anecdotario político* (Barcelona, 1976), 228–29.
5. J. Díaz, *Tres años de lucha* (Barcelona, 1978), 2:190. These statistics may be considered only approximations. Slightly different ones were discussed by the Comintern adviser "Moreno" (Artur Stepanov) in his report to Moscow dated Mar. 28, 1937, in Rossiiskaia Akademiia Nauk, *Komintern i grazhdanskaia voina v Ispanii* (Moscow, 2001), 223–47. (Hereafter cited as RAN.)
6. S. Carrillo, *Frente rojo* (Valencia), Apr. 2, 1937.
7. The sections were General, Party Organization, Syndical Affairs, Agrarian Affairs, Agitation and Propaganda, Women's Affairs, Politico-Military Affairs, and Financial Affairs.
8. Report of Artur Stepanov, Mar. 28, 1937, in RAN, 223–47.
9. These problems are emphasized (and perhaps slightly exaggerated) in T. Rees, "The Highpoint of Comintern Influence? The Communist Party and the Civil War in Spain," in *International Communism and the Communist International, 1919–1943*, ed. T. Rees and A. Thorpe, 143–67 (Manchester, 1999).
10. Report of André Marty, Oct. 14, 1936, in *Spain Betrayed: The Soviet Union in the Spanish Civil War*, ed. R. Radosh, M. Habeck, and G. Sevostianov, 35–40 (New Haven, Conn., 2001); RAN, 171–76, 223–47.
11. In his report of Oct. 14, 1936 (in Radosh et al., *Spain Betrayed*), Marty judged that Gero's methods in Barcelona were "not as authoritarian" as Codovilla's but still inappropriate. Marty attempted to present himself as an adviser of greater discretion, though this assessment is scarcely corroborated by other sources.
12. D. Ibárruri et al., eds., *Guerra y revolución en España, 1936–39* (Moscow, 1966), 1:271.
13. See the discussion in Bolloten, *Spanish Civil War*, 236–45.
14. S. Carrillo, *En marcha hacia la victoria* (Valencia, 1937), 4.
15. Cf. the remarks in F. Olaya Morales, *El oro de Negrín* (Madrid, 1998), 405.
16. J. Aróstegui Sánchez and J. A. Martínez, *La Junta de Defensa de Madrid* (Madrid, 1984), present the basic data. Gen. Vicente Rojo, at that time Republican chief of staff for the central front, has presented his account of the defense in his memoir, *Así fue la defensa de Madrid* (Madrid, 1987).
17. There are two works on this controversy: I. Gibson, *Paracuellos, cómo fue* (Barcelona, 1983), and C. Fernández, *Paracuellos del Jarama, ¿Carrillo culpable?* (Barcelona, 1983). In his *Memorias* (Barcelona, 1993), Carrillo denies everything,

but see also R. Casas de la Vega, *El terror: Madrid 1936* (Madrid, 1994), and R. de la Cierva, *Carrillo miente: 156 documentos contra 103 falsedades* (Madrid, 1994), 137–230.

18. W. Krivitsky, *In Stalin's Secret Service* (New York, 1939), 102.

19. The full text is presented in Ibárruri et al., *Guerra y revolución,* 1:271.

20. RAN, 176–99.

21. Quoted in Radosh et al., *Spain Betrayed,* 60, 55. The Russian text in RAN, 149–71, is dated Oct. 11.

22. See J. Casanova, *Anarquismo y revolución en la sociedad rural aragonesa, 1936–1938* (Madrid, 1985), and G. Kelsey, *Anarchosyndicalism, Libertarian Communism, and the State: The CNT in Zaragoza and Aragon, 1930–1937* (Boston, 1991).

23. POUM's membersip figures, according to a report to the party's central committee, are cited in A. Nin, *La revolución española* (Barcelona, 1978), 232.

24. Published in the pamphlet *El proletariado español ante la revolución en marcha,* then reprinted in Nin's *Los problemas de la revolución española* (Paris, 1971), 173–91.

25. *La Batalla,* Sept. 18, 1936.

26. A. Paz, *La cuestión de Marruecos en la República española* (Madrid, 2000); S. E. Fleming, "Spanish Morocco and the Alzamiento Nacional," *Journal of Contemporary History* 18 (1983): 21–39; A. al-Fasi, *The Independence Movements in Arab North Africa* (Washington, D.C., 1954), 150–53; and R. A. Friedlander, "Holy Crusade or Unholy Alliance? Franco's 'National Revolution' and the Moors," *Southwestern Social Science Quarterly* 44 (1964): 341–62. Years later in Moscow, after the Soviet Union had again taken a revolutionary anticolonial position, the Communist leaders who edited *Guerra y revolución en España* (1:223) blamed the failure to use the Moroccan card on the Socialists, but this is a falsification, for Soviet policy also opposed this move in 1936.

27. A. Elorza and M. Bizcarrondo, *Queridos camaradas: La Internacional Comunista y España, 1919–1939* (Barcelona, 1999), 334, 363–64.

28. L. Trotsky, *The Spanish Revolution* (New York, 1972), 206–18, 233–42.

29. The SB-L may never have had more than thirty or so members. This was the number they represented at the founding of the Fourth International at Lausanne in September 1938. *Documents from the Fourth International: The Formative Years, 1933–40* (New York, 1973), 289. See Bolloten, *Spanish Civil War,* 405–10.

30. J. Comorera, *Cataluña en pie de guerra* (Valencia, 1937) and *Informe presentado en la primera conferencia nacional del Partido Socialista Unificado de Cataluña* (Barcelona, 1937), cited in Bolloten, *Spanish Civil War,* 857n22.

31. D. Ballester, *Els anys de la guerra: La UGT de Catalunya (1936–1939)* (Barcelona, 1998), calculates a maximal membership of approximately 486,000.

32. Bolloten, *Spanish Civil War,* 400–401.

33. The most graphic accounts are by Luis Araquistain (who was ambassador in Paris during these months but presumably was fully informed by Largo and others) in *La intervención de Rusia en el conflicto español* (San José, C.R., 1939);

El comunismo y la guerra de España (San José, C.R., 1939), 11; and *Hoy* (Buenos Aires), Dec. 5, 1942, in D. L. Kowalsky, "The Soviet Union and the Spanish Republic, 1936–1939: Diplomatic, Military, and Cultural Relations" (Ph.D. diss., University of Wisconsin–Madison, 2001), 110. And see Kowalsky's account on pp. 109–13.

34. This account of the Republican mission to Moscow is based on the thorough treatment in Kowalsky, "Soviet Union," 126–66, itself founded on the first careful investigation of Pascua's papers in the Archivo Histórico Nacional.

35. This letter was originally transmitted in French by the Soviet government. The first publication was an English translation, with a partial facsimile reproduction of the French original, in an article by Luis Araquistain in the *New York Times*, June 4, 1939. The original French text first appeared fully in Salvador de Madariaga's *Spain* (New York, 1958), 672–74. It was subsequently published in both Russian and Spanish in Ibárruri et al., *Guerra y revolución*, 2:100–102.

36. From the photostat of the French original in Ibárruri et al., *Guerra y revolución*, 2:102–3.

37. Quoted in Kowalsky, "Soviet Union," 118. As Kowalsky says, it was a matter not merely of arrogance but of Rosenberg's overall "poor management style."

38. Ibid., 118–25.

39. Ibid., 122,

40. RAN, 176–99.

41. In reports during October and November, Antonov-Ovseenko registered a certain amount of progress in achieving partial cooperation from the CNT. Radosh et al., *Spain Betrayed*, 73–84.

42. Report of Erno Gero, Oct. 29, 1936, cited in P. Broué, *Staline et la révolution* (Paris, 1993), 167.

43. Antonov-Ovseenko's report of Oct. 6, 1936, in Radosh et al., *Spain Betrayed*, 97–98. The speculation about a deal with Italy was somewhat less benign than the consul concluded. One Generalitat official did attempt negotiations with Rome. The attempt quickly failed and, after word leaked out, required him to flee to France. This initiative, known as *l'afer Revertés*, has drawn attention in B. de Riquer, *L'últim Cambó (1936–1947)* (Vich, 1996), 81–83.

44. E. H. Carr, *The Comintern and the Spanish Civil War* (New York, 1984), 34.

45. *La Batalla* made this charge on Nov. 29, and there is evidence that Rosenberg personally vetoed the participation of the POUM. Aróstegui and Martínez, *Junta de Defensa de Madrid*, 82.

46. Radosh et al., *Spain Betrayed*, 107; Elorza and Bizcarrondo, *Queridos camaradas*, 364, who note (368) that the Comintern vetoed any cooperation even with the POUM section in Valencia, which was strongly oriented toward Maurín, less insistent on following Nin's line, and willing to work directly with the PCE.

47. According to Miquel Serra Pàmies, one-time PSUC intimate of Comorera, in an interview with Bolloten in Mexico in 1944. Bolloten, *Spanish Civil War*, 411, 633–34.

48. See the analysis in R. Alexander, *The Anarchists in the Spanish Civil War* (London, 1999), 2:775.

49. From a British intelligence decrypt quoted by G. Roberts in C. Leitz and D. J. Dunthorn, *Spain in an International Context, 1936–1959* (New York, 1999), 102n.

50. For further treatment of the POUM during the first year of the Civil War, see V. Alba, *El marxismo en España (1919–1939)*, Historia del B.O.C. y del P.O.U.M., vol. 1 (Mexico City, 1973), and W. Solano, *El POUM en la historia: Andreu Nin y la revolución española* (Madrid, 1999).

51. Interview of Bolloten with Miquel Serra Pàmies in Mexico City in 1944. Bolloten, *Spanish Civil War*, 181, 316.

52. J. Hernández, *Yo fui un ministro de Stalin* (Mexico City, 1953), 75. My account here partly follows the research of Bolloten, *Spanish Civil War*, 180–83.

53. The text of the proposal is in P. de Azcárate, *Mi embajada en Londres durante la guerra civil* (Barcelona, 1976), 266–68.

54. These negotiations have never been fully investigated. See the treatment of the Largo Caballero government's foreign policy by Julio Aróstegui in the series published by Historia 16, *La guerra civil* (Madrid, 1986), 18:22–49, as well as L. Araquistain, *Sobre la guerra civil y la emigración*, ed. J. Tusell (Madrid, 1983), 30–39.

55. D. Ibárruri, *Speeches and Articles, 1936–1938* (New York, 1938), 50–51.

56. F. Montseny to B. Bolloten, May 31, 1950, in Bolloten, *Spanish Civil War*, 230.

57. S. Carrillo, *En marcha hacia la victoria* (Valencia, 1937).

58. A. Sesé, J. del Barrio, and J. Comorera, *Nuestra situación política actual* (Barcelona, 1936).

59. The text is from an interview of Carrillo in 1974, published in his *Demain l'Espagne* (Paris, 1974), 53, cited in Bolloten, *Spanish Civil War*, 227, 387.

60. *El día gráfico* (Barcelona), Jan. 31, 1937, quoted in Bolloten, *Spanish Civil War*, 180, 316.

61. *Treball* (Barcelona), Feb. 2, 1937.

62. This speech has been reprinted various times, most recently in J. Díaz, *La guerra y el Frente Popular* (Madrid, 1990), 37–131.

63. Hernández, *Yo fui un ministro de Stalin*, 135.

64. F. Largo Caballero, *Mis recuerdos* (Mexico City, 1954), 223–26, and "Notas históricas sobre la guerra de España," Fundación Pablo Iglesias, 264–65, cited in Bolloten, *Spanish Civil War*, 350–52.

65. Cf. H. Graham, *Socialism and War: The Spanish Socialist Party in Power and Crisis, 1936–1939* (Cambridge, Mass., 1991), 74–81.

66. André Marty had reported rather routinely to the Secretariat of the ECCI on Oct. 10, 1936, that the PCE was operating its own jail. Radosh et al., *Spain Betrayed*, 40–55.

67. For eyewitness testimony to the execution of three young Spaniards in a Soviet prison maintained for the International Brigades in Murcia in 1937, see W. Herrick, *Jumping the Line* (Madison, Wis., 1998), 200–202.

68. According to the KGB documentation copied during the 1980s by Vasily Mitrokhin. See C. Andrew and V. Mitrokhin, *The Sword and the Shield: The Mitrokhin Archive and the Secret History of the KGB* (New York, 1998), 74. The immediate superintendent of the crematorium was a PCE member named José Castelo Pacheco. After he died in 1982, a female relative tried to claim a pension from the KGB, but received only a lump-sum payment of less than $7,000 from the Soviet embassy in Madrid.

Vaupshasov was already a specialist in guerrilla operations and commando-style raids, having participated in such actions in eastern Poland during the late 1920s. Somewhat psychopathic, he had earlier been imprisoned in the Soviet Union for murdering an NKVD colleague, but was soon released. His main responsibility in Spain was not the crematorium but to serve as one of Orlov's chief lieutenants, under Leonid Eitingon, in developing Republican guerrilla operations; he even personally led a few operations behind Franco's lines. During World War II he became a major Soviet hero for his exploits in guerrilla operations, and was said to have become the most heavily decorated Soviet civilian of the war. His subsequent memoir, *Na trevozhnikh perekrestkakh: Zapiski chekista* (Moscow, 1971), gives a sanitized account of his operations in Spain.

69. J. Costello and O. Tsarev, *Deadly Illusions* (New York, 1993), 269–72. Orlov refers to the disposition of corpses in the work he prepared years later while a consultant on Soviet law at the University of Michigan, *A Handbook of Intelligence and Guerrilla Warfare* (Ann Arbor, 1962).

70. Costello and Tsarev, *Deadly Illusions*, 272, 275.

71. Ibid., 288.

72. Ibid., 275–77, 285–87. Most of Orlov's students were dispatched abroad during 1938. They included two men who later played key roles in the Rote Kapelle network in Berlin and the American Morris Cohen, one of the leading agents involved in transmitting secrets of the atomic bomb to Moscow.

73. Ibid., 274–75.

74. Ibid., 280–82.

75. Costello and Tsarev, *Deadly Illusions*, 284. Cf. P. and A. Sudoplatov with J. L. and L. P. Schecter, *Special Tasks: The Memoirs of an Unwanted Witness, a Soviet Spymaster* (Boston, 1995), 44. The report that Stalin had been a police informer is entirely possible, indeed perhaps likely. Before 1917 the Russian revolutionary organizations had been heavily penetrated by tsarist police informers. There is circumstantial evidence that Stalin was one of them. See E. Radzinsky, *Stalin* (New York, 1996), 47–86, and R. Brackman, *Stalin's Secret File* (London, 2001).

76. Costello and Tsarev, *Deadly Illusions*, 265.

77. Ibid., 267.

78. Krivitsky, *In Stalin's Secret Service*, 106.

79. In a letter of Apr. 15, 1937, Semyon Uritsky, Berzin's successor as head of the GRU, gently takes Berzin to task for failing to implement his orders fully. Radosh et al., *Spain Betrayed*, 278–81.

80. Elorza and Bizcarrondo, *Queridos camaradas*, 337–38.

81. Ibid., 340.

82. See Bolloten, *Spanish Civil War*, 348–49.

83. Radosh et al., *Spain Betrayed*, 129–41, 146–50.

84. H. Thomas, *The Spanish Civil War* (New York, 1986), 381.

85. A. Dallin and F. I. Firsov, eds., *Dimitrov and Stalin* (New Haven, Conn., 2000), 50.

86. RAN, 176–99, 223–47, 253–76.

87. K. L. Maidanik, *Ispanskii proletariat v natsional'no-revoliutsionnoi voine* (Moscow, 1960), 310. For further quantitative data on the political identity of the officer corps, see ibid., 172–73, and my *Spanish Revolution* (New York, 1970), 332–33, 336, 338.

88. *La Humanitat* (Barcelona), Dec. 29, 1936.

89. Radosh et al., *Spain Betrayed*, 154–55. Radosh and his colleagues conjecture (pp. 150–51) that Antonov-Ovseenko had begun to adopt a more extremely militant posture in Barcelona to demonstrate his absolute loyalty to Stalin, given his identification years earlier with Trotsky and their friendship during the 1920s. If that was his motive, his actions were not enough to save him.

90. Krivitsky, *In Stalin's Secret Service*, 107.

91. RAN, 209–13, 213–23, 223–47, 253–76, 276–86.

92. Radosh et al., *Spain Betrayed*, 155–70.

93. Ibid., 184–95.

94. See Bolloten, *Spanish Civil War*, 381–85.

95. Radosh et al., *Spain Betrayed*, 184–95.

96. Ibid.

97. R. J. Alexander, *The Anarchists in the Spanish Civil War* (London, 1999), 2:938–42.

98. Krivitsky, *In Stalin's Secret Service*, 108–9.

99. See, in addition to Costello and Tsarev, *Deadly Illusions*, 280–81, the remarks of Franco to German Ambassador Wilhelm von Faupel in Salamanca on May 11, 1937, in *Documents on German Foreign Policy, 1918–1945* (Washington, D.C., 1950), ser. D, 3:284–86.

100. The best brief analytic reconstruction of the May Days in Barcelona will be found in Bolloten, *Spanish Civil War*, 430–60. For more detail, see F. Bonamusa, *Els fets de maig* (Barcelona, 1977).

101. Cf. J. Gorkín, *Caníbales políticos* (Mexico City, 1941), 69. Bolloten also draws attention to the party's position as expressed in *The Spanish Revolution*, May 19, 1937, which not inaccurately portrays the initial action as a "Stalinist" provocation, and goes on to declare that during the fighting the POUM called for formation of a "revolutionary workers' front." It claimed that "the workers stood ready, vigilant, awaiting the CNT's order to attack," which never came—through no fault of the POUM.

102. This was the conclusion of the account in *The Spanish Revolution*, May 19, 1937.

103. Radosh et al., *Spain Betrayed*, 195–208.

104. Ibid. The role of the People's Army as the true vanguard of revolution had become dogma. Even before this speech, the report that Stepanov had sent to Moscow on May 4, in the middle of the May Days, had declared: "The People's Army is the most organized, the most responsible, and the most disciplined power of the revolution. The People's Army is the best organized foundation of the new government structure, of the new political development." RAN, 253–76. This orthodox Marxist-Leninist dogma was followed in practice by such new regimes down to the end in the 1980s.

105. Krivitsky, *In Stalin's Secret Service,* claimed that Stashevsky had confidently told him months earlier that Negrín would be the next prime minister.

106. Radosh et al., *Spain Betrayed,* 202.

107. Ibid., 203.

108. Relevant documentation is provided by J. M. Martínez Bande, *La ofensiva sobre Segovia y la batalla de Brunete* (Madrid, 1972), 56n60. See also Araquistain, *Comunismo y la guerra de España,* 13; Largo Caballero, *Mis recuerdos* (Mexico City, 1954), 215; Salas Larrazábal, *Historia del Ejército Popular* (Madrid, 1973), 1:1075–83; and Casado, *Last Days of Madrid,* 72–73.

109. Hernández, *Yo fui un ministro de Stalin,* 79–85. Later, in a report of Aug. 30, Dimitrov's chief West European lieutenant, Palmiro Togliatti, by then the chief Comintern adviser in Spain, reported that the prietistas were very helpful to the Communists throughout this crisis. Togliatti, *Escritos sobre la guerra de España* (Barcelona, 1980), 136. This was confirmed by Vicente Uribe in *España popular* (Mexico City), Mar. 11, 1990, in Bolloten, *Spanish Civil War,* 472–73.

CHAPTER 10. THE NEGRÍN GOVERNMENT

1. Araquistain to Diego Martínez Barrio, in *Vía libre* (New York), May 15, 1939, quoted in B. Bolloten, "El extraño caso del doctor Juan Negrín," *Historia 16* 10 (January 1986): 11–24. The most scholarly critique of Negrín will be found in this article and in B. Bolloten, *The Spanish Civil War* (Chapel Hill, N.C., 1991).

2. In an article in *Tiempo de historia,* May 1979, cited in Bolloten, "Extraño caso."

3. The most serious scholarly writing favorable to Negrín will be found in M. Tuñón de Lara et al., *Juan Negrín López: El hombre necesario* (Las Palmas, 1996); R. Miralles, "Juan Negrín: Resistir, ¿para qué?" *Historia 16* 22 (May 1997): 8–23; and H. Graham, "War, Modernity and Reform: The Premiership of Juan Negrín, 1937–1939," in *The Republic Besieged: Civil War in Spain 1936–1939,* ed. P. Preston and A. L. Mackenzie, 163–96 (Edinburgh, 1996).

4. On his scientific career, see Tuñón de Lara et al., *Juan Negrín López,* 193–243.

5. Cf. his sometime friend and leader Indalecio Prieto, "Un hombre singular," in his *Convulsiones de España* (Mexico City, 1967), 3:219–21. In his eulogy of Azaña, *The Tragedy of Manuel Azaña and the Fate of the Spanish Republic* (Columbus, Ohio, 1963), 183, Frank Sedwick calls him a "tactless, indecorous, disorganized and unscrupulous man, whom even his friends admit to have been a kind of Rasputin-of-the-stomach-and-sex in his personal life."

6. *El Socialista*, Sept. 24, 1933, in P. Moa, *Los orígenes de la guerra civil española* (Madrid, 1999), 162.

7. On the special relationship between Stashevsky and Negrín, see Louis Fischer in *The Nation* (New York), Jan. 13, 1940; J. Alvarez del Vayo, *The Last Optimist* (New York, 1950), 291; and M. Ansó, *Yo fui ministro de Negrín* (Barcelona, 1976), 198. Santiago Garcés Arroyo, whom Negrín made head of SIM, later wrote that until Stashevsky was recalled from Spain in June 1937, he and Negrín lunched together almost every day. *Indice*, June 15, 1974, cited in Bolloten, *Spanish Civil War*, 474–75, 881.

8. W. Krivitsky, *In Stalin's Secret Service* (New York, 1939), 87. Pascua to Negrín, Jan. 15, 1937, reported that the son was doing well but thus far not learning much Russian. Carpeta 33, Archivo de la Fundación Nacional Francisco Franco (hereafter AFNFF). Negrín, who could read some Russian, also had Pascua send him a copy of the current annual budget of the Soviet Union.

9. Communications concerning a considerable number of these purchases and transactions are contained in Carpeta 33, AFNFF. On Feb. 25, 1937, the Republican embassy in Paris complained of having been starved of funds since December, though Negrín insisted that he had always supplied funds for any specific purchases. Apparently from approximately the end of 1936 the Ministry of Finance attempted to tighten its accounting. Thus Soviet agents in Paris might occasionally query Negrín concerning an individual order or purchase. A query of Feb. 20, for example, is contained in this file. In a message of Mar. 2 the embassy in Paris reported that "la única gestión relativamente afortunada de las de tipo directo ha sido la de los comunistas," apparently referring to sizable purchases of Polish arms, and on Mar. 21 the Soviet Banque Commerciale pour l'Europe du Nord informed Negrín of large-scale purchasing by the PCF. The Ministry of Finance paid for arms and other goods purchased from a wide variety of countries, and on Mar. 4, 1937, prepared an eight-page memorandum about the need to coordinate and centralize payments more fully. The embassy in Paris, however, continued to complain of the disorganization in purchasing and the unreliability of payments. On May 22, 1937, the Banque Commerciale complained of the multiplicity of individual Republican accounts and announced that it was consolidating them into one general Republican account. Nonmilitary goods were also in great demand, as exemplified by the request of Julio Just, minister of public works, for the deposit of £100,000 sterling in the Soviet Mosnarodny Bank in London to purchase vital railroad equipment.

One of the more curious communications in this file is an apparently autograph letter of Winston Churchill to Negrín on Feb. 22, 1937, with recommendations about how to purchase certain military supplies. This may indicate that Churchill, who originally favored the Spanish insurgents for conservative political reasons, came to favor the Republicans for military and geostrategic reasons from a fairly early date.

10. The orders of Feb. 16 and 23 for the sale of gold to be used in payment amounted to $115 million. Negrín to Stashevsky, Feb. 23, 1937, in Carpeta 33, AFNFF.

11. Manuel Azaña, *Obras completas*, 4 vols. (Mexico City, 1965–68), 4:602.

12. Krivitsky, *In Stalin's Secret Service*, 87, and Bolloten's interviews with PCE leaders, March 1937, in his "Extraño caso."

13. Francisco Largo Caballero, "Notas históricas," 1198, cited by J. Aróstegui in *La guerra civil española: Cincuenta años después*, ed. M. Tuñón de Lara (Barcelona, 1985), 90.

14. As explained in the Comintern report of May 11, 1937, in *Spain Betrayed: The Soviet Union in the Spanish Civil War*, ed. R. Radosh et al., 195–204 (New Haven, Conn., 2001).

15. Azaña, *Obras completas*, 4:832.

16. Krivitsky, *In Stalin's Secret Service*, 87–88. The most negative reaction to the Negrín government came from the moderate and anticommunist sector of the French Socialist Party. By this point Paul Faure, its secretary general, had become convinced that the Soviet Union was trying to take over Spain. *Le Bulletin socialiste* of May, 31, 1937, "openly suggested that fascism and communism were opposite sides of the same coin," and denied that war would lead to revolution. Faure privately told other Socialist leaders that Soviet policy was to promote a general war. Georges Dumoulin, secretary general of the CGT in the department of the Nord, feared that the Republic had become "totally Bolshevized" and its liberties destroyed. N. Greene, *Crisis and Decline: The French Socialist Party in the Popular Front Era* (Ithaca, N.Y., 1969), 115n122.

17. As in his reports of Mar. 28 and May 4, 1937. Rossiiskaia Akademiia Nauk, *Komintern i grazhdanskaia voina v Ispanii* (Moscow, 2001), 223–47, 253–76. (Hereafter cited as RAN.)

18. The high-ranking Communist commander Antonio Cordón, in his *Trayectoria* (Paris, 1971), 411, testifies that Martínez's appointment was "following party orders."

19. According to his conversations with Louis Fischer while finance minister. Fischer, *Men and Politics* (New York, 1941), 421.

20. Something of the spirit behind the formation of the new government may be gleaned from a letter that the ambassador to Washington, Fernando de los Ríos, wrote to PSOE party secretary Lamoneda on May 22. De los Ríos is usually described as a "humanist" and a "social democrat," but in this letter he expressed a great passion for the triumph of the revolution: "I am at the service of the revolution and the war for everything, absolutely everything. . . ." "The great error . . . has been to criticize the revolution for concrete injustices committed in its course; that is its pathological, lamentable, and sad element, but is what makes it fruitful or sterile." What really matters is "its really vital impetus," "without the sadness for the deaths in my family or the injustices suffered being an obstacle. That is important for me, but not for the Revolution, which is something so deep that with regard to Spain it has been developing since the seventeenth

century. I trust that it will be the light of dawn." Quoted in R. Gil Bracero, *Revolucionarios sin revolución: Marxistas y sindicalistas en guerra, Granada-Baza, 1936–1939* (Granada, 1998), 219–20.

21. Quoted in A. Elorza and M. Bizcarrondo, *Queridos camaradas: La Internacional Comunista y España, 1919–1939* (Barcelona, 1999), 342.

22. As Stepanov declared in his report of May 4, 1937. RAN, 253–76.

23. As in Codovilla's formulation of Dec. 24, 1937, ibid., 176–99.

24. J. Hernández, *Yo fui un ministro de Stalin* (Mexico City, 1953), 87–88; P. Togliatti, *Los escritos sobre la guerra de España* (Barcelona, 1980), 229–34. The text of the Russian version of this report, filed in the Comintern archive, appears in RAN, 416–73.

25. J. S. Vidarte, *Todos fuimos culpables* (Mexico City, 1973), 751.

26. *Castilla libre*, Apr. 10, 1937, quoted in Bolloten, *Spanish Civil War*, 523; J. García Pradas, *¡Teníamos que perder!* (Madrid, 1974), 157. From the end of March forward, the CNT press was full of denunciations of this new policy. Later Enrique Líster admitted that it was necessary "to adopt some very harsh, very serious measures. I have responded that yes, I have had people executed, and I am ready to do it as many times as necessary," as far as "bandits" were concerned. *Triunfo*, Nov. 19, 1977, cited in Bolloten, *Spanish Civil War*, 241.

27. A. Nin, *Los problemas de la revolución española* (Barcelona, 1977), 223.

28. According to a report by Stepanov to the Comintern. Elorza and Bizcarrondo, *Queridos camaradas*, 361.

29. According to Dimitrov, Stalin had told him on Feb. 11: "All of you there in the Comintern are working in the hands of the enemy." Quoted in K. McDermott and J. Agnew, *The Comintern* (London, 1996), 145.

30. J. Costello and O. Tsarev, *Deadly Illusions* (New York, 1993), 288–89.

31. Prieto, *Convulsiones de España*, 2:7.

32. G. Morón, *Política de ayer y política de mañana* (Mexico City, 1942), 100–105.

33. Azaña, *Obras completas*, 4:692.

34. The best account of the political reaction to the suppression of the POUM is Bolloten, *Spanish Civil War*, 498–515. See also V. Alba and M. Ardévol, eds., *El proceso del POUM* (Barcelona, 1989); V. Alba and S. Schwartz, *Spanish Marxism versus Soviet Communism: A History of the P.O.U.M.* (New Brunswick, N.J., 1988), 210–79; V. Alba, *El marxismo en España (1919–1939)*, vol. 2 (Mexico City, 1973); and Vidarte, *Todos fuimos culpables*, 732–33.

35. Orlov rather cryptically described the killing in his NKVD report of July 24, according to Costello and Tsarev, *Deadly Illusions*, 291–92. The full story of Nin's execution as revealed by surviving KGB documentation was presented in the report "Operación Nikolai" (NKVD code name for the Nin case) prepared by M. D. Genovés and L. Ferri for presentation on Barcelona's TV 3 on Nov. 5, 1992. It clarifies details but also in considerable measure substantiates the pamphlet *El Asesinato de Andreu Nin*, written by the POUMist leader Juan Andrade in 1939 and eventually published in René Lefebre, *L'Espagne: Les fossoyeurs de la révolution sociale* (Paris, 1975). According to that account, two of Irujo's agents managed

to speak to Nin in the basement of Hidalgo de Cisneros's home in Alcalá, and even enlisted the support of the Madrid military commander, Gen. José Miaja, but Orlov stalled long enough to carry out the execution. See L. Ferri's account of producing the documentary *Nikolai: Claror, ombra i penombra*, in *L'Avenç*, January 1993; the brief account in W. Solano, *El POUM en la historia* (Madrid, 1998), 164–66; and the lucid summary in J. Cervera, *Madrid en guerra* (Madrid, 1998), 302–6.

36. Greene, *Crisis and Decline*, 195. Trotsky, on the other hand, was his usual charitable and magnanimous self, continuing to denounce Nin and the POUM leaders categorically even after their demise, saying that they themselves were responsible for their fate. On Dec. 17, 1937, he wrote that "the POUM proved to be, in the final analysis, the chief obstacle on the road to the creation of a revolutionary party." It had failed to unite the workers in a direct seizure of power and had not initiated the creation of a true worker revolutionary army. It was typical of Trotsky's obsessive fixations that at the time of his assassination by a Catalan PSUquista in 1940 he left unfinished a manuscript titled "The Treachery of the POUM." L. Trotsky, *The Spanish Revolution* (New York, 1973), 318, 363.

37. "Verbali di riunioni e appunti redatti a mano da P. Togiatti nel corso della sua presentazione in Spagna (1937–1939)," in Archivio della Fondazione Antonio Gramsci (Rome), cited in Elorza and Bizcarrondo, *Queridos camaradas*, 279.

38. Bolloten, *Spanish Civil War*, 512–14.

39. This more moderate line was more in keeping with the criteria of the POUM's chief founder, Maurín, who would languish for a decade in Franco's prisons. He later wrote that the chief priority of the POUM ought to have been to win the military struggle. V. Alba, *Dos revolucionarios: Andreu Nin, Joaquín Maurín* (Madrid, 1975), 288–89.

40. P. Togliatti, *Opere* (Rome, 1979), 4:306.

41. See Bolloten, *Spanish Civil War*, 518–19.

42. See Alba and Ardévol, *Proceso del POUM*, and A. Suárez (I. Iglesias), *Un episodio de la revolución española: El proceso contra el POUM* (Paris, 1974).

43. P. Togliatti, *Escritos sobre la guerra de España* (Barcelona, 1980), 232.

44. On the Consejo and anarchism in Aragon generally, see J. Casanova, *Anarquismo y revolución en la sociedad rural aragonesa, 1936–1938* (Madrid, 1985), and G. Kelsey, *Anarchosyndicalism, Libertarian Communism, and the State: The CNT in Zaragoza and Aragon, 1930–1937* (Boston, 1991).

45. C. M. Lorenzo, *Les anarchistes espagnols et le pouvoir, 1868–1969* (Paris, 1969), 310.

46. See the account of this operation in Bolloten, *Spanish Civil War*, 522–31, and in R. J. Alexander, *The Anarchists in the Spanish Civil War* (London, 1999), 2:1013–19.

47. Cf. A. Bosch Sánchez, *Ugetistas y libertarios: Guerra civil y revolución en el País Valenciano, 1936–1939* (Valencia, 1983), 306–28.

48. Azaña, *Obras completas*, 4:733.

49. One of them, Manuel Almudí, said "Líster did not kill many." Bolloten, *Spanish Civil War*, 526–27.

50. In J. Silva, *La revolución popular en el campo* (Valencia, 1937), cited ibid., 528.

51. R. Fraser, *Blood of Spain* (New York, 1979), 391.

52. J. Peirats, *Los anarquistas en la crisis política española* (Buenos Aires, 1964), 300–301.

53. Quoted in Elorza and Bizcarrondo, *Queridos camaradas*, 390.

54. Radosh et al., *Spain Betrayed*, 387.

55. *Frente rojo*, July 7, 1937.

56. Radosh et al., *Spain Betrayed*, 213–16.

57. Bolloten, *Spanish Civil War*, 539.

58. Radosh et al., *Spain Betrayed*, 216–19.

59. Ibid., 219–20.

60. Ibid., 220–24.

61. Ibid., 381–86.

62. Ibid., 389–90.

63. Ibid., 391.

64. Ibid., 396, 402–5.

65. Ibid., 392–93; Elorza and Bizcarrondo, *Queridos camaradas*, 396–97.

66. Radosh et al., *Spain Betrayed*, 375–81; A. Dallin and F. I. Firsov, eds., *Dimitrov and Stalin, 1934–1943* (New Haven, Conn., 2000), 61.

67. The Comintern bosses seemed to be unaware that calling for elections was constitutionally the president's prerogative, in any case.

68. Dallin and Firsov, *Dimitrov and Stalin*, 62–71. Cf. M. V. Novikov, *SSSR, Komintern i grazhdanskaia voina v Ispanii, 1936–1939 gg.* (Yaroslavl, 1995), 2:87.

69. Radosh et al., *Spain Betrayed*, 391.

70. Elorza and Bizcarrondo, *Queridos camaradas*, 202.

71. Ibid., 403–4.

72. The Soviet leaders' discouragement of assistance to the north of course did not prevent them from bitterly resenting and denouncing any criticism of this policy, which they denied ever adopting. RAN, 272–76.

73. Gorev himself briefly went to Bilbao in May and returned a very negative report on the Soviet advisers in Vizcaya, recommending that their number be increased. Radosh et al., *Spain Betrayed*, 276–78. Soviet advisers served in all three northern sectors; those in Asturias remained until the very end. Prieto, whose political base was originally in Bilbao, was more concerned about the north than were most of the government leaders, but after five of six new Soviet fighters sent to Bilbao were destroyed on the ground soon after they had landed, he agreed with the Communist air force commander, Hidalgo de Cisneros, that warplanes could not be sent usefully to the north, where their small numbers would have to face the bulk of Franco's air force. Prieto was nonetheless shaken by the fall of Bilbao and ready to submit his resignation. Prieto to Negrín, June 6 and 30, 1937, Carpeta 33, AFNFF.

74. According to J. Salas Larrazábal, *Guerra aérea, 1936/39* (Madrid, 1999), 2:271.

75. It was probably a mistake for the original structure of the Ejército Popular to have eliminated the very lowest officer ranks of *brigada* and *alférez*, reducing the cohesiveness of small units. Cf. M. Alpert, *El ejército republicano en la guerra civil* (Paris, 1977), 130, 147.

76. Detailed in a report by the Polish Red Army colonel Karol Sverchevsky, transmitted to Voroshilov on Aug. 2, 1938. Radosh et al., *Spain Betrayed*, 481. Sverchevsky added that on the second night of the battle Líster executed a divisional commissar and a regular brigade commander, both anarchists, for refusing to obey orders.

77. This, for example, was the judgment of Togliatti in a report of Aug. 29, 1937. This and other Soviet military and Comintern reports from the summer of 1937 dealing with the decline of the International Brigades may be found ibid., 237–61.

78. The internal and administrative problems are highlighted in M. T. Meshcheriakov, "Sud'ba Interbrigad v Ispanii po novym dokumentam," *Novaia i noveishaia istoriia* 5 (1993): 18–41.

79. Radosh et al., *Spain Betrayed*, 275–76.

80. J. Hernández, *Yo fui un ministro de Stalin*, 113–19. For a clear account of these naval incidents, see W. C. Frank Jr., "Misperception and Incidents at Sea: The *Deutschland* and *Leipzig* Crises, 1937," *Naval War College Review* 43 (Spring 1990): 31–46.

81. Admiral Francisco Basterreche, commander of the elite cruiser *Canarias* during the Civil War, later wrote that the Nationalist navy sank 53 merchant ships totaling 129,000 tons during the conflict, and seized or searched 324 other vessels. Most of the ships sunk belonged to the Republic, but the figure also included a good many vessels from other countries. "De nuestra guerra en el mar," in *La Guerra de Liberación Nacional* (Zaragoza, 1961), 402–3.

82. According to Novikov, *SSSR, Komintern*, 2:47.

83. A. A. Grechko, ed., *Istoriia vtoroi mirovoi voiny, 1939–1945* (Moscow, 1974), 2:54.

84. Franco's intelligence services intercepted a report from Ambassador Pascua in Moscow in midsummer in which he relayed renewed assurances from Stalin and Voroshilov that the Republic would not be abandoned. Carpeta 33, 14–619, AFNFF. By late summer, however, Soviet priorities had clearly changed. Orlov has written that whereas previously "the policy of the politburo was to assist the Spanish Republican Government to the utmost . . . in order to secure for the Republicans a speedy victory over Franco," "now the politburo had come to the conclusion that it would be more advantageous to the Soviet Union if neither of the warring camps gained preponderant strength and if the war in Spain dragged on as long as possible and thus tied up Hitler for a longer time." A. Orlov, *The Secret History of Stalin's Crimes* (New York, 1953), 238.

85. U.S. Department of State, *Documents on German Foreign Policy, 1918–1945* (Washington, D.C., 1949–83), ser. D, 4:37.

86. Radosh et al., *Spain Betrayed*, 281–95.

87. Some details are given in D. L. Kowalsky, "The Soviet Union and the Spanish Republic, 1936–1939: Diplomatic, Military, and Cultural Relations" (Ph.D. diss., University of Wisconsin–Madison, 2001), 172–75, and in Novikov, *SSSR, Komintern*, 2:116–20.

88. These figures are taken from D. S. Allen, "The Soviet Union and the Spanish Civil War" (Ph.D. diss., Stanford University, 1952), 410–18. Barcelona anarchists became convinced that the industrial wealth of Catalonia was flowing out to the Soviet Union without adequate compensation, and even that Catalan industrial secrets had been purloined. Comité Peninsular de la FAI, "Informe," September 1938, cited in Bolloten, *Spanish Civil War*, 612.

89. On the large-scale cultural and propaganda exchange, see Kowalsky, "Soviet Union," 274–324, and also Allen, "Soviet Union," 450–77. For the success of the visiting Basque football team in 1938, E. Radzinsky, *Stalin* (New York, 1996), 389–90.

90. A. Alted Vigil et al., *Los niños de la guerra de España en la Unión Soviética: De la evacuación al retorno (1937–1999)* (Madrid, 1999). See also Kowalsky, "Soviet Union," 199–241, and J. Fernández, *Memorias de un niño de Moscú* (Barcelona, 1999).

91. For example, Voroshilov dispatched a memo to Stalin saying that their agents had an opportunity to purchase seven transport planes and one hundred airplane engines in the United States, noting that all the matériel would be paid for with Spanish funds. Radosh et al., *Spain Betrayed*, 425.

92. A. Viñas, *El oro de Moscú* (Madrid, 1979), 329–39, 194–245, 358.

93. Ibid., 359–86, 408–15.

94. On Sept. 15, 1937, Togliatti had reported that a "very dangerous" situation was developing in the Ejército Popular because of the inadequacy of politicization. Even the "Communist cadres" in the army "do not feel the authority of the Central Committee." Radosh et al., *Spain Betrayed*, 419.

95. D. Ibárruri, *El único camino* (Paris, 1962), 389. Togliatti reported in November 1937 that Communists commanded twenty-nine of the fifty-two Republican divisions (with one more commanded by a sympathizer) and seven of the twenty-one army corps (with five more corps commanded by sympathizers). Togliatti, *Escritos sobre la guerra*, 180.

96. Orlov's response to the questionnaire I sent him, which he dated Apr. 1, 1968. Orlov claims, however, that Prieto telephoned him to obtain his approval of the latter appointment.

97. I. Prieto, *Cómo y por qué salí del Ministerio de Defensa Nacional* (Mexico City, 1940), 78. After the Civil War the talented Durán became a United States citizen and an adviser to the U.S. State Department. As Bolloten points out, he testified under oath that he had never been a member of the Communist Party, but years later his membership was admitted by the official *Guerra y revolución en España, 1936–39*, ed. D. Ibárruri et al. (Moscow, 1966), 4:230.

98. J. Hernández, *Yo fui un ministro de Stalin*, 130–31.

99. Radosh et al., *Spain Betrayed*, 390.

100. *Frente libertario*, Aug. 29, 1937, quoted in Bolloten, *Spanish Civil War*, 553.
101. Radosh et al., *Spain Betrayed*, 417.
102. On the internecine struggle among the Socialists, see H. Graham, *Socialism and War: The Spanish Socialist Party in Power and Crisis, 1936–1939* (Cambridge, Mass., 1991), 107–97.
103. Togliatti, *Escritos sobre la guerra*, 162.
104. Kowalsky, "Soviet Union," 353.
105. Cf. M. Valdés, *El Partido Socialista Unificado de Cataluña, partido único revolucionario bolchevique de Cataluña* (Barcelona, 1937).
106. E. Ruiz i Ponsetí, *Les empreses collectivitzades i el nou ordre económic* (Barcelona, 1937).
107. Elorza and Bizcarrondo, *Queridos camaradas*, 408–9.
108. Quoted in Dallin and Firsov, *Dimitrov and Stalin*, 71–72.
109. Elorza and Bizcarrondo, *Queridos camaradas*, 408–9.
110. Ibárruri et al., *Guerra y revolución*, 4:75–76.
111. Dallin and Firsov, *Dimitrov and Stalin*, 72.
112. Hernández declared that these were the instructions brought back from Moscow in mid-February. *Yo fui un ministro de Stalin*, 158. If his memory is accurate, this might have been just before the 17th.
113. Elorza and Bizcarrondo, *Queridos camaradas*, 417.
114. Ibid., 415.
115. Hernández has emphasized that the success of these "salami" tactics, slicing off opponents one at a time, was due above all to the opponents' internal division and disunity: "Thus to eliminate Francisco Largo Caballero we chiefly relied on Negrín and, in part, on Prieto. To get rid of the latter we used Negrín and other leading Socialists, and if the war had continued, we would not have hesitated to ally ourselves with the devil himself if necessary to eliminate Negrín, had he become an obstacle. . . .

"Our attack on Prieto especially wounded the various Republican parties, who traditionally saw in this Socialist leader, more than in any other, the orchestrator who projected their Republican policy in Spain. . . . If at that time a total collapse of our position did not occur, it may be attributed to the fact that all these forces that hated the Communists were incapable of uniting in a common front." (*Yo fui un ministro de Stalin*, 135–36, 140.)
116. In the *Epistolario Prieto-Negrín* (Paris, 1939), 15, Prieto refers to the CNT offer of support, but says nothing about the use of force.
117. Quoted by Prieto's son César M. Lorenzo in his book *Les anarchistes espagnols et le pouvoir, 1868–1939* (Paris, 1969), 315–16.
118. Togliatti, *Escritos sobre la guerra*, 195.
119. In this post Zugazagoitia was so completely ignored that he complained to the executive commission of the PSOE, "When I want to know something about the war, I have to buy a newspaper or ask a friend," according to Prieto in the *Epistolario Prieto y Negrín*, 101.

120. For references, see the sources cited in B. Bolloten, "El extraño caso del doctor Juan Negrín," *Historia 16* 10 (January 1986): 11–24nn32–33.

121. Elorza and Bizcarrondo, *Queridos camaradas*, 417–18.

122. On this problem, see M. Seidman, "Work and Revolution: Workers' Control in Barcelona in the Spanish Civil War, 1936–38," *Journal of Contemporary History* 17 (1982): 409–33, and especially his *Republic of Egos: A Social History of the Spanish Civil War* (Madison, Wis., 2002).

123. Togliatti, *Escritos sobre la guerra*, 229.

124. Bolloten, *Spanish Civil War,* 587

125. Togliatti, *Escritos sobre la guerra*, 234, 231, 288, 231, 236.

126. Ibid., 154, 231; J. Martínez Amutio, *Chantaje a un pueblo* (Madrid, 1974), 368; Bolloten, *Spanish Civil War,* 589.

127. In a letter to Bolloten in his *Spanish Civil War,* 589.

128. In his report of Nov. 25, 1937, in Togliatti, *Escritos sobre la guerra*, 154.

129. Bolloten, *Spanish Civil War,* 591.

130. A. Cordón, *Trayectoria* (Paris, 1971), 391.

131. H. Thomas, *The Spanish Civil War* (New York, 1986), 669; Vidarte, *Todos fuimos culpables,* 855.

132. Graham, "War, Modernity and Reform."

133. For the aversion of the Spanish left to nationalism, see C. Alonso de los Ríos, *La izquierda y la nación* (Madrid, 2000). In a patriotic appeal late in the war, Negrín declared: "I neither deny nor renounce the history of my country. We have inherited a magnificent history. With stains and blemishes, like any, yes, but also with a proud grandeur like no other. That is a weighty responsibility." Quoted in Tuñon de Lara et al., *Juan Negrín López*, 7. This statement may be dismissed as wartime propaganda, but in my judgment it reflects his genuine personal attitude.

134. Zugazagoitia, *Historia de la guerra*, 428–29.

135. Hernández, *Yo fui un ministro de Stalin*, 159.

136. Togliatti, *Escritos sobre la guerra*, 196–97; Novikov, *SSSR, Komintern*, 2:84.

137. Bolloten, *Spanish Civil War,* 635–36; Seidman, forthcoming.

138. L. Fischer, *Men and Politics* (New York, 1941), 491–92; Doc. 59 of the Rocker Collection, International Institute of Social History (Amsterdam), cited in Bolloten, *Spanish Civil War,* 647, 917.

139. Elorza and M. Bizcarrondo, *Queridos camaradas*, 419; Bolloten, *Spanish Civil War,* 642.

140. D. Ibárruri, *En la lucha: Palabras y hechos, 1936–1939* (Moscow, 1968), 277.

141. Vidarte quotes Azaña as saying: "I know that some of you think that in a world war the just cause of the Republic would be saved. Such a war would be a catastrophe of inconceivable dimensions and it would be wrong to seek our salvation in the martyrdom of millions of human beings. . . . I see that you too have been infected with Negrín's thesis. . . . Suppose that the result of such a war was the implantation of communism in Western Europe just as the result of the previous one was its implantation in Eastern Europe. Such a solution

would be repugnant to the majority of Republicans and I suppose to the Socialists, as well." *Todos fuimos culpables,* 894–95.

142. For Negrín's attitude, see D. T. Cattell, *Communism and the Spanish Civil War* (Berkeley, Calif., 1956), 186, and Graham, "War, Modernity and Reform," 189–90.

143. Elorza and Bizcarrondo, *Queridos camaradas,* 419.

144. Togliatti, *Escritos sobre la guerra,* 230–36; Dallin and Firsov, *Dimitrov and Stalin,* 73–76.

145. Cordón, *Trayectoria,* 380, 389.

146. Hernández, *Yo fui ministro de Stalin,* 144.

147. Ibárruri et al., *Guerra y revolución,* 4:229–30.

148. From an unpublished CNT document in the Rocker collection cited by Bolloten, *Spanish Civil War,* 594.

149. J. Peirats, *Los anarquistas en la crisis política española* (Buenos Aires, 1964), 357.

150. Cf. D. Pastor Petit, *La cinquena columna a Catalunya, 1936–1939* (Barcelona, 1978), 222.

151. Quoted in Costello and Tsarev, *Deadly Illusions,* 300.

152. According to P. and A. Sudoplatov, with J. L. and L. P. Schecter, *Special Tasks: The Memoirs of an Unwanted Witness, a Soviet Spymaster* (Boston, 1995), 44. One flaw in his reports to Moscow was their tendency to hyperbole, as at the end of 1937 when he had gushingly informed his superiors that the capture of Teruel marked "a turning point for both the army and the country." Quoted in Costello and Tsarev, *Deadly Illusions,* 271.

153. A half century later, the onetime high-ranking NKVD official Sudoplatov would claim that the person awaiting Orlov was his new superior, Aleksandr Shpigelglas, who had succeeded Slutsky. Shpigelglas had visited the Republican zone several times but allegedly dared not enter France because he was personally implicated in a recent high-profile NKVD kidnapping. Sudoplatov, *Special Tasks,* 45. On Shpigelglas during this period, see V. and E. Petrov, *Empire of Fear* (New York, 1956), 57. This account, however, is not altogether convincing because Shpigelglas had apparently not been identified by his NKVD code name.

154. In Costello and Tsarev, *Deadly Illusions.* Orlov's lies in regard to Spain were most notable in, but not at all restricted to, my questionnaire (see n. 96). E. P. Gazur, *Alexander Orlov: The FBI's KGB General* (New York, 2001), by Orlov's FBI control agent, accepts a great many of his lies at face value.

155. Radosh et al., *Spain Betrayed,* 496.

156. Dallin and Firsov, *Dimitrov and Stalin,* 73.

157. Radosh et al., *Spain Betrayed,* 488–96. Sverchevsky was highly regarded in Spain. When he was recalled to the Soviet Union very soon after this, Orlov went out of his way to obtain testimonials concerning his loyalty and good work. Costello and Tsarev, *Deadly Illusions,* 301. Whether these actions were instrumental or not, Sverchevsky was not purged, as Berzin and Gorev were.

158. See Radosh et al., *Spain Betrayed*, 428–30. A report to Voroshilov of Apr. 20 indicated that three DC-3s being purchased for Spain would first be diverted to China to help evacuate Soviet personnel there. The information about Roosevelt, supplied by the Spanish ambassador, De los Ríos, to Litvinov on Apr. 13, 1938, was substantially correct, as Roosevelt briefly conspired to arrange shipments through his brother-in-law G. Hall Roosevelt. This initiative apparently came to an end after the French border was officially closed again in June 1938. F. Freidel, *Franklin D. Roosevelt: A Rendezvous with Destiny* (Boston, 1990), 271–72.

159. Hitler passed on his concern about Western intervention through Col. Erwin Jaenecke, who supervised supplies to Nationalist Spain. R. H. Whealey, *Hitler and Spain: The Nazi Role in the Spanish Civil War* (Lexington, Ky., 1989), 60.

160. G. Howson, *Arms for Spain: The Untold Story of the Spanish Civil War* (London, 1998), 239–41.

161. For Irujo's own references on this matter, see Bolloten, *Spanish Civil War*, 605–6, 910.

162. U.S. Department of State, *Documents on German Foreign Policy*, 3:698–99.

163. Ibid., 699, 715.

164. G. Hilger and A. G. Meyer, *The Incompatible Allies: A Memoir-History of German-Soviet Relations, 1918–1941* (New York, 1953), 288.

165. U.S. Department of State, *Documents on German Foreign Policy*, 3:713–15.

166. Elorza and Bizcarrondo, *Queridos camaradas*, 421–22.

167. Cf. Novikov, *SSSR, Komintern*, 2:86.

168. See the negative reports on the brigades by Sverchevsky and others in 1938 in Radosh et al., *Spain Betrayed*, 431–73. Sverchevsky complained that some of the most recent volunteers had been "simply criminals." Disciplinary violence was increased early in 1938 and numerous secret executions were carried out, primarily by the SIM. This further indicates the extent to which the SIM, particularly in Catalonia, was not limited to intelligence but carried out full NKVD-type functions. See S. Voros, *American Commissar* (Philadelphia, 1961), 410–11; C. Penchienati, *Brigate Internazionali in Spagna: Delitti della "Ceka" comunista* (Milan, 1950), 125; and Gustav Regler to B. Bolloten, May 10, 1948, in Bolloten, *Spanish Civil War*, 571.

169. Radosh et al., *Spain Betrayed*, 469.

170. Elorza and Bizcarrondo, *Queridos camaradas*, 424–25.

171. RAN, 396–99.

172. Dallin and Firsov, *Dimitrov and Stalin*, 76–78.

173. M. Aznar, *Historia militar de la guerra de España* (Madrid, 1958), 3:264.

CHAPTER 11. DEFEAT

1. A. Elorza and M. Bizcarrondo, *Queridos camaradas: La Internacional Comunista y España, 1919–1939* (Barcelona, 1999), 423–24.

2. D. Kowalsky, "The Soviet Union and the Spanish Republic, 1936–1939: Diplomatic, Military, and Cultural Relations" (Ph.D. diss., University of Wisconsin–Madison, 2001), 401.

3. J. Peirats, *La CNT en la revolución española* (Cali, 1988), 3:304.

4. P. Togliatti, *Escritos sobre la guerra de Espana* (Barcelona, 1980), 244.

5. J. Peirats, *Los anarquistas en la crisis política española* (Buenos Aires, 1964), 351–52.

6. Quoted in B. Bolloten, *The Spanish Civil War* (Chapel Hill, N.C., 1991), 630.

7. D. Ibárruri et al., eds., *Guerra y revolución en España, 1936–1939* (Moscow, 1977), 4:166.

8. D. Ibárruri, *El único camino* (Paris, 1962), 410–11; Elorza and Bizcarrondo, *Queridos camaradas,* 425.

9. Bolloten, *Spanish Civil War,* 613; G. Morán, *Miseria y grandeza del Partido Comunista de España, 1939–1985* (Barcelona, 1986), 30.

10. R. Gil Bracero, *Revolucionarios sin revolución: Marxistas y anarcosindicalistas en guerra: Granada-Baza, 1936–1939* (Granada, 1998), 241.

11. R. Radosh, M. Habeck, and G. Sevostianov, eds., *Spain Betrayed: The Soviet Union in the Spanish Civil War* (New Haven, Conn., 2001), 503–11.

12. Ibárruri et al., *Guerra y revolución,* 4:328–29.

13. Ibid., 197–201. Hidalgo de Cisneros presented his version of this mission in his memoir, *Cambio de rumbo* (Bucharest, 1964), 242–50. Part of his account, including some of the dates, clearly seem to be inaccurate. For example, a letter of Voroshilov to Stalin on Nov. 27 indicates that he was already in Moscow by that date. G. Howson, *Arms for Spain: The Untold Story of the Spanish Civil War* (London, 1998), 242.

14. M. V. Novikov, *SSSR, Komintern i grazhdanskaia voina v Ispanii, 1936–1939 gg.* (Yaroslavl, 1995), 55. A. Grechko, ed., *Istoriia vtoroi mirovoi voiny* (Moscow, 1974), 2:54, mentions only three antitank guns, 35,000 rifles, 2,772 machine guns, and much ammunition and other supplies, but probably through an oversight leaves out the 30 Polikarpov I-16bis Superchatos, which are included in the original Soviet records, according to Howson, *Arms for Spain,* app., 302. Conversely, M. T. Meshcheriakov, perhaps the most careful of the Soviet historians who dealt with the Spanish war, found indication in the Soviet archives of the arrival of 27 planes, 20 pieces of artillery, 2,400 machine guns, 40,000 rifles, and a sizable quantity of ammunition. "Sovietskii Soiuz i antifashistskaia voina ispanskov naroda (1936–1939)," *Istoriia SSSR* 1 (January–February 1988): 31.

15. The veteran *New York Times* journalist Herbert Matthews, an admirer of Negrín since the Civil War, wrote that "Dr. Negrín told me in 1954 that the purchases from the Soviet Union did not use up the full amount of the gold sent and that Moscow therefore owed Spain a sum that had to be calculated, partly because the Russians, without asking permission, had melted down the more valuable English gold sovereign coins into bars, and partly because Spanish raw materials were shipped to Russia in partial payment of the purchases." *Half of Spain Died: A Reappraisal of the Spanish Civil War* (New York, 1973), 171.

There is undoubtedly some truth to both of Negrín's allegations in 1954. Not only do serious unanswered questions remain about the ways the Soviet government disposed of the gold—and thus how much it was really worth—but also about all the Soviet accounting and financial procedures during the war, as indicated in Chapter 8. In addition, a thorough study is needed of all the additional commercial exchanges between the Republic and the Soviet Union. Negrín's allegation of special shipments of raw materials to pay for the loans of 1938 constitutes only one of a number of points at issue. The CNT particularly, with its strong suspicion of the Soviet Union, always claimed that proper credit was not received for the export of finished goods, and even that certain Catalan industrial secrets passed into Soviet hands. Cf. D. Abad de Santillán, *Por qué perdimos la guerra* (Buenos Aires, 1940), 253.

16. Elorza and Bizcarrondo, *Queridos camaradas*, 426; Radosh et al., *Spain Betrayed*, 391.

17. Quoted in Bolloten, *Spanish Civil War*, 671.

18. Radosh et al., *Spain Betrayed*, 498.

19. Ibid., 499–500.

20. Elorza and Bizcarrondo, *Queridos camaradas*, 427.

21. These figures follow the statistics in H. Thomas, *The Spanish Civil War* (New York, 1986), 867–68, which appear to be roughly accurate. The Soviet figures given by Grechko, *Istoriia vtoroi mirovoi voiny*, 2:62, are 176,000 troops, 134 planes, 240 tanks and armored cars, and 280 cannon. The latter troop statistic may not be far off in respect to fully trained and equipped troops.

22. Elorza and Bizcarrondo, *Queridos camaradas*, 429.

23. Voroshilov to the Soviet Politburo and to Stalin, Feb. 16, 1939, in Radosh et al., *Spain Betrayed*, 512.

24. Kowalsky, "Soviet Union," 373.

25. Bolloten, *Spanish Civil War*, 668, points out the urgent appeal for international assistance made by *World News and Views*, a Comintern organ published in several languages.

26. Kowalsky, "Soviet Union," 401–2. J. Fernández Sánchez, "Los últimos consejeros rusos en España," *Historia 16*, April 1984, claims that by the end of January remaining Soviet military personnel totaled only about thirty.

27. Togliatti, *Escritos sobre la guerra*, 265.

28. E.g., Grechko, *Istoriia vtoroi mirovoi voiny*, 2:62.

29. Elorza and Bizcarrondo, *Queridos camaradas*, 430, based on Stepanov's postwar manuscript.

30. Stepanov's report is quoted in Bolloten, *Spanish Civil War*, 692.

31. Quoted from Togliatti's notebook in Elorza and Bizcarrondo, *Queridos camaradas*, 431, 430.

32. Quoted in Bolloten, *Spanish Civil War*, 693.

33. Quoted ibid.

34. Elorza and Bizcarrondo, *Queridos camaradas*, 431–32.

35. F.-F. Montiel, *Un coronel llamado Segismundo: Mentiras y misterios de la guerra de Stalin en España* (Madrid, 1998).

36. Bolloten, *Spanish Civil War*, 686. A brief account of the development and outcome of the so-called *casadazo*, in which I collaborated with Bolloten, will be

found ibid., 702–43. Casado's own account quickly appeared in English as *The Last Days of Madrid* (London, 1939).

37. Elorza and Bizcarrondo, *Queridos camaradas*, 432.

38. Thus Ibárruri et al., *Guerra y revolución*, 4:258, claims that the PCE politburo on the 24th repeated to Negrín the request to reassign Casado.

39. Elorza and Bizcarrondo, *Queridos camaradas*, 433.

40. Ricardo de la Cierva points out that the new *Diario oficial del Consejo de Defensa*, which appeared on Mar. 15, canceled the appointments published in the preceding *Diario oficial* on both Mar. 3 and 4. Cancellations of appointments for both dates were also published in the *Gaceta de la República* on Mar. 27. *La victoria y el caos: A los sesenta años del 1 de abril de 1939* (Madrid, 1998), 421–24.

41. This was the criticism subsequently leveled by Togliatti, *Escritos sobre la guerra*, 284.

42. The most thorough account of the origins, development, and carrying out of the revolt in Madrid is A. Bahamonde and J. Cervera Gil, *Así terminó la guerra de España* (Madrid, 1999).

43. Manuel Tagüeña Lacorte, *Testimonio de dos guerras* (Mexico City, 1973), 309–10; Hernández, *Yo fui un ministro de Stalin*, 192–95.

44. In his postmortem to the Comintern on May 31, Togliatti criticized some Communist commanders who he said were unresponsive, claiming they failed to cooperate because they were Masons and hence not true Communists. *Escritos sobre la guerra*, 292. Some of this criticism was unwarranted, though it was true that some Communist officers did fail to act against Casado.

45. S. A. Vaupshasov, *Na trevozhnykh perekrestkakh: Zapiski chekista* (Moscow, 1971), 180–86. This sinister NKVD personage, aside from having maintained the Soviet crematorium in Spain for the disposal of corpses, was used to being in tight situations in guerrilla operations.

46. Togliatti, *Escritos sobre la guerra*, 206–7. Referring more broadly to the situation from mid-February down to the coup, Togliatti further explained: "For an act of force . . . we could not count on a single ally; everyone would have been against us. We would have had to seize power as a single party. That would have meant that the party assumed the political responsibility of breaking up the Popular Front by force.

"The entire leadership of the party was opposed to that. Moreover, in my personal opinion, there was yet another more profound reason. . . . I was convinced . . . that we would have been quickly and hopelessly defeated, because the masses, disoriented and desiring only peace, would not have followed us, and not even the military forces commanded by Communists would have supported us with the necessary energy and determination. Very probably, part of them would have lined up against us. And it is even very probable that part of the party would have vacillated" (pp. 280–81).

Rafael Gil Bracero points out that the party was becoming so weak in Andalusia during the last phase of the war that it was relying above all on the Communist officers and commanders of the Ejército de Andalucía, most of whom ended up by going over to Casado. *Revolucionarios sin revolución: Marxistas y anarcosindicalistas en guerra: Granada-Baza, 1936–1939* (Granada, 1998), 312.

47. Togliatti, *Escritos sobre la guerra*, 205.

48. Hernández, *Yo fui un ministro de Stalin*, 255–56.

49. Dallin and Firsov, *Dimitrov and Stalin*, 79. The key work on Spanish Communists in the years after the Civil War is D. W. Pike, *In the Service of Stalin: The Spanish Communists in Exile, 1939–1945* (Oxford, 1993).

50. Elorza and Bizcarrondo, *Queridos camaradas*, 437–42. Stepanov was probably encouraged to prepare his own report, "Les causes de la défaite de la République espagnole," cited frequently ibid. The final "Resolution" of the ECCI of Aug. 5, detailing the official criticism, may be found in RAN, 474–79.

CHAPTER 12. CONCLUSION

1. W. Krivitsky, *In Stalin's Secret Service* (New York, 1939), 65; G. Howson, *Arms for Spain: The Untold Story of the Spanish Civil War* (London, 1998), 119.

2. G. Roberts, "Soviet Foreign Policy and the Spanish Civil War," in *Spain in an International Context, 1936–1959*, ed. C. Leitz and D. Dunthorn (New York, 1999), 84.

3. "The fact that today bourgeois historians devote themselves to defining what was 'revolutionary' and what was 'counterrevolutionary' in the Spanish war is eloquent and expressive. It is easy to point out the basic falsification committed by these historians: The struggle to put an end to essays of 'libertarian communism' did not lead to reestablishment of the 'old order,' the predominance of the landowning bourgeois oligarchy. It was not a matter of returning to the Republican institutions before the 18th of July, but of reconstructing them with a completely new content that would respond to the requirements of the antifascist war and the democratic character of the revolution being developed in Spain.

"Suppression of the 'committees' was not a step backward; it was a step forward. It served, on the one hand, to strengthen the unity of the people in the war; and on the other, to solidify the democratic republic of a new type; to structure a people's democracy, which appeared for the first time in Europe; to develop the Spanish democratic revolution through its own original channels, with its own specific features." (Ibárruri et al., eds., *Guerra y revolución en España, 1936–1939* [Moscow, 1966], 2:271.)

4. W. Solano, *El POUM en la historia: Andreu Nin y la revolución española* (Madrid, 1999), 174.

5. Krivitsky, *In Stalin's Secret Service*, 76; E. H. Carr, *The Comintern and the Spanish Civil War* (New York, 1984), 44.

6. O. Sarin and L. Dvoretsky, *Alien Wars: The Soviet Union's Aggressions against the World, 1919 to 1989* (Novato, Calif., 1996), 17.

7. J. Díaz, *Tres años de lucha* (Paris, 1969), 349.

8. D. Ibárruri, *El único camino* (Paris, 1962), 436.

9. Ibárruri et al., *Guerra y revolución*, 1:256–58; J. Sandoval and M. Azcárate, *Spain, 1936–1939* (London, 1963), 85.

10. Solano, *POUM en la historia*, 180; S. Carrillo, *El comunismo a pesar de todo*, cited in A. Elorza and M. Bizcarrondo, *Queridos camaradas: La Internacional Comunista y España, 1919–1939* (Barcelona, 1999), 384. Carrillo expanded on the theme in his introduction to the 1978 edition of Díaz's collected speeches, declaring that "the 'Popular Front'—which at first was called 'Bloque Popular'—presented in Spain *specific characteristics*, which went much further than a *tactical concept* to transform themselves into a *strategy* of *popular* democratic revolution and of Revolution *tout court*." The wartime Republic was not like one of the normal "formal democracies," because "it underwent an original revolutionary experience." "It seems to me beyond doubt that the Giral government, like the two Largo Caballero governments and the two [*sic*] governments of Negrín, exemplified, despite certain qualifications, a form of popular dictatorship," though he adds that it was *"a profoundly and openly democratic dictatorship"* (J. Díaz, *Tres años de lucha* [Barcelona, 1978], 1:11–14; italics in original).

11. K. L. Maidanik, *Ispanskii proletariat v natsional'no-revoliutsionnoi voine* (Moscow, 1960), 3.

12. *Kommunisticheskii Internatsional: Kratkii istoricheskii ocherk* (Moscow, 1969), 444, cited in B. Bolloten, *The Spanish Civil War* (Chapel Hill, N.C., 1991), 315.

13. A. A. Grechko, ed., *Istoriia vtoroi mirovoi voiny, 1939–1945* (Moscow, 1974), 2:51.

14. P. and A. Sudoplatov, with J. L. and L. P. Schecter, *Special Tasks: The Memoirs of an Unwanted Witness, a Soviet Spymaster* (Boston, 1995), 30.

15. Sarin and Dvoretsky, *Alien Wars*, 19. The authors have overlooked the Soviet conquest of Outer Mongolia in 1921.

16. D. T. Cattell, *Communism and the Spanish Civil War* (Berkeley, Calif., 1956), 211.

17. Elorza and Bizcarrondo, *Queridos camaradas*, 386, 454–55.

18. F. Furet, *El pasado de una ilusión: Ensayo sobre la idea comunista en el siglo XX* (Mexico City, 1995), 296, 297.

19. R. Radosh, M. Habeck, and G. Sevostianov, eds., *Spain Betrayed: The Soviet Union in the Spanish Civil War* (New Haven, Conn., 2001), xxiii.

20. Quoted in F. Montiel, "España fue una República popular y volverá a serla," *Nuestra bandera* 23 (December 1947): 1027–49.

21. J. Dimitrov, *Obras escogidas* (Madrid, 1977), 2:64–65, 78, 176–78, 690, as cited in Elorza and Bizcarrondo, *Queridos camaradas*, 510.

22. Grechko, *Istoriia vtoroi mirovoi voiny*, 2:54.

23. For a slightly different analysis, see P. Broué, "Premier essai de démocratie populaire," chap. 15 of his *Staline et la révolution: Le cas espagnol (1936–1939)* (Paris, 1993), 353–60.

24. The nine vessels, valued at approximately $8 million, are listed in F. Olaya Morales, *El oro de Negrín* (Madrid, 1998), 17, 430.

25. Sarin and Dvoretsky, *Alien Wars*, 5–6.

26. R. H. Whealey, *Hitler and Spain: The Nazi Role in the Spanish Civil War, 1936–1939* (Lexington, Ky., 1989), and P. Elstob, *La Legión Condor* (Madrid, 1973), both present extensive lists of new techniques invented or perfected by the Germans in Spain, such as the operation of combined air-to-ground communications and

cooperation, mobile air action in support of a moving offensive, intensive air bombardment to supplement artillery, radio use, sustained consecutive attacks to open a breach or take out a strong position, first use of napalm bombs, carpet bombing, and new use of anti-aircraft and antitank guns.

27. Mary R. Habeck, "Storm of Steel: The Development of Armor Doctrine in Germany and the Soviet Union" (forthcoming), 344, 345, and "Dress Rehearsals, 1937–1941," in *The Military History of the Soviet Union*, ed. R. Higham and F. W. Kagan, 93–108 (London, 2000). Habeck has photocopied an extensive cross section of these documents, which now form a special collection at Yale University.

28. Sarin and Dvoretsky, *Alien Wars*, 3.

29. Iu. Rybalkin, *Operatsiia "Kh": Sovetskaia voennaia pomoshch respublikanskoi Ispanii (1936–1939)* (Moscow, 2000), 104–10.

30. The most thorough inventory will be found ibid., 110–21.

31. The chief study of this problem is Habeck, "Storm of Steel."

32. R. W. Harrison, *The Russian Way of War: Operational Art, 1904–1940* (Lawrence, Kans., 2001), 225.

33. The Soviets learned to improve specific features of tank design that they might not have corrected so rapidly otherwise. Improvements included enclosing and protecting tank motors from the rear and reducing their inflammability, and improving the tread design on the BT-5s, which was important in developing the T-34. Cf. P. Héricourt, *Les Soviets et la France* (Paris, 1938), 64, and T. Wintringham, *Deadlock War* (London, 1940), 226–27.

On the character and limitations of the employment of armor in Spain, see J. L. S. Daley, "The Theory and Practice of Armored Warfare in Spain, October 1936–February 1937," *Armor*, March–April 1999, 30–43, and "Soviet and German Advisors Put Armor to the Test: Tanks in the Siege of Madrid," *Armor*, May–June 1999, 33–37; and Col. A. J. Candil, "Soviet Armor in Spain: Aid Mission to Spain Tested Doctrine and Equipment," *Armor*, March–April 1999, 31–38.

The light German and Italian tanks and tankettes sent to Spain were not very effective, but that fact made comparatively little impression on the Italians, perhaps because of Franco's overall success. The most useful tanks that the Nationalist army ever acquired were the Soviet T-26s and B-5s, which eventually formed two whole battalions of captured Soviet tanks. The Nationalist government announced the capture of eighty-four of these tanks from July 1937 to August 1938, according to A. J. Toynbee and V. M. Boulter, *Survey of International Affairs: 1938* (London, 1941), 1:315n. Even more were captured during the final phases of the war. A final report of June 15, 1939, listed a total of 150 Soviet tanks recovered. Carpeta 33, Archivo de la Fundación Nacional Francisco Franco (hereafter AFNFF), 124-6322.

34. The Spanish Nationalist army itself incorporated Soviet warplanes at the end of the war, both those manufactured in the Soviet Union and the small number produced in Catalonia and the Levant. At the end, the Nationalists recovered nearly 200 planes from the final Republican zone, but they consisted of nearly

forty types of aircraft, mostly in poor condition. J. Arráez Cerdá, "Aviones recuperados en el sureste al final de la guerra civil," *Revista española de historia militar* 1 (January–February 2000): 56–64.

Franco's first air minister, Gen. Juan Yague, at first proposed to sell off the Soviet planes and replace them with models derived from Germany and Italy. In a memo to Franco of Oct. 4, 1939, Yague proposed to sell, inter alia, seventeen Polikarpov I-16s, eighteen Katiuska medium bombers, and thirty-one Natacha biplanes. AFNFF, 67-2673. However, those I-16s in relatively good condition proved useful, and at least two squadrons made up of them long served in the Nationalist air force. Some continued to fly until 1953, when they were finally replaced with relatively late-model American planes. Cf. J. A. Guerrero, *Polikarpov I-16 "Mosca"* (Madrid, 1978).

35. Here I draw on a forthcoming monograph on the bolshoi flot by Milan Hauner. The best brief treatment of the naval aspects of the war is W. C. Frank, "Naval Operations in the Spanish Civil War, 1936–1939," *Naval War College Review* 38 (1984): 24–55.

36. Cf. Gen. M. Duval, *Les leçons de la guerre d'Espagne* (Paris, 1938); C. Rougeron, *Les enseignements aériens de la guerre d'Espagne* (Paris, 1939); R. A. Doughty, *The Development of French Army Doctrine* (Hamden, Conn., 1985), 89; and particularly J. Martínez Parrilla, *Las fuerzas armadas francesas ante la guerra civil española (1936–1939)* (Madrid, 1987).

37. G. Roberts, *The Unholy Alliance: Stalin's Pact with Hitler* (Bloomington, Ind., 1989), 116–19, and A. Read and D. Fisher, *The Deadly Embrace: Hitler, Stalin, and the Nazi-Soviet Pact, 1939–1941* (New York, 1988), 58–59.

38. According to E. Nolte, *La guerra civil europea, 1917–1945: Nacionalsocialismo y bolchevismo* (Mexico City, 1994), 413.

39. G. Roberts, "The Alliance That Failed: Moscow and the Triple Alliance Negotiations, 1939," *European History Quarterly* 26, no. 3 (1996): 383–414.

40. A. Nekrich, *Pariahs, Partners, Predators: Stalin's Pact with Hitler: German-Soviet Relations, 1922–1941* (New York, 1997), 134–41.

41. Cf. V. B. Johnston, *Legions of Babel* (University Park, Pa., 1967), 149.

42. K. Rentola, "The Finnish Communists and the Winter War," *Journal of Contemporary History* 33, no. 4 (1998): 591–607.

43. N. S. Lebedeva and M. M. Narinskii, eds., *Komintern i vtoraia mirovaia voina* (Moscow, 1998), 1:10–11.

44. Quoted in A. C. Brown and C. B. MacDonald, *On a Field of Red: The Communist International and the Coming of World War II* (New York, 1981), 508.

45. P. Renouvin, *Histoire des relations internationales* (Paris, 1965), 8:112.

46. During World War II, the Carlists, for example, were divided into pro-Allied, pro-German, and neutral sectors. Don Javier, the Carlist regent, joined the anti-German resistance and ended up in a Nazi concentration camp.

47. In the preceding paragraphs I have reformulated some of the arguments in the excellent article by W. C. Frank Jr., "The Spanish Civil War and the Coming of the Second World War," *International History Review* 9 (August 1987): 367–409.

Index